DEVOTION TO THE SACRED HEART

DEVOTION

TO

THE SACRED HEART

OBJECT   ENDS   PRACTICE   MOTIVES

By

LOUIS VERHEYLEZOON, s.j.

With Foreword by
The Rev. C. C. Martindale, s.j.

TAN BOOKS AND PUBLISHERS, INC.
Rockford, Illinois 61105

Nihil obstat:

DANIEL DUIVESTEIJN, S.T.D.

Censor deputatus

Imprimatur:

E. MORROGH BERNARD

Vic. Gen.

Westmonasterii,
die 18a Octobris, 1954.

First published March 1955
Second impression April 1956

Third Printing, 1978

Printed and bound in the United States of America

TAN BOOKS AND PUBLISHERS, INC.
P. O. Box 424
Rockford, Illinois 61105

1978

Contents

CHAPTER II

ENDS OF THE DEVOTION

CHAPTER III

PRACTICE OF THE DEVOTION

CHAPTER IV

MOTIVES FOR PRACTISING THE DEVOTION

APPENDICES

Preface

This work was originally published in Flemish, in 1946, under the title of *De Devotie tot het Heilig Hart*. It met with a ready acceptance in Belgium and Holland. Surely there is no lack of excellent books on devotion to the Sacred Heart in the English language; yet we have reason to hope that room may be found for an essay at systematization, which embraces the Devotion to its full extent and presents it as an harmonious and logical whole.

This treatise then is neither a book for mere reading nor a 'devotional book'. It is a book of study. It is intended for all those —priests, religious and laymen—who wish to acquire a reasoned and exhaustive knowledge of the great devotion of modern times, which contains 'the summary of the whole religion, and the rule of a life of greater perfection' (Encyclical *Miserentissimus* by Pope Pius XI).

This knowledge will lead them to a higher esteem and a more intense practice of this comprehensive and beneficial devotion. Such is our ardent wish. May the Sacred Heart realize it!

L. VERHEYLEZOON, S.J.

Ghent, Belgium.

Foreword

We can learn about a country by studying its map, by looking at pictures or reading descriptions of it, or finally by living in it. This book corresponds, on the whole, to the 'map': it is a theological dissection of its subject. There is much literature concerned with the same subject—some noble indeed, like the *Ancient Devotions to the Sacred Heart of Jesus*, written by Carthusian Monks of the fourteenth to the seventeenth centuries, prefaced by the Prior of Parkminster; and much pictorial decoration of the 'devotion', most of it, we fear, calculated to repel rather than attract, so does it weaken and sentimentalize what it professes to represent. Finally, there are those who know, quite simply, that Christ is loving them and who love Him in return, and these are they who may indeed be said to 'live in His Sacred Heart'.

Dom Aelred Watkin, o.s.b., of Downside, in *The Heart of the World*, integrates, so to say, all that is meant by 'devotion to the Sacred Heart', while acknowledging that 'devotion' is not, perhaps, the best word that we could use. Thus we speak of having 'a devotion' to a certain picture, or to Our Lady 'of' such or such a shrine: this is an 'exercise of the pious', optional, a matter may be of instinct or temperament, whereas the true 'devotion' to the Sacred Heart is 'a profound dedication to a mystery, a fact, a Person; it is Christ redeeming the world in and through each of us. And in Christ, as God, there is no distinction between what He does and what He is'.

This book, however, concentrates on that aspect of the cult of the Sacred Heart which St. Margaret Mary was supernaturally guided to make popular. We do not intend to add anything to what the author has written, but we would wish to single out, for the sake of clearness, a few very important points that he himself has made.

First, the Heart is not merely a metaphor, as a rose would be if we called it 'love'; or a flag, if we called it 'England'; or like the 'laughter of the sea' that the old Greek poet wrote about.

But it is most certainly a 'symbol'. Our cult does not stop short at the Heart of flesh—and indeed it is difficult to imagine anyone's

...

worship doing so. The heart, strictly speaking, is not 'the seat of emotions': love, sorrow, joy are not placed in, or produced by, the heart, even though we say: 'I love you with all my heart—my very heart grieves for you—my heart leaps up with joy.' Emotions affect the heart; but the literature of other nations shows that the names of quite different organs were regularly used when we might say 'heart'; and our Lady could have said that her 'heart' thrilled with joy in God her Saviour as naturally as that her 'spirit' did so.

It follows that the Heart should not be thought of, or represented, apart from the Person of our Lord.[1] Artists must not be at pains to depict it 'realistically', anatomically, in the place which it would correctly occupy in the human body. The image of the Heart is symbolical, we repeat, as indeed the wreath of thorns and the radiance which surround it, the cross which surmounts it, suffice to prove. We shall not, therefore, be tempted to treat the Sacred Heart as it were in isolation from the whole of the Sacred Humanity. The Holy See has shown no favour to those who would seem to 'departmentalize' the worship due to our Lord—to pay a separate cult to His Hands, His Head and so forth. (The cult of the Holy Face has a special and easily understood position.) Hence, for my part, I cannot feel comfortable when the Sacred Heart is written of both in terms proper to a person, and yet as 'It'—Its intentions, desires, distresses; even Its sighs and Its tears. There is here, surely, a real confusion both of thought and of imagination, or at any rate of the latter.

Hence while the author most rightly will not permit the Heart to be pictured apart from the 'Man, Jesus Christ', as St. Paul says (1 Tim. ii, 5), so will he insist that even the Sacred Humanity must not be thought of in isolation: we must not 'divide Christ' (1 John iv, 3). We cannot but fear that there are some to whom 'the Sacred Heart' is almost a sort of super-Saint. We read of thanks being offered to Our Lady, the Sacred Heart, St. Anthony and the Little Flower. But the Sacred Heart cannot mean less than our Lord Himself, that is, the One Person in whom the Divine and Human Natures are indissolubly joined. No doubt most of those who thus seem to treat 'the Sacred Heart' as if it

---

[1] In two decrees, of the Sacred Congregation of Rites (April 5th, 1879) and the Holy Office (August. 26th, 1891), it was ruled that the Heart must not be exhibited for public worship apart from the figure of our Lord: but it may be so pictured as decoration, on tabernacles, room-doors, badges and the like.

were one among a number of 'devotions' do not really think about what they are doing at all. It may certainly be that they are actually attracted by the representations of our Lord which presumably aim at expressing Him as 'meek and humble of heart' and, in their uninspired commercialism, succeed only in making an image of effeminacy. Those who are sophisticated enough to criticize such naïve piety should be able to allow for it, and probably to wish that their own devotion were as childlike.

We have, therefore, to ask if the 'devotion' to the Sacred Heart, as now practised, is simply devotion to our Lord Jesus Christ. That it is that, and how much that means, the recent book already mentioned, *The Heart of the World*, amply shows. But the pages that follow concentrate on that special aspect of this cultus which was made known to the world by St. Margaret Mary. The 'devotion' to the Sacred Heart had been practised long before her time, but rather by individual Saints than by the Faithful at large. Even when St. Francis de Sales told his Visitation nuns to be worthy 'daughters of the Sacred Heart', I doubt if he dwelt on any particular quality (so to say) of our Lord's interior life. But when St. John Eudes wrote so much about the Hearts of Jesus and Mary, he dwelt above all (though not exclusively) on their life as lived towards God. He could have said of our Lord's Heart: 'Behold this Heart that has so much loved God', and it was primarily in this sense that he inaugurated the liturgical devotion of which the Church speaks in his Office. But St. Margaret Mary definitely changed the whole graph, if I may so call it, of the devotion, when she repeated our Lord's words: 'Behold this Heart which has so much loved *men*.'

She contemplates, therefore, the divine and human love felt by our Lord for us men, and sees how terribly it is rebuffed. She dwells especially on His sense of our ingratitude and failure to return love for love and speaks throughout as if He were actually among us and experiencing that bitterness now.

But the very expression 'as if' suggests unreality; and it is true that our Lord, now in glory, suffers no more: neither death nor pain have any 'dominion over Him'. And even if we recall that during His Passion He suffered for all sin, past or yet to be, the imagination is baffled and we cannot assimilate the truth that then He bore my sins, and the sins of each and every man in every age. We have, therefore, to renew our hold upon the doctrine of which we have heard so much in modern times—a doctrine, however, stated so clearly by St. Paul, nay, by our Lord Himself, not only as recorded by St. John but as taught by Him when He insisted that what was done to others was done to Himself (Matt. xxv, 34–45)—the doctrine, that is, of His Mystical Body which consists of all who are incorporated with Him by grace; and His love does not stop short even at these, but stretches forth to all men even when they are obdurate and refuse to listen to His call —for there is none whom in some way it does not reach. And if He would have us sorry for the sick, who are so sick as those who are sick in soul, and are wilful sinners?

So it is true not only that in virtue of this 'incorporation' I am living in Christ, but, by virtue of that same mysterious 'trans-action', *commercium*, as the Breviary keeps calling it in the Christ-mas-tide offices, Christ is living in me, so that in me He is desiring, grieving, grateful, pitying. It is this fact that lies behind the visions —far from infrequent in the lives of Saints—in which an 'exchange' takes place, and the Saint sees her heart taken by Christ into Himself, while He gives her His own, or a flame from His own, and so forth, instead. We are not to suppose that a physical trans-action occurs—the visions are 'imaginative' and symbolical—but they express in such terms the union between Christ and Christian, which exists in a superlative degree in one so purified from all wrongful attachments as a St. Catherine of Siena or St. Margaret Mary. The author does not seek to 'analyse' the Saint's experiences or writings: it would be an easy task to describe her personal style, catalogue her favourite words, indicate how she could not but put the divine communications that she received into a diction proper to herself. The Liturgy likes to use the word 'ineffable', 'unutterable', in connection with the Mystery of the Sacred Heart, and St. Paul (2 Cor. xii, 4) tells how he in ecstasy heard 'words unspeakable'—nor does he try to translate them into human utterance; but St. Margaret Mary was given a mission, and it was her duty to tell to the world, as best she could, what she had learnt of the love of Christ.

One not seldom hears people say that they believe in God, that they do not wish to offend Him, even, that they want to do His will and so save their souls; but they may frankly say that they do not love Him. They may simply mean that they do not see how they can love the Invisible—and St. John indeed says much the same thing—but on the whole they mean that they cannot feel the same sort of love for God as that which they feel for some human person dear to them. Nor will they be much helped by being told that love consists in the will and not in the emotions. Still less, maybe, can they understand how God can possibly love them, and this, not out of false humility but because they simply cannot see how God can really love the myriad myriad individuals who have lived, or even one of them, so tiny is each one. But it was because God does love the world that the Incarnation took place; and we as Christians are taught to seek and find God in His Son, Jesus Christ. And so urgent is His love for us, that He has sought every way of assuring us that He does love us—the supreme among such 'ways' being the institution of the Blessed Sacrament, and, among less universally cogent, less authoritative, 'private Revelations' like those given to St. Margaret Mary. Artistically, the writings transmitted by, or through, St. Gertrude, may be the more appealing; it remains that St. Margaret Mary had a public mission, which others, who wrote so beautifully about the Sacred Heart, had not; and it is not for us to resent the literary taste of the seventeenth century any more than the strange forms in which the Hebrew Prophets wrote. If, then, in spite of all we are not sure how truly we love God even in the person of His Son, our fellow-man, Jesus Christ, but are quite sure that we should love Him very much better, we must remember that we cannot be holier than God's actual gift of Grace enables us to be, and we must learn the Psalmist's constantly repeated doctrine of waiting. Yet we wait, not dispassionately, but in hope. True, only God can give us the 'new heart', but He wishes and has promised to do so: 'I will give you a new heart, and put a new spirit within you: and I will take away the stony heart out of your flesh, and will give you a heart of flesh, and I will put *My* spirit in the midst of you' (Ezech. xxxvi, 26, 27). Such is the change that a deeper love for our Lord will, please God, bring about in us.

C. C. MARTINDALE, S.J.

B

Introduction

1. What is Meant by Devotion to the Sacred Heart

Devotion, in the proper sense of the word, is, in general, an inclination and readiness for all that relates to the service and worship of God. We distinguish substantial devotion which has its seat in the will and consists in the willingness and readiness to serve and revere God[1], and accidental or sensible devotion which resides in man's sensitive or emotional nature and consists in a disposition of the soul, which makes us find a relish in the service and worship of God.[2]

In a derived sense, devotion is the propensity and readiness to pay honour in particular to one of the three Persons of the Most Blessed Trinity, or to one Saint or another. The object of this cult may be either the person taken as a whole—such is devotion to God the Father, to Jesus, the Holy Ghost, the Blessed Virgin or some Saint; or that person, considered under some special aspect —such is devotion to the Holy Eucharist, the Sacred Passion of our Lord, His Sacred Wounds, the Child Jesus, the Immaculate Conception, the Immaculate Heart, the Seven Dolours of the Blessed Virgin, etc. Such is also devotion to the Heart of Jesus. Hence by devotion to the Heart of Jesus is meant, first, a certain propensity and readiness to worship the Sacred Heart; it is in this sense that one may be said to have a tender devotion to the Sacred Heart; it is the subjective sense of the word.

But the word has yet another derived sense, an objective sense, closely connected with the previous one; it also denotes actual worship of a Divine Person, or of some Saint, with all its constituents. It is in this sense that we use the word 'devotion' throughout this book.

Hence by 'devotion to the Sacred Heart' is meant here the cult of the Heart of Jesus, with all that constitutes this cult.

2. Origin and Development of the Devotion

The Heart of Jesus has been worshipped in many ways. It is

---

[1] St. Thomas defines it: 'Voluntas quaedam prompte tradendi se ad ea quae pertinent ad Dei famulatum' (2.2. q. 82, art. 2).

[2] Cf. *Dictionnaire de théologie catholique*, art. *Dévotion*, col. 680; and Vermeersch, s.j., *Pratique et doctrine de la dévotion au Sacré-Cœur*, 1930, vol. II, p. 4.

not our intention to examine and expound the different forms the devotion has taken in the course of time.[1]

We confine ourselves to studying a well-defined form, a definite devotion to the Sacred Heart, namely, that which nowadays is universally spread among the faithful, which owes its origin and rapid propagation to the apparitions made by our Lord to St. Margaret Mary[2] and which the Church has not only approved and encouraged but has made her own. And this devotion we consider as it actually exists, as it is viewed and proposed by the Church, and as it is commonly practised by the faithful.

Nevertheless it will not be inappropriate to sketch in broad outlines its origin and development. This summary is derived from the second Nocturn of the Office of the Feast of the Sacred Heart.[3]

'Among the marvellous developments of sacred doctrine and of piety, whereby the designs of the Divine Wisdom manifest themselves to the Church ever more clearly, there is scarcely any other more outstanding than the triumphant progress of the cult of the Most Sacred Heart of Jesus.

'True, in the course of former times, the Fathers, the Doctors and the Saints have again and again celebrated the love of our Redeemer; they called the open wound in the side of Christ the hidden source of all graces. But, since the Middle Ages, when the faithful began to have a more tender affection towards our

---

[1] For the history of the Devotion see especially Hamon, s.J., *Histoire de la dévotion au Sacré-Cœur*, 5 vol.; and Bainvel, s.J., *La dévotion au Sacré-Cœur*, pt. III.

[2] Cf. Vermeersch, vol. II, p. 16; and Bainvel, p. 159. Margaret Mary Alacoque was born on July 22nd, 1647, at Lautecourt, a village belonging to the parish of Verosvres, France. After a childhood and youth spent in piety and innocence, she entered, at the age of twenty-four, the order of the Visitation of our Lady, at Paray-le-Monial. Our Divine Saviour frequently appeared to her and made known to her His wishes. When she was sufficiently prepared for the execution of His loving designs, He revealed to her the devotion to His Sacred Heart and ordered her to propagate it. From that time forward she only lived to fulfil the mission entrusted to her of honouring and consoling the Sacred Heart, and making it known, honoured and loved by others. She died in odour of sanctity on October 17th, 1690. Her feast is celebrated on October 17th. (See *Bull of canonization* in *Vie et Oeuvres*, vol. III, p. 699. Cf. also Hamon, vol. I, *Vie de sainte Marie-Marguerite*; Gauthey, *Vie et Oeuvres de sainte Marguerite-Marie Alacoque*, 1920, vol. I, *Mémoire des Contemporaines*; vol. II, *Autobiographie*; Croiset, s.J., *La dévotion au sacré Cœur de Jésus*; Mgr. Languet, *La vie de la vén. Marguerite-Marie*; Mgr. Bougaud, *Histoire de la B. Marguerite-Marie.*

[3] According to liturgical usage, the lessons of the Second Nocturn briefly recall the life of the Saint or the object of the mystery celebrated. Their historical value is very different. Among those of ancient offices some transmit but mere legends. In the more recent ones, generally more exactitude is observed. The lessons of the present Office summarize a history which has been carefully studied in recent times. Moreover, they are fully in accordance with the views exposed by Pope Pius XI in his Encyclical *Miserentissimus*. (Galtier, s.J., *Le Sacré-Cœur*, p. 3.)

Saviour's Sacred Humanity, contemplative souls used to penetrate as it were through this Wound into the Heart itself, wounded for love of men.

'From that time forward, this contemplation became familiar to all those who excelled in sanctity, so that there is neither country nor religious order where there are not to be found testimonies for that, which, for that period, are very remarkable. Finally, especially at the time when heretics, under the guise of false piety, were bent on deterring Christian people from the Blessed Eucharist, public worship began to be paid to the Sacred Heart, particularly by means of St. John Eudes who, not without reason, is called "the author of the liturgical cult of the Sacred Hearts of Jesus and of Mary".[1]

'Yet, in order to give the cult of the Sacred Heart its full and perfect form, and to propagate it throughout the world, God Himself chose as instrument a humble virgin of the Visitation order, St. Margaret Mary Alacoque. From her early youth she had been animated with an ardent love towards the Blessed Sacrament, and Christ our Lord, in many apparitions, deigned to manifest to her the riches and the wishes of His Divine Heart.

'Of these apparitions the most famous is that in which, whilst she was praying before the Eucharist, Jesus presented Himself to her and showed her His Sacred Heart. He complained that, in return for His boundless charity, He received from ungrateful men nothing but outrages, and He ordered her to work for the institution of a new feast on the Friday after the octave of Corpus Christi, by which due honour should be paid to His Heart, and the outrages offered Him by sinners in the Sacrament of His love should be expiated by worthy homage.

'There is no one who does not know of the great difficulties

---

[1] St. John Eudes, the founder of the Eudists (officially: the Congregation of Jesus and Mary) was born at Ri, a village of the district of Argentan, on November 14th, 1601. He was the first apostle of the devotion to the Sacred Heart of Mary, and wrote a great work entitled *Le Cœur admirable de la très sacrée Mère de Dieu.* He was also the first apostle of the devotion to the Sacred Heart of Jesus. At the beginning he joined the two Hearts, but later on he separated the two cults. He also composed a Mass and Office in honour of the Sacred Heart. His devotion differs from that which our Lord revealed to St. Margaret Mary, yet he prepared the way for the movement that started from Paray-le-Monial. He died on August 19th, 1680. His feast is celebrated on 19th August. (See Boulay, *Vie du Vénérable Jean Eudes*; Lebrun, *Le Bienheureux Jean Eudes et le culte public du Cœur de Jésus*; Le Doré, *Les Sacrés-Cœurs et le Vénérable Jean Eudes*; Hamon, op. cit., vol. III, chap. vii and viii; Bremond, *Histoire littéraire du sentiment religieux en France*, vol. III, pt. III; Bainvel, op. cit., pt. III, chap. v, p. 453; Vermeersch op. cit., vol. II, pp. 17–18.)

God's servant experienced in executing Christ's commands. But our Lord Himself was her strength; and vigorously supported by her spiritual directors, who were animated with an incredible ardour to promote this cult, she never ceased even to her death faithfully acquitting herself of the task entrusted to her.

'In 1765, finally, the Sovereign Pontiff Clement XIII approved an Office and Mass in honour of the Most Sacred Heart of Jesus. Pius IX extended the feast to the universal Church.[1]

'Ever since that time, this cult of the Sacred Heart, like an over-flowing stream sweeping away all obstacles, has spread abroad throughout the world. At the dawn of the new century, after he had proclaimed the Jubilee, Leo XIII desired that the whole human race should be consecrated to the Sacred Heart. This Consecration, which was made with great solemnity in all the churches of the Catholic world, brought about an immense increase of the devotion. It won nations as well as single families; those that consecrate themselves to the Divine Heart and submit to Its royal empire are innumerable.

'Finally, in order that the solemnity of the Feast might correspond more fully to the devotion which was so widespread among Christian people, Pope Pius XI raised the Feast to the rite of Double of the first class with octave. Moreover, to make up for the violated rights of Christ, our supreme and loving Lord, and to atone for the sins of nations, he prescribed that every year, on the same feast day, an Act of Reparation should be recited in all the churches of the Christian world.'

The chief historical dates of the Devotion are:

December 27th, 1673: The first great apparition.
Beginning 1674: The second great apparition.
July 2nd (?), 1674: The third great apparition.

---

[1] The feast, then, of the Sacred Heart was not instituted until ninety years after it was demanded by our Lord. The Church, as we know, proceeds cautiously in making decisions. At the very outset the Devotion met with violent opposition, not only on the part of Jansenist priests and laymen, but even in the highest ranks of the hierarchy. The cult was considered an unsound novelty, superstitious, sensual, or at least too material. Even bishops and cardinals openly took a hostile attitude. At first the Sovereign Pontiffs themselves were extremely reserved and little inclined to approve the devotion which was presented as unusual and new. Gradually, however, as their prejudices faded away, they began to grant indulgences and other spiritual favours to Confraternities established in honour of the Sacred Heart. Already under Innocent XII (1691–1700) Bulls of that kind reached the number of 32; no less than 214 were issued by Clement XI (1700–21), 39 by Innocent XIII (1721–24), more than 200 by Benedict XIV (1740–58).

June 16th (?), 1675: The fourth great apparition.

January 26th and February 6th, 1765: Institution of the Feast of the Sacred Heart by Pope Clement XIII.

August 28th, 1794: Publication of the Bull *Auctorem fidei* by Pope Pius VI against the false accusations of the Jansenists.

August 23rd, 1856: Extension of the Feast of the Sacred Heart to the universal Church by Pope Pius IX.

September 18th, 1864: Beatification of Margaret Mary.

June 16th, 1875: General consecration of the faithful to the Sacred Heart, at the invitation of Pope Pius IX.

May 25th, 1899: Encyclical *Annum sacrum* by Pope Leo XIII on the Consecration of mankind to the Sacred Heart.

June 11th, 1899: Consecration of the human race to the Sacred Heart by Pope Leo XIII.

May 13th, 1920: Canonization of Margaret Mary by Pope Benedict XV

May 8th, 1928: Encyclical *Miserentissimus* by Pope Pius XI on the universal duty of reparation to the Sacred Heart.

January 29th, 1929: Raising of the Feast of the Sacred Heart to the rite of Double of the first class with privileged octave of the third order, by Pope Pius XI.

June 16th, 1929: Beatification of Claude de la Colombière by Pope Pius XI.

3. The Apparitions of Jesus to St. Margaret Mary

I. THE FOUR GREAT APPARITIONS

The Devotion which we are studying here owes its origin, from an historical point of view, to our Lord's apparitions to St. Margaret Mary. Among these there are four of greater importance, which for that reason are commonly called 'the great apparitions'.[1]

The first apparition took place on the feast of St. John the Evangelist, that is, on December 27th, probably in 1673. The Saint relates it as follows:

'One day, being before the Blessed Sacrament, as I had some leisure time, I was so overwhelmed by this Divine presence as to

---

[1] For the progressive revelation of the Devotion as it is developed in these four apparitions, see Bainvel, op. cit., pt. I, chap. ii; and Hamon, op. cit., vol. III, p. 270.

forget myself and the place where I was. I abandoned myself to this Divine Spirit, surrendering my heart to the might of His love. He (our Lord) allowed me to recline for a long time on His divine breast, where He disclosed to me the marvels of His love and the unutterable secrets of His Sacred Heart, which He had always concealed from me, until He opened It to me now for the first time. This He did so effectually and so sensibly as to leave me no reason to doubt it, because of the effects which this grace produced in me, though I am always afraid of being mistaken in all that I say is going on in me. It happened, as it seems to me, in this way:

'He said to me: "My Divine Heart is so passionately inflamed with love for men, and for you in particular, that, not being able any longer to contain within Itself the flames of Its ardent charity, It must needs spread them abroad through your means, and manifest Itself to men, that they may be enriched with Its precious treasures which I unfold to you, and which contain the sanctifying and salutary graces that are necessary to hold them back from the abyss of ruin. And I have chosen you, an abyss of unworthiness and ignorance, for the accomplishment of this great design, that all this may be My work." Thereupon He demanded my heart, which I entreated Him to take. He took it from my breast and plunged it into His own adorable Heart where it appeared as but an atom in the midst of an immense ocean of fire. Then drawing it forth, in appearance like a flame in the shape of a heart, He replaced it in my breast, saying as He did so: "Behold, My beloved, a precious pledge of My love; it contains within your breast a little spark of Its most ardent flames, to serve you as a heart and to consume you up to your last moment. . . . Hitherto you have taken but the name of My slave; I give you now the title of the beloved disciple of My Sacred Heart." '[1]

The second apparition took place shortly afterwards, probably on a first Friday of the month, in 1674.[2]

'After that, this Divine Heart was shown to me as on a throne of flames, more dazzling than the sun and transparent as crystal, with that adorable wound, and surrounded with a crown of thorns signifying the pricks caused to It by our sins; and above there was a cross, which meant that from the first moment of His Incarna-

[1] *Vie et Oeuvres*, vol. ii, *Autobiographie*, n. 53 and 54, pp. 69 and 71.
[2] Cf. Hamon, op. cit., vol. i, p. 149, note.

tion, that is as soon as this Sacred Heart was formed, the cross was planted in It, and that It was filled at once with all the bitterness which humiliations and poverty, pains and scorn, would cause to It, and which His Sacred Humanity was to suffer throughout all His lifetime and in His Sacred Passion.

'And He showed me that it was His great desire of being loved by men and of withdrawing them from the path of ruin into which Satan hurls such crowds of them, that made Him form the design of manifesting His Heart to men, with all the treasures of love, of mercy, of grace, of sanctification and salvation which It contains, in order that those who desire to render Him and procure for Him all the honour and love possible, might themselves be abundantly enriched with those divine treasures of which this Heart is the source. He should be honoured under the figure of this Heart of flesh, and Its image should be exposed. He wished me to wear this image on my own heart, that He might impress in it His love and fill it with all the gifts with which His Heart is replete, and destroy in it all inordinate affections. He promised me that wherever this image should be exposed with a view to showing It special honour, He would pour forth His blessings and graces. This devotion was the last effort of His love that He would grant to men in these latter ages, in order to withdraw them from the empire of Satan which He desired to destroy, and thus to introduce them into the sweet liberty of the rule of His love, which He wished to restore in the hearts of all those who should embrace this devotion.

'Thereupon the Lord of my soul said to me: "These are the designs for which I have chosen you, and for which I have bestowed upon you so many graces and such particular care. I Myself have become your Master and Director, to prepare you for the accomplishment of that great design, and to entrust you with the great treasures I unfold to you here." Then, prostrate on the ground, I said to Him with St. Thomas of old: "My Lord and my God!", being unable to give utterance to my feelings at that moment, and not knowing whether I were in Heaven or on earth.'[1]

The third apparition took place probably on July 2nd, 1674, the feast of the Visitation of our Lady.[2]

---

[1] *Vie et Oeuvres*, vol. II, *4e Lettre au P. Croiset*, 1689, pp. 571–73.
[2] Cf. Bainvel, op. cit., p. 25.

'One day, as I knelt before the Blessed Sacrament exposed on the altar, after feeling withdrawn within myself by an extraordinary recollection of all my senses and faculties, Jesus Christ, my sweet Master, presented Himself to me, all resplendent with glory, with His five wounds shining like so many suns. From all parts of His Sacred Humanity there issued flames but especially from His adorable breast, which was like a furnace. Opening it, He showed me His loving and lovable Heart as the living source of those flames. Then He revealed to me all the unspeakable marvels of His pure love, and the excess of love He had conceived for men from whom He received nothing but ingratitude and contempt. "This is more grievous to Me," He said, "than all that I endured in My Passion. If they would only give Me some return of love, I should not reckon all that I have done for them, and I would do yet more if possible. But they have only coldness and contempt for all My endeavours to do them good. You, at least, can give Me the happiness of making up for their ingratitude, as much as you can."

'And as I pointed out my inability to do so, He replied: "Behold, this is how I will supply for all that is wanting on your part." At the same time this Divine Heart opened Itself, and there issued forth a flame so ardent that I thought I should be consumed by it. I was so overwhelmed as to be unable to bear it any longer, and I asked Him to take pity on my weakness. "I shall be your strength", He said to me, "fear not, but be attentive to My voice and to what I demand of you to make you fit for the accomplishment of My designs.

' "First, you are to receive Me in the Blessed Sacrament as often as obedience will allow, no matter what mortification or humiliation it may entail. Moreover, you are to receive Holy Communion on the first Friday of each month, and every night between Thursday and Friday I will make you partaker of that sorrow unto death which it was My will to suffer in the Garden of Olives. This sorrow will reduce you, without your understanding how, to a kind of agony more bitter than death. To join with Me in the humble prayer which I then offered to My Heavenly Father in agony you are to rise between eleven and twelve o'clock, and remain with Me upon your knees for an hour, with your face to the ground, to appease the anger of My Eternal Father, and to ask of Him pardon for sinners. You will thus also share with Me, and in a manner soothe, the bitter grief I suffered when My disciples abandoned Me and I was constrained to reproach them that they could not watch with Me even one hour. During that hour you are to do what I will teach you." '[1]

The fourth apparition, the most important, and for that reason called the 'great' apparition, took place in 1675, during the octave of Corpus Christi, probably on June 16th.[2] The Saint relates it as follows:

'One day, during the octave of Corpus Christi, when being before the Blessed Sacrament, I received from my God extra-ordinary proofs of His love. As I earnestly desired to make some return of love, He said to me: "You could not show Me greater love than by doing what I have already so many times demanded of you." And discovering to me His Divine Heart: "Behold this Heart which has so loved men that It spared nothing, even going so far as to exhaust and consume Itself, to prove to them Its love. And in return I receive from the greater part of men nothing but ingratitude, by the contempt, irreverence, sacrileges and coldness with which they treat Me in this Sacrament of Love. But what is still more painful to Me is that even souls consecrated to Me are acting in this way. Therefore I ask of you that the first Friday after the octave of Corpus Christi be dedicated as a feast in honour of My Heart, and amends made to It in an Act of Reparation offered to It and by the reception of Holy Communion on that day, to atone for the outrages It has received during the time It has been exposed on the Altars. I promise you that My Heart will open wide to pour forth lavishly the influence of Its Divine love on all who will render and procure for It this honour.

' "But, O Lord, to whom do you address Yourself? To so frail a creature and poor sinner, whose unworthiness might even be capable of preventing the accomplishment of Your designs? You have so many generous souls to carry out Your designs." ' "Ah! poor innocent, do you not know that I employ those who are weak to confound those who are strong, and that it is usually in the poor in spirit that I show My power with more splendour, that they may not ascribe anything to themselves?" "Give me then," I said, "the means of doing what You command me."

---

[1] *Vie et Oeuvres*, vol. II, *Autobiographie*, n. 55–57, pp. 72–73.
[2] Cf. Hamon, op. cit., vol. I, p. 173, note.

Thereupon He said: "Address yourself to My servant N.[1] and tell him from Me to do his best to establish this devotion and afford this pleasure to My Divine Heart. He should not lose courage because of the difficulties he will experience; he should know that he is all-powerful who is distrustful of himself and commits himself to Me only." '[2]

II. AUTHENTICITY OF THE REVELATIONS

Are we certain of the reality of these apparitions and of the revelations which accompanied them?

Absolutely certain, no. We know them only by a human witness, the witness of the Saint. Yet, a human testimony, especially

---

[1] Here our Lord indicates Fr. Claude de la Colombière, s.j., the then Superior of the Jesuit house at Paray-le-Monial. He calls him 'His faithful servant and perfect friend' (*Vie et Oeuvres*, vol. II, *Lettre au P. Croiset*, p. 545).

Claude de la Colombière was born on February 2nd, 1641, at Saint-Symphorien-d'Ozon, France. At the age of seventeen he entered the Society of Jesus and on February 2nd, 1675, came to Paray-le-Monial as Superior. Highly appreciated as preacher and spiritual director, he was also considered a holy religious. Pope Benedict XV calls him 'a man of eminent holiness' (Office of the feast of St. Margaret Mary). Chosen by our Lord Himself as counsellor of St. Margaret Mary, he soon recognized the genuineness of the apparitions and became, together with the Saint, the first apostle of the new devotion. Being appointed court chaplain of the catholic Duchess of York he set out for London in 1676. Two years later he was detained in prison by the protestant government and then banished. He returned to France with broken health, and died at Paray on February 15th, 1682. On June 16th, 1929, he was beatified by Pius XI. His feast is celebrated on February 15th.

The particle 'de' before Bl. Claude's surname denoting nobility seems to be wrongly used. True, his ancestors did belong to the nobility, but the la Colombières of Saint-Symphorien had lost the title and privileges of this rank. (Cf. Guitton, s.j., *Le Bienheureux Claude La Colombière*, 1943, p. 29.)

[2] Cf. *La Retraite spirituelle du bienheureux Claude de la Colombière*, p. 128. See also *Vie et Oeuvres*, II, *Autobiographie*, p. 103, and I, n. 136, where this quotation, slightly altered, also occurs. The narration we have quoted is that which the Saint put in writing by order of her confessor, Fr. de la Colombière, almost immediately after the apparition had taken place. (Cf. *Vie et Oeuvres*, II, n. 93.) It was inserted by the Father in the Journal of his retreat of 1677. This Journal, joined to that of his thirty days' retreat in 1674, was published in 1684, hence still during the lifetime of the Saint, and was entitled *Retraite spirituelle*. (See *Oeuvres complètes du Vén. Père de la Colombière*, VI, p. 118; Monier-Vinard et Condamin, *Le bienheureux Claude de la Colombière. Notes spirituelles et pages choisies*, n. 135.)

The *Retraite spirituelle* acqauints us with the marvellous working of Divine grace, preparing Fr. de la Colombière for his special mission. Pope Benedict XV speaks of it as follows: 'His manuscripts, really worthy of being edited, were published shortly after his death. Among those writings there was found the above-mentioned book, so full of most admirable sentiments of piety. It has been eagerly received by all nations, and it is still read everywhere in Europe by pious persons with great profit for their souls' (Brief of Beatification). This Journal was the means which God employed for making known the apparitions. The eminent moral authority of its author and the profound impression made by the reading of it, won many to belief in the apparitions and to practice of the new devotion. Cf. Hamon, op. cit., I, chap. vi, vii, ix and xi.

in such matters as this, is by no means infallible and so cannot carry with it absolute certainty.

The Church, it is true, in view of the beatification of Margaret Mary, examined her writings and hence also the revelations related therein, and she approved them. From this approval we may deduce that these revelations do not contain anything contrary to Faith and morals, but by no means that they are necessarily authentic, or that our Lord really made them to the Saint. Yet, if we have no absolute certainty, we possess at least reliable guarantees which permit of our believing in the reality and genuineness of these revelations, without incurring the reproach of credulity and imprudence.

There is, first, the attitude of the Church with reference to them. Although she makes no explicit pronouncement on them in virtue of her infallible teaching authority, yet she clearly shows belief in them: not with an assent of divine faith, founded on the word of God, but with a human belief as in a duly established historical fact.

The Popes in their Letters, Encyclicals, Briefs and Bulls mention them as unquestionable realities. Pope Pius IX, for instance, in the Brief of beatification of Margaret Mary (September 18th, 1864) states: 'One day, while she was praying most fervently before the Blessed Sacrament, Our Lord Jesus Christ made known to her that it would be most agreeable to Him that the cult of His Most Sacred Heart, all-glowing with love for mankind, should be established and that He would entrust her with this mission. The Venerable Servant of God, humble as she was, was overwhelmed by it, deeming herself unworthy of such a task. But, in order to obey the command of Jesus, and urged on by her desire of enkindling the Divine love within the hearts of men, she exerted herself among the Sisters of her convent and among all those on whom she might exercise some influence, that this Most Sacred Heart, the seat of the Divine charity, should receive from them all kinds of homage and adoration.'[1]

Pope Leo XIII, in his Encyclical *Annum sacrum* on the Consecration of mankind to the Sacred Heart (May 25th, 1899), mentions 'the mission which Blessed Margaret Mary received from Heaven of propagating the cult of the Divine Heart'.

In the Bull of canonization of St. Margaret Mary (May 13th,

[1] *Vie et Oeuvres*, vol. III, p. 151.

1920), Pope Benedict XV briefly relates the principal apparitions of the Sacred Heart made to His chosen servant, and what He revealed to her in these apparitions.[1]

In his Encyclical *Miserentissimus* (May 8th, 1928, Pope Pius XI writes: 'Perhaps many of the faithful are still ignorant of the complaints of our most loving Lord in His apparitions to Margaret Mary Alacoque, and of the desires He expressed and the requests He made of man, for man's benefit' (n. 3). 'When the most insidious and pernicious of all heresies, Jansenism, was creeping in, . . . the loving Jesus showed His Heart to all nations as a token of peace and love' (n. 5). And further: 'When Christ showed Himself to Margaret Mary, He pointed out to her His boundless love, and at the same time, in an afflicted tone, He complained of the numerous outrages inflicted on Him by the ingratitude of men . . .' and then the Pope quotes Our Lord's own words: 'Behold this Heart which so loved men, etc.'(n. 22). Then he indicates two important exercises of reparation which Jesus asked of the Saint (n. 23).

This conviction of the Church is apparent also from her liturgy. In the Office of the Feast of St. Margaret Mary we read: 'She was endowed by God with the gift of an elevated prayer, and with other priceless graces. Among the various apparitions the most famous was that in which Jesus presented Himself to her while she was praying before the Blessed Sacrament, and showed her His Divine Heart in His opened breast, burning with flames and surrounded with thorns, and He enjoined on her to bring about that public worship should be paid to His Heart.'[2]

Again, in the Office of the Feast of the Sacred Heart: 'In order to give the cult of the Sacred Heart its full and perfect form, and to propagate it throughout the world, God Himself chose as instrument a most humble virgin of the Visitation order, St. Margaret Mary. . . . Christ, Our Lord, in many apparitions, deigned to manifest to her the riches and the desires of His Heart.' And we are reminded in particular of the fourth great apparition.

Finally, in the Office of the Feast of Bl. Claude de la Colombière, we read: 'Soon, after his solemn profession of the four vows, he was sent to Paray-le-Monial as Superior of that house. Not without reason it is believed that this happened by divine inspira-

---

[1] Cf. *Vie et Oeuvres*, vol. III, p. 699.
[2] *Off. in festo S. Marg. Mariae*, lect. 2 Noct.

tion, that St. Margaret Mary might find in Blessed Claude the suitable help promised to her by Our Lord, in order to constitute fully and perfectly the cult of the Most Sacred Heart, and by the institution of a liturgical feast to spread it throughout the world.'[1]

We, too, then may, without any fear of being mistaken, believe in the reality of those apparitions and revelations. For though the Church does not pledge her infallibility in this matter, she is nevertheless, as we know, an absolutely reliable guide, even as regards the piety of the faithful.

Yet, though the Church imposes no belief, no more than in any private and individual revelation, one would behave imprudently and even temerariously in opposing one's own judgment to that of the Church, which even in such matters as this never proceeds incautiously.[2]

The view of the Church concerning the revelations of the Sacred Heart is based indeed on valid arguments which, even apart from her doctrinal authority, afford us on this point the moral certainty, commonly inspired by the account of a reliable witness.

In the first place, the character itself of our Lord's chosen servant affords such proof. Margaret Mary, as it appears from her writings and from the testimonies of her Superiors and Sisters in religion, was a woman of great common sense, deemed worthy to be charged with the training of the young Sisters for religious life. Being profoundly humble, she showed herself distrustful of the extraordinary, supernatural favours bestowed upon her; it was but reluctantly, and only by order of her Superiors, that she consented to speak of those graces. Perfectly obedient and open-hearted towards her Superiors and spiritual directors she readily submitted to their guidance in all things. Are not all these qualities sufficient to preclude the probability of supposed hallucination or self-illusion?[3]

Further, the judgment of her spiritual directors gives like evidence, particularly that of Bl. Claude de la Colombière[4] and

---

[1] *Off. in festo B. Claudii de la Colombière*, lect. 2 Noct.

[2] Cf. Terrien, s.j., *La dévotion au Sacré-Cœur de Jésus*, pp. 365–68; Vermeersch, op. cit., vol. II, pp. 152–55.   [3] Cf. Hamon, op. cit., vol. I, pp. 305–18.

[4] The Brief of Beatification bears witness to him: 'So admirable, prudent, and full of the spirit of God, was the way in which the Venerable Servant of God guided St. Margaret Mary, that he was considered, not without reason, to have been chosen by God for this task. Even during his lifetime he was held to be a saint, not only by St. Margaret Mary and by other Sisters of the Visitation convent at Paray-le-Monial, but also by other persons of every condition, who were under his direction' (*Acta Apost. Sedis*, 1929, p. 479).

of Fr. Ign. Rolin, s.j.,[1] both of them highly esteemed for their knowledge, their perspicacity, their prudence in the direction of souls, and both of them convinced of the reality of the revelations.

Yet another proof is afforded by the fact of the rapid and world-wide spread of the Devotion which owes its origin to those revelations. Is there now any true Catholic who does not practise it to some degree? Is there any church or chapel or true Catholic home without a picture or statue of the Sacred Heart? The Devotion has really become Catholic, that is, universal. It knows no other limits than those of the Catholic Church herself. Now, can we account for such a propagation as this, and for that universal belief of so many generations of the faithful, if its origin is due to the hallucination of a woman's imagination?

A last proof is the beneficial fruits yielded by the Devotion in the hearts of the faithful: fruits of conversion, of fervour, generosity, self-sacrifice, zeal for souls, heroic charity and true sanctity. Once more, is it admissible that the self-delusion of a pretended visionary could have yielded such marvellous results?

Hence, to the apparitions and revelations of the Sacred Heart vouchsafed to St. Margaret Mary, we not only may, but even must give credence, lest we should act rashly and unreasonably.[2] Yet the objection may be raised: how are we to have moral certainty on this point, since St. Margaret Mary herself was, or at least seemed to be, in doubt? For in her letters and autobiography the narrative of these apparitions usually starts with these words: 'It seems to me', or 'If I am not mistaken'.

In fact, these phrases express no real doubt on the part of the Saint. The explanation of her use of them is very simple. She was told to do so by her Superiors. Mother Greyfié, who was her Superior from 1678 to 1684, stated: 'I told her not to speak of these extraordinary graces which she received except in terms of

---

[1] Fr. Ign. Rolin was the Saint's confessor in 1685–86. To him we owe the precious document, her *Autobiography*, which permits us to penetrate into the interior life of such a generous and favoured soul as this. At first, as we read in a biography of the Saint, composed by the Sisters of the convent, *Mémoire des Contemporaines* (in *Vie et Oeuvres*, vol. I, p. 229), he was prejudiced against her; but when he had learned to know her, he changed his mind and held her to be a soul highly favoured by Our Lord. This is the judgment passed upon him by his Superiors: 'An intelligent man, of common sense, great prudence, experienced in matters of government, of tried virtue, and of a kindly nature. (Cf. Hamon, op. cit., vol. I, p. 363, note.)

[2] Cf. Bainvel, op. cit., p. 159; *Vie et Oeuvres*, vol. I, preface, pp. 17–22; Vermeersch, op. cit., vol. II, p. 155.

doubt, such as "It seems to me", or "If I am not mistaken".'[1]
And Fr. Rolin, in his turn, wrote to her (September 8th, 1686):
'Rejoice in the Lord if they take you to be a visionary. When you
say anything, you should simply add: "That is what I think;
perhaps I am mistaken." '[2]

The Saint always remained faithful to this line of conduct.
Mother Greyfié attested to it: to the statement quoted above she
added: 'She always appeared to me most faithful to this advice.'[3]
In her heart of hearts, however, St. Margaret Mary had no doubt
whatever, especially after her spiritual directors had set her mind
at rest concerning the Divine character of her revelations. This is
witnessed by the courage, confidence and constancy with which
she supported the opposition and humiliations they caused her,
and by the unflagging zeal with which she exerted herself to make
known and promote the devotion which had been revealed to her.

III. THEIR CONNECTION WITH THE CHURCH'S APPROVAL OF THE DEVOTION

Although our devotion to the Sacred Heart, from the historical
point of view, owes its origin and propagation to the apparitions
and revelations made by Jesus to St. Margaret Mary, yet, viewed
theologically, it is not based on them. No doubt our Lord's desire
and magnificent promises should strongly urge us on to practise
it, but they are not the intrinsic reason for it. This is, as we shall
see, twofold: the Divinity of the Heart of Jesus, and the relation
between His Heart and His love. It is not because of her belief in
the genuineness of the apparitions of the Sacred Heart that the
Church approved the Devotion and made it her own,[4] but because
she recognized that the devotion was adequately in keeping with
the Catholic Faith and constituted a logical consequence of certain
revealed truths, particularly of the Divinity of Christ, the reality
of His human nature, its hypostatic union with the Person of the
Word, His boundless love for men, etc.[5]

---

[1] *Vie et Oeuvres*, vol. i, *Mémoire des Contemporaines*, p. 175.
[2] Ibid., n. 9, p. 233.
[3] Ibid., p. 175.
[4] The Church had already approved the Devotion by instituting the Feast of the
Sacred Heart (1765), a long time before she took into consideration the writings of
St. Margaret Mary. It was not until 1825 that, in view of her beatification, she submitted them to a canonical examination.
[5] Cf. Bainvel, op. cit., Fondements historiques, p. 159–61.

c

4. Sources from which the Doctrine of the Devotion is to be Drawn

Where are we to seek the data necessary to form an accurate idea of the Devotion to the Sacred Heart?

The nature of the Devotion clearly shows it.

The Devotion owes its origin to the apparitions and revelations made by Jesus to St. Margaret Mary. Hence we have to examine what Jesus said to her and demanded of her, and how she understood, realized and taught it. This we find in her writings and particularly in her Autobiography.

The Devotion rests on dogmatic grounds. Hence we have to inquire how theologians have explained and justified it.

The Devotion has been approved and encouraged by the Church and admitted to her liturgy. Hence we have to investigate how the Church understands, presents and practises it.

It is, finally, a living devotion. Therefore we have to take into account its development among the faithful, that is, the manner in which, under the control and guidance of the Church, it has been understood and practised by the faithful.

I. THE WRITINGS OF ST. MARGARET MARY

Among the writings of the Saint the most important are:

1. Her Autobiography, composed by order of Fr. Rolin, her spiritual director. It is from this work, together with her Letters, that we know the Saint most intimately. During her last illness she humbly begged that it should be burnt. God, however, did not permit her wish to be carried out, thus 'this masterpiece of humility and simplicity' has been preserved.[1]

2. One hundred and forty-two letters[2] addressed for the greater part to her former Superiors, Mother de Saumaise and Mother Greyfié, to Sisters of the Visitation order, and to Fr. Croiset.

3. Advice and instructions, nearly all intended for her novices.[3]

4. A collection of writings in which the Saint renders an account to her Superior, Mother de Saumaise, of the graces received between 1672 and 1678.[4]

---

[1] *Procès de 1715: Déposition de la Sœur de Farges.* Cf. Hamon, op. cit., vol. I, p. 482. Cf. also *Vie et Oeuvres*, vol. II, *Avertissement*, p. 23.

[2] Cf. *Vie et Oeuvres*, vol. II, *Avertissement aux lettres*, p. 209.

[3] Cf. *Vie et Oeuvres*, vol. II, p. 633.

[4] Cf. ibid., p. 121.

5. A booklet containing prayers and pious exercises, nearly all relating to the Sacred Heart. It is entirely in her own handwriting; yet this does not imply that all the prayers are composed by herself.[1]

All the writings of the Saint were edited in 1915 by Mgr. Gauthey, Archbishop of Besançon, under the title of *Vie et Oeuvres de la bienheureuse Marguerite-Marie*. A new edition was issued in 1920. This work will be referred to hereafter as *Vie et Oeuvres* for all quotations.

In addition to these writings the work contains a biography of the Saint, entitled 'Mémoire des Contemporaines', and composed by two of her former novices, Sister Verchère and Sister de Farges. Mother Greyfié attested to its entire veracity.[2]

II. THE WORKS OF THEOLOGIANS

The works which treat of the devotion to the Sacred Heart are countless. Yet among them there are two that are deserving of special mention—namely, that by Fr. Croiset, *La dévotion au Sacré-Cœur de Jésus*, and that by Fr. de Galliffet, *De l'excellence de la dévotion au Cœur adorable de Jésus-Christ*.

(a) The Book by Fr. Croiset

The book by Fr. Croiset, s.j.,[3] was written at the request, under the direct control, and as it were dictated by St. Margaret Mary; it may be added, it was as a result of a particular wish of the Sacred Heart, as may be inferred from many passages of her letters to Fr. Croiset: 'If you only knew the ardent desire I have that the Sacred Heart should be known, loved and honoured, you would not refuse to apply yourself to it, as He demands of you, and to write on such a worthy subject when He will give you the leisure and the inspiration for doing so.'[4] Again: 'Our Lord wishes me to assure you that this beginning has pleased Him so much, that He wishes to impart to you the graces which He had destined

---

[1] Cf. *Vie et Oeuvres*, vol. ii, p. 771. Cf. Bainvel, op. cit., p. 14.
[2] Ibid., vol. i, p. 63. Cf. Bainvel, op. cit., p. 6, note.
[3] Jean Croiset was born at Marseilles on August 28th, 1656. He entered the Society of Jesus on December 16th, 1677. His virtue was held in high esteem by St. Margaret Mary. He displayed extraordinary energy and zeal in preaching and propagating the new devotion. As foretold to him by the Saint, he had to suffer much on account of it. (Cf. Hamon, op. cit., vol. iii, p. 362.)
[4] *Vie et Oeuvres*, vol. ii, *Lettre au P. Croiset*, p. 520.

for another, who excused himself on account of his occupations, that you may do what you have done and what He wishes you to do in the future.'[1] Again: 'The plan you have conceived of honouring this Divine Heart is so agreeable to Him, that this will be, I think, one of the means which He intends to use in this devotion. . . . I cannot doubt any more that He has destined you for it.'[2] 'I say particularly to you, as He gave me to understand, that the treasures of His Sacred Heart are open to you; and I see that He will allow you to draw from that source abundantly for the accomplishment of this great work, for which I can no longer doubt that He has destined you.'[3] 'The first time that I saw you, He gave me such great certainty that He had chosen you for this design. . . . I was set at rest by the words that He would not have given you either such liking for this devotion nor such fitness for working for it if He had not chosen you for it.'[4] 'If He had not chosen you to procure for Him the honour and glory which He expects of you by means of the work which you have undertaken, He would never have allowed me to talk to you so confidently . . .'[5]

The Saint had not the good fortune to see the book so ardently desired appear in print; she died on October 17th, 1690, and the book was not published until June 10th, 1691. It met with a great success, particularly because of the Saint's biography which was joined to it. It had already gone through several editions when, in 1704, contrary to expectation, it was placed on the Index, not on account of its contents but apparently because of the omission of certain formalities.[6] Yet the book continued to be reprinted; having undergone a slight change it was translated into Italian.[7] The prohibition, however, remained in force till August 24th, 1887, when the Sacred Congregation of Inquisition removed it and recommended the book as most suitable to enkindle the piety of the faithful through the devotion to the Sacred Heart.[8]

---

[1] *Vie et Oeuvres*, vol. II, *Lettre au P. Croiset*, p. 530.
[2] Ibid., p. 550.
[3] Ibid., p. 560.
[4] Ibid., p. 597.
[5] Ibid., p. 619. See in other passages of her letters how she urges him to set to work without delay, how she encourages and advises him, approves what he has written, etc., for instance, pp. 531, 536, 583, 584, 602, 606, 617, 621, 622, 623.
[6] Cf. Hamon, op. cit., vol. III; Bainvel, op. cit., p. 523.
[7] Cf. Bainvel, op. cit., p. 523.
[8] See in the Preface of the new edition, published in 1891 by Vromant (Brussels), the circumstances in which the prohibition was withdrawn.

(b) The Book by Fr. de Galliffet

The book by Fr. de Galliffet, s.j.,[1] was published in 1726, in Latin, under the title of *De cultu sacrosancti Cordis Dei ac Domini nostri Jesu Christi*. The author intended first and foremost to inform the Sacred Congregation of Rites accurately and completely about the bearing and purport of the requested Feast of the Sacred Heart, as well as of the Devotion to which the institution of this Feast would attach the approval of the Church. 'It is the first work that treats doctrinally and profoundly of the Devotion to the Sacred Heart. Theology, philosophy, physiology, history, nothing has been omitted by the author to make this study a definitive work. And he succeeded in it. Without venturing to contend that no one after him did better, it is certain that those who surpassed him could succeed in doing so only because of his book.'[2] Some of his assertions, it is true, need elucidation; others are, as we shall see, open to discussion, but the whole is a masterly account of the doctrine of the Devotion.

The value and authority of this book are still further enhanced by the part it played in the publication of the Decree of the Congregation of Rites in 1765, whereby the Feast requested was finally instituted. This Decree set forth that the Feast was granted in the sense of the request, presented by the *Memoriale* of the Bishops of Poland.[3] Now this *Memoriale* is entirely based on Fr. de Galliffet's book and quotes it literally in many passages. If then we wish to

---

[1] Joseph de Galliffet was born at Aix, in Provence, May 3rd, 1663. He entered the Society of Jesus, September 17th, 1678. In 1680, while studying philosophy, he lived for one year under the spiritual direction of Bl. Claude de la Colombière. 'It was from this Servant of God,' he wrote afterwards, 'that I received the first instructions concerning the devotion to the Sacred Heart of Jesus Christ, and from that time forward I began to appreciate and cherish it.' Ten years later he recovered from a mortal illness, contrary to all expectations, after Fr. Croiset had promised in his name that, if he were restored to health, he would devote his life to the propagation of the devotion to the Sacred Heart. Fr. de Galliffet ratified the promise, and henceforth considered himself entrusted by Our Lord with the mission of making known the Devotion. This he did to the best of his power in his capacity as Superior at Grenoble and at Lyons, and as Provincial. In 1723 he came to Rome as Assistant of the General of the Society. There he tried every possible means in order to obtain the institution of a feast in honour of the Sacred Heart, but his efforts failed. The Sacred Congregation of Rites refused to comply with his request: the devotion was said to be new; there seemed to be no sufficient evidence that the feast was willed by God, as the holiness of Margaret Mary was not yet proved by any miracle; moreover, Fr. de Galliffet, as we shall see in the next chapter, founded the devotion to the Sacred Heart on grounds as to which opinions were divided. He died on August 31st, 1749, 'having always lived as a saint, he died as such', wrote his Superior. (Cf. Hamon, op. cit., vol. IV, chap. i and ii.)

[2] Cf. Hamon, op. cit., vol. IV, p. 16. There will be found the summary of this work.

[3] See p. xxxviii.

know accurately how the Devotion has been understood and approved by the Church, we have only to consult the work of Fr. de Galliffet.

The author published in 1733 the French version of his book, entitled *De l'excellence de la dévotion au Cœur adorable de Jésus-Christ.*

III. OFFICIAL DOCUMENTS

(a) *Papal Letters and Decrees*

Among the Papal documents the most important are: the Decree of the Sacred Congregation of Rites, in 1765; the Bull *Auctorem fidei* by Pope Pius VI; the Encyclical *Annum sacrum* by Pope Leo XIII; and the Encyclical *Miserentissimus* by Pope Pius XI.

1. *The Decree of 1765*

The Decree of the Sacred Congregation of Rites was issued on February 6th, 1765, under the pontificate of Clement XIII. As Fr. de Galliffet had not succeeded in obtaining the institution of a feast in honour of the Sacred Heart, the Bishops of Poland, some thirty years later, made a new attempt and presented to the Roman Congregation a *Memoriale*, or explanatory memorandum, in which they advanced at length all that might be pleaded in favour of the Feast requested and of the devotion which was connected with it. At the same time they answered the objections which might be raised, and in fact were raised, against the new feast. Explanation, arguments and answers were, for the greater part, derived and even quoted word for word from Fr. de Galliffet's book.[1]

The request was supported by the King of Poland, by the Duke of Bavaria, by more than a hundred and forty Bishops, and many religious Orders and Confraternities. Personally the Pope was favourably disposed to the Devotion. The Sacred Congregation took the request into consideration and resolved also, in its session of January 26th, 1765, to give a favourable answer.

The Decree, approved by the Sovereign Pontiff, was issued on February 6th. It said: 'Having been requested to grant a Mass and an Office of the Sacred Heart by the greater part of the most

---

[1] See the analysis of the *Memoriale* in Hamon, op. cit., vol. IV, p. 207–13. The Latin text is to be found in Nilles, *De rationibus festorum Beatissimi Cordis Jesu et Purissimi Cordis Mariae*, editio 3a, Liber I, cap. iii, § iii, A.

Reverend Bishops of Poland and by the Roman Archconfraternity erected under this title, the Sacred Congregation of Rites, in its session of January 26th, 1765, recognizing that the cult of the Heart of Jesus is already spread in almost all parts of the Catholic world, favoured by Bishops and enriched by the Apostolic See with a thousand Briefs of indulgences granted to nearly innumerable Confraternities canonically erected in honour of the Heart of Jesus; moreover, understanding that by allowing this Mass and Office nothing else is aimed at than to develop a cult already established and to renew symbolically the memory of the divine love by which the Only-begotten Son of God took upon Himself a human nature and, obedient unto death, wished to prove to men by His example that He was, as He had said, meek and humble of heart; for these reasons, acting on the report of His Eminence Cardinal Bishop of Sabinum, after hearing the Right Reverend Cajetanus Fortis, promoter of the Faith, and putting aside the decisions of July 30th, 1729, the said Sacred Congregation has deemed it right to accede to the request of the Bishops of the Kingdom of Poland and of the said Roman Archconfraternity. It will later on make a decision as to the Mass and Office which can be fittingly approved. This prescription of the Sacred Congregation has been submitted to our Holy Father the Pope Clement XIII. His Holiness, having given it his attention, has approved it in every respect.'[1]

This Decree is a document of great importance. It is the first time a Roman Congregation and the Sovereign Pontiff clearly manifested their opinion on the Devotion to the Sacred Heart. When we study the nature of the Devotion, we shall have the opportunity of expounding the text of the Decree. Meanwhile it is to be noted that the Sacred Congregation stated that it 'has deemed it right to accede to the request of the Bishops of Poland' without making any observation. From this we must conclude that the Congregation understood the Feast requested and the devotion connected with it, as they were set forth in the *Memoriale* of the Bishops, and that both were approved for the reasons laid down in it. 'Hence it appears that all questions referring to the nature, object and aim of this cult approved by the Church cannot be wisely and fully resolved, except in the light of the *Memoriale* from which the Sacred Congregation has drawn the reasons for its

[1] Nilles, op. cit., ibid., § iv, p. 135. Cf. Hamon, op. cit., p. 214.

decision. To be sure, the *Memoriale* has not the force of law, yet it helps us to understand the sense of the decree and the sense of the Feast. The reasons of a decree must be those of its interpretation.'[1]

2. *The Bull 'Auctorem fidei'*

The Bull *Auctorem fidei* by Pope Pius VI was issued on August 28th, 1794. It condemned the decrees of the diocesan synod, convoked by Ricci, the Jansenist bishop of Pistoia, Italy. This synod contended, among other things, (1) that to adore Christ's Humanity or a part of it was to pay divine worship to a mere creature; (2) that the devotion to the Sacred Heart was something new, false, or at least dangerous; (3) that it was wrong for the faithful to adore the Heart of Jesus, separate or apart from His divinity.

The Pope condemned those contentions in the three following decrees:

Proposition 61. 'The proposition which asserts that the *direct adoration of the Humanity of Christ, and especially a part of this Humanity, is always the rendering to a creature of an honour due to God alone*, in so far as by the word "*direct*" is meant to blame the cult of adoration which the faithful pay to the Humanity of Christ; as if it could be said that the adoration rendered to the humanity and living flesh of Christ, not considered in itself and as mere flesh, but as united with the Divinity, was divine honour paid to a creature, and not rather one and the same adoration by which the Word Incarnate with its own flesh is adored;—this proposition is false, fallacious, injurious and offensive to the pious cult which is due to the Humanity of Christ and which the faithful have always rendered to it and are bound to render to it.'

Proposition 62. 'The doctrine which rejects the devotion to the Most Sacred Heart of Jesus among the devotions which it qualifies as new, false, or at least dangerous;—if this devotion is understood to be such as is approved by the Apostolic See, this doctrine is false, temerarious, pernicious, offensive to pious ears, injurious to the Apostolic See.'

Proposition 63. 'Likewise the devout clients of the Heart of Jesus are reproached with paying no heed to the fact that neither the most sacred flesh of Christ, or any part of it, nor even the whole

[1] Hamon, op. cit., vol. IV, p. 216.

human nature, if separate or apart from the Divinity, may be adored with the supreme worship (*cultu latriae*); as though the faithful adored the Heart of Jesus, separate or apart from the Divinity;—whereas they adore it as the Heart of Jesus, that is, as the Heart of the Person of the Word, with whom It is inseparably united; in the same way as the inanimate body of Christ, during the three days of His death, was to be adored in the tomb, not as separate nor as apart from the Divinity. This doctrine is fallacious, injurious to the devout worshippers of the Heart of Christ.'[1]

3. *The Encyclical 'Annum sacrum'*

The Encyclical *Annum sacrum* by Pope Leo XIII (May 25th, 1899) treats of the Consecration of mankind to the Sacred Heart, which he intended to carry out on the occasion of the coming Holy Year (1900). The Sovereign Pontiff sets forth in it the motives prompting him to perform this act, and the beneficial fruits he expects of it. At the same time he expounds the meaning and purport of the Consecration to the Sacred Heart, and Jesus' claim to the total donation of ourselves. When we treat of this practice of devotion we shall see what persuaded the Pope to put this solemn act into effect.[2]

4. *The Encyclical 'Miserentissimus'*

The Encyclical *Miserentissimus* by Pope Pius XI (May 8th, 1928), according to its title, treats of 'the universal duty of reparation towards the Sacred Heart of Jesus'.[3] It lucidly sets forth the peculiar form and character of the Devotion, and brings into special prominence its two main features: Consecration and Reparation. As Pope Leo XIII had already treated of the former in his Encyclical *Annum sacrum*, Pius XI confines himself to repeating and completing what was there said on that score, and to emphasizing the duty of reparation, pointing out what is required by justice and demanded by love in this respect. The reparation proper and peculiar to the Devotion to the Sacred Heart is a reparation of love. The Sovereign Pontiff indicates the motives which should urge us on to practise it, and finally expresses the

---

[1] Denziger-Bannwart, *Enchiridion Symbolorum*, n. 1561, 1562, 1563. Cf. Hamon, op. cit., vol. IV, pp. 276-277.
[2] See p. 144.
[3] '*De communi expiatione Sacratissimo Cordi debita*' (*Acta Apost. Sedis*, vol. XX (1928), pp. 165-78). English translation in appendix II, 2.

wish that the whole Catholic world should join in it by solemnly celebrating the Feast of the Sacred Heart in a spirit of atonement and reparation. This encyclical is the only one specially consecrated to the devotion to the Sacred Heart, and thus it is the chief document which we must consult if we want to know how the Church wishes this devotion to be understood and practised.

5. *Other Documents*

In addition to those four official documents there are still others which, though less important as regards doctrine, contain valuable information concerning the practice of the devotion. We mention the following:[1]

1. Letter of Cardinal Mazella (July 21st, 1899), written in the name of Pope Leo XIII, on the means of promoting the devotion to the Sacred Heart.

2. Letter of Pope Benedict XV (April 27th, 1915) on the Consecration of Families to the Sacred Heart.

3. Letter of Pope Benedict XV (October 7th, 1919) on the occasion of the solemn dedication of the basilica of Montmartre, Paris, on Devotion to the Sacred Heart and on the universal charity which it should enkindle in souls.

4. The Encyclical *Caritate Christi compulsi* by Pope Pius XI (May 3rd, 1932) 'on offering prayer and expiation to the Sacred Heart of Jesus in the present distress of the human race' (*Acta Apost. Sedis*, vol. XXIV (1932), pp. 177–194).

(b) *The Liturgy*

The Church not only teaches by means of Decrees and Letters of the Apostolic See, but also, among other things, by her Liturgy, which is as the echo of her belief.

The liturgical practices connected with the devotion to the Sacred Heart are: the Mass for the Feast of the Sacred Heart, the Office of this Feast, and the Litany of the Sacred Heart.[2]

1. *The Mass of the Sacred Heart*

The Sacred Congregation of Rites, in its decree of February 6th,

---

[1] They are to be found in Galtier, op. cit.
[2] To these might be added: the Consecration of mankind to the Sacred Heart, prescribed by Pope Leo XIII, and the Act of Reparation, prescribed by Pius XI.

1765,[1] had promised a Mass and an Office of the Sacred Heart. It redeemed its promise on May 11th of the same year.

The form of the Mass then approved is known by the name of Mass *Miserebitur* after the first word of the Introit. The Collect is as follows: 'Grant, we beseech Thee, O Almighty God, that we, who glory in the Most Sacred Heart of Thy beloved Son, and celebrate the singular benefits of His love towards us, may rejoice both in their accomplishment and in the fruit they produce. Through the same Christ Our Lord.'[2]

In consequence of his Encyclical *Miserentissimus*, Pope Pius XI charged a special committee with the composition of a new Mass and a new Office. The Mass, open with the words *Cogitationes Cordis Ejus*, was approved by him (January 29th, 1929), and made obligatory for the universal Church. It brings out the two leading ideas of the Encyclical, especially in the Collect, the Epistle and the Preface.[3] The Collect, in particular, says: 'O God, who in the Sacred Heart of Thy Son, wounded by our sins, dost deign mercifully to bestow on us infinite treasures of love, grant, we beseech Thee, that whilst we render It the devout homage of our affection, we may also discharge our duty of worthy satisfaction. Through the same.'[4]

2. *The Office of the Feast of the Sacred Heart*

The new Office, composed by the Sacred Congregation of Rites in 1929, together with the new Mass, is obligatory for all priests. The three lessons of the Second Nocturn contain an outstandingly good sketch of the origin and development of the Devotion to the Sacred Heart.[5]

3. *The Litany of the Sacred Heart*

The Litany, in its present form, was approved by Pope Leo XIII

[1] See p. xxxix.

[2] 'Concede, quaesumus, omnipotens Deus: ut, qui in sanctissimo dilecti Filii tui Corde gloriantes, praecipua in nos caritatis ejus beneficia recolimus, eorum pariter et actu delectemur et fructu. Per eumdem Dominum.'

[3] An excellent paraphrase of the Mass is to be found in Vermeersch, op. cit., vol. I, pp. 64–79. Cf. also Galtier, op. cit, pp. 199–211.

[4] 'Deus, qui nobis, in Corde Filii tui, nostris vulnerato peccatis, infinitos dilectionis thesauros misericorditer largiri dignaris, concede, quaesumus, ut illi devotum pietatis nostrae praestantes obsequium, dignae quoque satisfactionis exhibeamus officium. Per eumdem Dominum.'

[5] Cf. p. xx. On the Office of the whole octave of the Feast, see Hugo Rahner, s.j., in *Zeitschrift für Aszese und Mystik*, 1943, 2. Heft, pp. 61–83.

(April 2nd, 1899) for the universal Church. It may be found useful to quote the decree of the Congregation of Rites in its entirety.

'Urbi et Orbi[1]

'By decree of the Sacred Congregation of Rites, dated June 27th, 1899, our Holy Father the Pope Leo XIII has approved the Litany of the Most Sacred Heart of Jesus and allowed it to be publicly recited or sung in the churches and chapels of the dioceses of Marseilles and Autun and of the Order of the Visitation of our Lady. Since then bishops, religious congregations and pious associations have addressed many similar requests to the Holy See, thus expressing the general wish that these pious invocations should be spread abroad everywhere, in order to procure more praise and glory to the Sacred Heart and to increase the devotion of the faithful, in the same manner as the Most Holy Name of Jesus is glorified throughout the Catholic world by common public homage, by the use of a special Litany inserted in the Roman ritual. Moreover, our Holy Father, animated with tender devotion towards the Sacred Heart and desirous to remedy the evils which afflict us ever more and more, intends to consecrate the whole world to the Sacred Heart of Jesus. To enhance the solemnity of this consecration, he has decided to prescribe a triduum of prayer during which this Litany will be recited. Therefore His Holiness has deigned to sanction in perpetuity the reciting or singing of the Litany of the Sacred Heart, in common or privately, already approved and enriched with an indulgence of three hundred days. Notwithstanding opposition or appeal.

'April 2nd, 1899.   CARDINAL MAZELLA,
'Prefect of the Sacred Congregation of Rites.'

By this solemn and universal approval, the Litany has taken a place in the official cult of the Church and become a liturgical prayer. It thus acquired high doctrinal value. 'Though this approbation is not the most solemn sanction given by the Church to the whole doctrine expressed in these invocations, yet it is sufficient to afford us full certainty that this doctrine is in every respect in accordance with the teaching of the Church, and hence that there is in it nothing false or exaggerated. It follows that the Sacred

[1] 'To the City and to the whole world', i.e. the decree is in force not only for Rome but for the whole Christian world.

Heart really possesses all the qualities and perfections which are attributed to It, that It is really worthy of all the eulogistic titles given It and of the worship paid to It, and that the motives enumerated for the special cult of the Sacred Heart are well founded.

'The teaching authority of the Church watches over the liturgical prayers most carefully, for they are one of the ordinary means it uses to convey religious truths to the minds of the faithful. In order to be profitable to the faithful as well as agreeable to God, these prayers must be fully in keeping with revealed truth; the Liturgy must be the rampart of the Faith; Faith must be the rule of prayer, of piety and worship, and must control and guide all its manifestations. Before approving any prayer, especially before admitting it to Her liturgy, the Church proceeds with the greatest caution, minutely examining the prayer, and accurately balancing the sense of each phrase and word. She has not acted otherwise in regard to the Litany of the Sacred Heart. For these reasons the Litany, in the form approved by the Sacred Congregation, is a valuable document which enables us to establish and understand the doctrine of the Church concerning the Sacred Heart and the special cult of the Sacred Heart, as well as the religious truths on which this cult is based and the motives which recommend it to the faithful.'[1]

[1] Leroy, *Les Litanies du Sacré-Cœur de Jésus*, p. 8. In chap. iii, when we treat of the practice of devotion, we shall study the origin of the Litany.

CHAPTER I

Object of the Devotion

GENERAL IDEA OF THE OBJECT

We ought first of all to form an accurate and clear idea of the object of the devotion to the Sacred Heart, that is to say, of what we intend to worship in and by this devotion.

It is evident that by the homage which we render to the Heart of Jesus we intend to honour, and we really do honour, Jesus Himself, the Person of Christ, with all that He is and all that He has. When we pay honour to a portion of the body of a person, we wish to render this homage to the person himself; for instance, when we kiss the hand of a prelate, we address this mark of respect to the prelate himself.[1]

So it is also with regard to the Heart of Jesus. Pope Leo XIII, in his Encyclical *Annum sacrum* (n. 10), recalls the fact: 'All homage of love paid to the Divine Heart is really and properly addressed to Christ Himself.'

Hence, the Person of Jesus is the ultimate object of devotion to the Sacred Heart.

He may also be said to be its general object. Indeed, all the devotions which honour one of the mysteries of the Life of our Lord, or some part of His sacred body, have for their common object His Divine Person. When, for instance, we venerate His sacred Wounds, or celebrate His Birth, His Resurrection, His Ascension, it is always the Divine Person of the Word Incarnate who receives the homage of our adoration and love.

But, although the Person of Jesus is but the ultimate and general object of the devotion, He is nevertheless also its principal object: for, by the homage which we pay to some part or to some quality of a person, it is his whole person whom we aim at, and whom we want to honour. The homage paid to the part or the quality is but the means; the cult of the person is its end.

[1] We find this principle formulated in St. Thomas (*Summa theol.*, pars III, q. 25, art. 1): 'Honour is, properly speaking, rendered to the entire person. Even when we honour the foot or the hand of a person, we do not venerate these parts in themselves, but only by reason of the entire person to whom they belong.'

But the question is: What distinguishes devotion to the Sacred Heart from all other devotions which have Jesus for their common object? What is its special and direct object? Our Lord Himself indicated this in His apparitions to St. Margaret Mary, especially in the fourth, called the 'Great' Apparition. To what did He draw attention in the first place? To the Heart that beats in His breast: 'Discovering to me His Heart, He said to me: "Behold this Heart . . ." ' And what did He declare concerning this Heart? That It ineffably loves us and is sensible to the manner in which men repay Its love: 'Behold this Heart which has so loved men. . . . And in return I receive from the greater part of them nothing but ingratitude. . . .' And what did He demand for this Heart? 'Therefore I ask of you that the first Friday after the octave of Corpus Christi be dedicated to a special feast in honour of My Heart. . . .'[1]

From this it appears that the special object of the devotion asked for by our Lord is His Heart: His Heart which loves us and complains of the neglect of Its love.

For the ordinary faithful this raises no difficulties. It is actually in this way that they understand the devotion; what they wish to honour is the Heart of Jesus, and this because It loves us and because Its love is despised.

Yet, if we want to form an accurate and adequate idea of the devotion, we ought closely to consider both this Heart and this love, and the relation that exists between them.

§ I. THE PHYSICAL HEART OF JESUS THE SYMBOL OF HIS LOVE AND, SECONDARILY, OF HIS WHOLE INNER LIFE

1. The Physical Heart of Jesus

The object of devotion to the Sacred Heart is in the first place the physical Heart of Jesus, the Heart which during His mortal life beat in His breast and still beats in His glorified body.

This is beyond all doubt. For it is this Heart which Jesus showed to St. Margaret Mary, this Heart to which He pointed when He asked for a special cult, a special devotion.

It is, moreover, this Heart of flesh which the Saint herself

[1] See p. xxvii.

honoured and caused to be honoured. It is sufficient to go through her writings to perceive that wherever she speaks of the devotion, she uses the word 'Heart' in its proper sense and designates the physical Heart of Jesus. Whatever she says of the Heart of Jesus she attributes to His Heart of flesh: this is evidenced by her zeal in spreading the veneration of the image of this Heart.

Thus it was understood by Fr. de Galliffet: 'Evidently,' he writes, 'the Heart of Jesus is to be taken in its *proper and natural sense* and by no means metaphorically. Jesus speaks of His Heart of flesh when He says: Behold this Heart, etc. He speaks of the Heart which He discovers and shows. This then is the Heart which He wished to see honoured and for which He asked a special Feast.'[1]

It was so understood by the Sacred Congregation of Rites when it granted in 1765 the institution of the Feast. Its decree stated that 'by allowing the Mass and Office nothing else was aimed at than to develop a cult already established.'[2] Now, what the faithful already honoured everywhere was actually the physical Heart of Jesus. Moreover, in unreservedly complying with the request of the Bishops of Poland, the Congregation showed that it understood the significance of the Feast requested, and the nature of the devotion connected with it, as this was set forth in the *Memoriale*, and that it approved both of them for the reasons laid down in it. Now the *Memoriale* stated that Jesus in His apparition to St. Margaret Mary spoke of His Heart 'not metaphorically, but *in the proper and natural sense* of the word, namely, of the noblest part of the Body of Christ', and hence that 'the object which Jesus presents for our veneration is His most Sacred Heart . . . , as It is in itself'.[3]

It was understood in this way by Pope Pius VI when, in 1794, by the Bull *Auctorem fidei*, he condemned the Jansenists who contended that the homage of adoration paid by the faithful to Jesus' Heart of flesh was illicit and contrary to Faith and truth, and when he solemnly declared that it was not wrong for the faithful to adore the Heart of flesh of Jesus, since they did not honour this

---

[1] De Galliffet, op. cit., Book I, pt. I, chap. iv, p. 95.

[2] See p. xxxix.

[3] 'Cor Jesu, non translatione sumptum, sed in propria ac nativa significatione, videlicet ut est pars corporis Christi nobilissima . . . En igitur quae sit res quam Jesus colendam proponit, nimirum Cor suum sacrosanctum . . . ut est in se.' (Nilles, op. cit., pars I, cap. iii, n. 32, p. 93; et pars II, cap. ii, p. 226.)

D

Heart separately and apart from the Divinity, but 'as the Heart of Jesus, that is, the Heart of the Person of the Word, with whom It is inseparably united, just as the inanimate body of Christ, during the three days of His death, was to be adored in the tomb, not as separate nor as apart from the Divinity'.[1]

It was so understood by Pope Pius IX when, in the Brief of beatification of Margaret Mary, he said: 'In order to enkindle ever more this fire of charity, He (Jesus) has willed that the veneration and cult of His Sacred Heart should be established in the Church and propagated. Who indeed could be so hard-hearted and insensible as not to be moved to make a return of love to this most sweet Heart, *wounded and pierced* by the lance, that our soul might have as it were a haven and refuge where it could find a shelter and refuge against the inroads and snares of the enemy? Who would not be incited to pay every kind of homage to this most Sacred Heart, *whose wound* shed water and blood, that is, the source of our life and our salvation?'[2]

It was understood in this way by Pope Leo XIII when, in his Encyclical *Annum sacrum* on the Consecration of mankind to the Sacred Heart, he proclaimed that this Heart would be a token and pledge of victory for the Church: 'In the early ages of the Church, a young emperor beheld in the heavens a cross, the herald of a magnificent and speedily approaching victory. Today, behold another emblem, sacred and divine, appears before our eyes. It is the Most Sacred Heart of Jesus, with the cross above it, glowing in the midst of flames. In It let us place all our hopes; to It let us look for the salvation of the human race.'

Thus was it understood by Pope Pius XI when, in his Encyclical *Miserentissimus* (n. 5), he recalled these encouraging words of Leo XIII and preceded them by this statement: 'Even as of old, when the human race came out of the ark, God gave "the bow shining in the clouds" as a sign of a covenant of friendship, so in the stormy times of a more recent age, when the most insidious of all heresies, Jansenism, was creeping in, contrary to love and devotion to God, representing Him not as a Father to be loved, but as a merciless judge to be feared, the most loving Jesus showed His Sacred Heart to all nations as a token of peace and love, and a pledge of victory.'

[1] See p. xli.
[2] *Vie et Oeuvres*, vol. III, *Bref de béatification*, p. 145.

Finally, it is so understood by the Church in her liturgy.

In the Invitatory of the Matins on the Feast of the Sacred Heart, she bids her priests pray: 'Come, let us adore the Heart of Jesus, *wounded* for love of us.'[1]

In the Hymn at Lauds, she sings to the Heart of Jesus: 'Love has willed Thee struck *with a visible wound* . . .'[2]

In the Collect, she bids us pray: 'O God, who, in the Heart of Thy Son, *wounded* by our sins, dost deign mercifully to bestow on us infinite treasures of love . . .'[3]

In the Gospel of the Mass, she relates how on the cross the sacred side of Jesus was *opened with a spear* (John xix, 34).

In the Preface, she emphasizes it again: 'Holy Lord, Father almighty, everlasting God, who didst will that Thine only-begotten Son as He hung upon the cross should be *pierced by a soldier's spear*, that this opened Heart, the treasury of the Divine bounty, might pour forth upon us streams of mercy and grace . . .'[4]

And in the Litany of the Sacred Heart, she bids us say: 'Heart of Jesus, formed by the Holy Ghost in the womb of the Virgin Mary,—hypostatically united to the Word of God,—pierced by the lance', invocations which evidently refer to the physical Heart of Jesus.

Thus, what we honour in the first place and directly in the Devotion which we are studying here, is the physical, living Heart of Jesus, His Heart of flesh.

This then is not what is meant by the expression 'Heart of Jesus' taken in a figurative or metaphorical sense: for instance, His spiritual emotional nature, and particularly His love. It is certainly open to anyone, for his personal piety, to conceive and practise devotion to the Sacred Heart in the way he prefers and, without attending to the physical Heart of Jesus, to address his homage directly to Christ's loving soul, to His love. But if we want to understand and practise devotion to the Sacred Heart as

---

[1] 'Cor Jesu, amore nostri vulneratum, venite adoremus.' As remarked by Pope Benedict XIV, in his immortal work on Beatification and Canonization of Saints, it is usually in the Invitatory of the Office that the Church points out the proper and peculiar character of the Feast.

[2] 'Te vulneratum caritas ictu patenti voluit.'

[3] 'Deus, qui nobis, in Corde Filii tui, nostris vulnerato peccatis, infinitos dilectionis thesauros misericorditer largiri dignaris.'

[4] 'Domine Sancte, Pater omnipotens, aeterne Deus, qui Unigenitum tuum in cruce pendentem lancea militis transfigi voluisti, ut apertum Cor, divinae largitatis sacrarium, torrentes nobis funderet miserationis et gratiae.'

it is asked for by Jesus and officially sanctioned by the Church, we are to address our homage to His Heart of flesh.[1]

The physical Heart of Jesus, therefore, is the direct and immediate object of the Devotion to the Sacred Heart.

And it is this Heart as It really is. It is not to be looked upon and honoured as something inanimate, as a relic, such being the case with the heart of some Saint or other.[2]

'To preclude all misinterpretation,' says the *Memoriale*, 'it should be noted and borne in mind that the Heart of Jesus, in this devotion, is by no means to be regarded as an inanimate and insensible thing, but as a *living and sensitive* Heart.'[3]

Nor do we consider It apart and separate from the rest of the body, from the entire human nature and the Divine Person of Jesus, but rather as united to this body, to this human nature, to this Divine Person. We look upon It as It was during the mortal life of Jesus and as It is still living in Heaven and in the Blessed Eucharist. 'Therefore', continues the *Memoriale*, 'the Heart of Jesus is to be considered as object of this devotion, not separate and apart, but in so far as It forms a unity with the soul of Jesus and His Divine Person.'[4]

2. Jesus' Love for Men

The object, then, of devotion to the Sacred Heart is in the first place the physical Heart of Jesus. It is not, however, this Heart considered in itself, as forming part of His body, of His sacred Humanity, and so belonging to His divine Person; nor is it this Heart, looked upon in its function of an organ keeping up the circulation of the blood; though under this twofold aspect It is worthy of adoring worship—and, as we shall see, in fact, the Devotion does not neglect these two claims of the Heart of Jesus to our veneration. But that is not the reason why His Heart is taken as the object of a special devotion, nor the peculiar aspect under which It is considered.

How then is It to be regarded? Chiefly in Its relation to Christ's

---

[1] See p. 3.

[2] For instance, the heart of St. John Berchmans, venerated in the Jesuit church at Louvain, Belgium.

[3] *Memoriale*, n. 33. Cf. Nilles, op. cit., p. 94.

[4] 'Itaque Cor Jesu non seorsum, non solitarie sumptum considerandum est, se quatenus cum anima Jesu eiusque divina Persona rem unam in ratione objecti huius cultus constituit' (*Memoriale*, n. 33). Nilles, op. cit., p. 94.

love for men. 'Behold this Heart which has so loved men . . .'
Thus our Lord has presented It as object of the devotion which
He demanded. 'Devotion to the Sacred Heart of Jesus,' writes
Fr. de Galliffet, 'is a practice of religion which has for its object
the adorable Heart of Jesus Christ all glowing with love for men.'[1]

We shall see further on in what sense Christ's love may be attributed to His Heart, and what is the relation that exists between
them. At the present moment it is sufficient to observe that the
Heart of Jesus, as object of this Devotion, is considered in Its
relation to the love of Jesus for men.

I. ITS PLACE IN THE DEVOTION

Hence it appears that Jesus' love for men also forms part of the
object of the Devotion. 'It should be noted,' writes Fr. de Galliffet,
'that this devotion, like all others, has two objects, joined together
and indivisibly honoured, one sensible and corporal, the other
invisible and spiritual. The sensible object is the divine Heart of
our Lord, the spiritual object is the boundless love with which
this Sacred Heart is inflamed.'[2]

Not only does the love of Jesus form part of the essential object
of the devotion, it is even the principal object.

For, on what did Jesus insist in His apparitions? On the excess
of His love. 'Behold this Heart,' He said, 'which has so loved men
that It spared nothing, going even so far as to exhaust Itself, in
order to testify Its love for them.' And of what did He complain?
Of the neglect and scorn of His love: 'And in return I receive from
the greater part of men nothing but ingratitude . . .' For what
purpose did He demand our love? In response to His own love:
'If they would only give Me some return of love, I should not
reckon all that I have done for them.' And for what did He ask
reparation? For the disdain of His love: 'At least, give Me the
happiness of making up for their ingratitude, as much as you
can.'[3]

Therefore, what Jesus wishes to see honoured first and foremost
is His love. This love, then, is really the chief constituent of the
essential object of devotion to the Sacred Heart.

'The particular object of this devotion,' writes Fr. Croiset, 'is

---

[1] De Galliffet, op. cit., Book I, chap. iv, p. 48.
[2] De Galliffet, op. cit., pp. 46–47.
[3] See p. xxvii.

the boundless love of the Son of God, which prompted Him to deliver Himself to death for us, and to give Himself entirely to us in the Blessed Sacrament of the Altar.' Again: 'Devotion to the Sacred Heart of our Lord Jesus Christ does not consist merely in honouring and loving this Heart of flesh, which is a part of the adorable body of Jesus Christ. . . . What we claim is that the word "Heart" is used here in the figurative[1] sense only, and that this divine Heart, considered as a part of the adorable body of Jesus Christ, is properly but the sensible object of this devotion, and that it is only the boundless love which Jesus Christ bears us, which is its principal motive.'[2]

II. ITS PRINCIPAL MANIFESTATIONS

We shall see further on to what extent Jesus loved and still loves us, how He has shown us His love, and what we owe to His love.

In devotion to the Sacred Heart, it is evident that we must consider the love of Jesus in all the proofs He has given of it, in all the benefits we owe it. Yet there are two which stand out specially: His sacred Passion and the institution of the Blessed Eucharist.

Fr. Croiset, as we have seen, begins his book as follows: 'The particular object of this devotion is the boundless love of the Son of God, which prompted Him *to deliver Himself to death for us* and to give Himself entirely to us in the *Blessed Sacrament of the Altar.*'

In like manner Fr. de Galliffet writes: 'The Heart of Jesus is to be regarded as glowing with that boundless love which induced Him to do and *to suffer* all that He did and suffered for us, and particularly *to institute the Sacrament of the Altar*, which has been the last effort of His love.'[3]

The Bishops of Poland in their *Memoriale* reproduce the views of Fr. de Galliffet almost word for word.[4]

And in the Office of the Feast of the Sacred Heart approved by Pope Clement XIII, in 1765, for several dioceses, we read that the Feast was granted 'in order that the faithful might recall with more devotion and fervour the love of Christ *suffering and*

---

[1] This adjective is inaccurate; the word 'Heart' here is used in the proper sense. Nor does it correspond to the author's mind, for he calls the Heart the sensible object of the devotion, thus using the word 'Heart' in its proper sense.

[2] Croiset, op. cit., pt. I, chap. i.

[3] De Galliffet, op. cit., Book I, chap. iv, p. 50.

[4] Nilles, *Memoriale*, n. 34.

dying for the Redemption of the human race, and, in memory of His death, *instituting* the Sacrament of His Body and Blood.'[1]

The supreme proof, indeed, which Jesus gave us of His love was to suffer and to die for us, nor can a greater one be imagined. He Himself declared: 'Greater love than this hath no man, that a man lay down his life for his friends' (John xv, 13). Hence to St. Margaret Mary He repeatedly expressed His wish 'to be honoured especially in His sacred Passion, and particularly in the sorrows of His Heart, which befell Him from the first moments of His lifetime and only ended at His death.'[2]

In all official documents which treat of the devotion to the Sacred Heart we find that this is always closely connected with the idea of our Lord's Passion and Death. The Mass *Miserebitur* and the former Office of the Feast of the Sacred Heart are full of it. The Litany, too, recalls it, in making us invoke the Heart of Jesus as 'atonement for our iniquities', 'overwhelmed with reproaches', 'bruised for our sins', 'made obedient unto death', 'pierced by the lance'.

Next to His Passion and Death, the Blessed Eucharist is surely the most magnificent manifestation of Christ's love for men. In the Eucharist indeed He went to the extreme of that love, so that He was willing to dwell in our midst, close by us, to the end of time; to renew unceasingly the Sacrifice of the Cross in an unbloody but real manner, and to unite Himself most intimately with each one of us in Holy Communion. The Eucharist is the masterpiece and the miracle of Jesus' love.[3]

On the other hand, the incredibly cold manner in which men repay the love He shows in the Blessed Eucharist is that to which He showed Himself the most sensitive and of which He complained the most grievously to St. Margaret Mary.

In the fourth apparition, to show their ingratitude, He points out particularly their conduct towards the Blessed Sacrament: 'In return I receive from the greater part of men nothing but ingratitude, by their irreverences and sacrileges, by the coldness and indifference with which they treat Me in this Sacrament of Love.' In another apparition He said to the Saint: 'I thirst, I burn with a consuming desire for men's love in the Blessed Sacrament, and

[1] 2nd Nocturn, 6th lesson.
[2] Cf. *Vie et Oeuvres*, vol. II, *Autobiographie*, n. 87, p. 99.
[3] See chap. ii, § i, 3.

I find none who, in accordance with My wish, strive to slake this thirst, by returning some love to Me.'[1]

Is the benefit of the Incarnation to be associated in a special way with the devotion to the Sacred Heart, in the same way as the Sacred Passion and the Eucharist?

It is clear that the Incarnation is one of the greatest proofs which the Son of God gave us of His love. In becoming Man He emptied Himself as it were of His Divinity and became like one of ourselves, in order to be able to atone for us, to reconcile us to His Father, and to merit for us the graces necessary to everlasting bliss and happiness.

But has this great gift a place in the devotion to the Sacred Heart?

The answer depends on the reply which is given to this other question: Does the love which Jesus bears us as God also form part of the object of the Devotion?

This question will be examined further on. In accordance with the solution which we there set out, we must say that it seems that the benefit of the Incarnation is not connected with the proper and direct object of the devotion to the Sacred Heart, but only with its object in a broad sense.

For the proper and direct object of the devotion is the human love of Jesus; His Divine love is but its object taken in a broad sense.

Now the Incarnation is not owing to Christ's human love, but to His Divine love, to the love He bears us as God. His human love presupposes the Incarnation; it is a consequence of it; for it is through the Incarnation that the Son of God assumed a human nature, capable of loving us with a human love.

Appendix: The Eucharistic Heart of Jesus

Lately stress has been laid on the gift of the Eucharist, on the love of the Sacred Heart to which we are indebted for it, and so there is frequently talk of devotion to the Eucharistic Heart of Jesus.

Having sprung up in France about the middle of the last century and having been approved by the Church at the beginning of the present one, this devotion was supported by the establishment of the Archconfraternity of the Eucharistic Heart of Jesus.[2]

---

[1] *Vie et Oeuvres*, vol. ii, Lettre cxxxiii, p. 580.   [2] See appendix ii, vii. p. 271.

By the title of 'Eucharistic Heart' is sometimes meant the Sacred Heart as present in the Eucharist. In this acceptation, however, the title is not justified. It seems to imply that there is a real distinction between the state in which It is in the Eucharist and that in which It is in Heaven. Such is definitely not the case. True, the Heart of Jesus is hidden in the Eucharist, but for the rest It is here as It is in Heaven, in infinite bliss and glory; nor has It here any sentiment or activity proper to this peculiar state. Hence it appears that no satisfactory reason can be advanced for designating by a special title the Heart of Jesus as present in the Eucharist.

Moreover, it is not in this sense that this devotion has been understood by the Church, but rather as a devotion to the Sacred Heart of Jesus in so far as we are indebted to Him for the institution of the Eucharist.

The *Raccolta*, i.e. the authentic collection of indulgenced prayers and pious works issued by the Sacred Penitentiary in 1898, and revised in 1937, precedes the invocations in honour of the Eucharistic Heart of Jesus by the following statement of the Sacred Congregation of Indulgences: 'The cult of the Most Sacred Heart of Jesus in the Eucharist is not to be considered as essentially different from that which is already rendered in the Church to the same Sacred Heart, but rather as a manifestation of special veneration and love, proceeding from a grateful heart, for the *supreme act of charity* whereby the Most Sacred Heart of Jesus *instituted* the adorable Sacrament of the Eucharist, and dwells in our midst to the end of ages.'[1]

In the same manner, the Brief whereby the Archconfraternity of the Eucharistic Heart of Jesus was erected, states that this devotion consists in 'rendering special marks of reverence, love and gratitude, appropriate to commemorate and pay homage to the act of supreme love, by which our Saviour *instituted* the adorable Sacrament of the Altar, in order to dwell in our midst to the end of time.'[2]

When, in 1914, the question was put before the Sacred Congregation of Rites as to whether it were permissible to dedicate a church to the Eucharistic Heart of Jesus and to place a statue or picture on the altar, the Sacred Congregation, by decree of March

---

[1] Cf. *Preces et pia opera indulgentiis ditata*, n. 235.
[2] The Latin text and French translation of the Brief are to be found in *Nouvelle Revue Théologique*, 1903, pp. 196 and 269.

28th, 1914, answered that, both for the church and the statue, the new title was to be replaced by a liturgical one, referring it all to some cult already approved. On July 15th this decree was followed by another which confirmed it and stated: 'The title of "Eucharistic Heart" is permitted only on behalf of Confraternities approved under this title, and subject to this condition, that it is understood in the sense of "Heart of Jesus as present in the Eucharist".' Since this decision caused some trouble in the souls of persons who practised this devotion, Cardinal Amette, Archbishop of Paris, addressed a request to the Sacred Congregation, asking for an explicit pronouncement concerning the question whether the title of 'Eucharistic Heart of Jesus' kept, none the less, the sense defined by the *Raccolta* of 1898 and by the Brief of February 16th, 1903. The Holy Office answered affirmatively (April 3rd, 1915), adding that the decree concerning the emblem and the liturgical part of the devotion remained in force; but "the devotion itself was to be regarded as approved by the Holy See, in the sense defined by the *Raccolta* of 1898".'[1]

Cardinal Merry del Val, Secretary of the Holy Office, who transmitted the decree to the Archbishop of Paris, commented on it as follows: 'This answer is entirely in keeping with the view of the Church. Do we not read in the Breviary that the feast of the Sacred Heart has for its purpose to remind us, under the symbol of this Sacred Heart, of the love of Christ, dying for us and instituting, in memory of His death, the Sacrament of His Body and Blood? And are not the feasts of Corpus Christi and that of the Sacred Heart so joined in the liturgy as to present the latter as the sequel and complement of the former? . . . No wonder, then, that when the devotion to the Eucharistic Heart grew up, the Holy See invariably declared that the cult of the Sacred Heart in the Eucharist was neither more perfect than the cult of the Eucharist, nor different from that of the Sacred Heart. . . . It follows that the devotion to the Eucharistic Heart was never disapproved by the Holy See; on the contrary, it was more than once positively recognized: but in that sense, and no other. As regards the new emblems, pictures, liturgical titles and feasts, relating to this devotion, they have been prohibited, lest some simple souls, seeking after novelties, should twist the devotion itself and expose so holy a thing to the malice of criticism. I beg of you, therefore,

---

[1] *Acta Apost. Sedis*, vol. VII (1915), p. 205.

prudently to inform the clients of this wholesome devotion of the true and genuine view of the Holy See, and to confirm them in their holy resolve.'[1]

A still more valuable approval was reserved for the devotion. In 1921 Pope Benedict XV allowed the celebration of the feast of the Eucharistic Heart of Jesus, with proper Office and proper Mass.[2] 'This feast', states the decree of the Congregation of Rites, 'has for its object to commemorate the love which Our Lord Jesus Christ shows us in the mystery of the Eucharist, to urge on the faithful to approach it with more confidence, and to enkindle in their hearts the fire of Divine love which inflamed the Heart of Jesus and prompted Him to institute the Blessed Eucharist'. By this decree, then, the devotion has taken a place in the public worship of the Church.[3]

From what precedes we must conclude that the devotion to the Eucharistic Heart of Jesus is not essentially different from the devotion to the Sacred Heart, but is a special form of it. In both devotions our homage is addressed to Christ's physical Heart and to His love for us. Yet, whereas the latter considers and honours this love in all its manifestations, the former regards and honours it in a well-defined manifestation, namely, in the institution of the Eucharist, which is as it were the summary of all the benefits for which we are indebted to His love.[4]

III. JESUS' LOVE ESPECIALLY CONSIDERED AS SCORNED

Thus what we intend to honour particularly in the devotion to the Sacred Heart is Jesus' love for men. Yet in this love there is a feature to which our attention is particularly drawn, a speciality that belongs to the intrinsic nature of the devotion as asked for

---

[1] *Acta Apost. Sedis*, vol. VII (1915), p. 205. See also Hamon, op. cit., vol. V, pp. 250–53; Bainvel, op. cit., pt. III, chap. viii, § ii, n. 3, p. 549; and Vermeersch, op. cit., vol. II, p. 136.

[2] The feast is celebrated on Thursday after the octave of Corpus Christi.

[3] *Acta Apost. Sedis*, vol. XIII (1921), p. 545. The Collect of the Feast is as follows: 'O Lord Jesus Christ, who, pouring forth the riches of Thy love for men, hast instituted the Sacrament of the Eucharist: grant us, we beseech Thee, that we may love Thy loving Heart and always worthily use so great a Sacrament.' The whole liturgy of the Office and Mass clearly speaks of Jesus as the Source and the Author of the Blessed Eucharist.

[4] Cf. Castelain, CssR, *De cultu Eucharistici Cordis Jesu: Historia, doctrina, documenta*; Card. Van Roey, *Le Cœur eucharistique de Jésus* in *La vie diocésaine*, 1920, pp. 23–28; Fr. Jansen, *Le Cœur eucharistique* in *Nouvelle Revue Théologique*, 1927; and *Rapports sur la dévotion au Cœur eucharistique de Jésus*, présentés aux Congrès eucharistiques internationaux de *Rome (1922) et de Carthage (1930)*.

by our Lord and as practised by the Church, a speciality which, as we shall see, impresses on the devotion a distinctive character —namely, the fact that this love is neglected, disdained and outraged by men.

On account of His love, because of all the proofs He has given us of it, because of all that He did and suffered for love of us, Jesus undoubtedly deserves that men should love Him in return with a grateful and devoted love.

The greater part of men, however, requite this love with coldness, indifference, ingratitude, slights and scorn, outrages and even hatred. Think, in particular, how they behave towards His Sacrament of Love, the Blessed Eucharist. What indifference, what disdain, what irreverence! And often even what unworthy and revolting behaviour!

Of this Jesus complained bitterly to St. Margaret Mary. In the fourth apparition, after recalling how His Heart is overflowing with the most generous love, He showed this love scorned and despised, even by those from whom He has a right to expect greater love and adoration: 'In return I receive from the greater part of men nothing but ingratitude, by their irreverence and sacrileges, by the coldness and contempt they have for Me in this Sacrament of Love. Yet what is more painful to Me is that even souls consecrated to Me are acting like this.'

He had already complained of it in the preceding apparition: 'Then He revealed to me all the unspeakable marvels of His pure love, and the excess of love He had conceived for men, from whom He received nothing but ingratitude and contempt. "This is more grievous to Me," He said to me, "than all that I endured in My Passion. If they would only give Me some return of love, I should not reckon all that I have done for them, and I would do still more, if possible. But they have only coldness and contempt for all My endeavours to do them good." '

Pope Pius XI reminds us of this lament in his Encyclical *Miserentissimus* (n. 22): 'When Christ showed Himself to Margaret Mary, He pointed out to her His boundless love, and at the same time, in an afflicted tone, He complained of the numerous outrages inflicted on Him by the ingratitude of men.'

After quoting the words of Our Lord, Fr. de Galliffet concludes: 'We must observe here an essential point of the nature of our devotion, namely, that this love of Jesus with which His Heart is glowing is to be regarded as a love *despised and offended* by the ingratitude of men. . . . The Heart of Jesus, then, is to be considered under two aspects: both as glowing with love for men and as cruelly offended by their ingratitude.'[1] And further on: 'It is not enough to have considered the infinite dignity and boundless love of the Heart of Jesus Christ, which make this sacred Heart worthy of our deepest adoration and tenderest love; we ought to consider It moreover as cruelly *outraged* by the ingratitude of men. . . .'[2]

3. The Physical Heart of Jesus: The Symbol of His Love

Both the physical Heart of Jesus and His love, then, form part of the essential object of the Devotion. They are not viewed, however, independently of each other, but in their mutual connection. What is this connection? That of symbolism. We consider the physical Heart of Jesus as the living symbol of His love.[3] It is in this way that it is represented by theologians.

Franzelin: 'The Heart of Jesus is the object of devotion because It is the *symbol* of His love and of His whole inner life.'[4]

Vermeersch: 'In devotion to the Sacred Heart, the Heart is not taken in a metaphorical sense, but as the real and natural *symbol* of His love.'[5] Again: 'The proper object of the devotion is the Heart, a real symbol of the love of Christ. . . . The Heart is honoured because and in so far as It is the real symbol of the love of Jesus Christ.'[6]

Bainvel: 'Devotion to the Heart of Jesus is addressed to this Heart, but does not stop here; it goes to It as to the *symbol* of His love, as to the expressive token of what He has been and suffered for love of us. . . . What we honour is neither love in itself, nor the Heart in Itself, but the love of Jesus under the figure of His Heart of flesh; it is the Heart of flesh, but as an emblem.'[7]

[1] De Galliffet, op. cit., Book I, chap. iv, p. 47.
[2] Ibid., p. 58.
[3] A symbol is something that can be perceived by the senses, especially by sight, and is regarded as naturally typifying or representing something by the possession of analogous qualities. Thus, for instance, the lion is the symbol of courage, the olive-branch the emblem of peace, the national flag the symbol of a country. Thus, too, the heart is generally regarded as the symbol of love: in seeing a heart we naturally think of love.
[4] Card. Franzelin, s.j., *De Verbo incarnato*, cap. vi, thesis xiv.
[5] Op cit., vol. II, p. 33.
[6] Ibid., p. 36.
[7] Op cit., p. 102.

Terrien: 'The tie that harmoniously joins the Heart to love, so as to make but one object, designated by one and the same word "Heart", is symbolism. The Heart, the real, physical Heart, this living and principal part of the humanity of our Saviour is presented to our homage of adoration; but It is presented to us as *symbolizing* love. The visible Heart carries us to the invisible love, and this love we contemplate in His heart.'[1]

Galtier: 'This then is doubtless the proper and direct object of the worship to be paid to the Sacred Heart: the Heart of flesh with the love of which It is the *symbol*, or the love of Christ symbolized by His Heart of flesh.'[2]

Leroy: 'The Heart of Jesus is honoured in Itself in so far as It is the *symbol* of His love.'[3]

It is in this way, moreover, that the Heart of Jesus is viewed by the Church.

In the decree of 1765, the Sacred Congregation of Rites sets forth that 'the allowing of the Mass and Office has no other aim than . . . to renew *symbolically* the memory of the Divine love whereby the Only-begotten Son of God assumed a human nature. . . .'[4]

In his Brief of June 29th, 1781, directed against Scipio Ricci, the Jansenist bishop of Pistoia, Pope Pius VI writes: 'The Holy See put a stop to the troubles and discussions, and has sufficiently shown what is the intrinsic nature of this devotion, free from all superstition and materialism. The devotion only intends to contemplate and venerate, under the *symbolical image* of His Heart, the boundless charity and overflowing love of our Divine Redeemer.'[5]

When the Provincial Synod of Quebec, in 1873, represented the Heart of Jesus as 'the source and origin of the love of Christ',[6] the Sacred Congregation of Rites substituted in the place of 'source and origin' the word 'symbol'.[7]

Pope Leo XIII, in his Apostolic Letter dated June 28th, 1889, stated: 'By this devotion we honour in a particular manner, under the *symbol* of the Most Sacred Heart, the principal benefits bestowed by our Redeemer on the human race.' And in his

---

[1] Op. cit., p. 35.
[2] Op cit., p. 121.
[3] Leroy, *De SS. Corde Jesu eiusque cultu*, cap. iii, q. xv, p. 176.
[4] See p. xxxix.
[5] Cf. Hamon, op. cit., vol. iv, p. 278.
[6] 'Christi caritatis fontem et originem in eius Corde existere.'
[7] Terrien, op. cit., p. 63.

Encyclical *Annum sacrum*: 'Since there is in the Sacred Heart a *symbol* and sensible image of the infinite love of Jesus Christ, which prompts us to make a return of love, therefore it is fitting that we should consecrate ourselves to His Most Sacred Heart.'

The sixth lesson of the former Office of the Feast of the Sacred Heart contained: 'Clement XIII allowed several churches to celebrate the Feast of the Sacred Heart, in order that the faithful, under the *symbol* of His Most Sacred Heart, might recall with more piety and devotion the love of Christ . . .'

In the hymn at Lauds in the new Office the Church sings: 'Under this *symbol* of love, suffering bloodily and mystically, Christ the Priest offered the twofold Sacrifice.'[1]

And did not Our Lord Himself, by the manner in which, in the second apparition, He showed His Heart to St. Margaret Mary, give her to understand that He wished to see His Heart honoured as the *symbol* of His love? 'This Heart was shown me,' she writes, 'as on a throne of flames, more dazzling than the sun and transparent as crystal, with that adorable wound, and surrounded with a crown of thorns which *signified* the pricks caused by our sins. And above there was a cross, which *signified* that from the first moment of His Incarnation, that is to say as soon as this Heart was formed, the cross was planted in It, and that It was filled with all the bitterness which humiliations and poverty, pains and scorn, would cause to It, and which His sacred humanity would have to suffer during His whole lifetime and in His sacred Passion.' Do not all these emblems with which Jesus showed His Heart—the flames, the wound, the cross, the thorns—give evidence that this Heart is to be taken as a symbol, as the symbol of His love?[2]

The Heart of Jesus is really the symbol, the natural symbol of His love.

There are two kinds of symbols. Some depend merely on convention and custom; they are called conventional symbols. Such is, for instance, the national flag; it is merely by general consent that a piece of bunting of a definite colour represents a definite country and it is, for the citizens of a State, the emblem of their country.

[1] 'Hoc sub amoris symbolo
Passus cruenta et mystica,
Utrumque sacrificium
Christus Sacerdos obtulit.'

[2] Cf. Terrien, op. cit., p. 167; and Bainvel, op. cit., p. 110.

Yet there are other symbols, which depend on something that from its very nature is proper to the object used as a symbol; on a natural quality or property of this object; and which for that reason are called natural symbols. Thus the lion, for instance, is the symbol of courage: the symbol being founded on an innate quality of the lion.

It is thus also with the heart as a symbol of love. An intimate connection exists between love and the heart: love has its reaction on the heart, the heart receives all the impressions of love; we feel our love in our heart; we love as it were with our heart.

This is true not only of sensible love but also of spiritual love. Striking proofs of it are found in the lives of the Saints: in many passages of their writings they speak of the impressions and effects produced on their hearts by their love for God. Nor is this always a mere appearance, but frequently a palpable reality. So violent at times may be the throbbings of the heart that it threatens to break; that the person faints away and is in peril of his life; so vehement sometimes may be the ardour of love, as to be unbearable, so that to slake this fire the person is obliged to bare his breast, to put pieces of wet cloth on it, or even to plunge into ice-cold water.[1]

The Heart, then, is really the natural symbol of love: by reason of its genuine connection with love, it typifies and represents it by its very nature.

It is in this way that the physical Heart of Jesus is looked upon in our devotion. Even as the heart in general is the natural symbol of love in general, so the Heart of Jesus is the natural symbol of His love in particular. In precisely the same manner as our own heart, the Heart of Jesus is in close connection with His love, experiences its influence and receives its impressions. It beats in unison with His love. Thus It typifies and represents His love quite naturally; It is its natural symbol.

It is thanks to the symbolism of the heart that Christ's love may be the object of a public worship. 'To constitute a real object of the Christian cult the love of Our Lord towards us must present itself under the appearance of a sensible expression. Thus it is required by a fundamental law of human nature, which true

---

[1] See in de Galliffet, op. cit., p. 119, a number of instances taken from the lives of Saints, as Philip Neri, Teresa, Magdalen of Pazzi, Rose of Lima, Catherine of Genoa, Margaret of Cortona, etc.

religion cannot fail to observe: we have no connection with spiritual things but by means and with the aid of sensible things. Where is this sensible sign of love to be found? There is one, self-evident, natural, usual and intelligible to all: the heart. The Heart of Our Lord, His physical Heart, is a material object which, while it is capable of being perceived by the senses and represented by the imagination, suggests to the mind the thought of the love which the Saviour has felt and with which He has been inspired.'[1]

It is also thanks to symbolism that Christ's physical Heart may be the object of a special devotion. It is true that His Heart, considered by itself, is worthy of the cult of adoration because of Its union to Jesus' Divine Person: but that feature It has in common with all the other parts of Christ's body. To be the object of a special devotion It must possess a special property. Now this property is Its capacity as a symbol of Christ's love.

Remarks

I. IS THE PHYSICAL HEART OF JESUS ALSO TO BE CONSIDERED THE ORGAN OF HIS LOVE?

We must distinguish His pure spiritual love and His sensible love, which emotion, as in our own case, usually accompanies His spiritual love.

The physical Heart of Jesus is certainly *not* the organ of His spiritual love. To arouse spiritual sentiments the soul does not need the help of a material organ. Moreover one does not see how a material organ could possibly serve as an instrument of the soul in producing these affections.

As for the sensible love of Jesus there have been some writers who held His Heart to be the organ of His love. So, among others, does Fr. de Galliffet in his book on devotion to the Sacred Heart.

In fact, in former times the heart was believed to be the organ of love, and ill-informed men still believe it. In common parlance it is considered in this way; does one not say, for instance, that one loves with one's whole heart? Yet this is mere appearance; according to modern science the heart has in reality no part in our affective life; it is not the instrument of the faculties of the soul in producing love. It only makes love sensible, felt, manifest. It may be said to be its revealing organ, but not its producing organ, its organ properly so called.

[1] De la Bégassière, in *Dictionnaire apologétique de la Foi catholique.*

E

The Church, moreover, never considered the physical Heart of Jesus the organ properly so called of His love.

When Fr. de Galliffet, in 1726, presented his request to obtain the institution of the feast of the Sacred Heart, he tried to justify the new cult by advancing his opinion about the physical Heart of Christ as the organ of His love. 'The soul,' he explained, 'depends on the organs of the body in producing the acts that are proper to it. The eyes are the organ of sight, the ears of hearing, and likewise the other senses. Now the chief organ of sensible affections, especially of love, of affliction and other similar emotions, is the heart. . . . As the soul may be said, in a proper sense, to see through the eyes and hear through the ears, so it may also be said to love through the heart.'[1]

Benedict XIV, at that time Cardinal, who was charged with the examination of the request, was particularly opposed to it because of that opinion on which Fr. de Galliffet based the worship of the Sacred Heart. In his famous book on Beatification and Canonization of saints, he himself made known the reason of his opposition. 'The Church,' he writes, 'has not yet made any pronouncement on that question, and very wisely abstains from settling such controversies. That is why I respectfully insinuated that a request based chiefly on an opinion of ancient philosophers should not be complied with, since it is contested by learned men today'.[2] And according to St. Alphonsus de Liguori this opinion of Fr. de Galliffet was the determinant reason why the request was refused. When some years later, in 1765, the Bishops of Poland renewed the request, they carefully abstained from making a stand concerning the rôle of the heart in producing love. And this time the request was granted.

II. MAY THE PHYSICAL HEART OF JESUS ALSO BE CALLED THE SEAT OF HIS LOVE?

Not when it is a question of His spiritual love. For a material thing cannot be the seat of a spiritual sentiment. Its seat is the spiritual appetitive faculty of His soul, namely, His will.

As for His sensible love, this has its seat, as is the case with us, in the sensible appetitive faculty which belongs to the compound formed by the soul and the body. In what portion of the body in

[1] De Galliffet, op. cit., Book I, pt. I, chap. iv, p. 52.
[2] Benedict XIV, op. cit., Liber IV, pars II, cap. xxxi, n. 25.

particular? According to modern science, in the nervous system, more precisely in the brain. Strictly speaking, then, it is the brain, not the heart, which is the seat of sensible love.

Yet this sensible love is chiefly manifested and perceived in the heart, which experiences its impressions in a special way. The heart, therefore, may be called its seat, at least in a broad sense.

It is the same with the love of Jesus. His physical Heart may be called the seat of it, not in the strict sense but broadly speaking, in so far as It experiences and manifests its impressions.

4. The Whole Inner Life of Jesus: Secondary Element of the Object

The love of Jesus, specially considered as neglected and despised, together with His physical Heart, is thus the essential constituent of the object of devotion to the Sacred Heart.

This object, however, comprises yet another element, secondary and accessory it is true, but nevertheless constituting a natural complement of the former.

Indeed, what the devotion of the faithful contemplates and honours in the Heart of Jesus is not only His love for men, but also His joys and sorrows, His love for His heavenly Father, His kindness, His mercy, His meekness, His humility, His generosity. In short, it refers all His sentiments and all His virtues to His Heart. In His Heart it sees His whole affective and moral life, His whole interior life. For Christian piety, therefore, the object of the devotion is not only His love for men but also His entire inner life. His love, together with His physical Heart, is its essential and primary constituent, but His whole inner life forms its secondary or accessory element.

It was understood in this way by the promoters of the devotion from the very outset.

Fr. de Galliffet summarizes his explanation as follows: 'This Heart, then, is to be considered, first, as closely and indissolubly united to the soul of the adorable Person of Jesus Christ, and exalted by this union to a divine state. Secondly, as the noblest and principal organ of the *sensible affections* of Jesus Christ, of His love, His zeal, His obedience, His wishes, His pains, His joys and His sorrows; as the principle and the seat of *those same affections and of all the virtues* of the God-Man. Thirdly, as the very centre of *all*

the interior sufferings which our salvation has cost Him; and moreover as cruelly wounded by the lance on the Cross. Finally, It is
to be viewed as sanctified by the most precious gifts of the Holy
Ghost, and by the infusion of all the treasures of grace of which
He is capable. All this really belongs to this Divine Heart; all this
is Its own; from this It derives Its dignity, Its value and excellence;
and hence all this forms part of the object of the devotion to the
Heart of Jesus.

  'It is this Heart, thus disposed, thus glowing with love, and thus
afflicted, which is the true object of the devotion now explained.
One should then contemplate this admirable compound which
arises from the Heart of Jesus, that is, of the soul and of the
Divinity united to it; of the gifts and graces which It contains; of
the virtues and affections of which It is the principle and seat;
and of the interior sorrows of which It is the centre. This then is
the complete object which is presented to the adoration and love
of the faithful: evidently the holiest, the noblest, the greatest, the
most sublime, the most Divine, and at the same time the sweetest,
most lovable and tenderest object that can be imagined.'[1]

  This explanation is taken almost word for word by the Bishops
of Poland in their request (1765): 'The Heart of Jesus is to be
considered, first, as constituting with His soul and His Divine
Person in a certain sense one object; secondly, as the symbol or
the natural seat of *all the virtues and interior affections* of Christ, and
especially of that immense love which He has borne to His Father
and to men; thirdly, as the centre of the interior sufferings which
our all-loving Redeemer endured during His life, but especially
in His Passion. . . . All this being most closely connected with the
Heart of Jesus, really constitutes, together with the Heart itself,
the object of this feast; it follows, and this is most noteworthy, that
this object, thus considered, really and truly comprises the whole
inner life of Christ our Lord.'[2]

  Mention is also made by Bl. Claude de la Colombière of this
inner life as the object of devotion, in his act of consecration to the
Sacred Heart: 'This offering,' he says, 'is made with the intention
of honouring the Divine Heart, which is the seat of all virtues, the
fountain of all blessings, and the refuge of all holy souls. The chief
virtues which we seek to honour in this Heart are: firstly, a most

---

[1] De Galliffet, op. cit., Book I, chap. iv, pp. 60–61.
[2] Nilles, op. cit., Liber I, pars I, cap. iii, n. 18.

tender love of God His Father, joined to perfect reverence and humility; secondly, an infinite patience under afflictions, an unspeakable grief and loathing for the sins He had taken upon Himself, the confidence of a most tender Son, and at the same time, shame and confusion for the guilt of the world; thirdly, a most sensitive compassion for our wretchedness. Yet despite these emotions, each of which reached the very depths of His Heart, an unalterable serenity, caused by so perfect a conformity to the will of God that no event whatsoever, no matter how contrary in appearance to Its zeal, love and humility, could in any way disturb It. . . .'[1]

In many passages of St. Margaret Mary's writings mention is made of Christ's virtues and affections as forming part of the object of the devotion.

As for the Church, although she did not explicitly recognize this extension of the object of the devotion, yet she sufficiently shows that she approves and admits it.

In granting the institution of the Feast of the Sacred Heart, in the sense in which it was asked for by the postulators, the Sacred Congregation of Rites approved, by that very fact, the devotion in the form represented in the request. Now the Bishops of Poland, as we have seen, indicated as its object not only Christ's love for men, but all His virtues and all His affections which included His whole inner life.

In the Litany of the Sacred Heart, the Church bids us invoke the Sacred Heart as 'abyss of all virtues,—full of kindness and love,—abode of justice and love,—in which are all the treasures of wisdom and knowledge,—patient and abounding in mercy,—rich unto all who call upon It,—obedient unto death'. In making this Litany her own, the Church not only recognizes that it contains nothing contrary either to Catholic Faith and morals, or to genuine Christian piety, but also approves and recommends the invocations addressed to the Heart of Jesus, and hence also those in which mention is made of Christ's virtues and sentiments, and of His inner life.

Is this extension of the object of the devotion justified?

There can be no doubt upon the point, for, being the symbol foremost of His love, the physical Heart of Jesus is therefore the

---

[1] *Retraite spirituelle du bienh. Cl. de la Colombière*, p. 135.

symbol also of His whole inner life. And on that account the latter may form part of the object of the devotion, at least as secondary element. Indeed, not only love, but also our whole inner life has a close and intimate connection with our heart.

This is true, in the first place, of our affective or emotional life. All our sentiments have a reaction on our heart: not only our love, then, but also our joys and our sorrows, our longings and our anxieties, our hopes and our disappointments. They produce in it impressions which modify its dispositions and its beat, and thus the heart manifests and reveals our emotions, making them sensible and as it were palpable. It may therefore be called the revealing or manifesting organ not only of our love but also of our whole affective or emotional life.

So much is this the case that, normally speaking, not only love, but all our emotions, are attributed to the heart, as though this were the organ, or at least the seat of them. Thus the Heart is said to rejoice, to be afflicted, to desire, to hope, to feel rancour or hatred, etc. True, this manner of speaking is scientifically inaccurate, but the fact which it is intended to convey, that is, the intimate connection between the affective life and the heart, is undeniable.

That is also true of our moral life, our moral dispositions, our virtues and vices. The moral life and the affective are so closely connected that the question may be raised as to whether they are really distinct from each other. Be that as it may, this much is certain, that our moral life reveals and expresses itself through our sentiments. So we speak of 'a heart of gold, a heart of stone, a contrite heart, a generous heart', etc. The heart is even spoken of as though it were the organ, or at least the seat, of moral life as well. Did not Jesus also represent Himself as 'meek and humble of heart?'[1]

If then the heart is in such close connection with our inner life, it is quite natural to employ it as its symbol, just as it is natural to use it as the symbol of love.

It is in this way that we consider the physical Heart of Jesus in our devotion: we regard It as the symbol not only of His love for us but also of His whole inner life. Hence this inner life has its due place in the devotion, and constitutes, together with His love and His Heart, the first element of its object. His love is its

---

[1] Cf. Bainvel, op. cit., pt. II, chap. i, n. vii, p. 126.

essential or primary, His whole inner life its secondary or accessory constituent. In the foreground we behold and honour His love for us, and beyond that, His whole inner life.

§ II. THE SPIRITUAL HEART OF JESUS THE PRINCIPLE AND SEAT OF HIS LOVE AND OF HIS WHOLE INNER LIFE

Therefore the physical Heart of Jesus, a symbol of His love and of His whole inner life, is in the first place the object of the devotion.

But does It constitute its entire object?

I do not think so. I hold that the object also comprises what is meant by the word 'Heart' in a certain figurative sense, namely, that which is the principle and seat of Jesus' love and of His whole inner life, the appetitive faculty of His soul,[1] or that which we shall call His spiritual Heart, in order to distinguish this acceptation from any other figurative sense of the word.[2]

In fact, not only the ordinary faithful, but also the prayer-books in their devotional exercises in honour of the Sacred Heart, preachers in the pulpit, theologians and ascetical writers in their treatises and books on devotion to the Sacred Heart, speak of the Heart of Jesus as though It were the principle and seat of His love and of His whole inner life. They speak, for instance, of the love of His Heart, of Its yearning for a return of love, of Its affliction because of the ingratitude of men and the neglect of Its love, of Its desire for reparation, of Its anguish at Gethsemane, of Its virtues, Its kindness, Its mercy, Its meekness and humility; in short, they attribute to His Heart all that belongs to His inner life.

The Church speaks in the same way: in her Litany she invokes the Heart of Jesus as 'glowing furnace of charity,—abode of justice and love,—full of kindness and love,—patient and abounding in mercy,—obedient unto death,—abyss of all virtues,—overwhelmed with reproaches,—rich unto all who call upon It,' etc.

[1] More precisely, its twofold appetitive faculty; both His spiritual appetitive faculty or His will, and His sensible appetitive faculty or His sensibility, the principle and seat of His emotions.

[2] Cf. Noldin, s.j., *Die Andacht zum heiligsten Herzen Jesu*, pp. 82 and 112.

And Jesus, too, in His apparitions to St. Margaret Mary, expresses Himself in the same way. He points to His Heart as loving men, as sparing nothing to show them Its love: 'Behold this Heart,' He says, 'which has so loved men that It spared nothing, even going so far as to exhaust and consume Itself, in order to testify to them Its love.' He shows His Heart as glowing with love, eager to pour Itself forth: 'My Divine Heart is so inflamed with love for men, and for you in particular, that, not being able any longer to contain within Itself the flames of Its ardent charity, It must needs spread them abroad.'

In all these expressions the Sacred Heart is presented as the principle and seat of His love and of His whole inner life.[1]

This principle and seat, however, is not His physical Heart, but the appetitive faculty of His soul; His spiritual Heart. It is then really His spiritual Heart that is meant.

But may Christ's qualities and sentiments not be said to be attributed to His physical Heart, considered as a symbol?

By no means. First, it is not true that to a symbol is attributable whatever belongs to the symbolized thing. When, for instance, the country is said to be proud of her children fallen upon a battlefield, is it permissible on that score to attribute this sentiment to the national flag, a symbol of the country? And in order that Christ's sentiments should be attributable to His physical Heart, considered as a symbol, it would be necessary that the thing symbolized by this physical Heart, i.e. His love, His inner life, etc., should be the subject of these qualities and sentiments. This, however, is not the case: it is His spiritual Heart that is their subject. Therefore they are not attributable to His physical Heart, considered as a symbol.

Consequently what we wish to honour in the devotion to the Heart of Jesus is not only His physical Heart but also His spiritual Heart. In other words, His physical Heart, the symbol of His love and of His whole inner life, does not make up the entire object of the devotion; this object also comprises His spiritual Heart, the principle and seat of His love and of His whole inner life.[2]

This conclusion is confirmed by the manner in which the devotion is practised. There are many ways in which we can show

---

[1] These expressions bear marks, it is true, of the obsolete opinion which, based on appearances, held the physical heart to be the organ of affective life (cf. p. 19). Yet, properly interpreted, they are fully justified.

[2] Cf. Noldin, op. cit., p. 90.

our love; among others, by consecrating ourselves to His Heart, by imitating Its virtues, by invoking It, by promoting Its reign, and especially by making reparation for the neglect of Its love. Now, nothing at all of this belongs to His physical Heart. Nothing is more proper than that It should be honoured as the symbol of His love and of His whole inner life; for, as we shall see, It deserves this homage in the highest degree. It is evident that It should be venerated, even with the worship of adoration, as forming part of His sacred Humanity and belonging to His Divine Person; for by Its union with His Divine Person It possesses a really Divine dignity, which we wish to recognize by our homage and adoration. Moreover, as this homage and adoration are ultimately directed to His Person, all the parts of His sacred Body may and even must be their object.

But there can be no question of consecrating ourselves to His physical Heart, of consoling It by our reparation, imitating It, calling upon It and extending Its reign. These tokens of love presuppose a spiritual subject capable of receiving them. More-over they are only consistent with a subject which is sensitive to love, consolation and reparation; they only appertain to a subject which really possesses these virtues which we wish to imitate, which really is able and willing to help us, which really is able to reign, etc. Therefore they do not appertain to the physical Heart of Jesus, but only to His spiritual Heart.

The objection may be raised: Are not these tokens of love which are shown towards the physical Heart of Jesus ultimately addressed to His Person? And is not this a sufficient reason for giving them to His physical Heart? By no means; for if it were sufficient, one might as well pay this homage to the other portions of His body, to His hands, His feet, etc.—and no one would make this claim.

But is there not a special reason for giving this homage to His physical Heart? Is not this Heart considered as a symbol? And may not all the tokens of love which are addressed to the sym-bolized thing be given to the symbol? The truth of this principle might perhaps be called in question. Be that as it may, it is not pertinent to the matter in hand. For, what is properly symbolized by the physical Heart of Jesus? His love and His whole inner life. The tokens of love however in question are not aimed at His inner life, but at what is the principle and seat of them, and, through this, His Person. These tokens of love therefore cannot be given to the physical Heart of Jesus, even in so far as It may be considered as a symbol.[1]

We may conclude, then, that it seems to us that the spiritual Heart of Jesus also forms part of the object of the devotion. The Church, it is true, in the way in which she presents the devotion, and spiritual writers in the definition which they give of it, mention solely the physical Heart of Jesus, the symbol of His love and, secondarily, of His whole inner life. Yet, as we have just seen, in practice they consider as also forming part of the object that which is the principle and seat of His love and of His entire inner life, namely, what we call His spiritual Heart.

§ III. THE TOTAL HEART OF JESUS AT ONCE THE SYMBOL, PRINCIPLE AND SEAT OF HIS LOVE AND OF HIS WHOLE INNER LIFE

Must we then conclude from what precedes that there is a double object: the physical and the spiritual Heart? By no means; otherwise there would also be a double devotion. The two Hearts form only one object. They are not regarded and honoured separately, but as closely united to each other, and forming a whole, a unity. For both of them play a part in Jesus' affective life; His spiritual Heart is the principle and seat of it, His physical Heart is the revealing organ.[2] His spiritual Heart produces love and the other sentiments; His physical Heart, by the impressions which It receives from them, makes them sensible and reveals them. They make up the compound of the factors which play a part in His love and other emotions. Hence, they may be considered as forming a whole, a totality. And to this totality is also given the name of 'Heart'.

Consequently, what in devotion to the Sacred Heart is meant by the word 'Heart' is not only Christ's physical Heart but also His spiritual Heart, or rather it is the whole which is formed by both of them, and which may be called His total Heart.[3]

---

[1] Cf. Noldin, op. cit., p. 91.
[2] See p. 19.
[3] Cf. Noldin, op. cit., p. 82. Is it not in this way that we are to understand the statement of the *Memoriale*: 'The Heart of Jesus is to be considered as forming, together with His soul and His Divine Person, only one object?' (Nilles, op. cit., pars I, cap. iii, *Disputatio habita in S.R.C.*; B. *Exceptiones*, n. 18).

If we take it in this way we understand how this Heart is said to love, to wish, to be grieved, to rejoice, to be merciful, meek, humble, etc. To be sure, strictly speaking, these sentiments and qualities belong to the spiritual Heart of Jesus, but they are attributed to His total Heart. And with justice; for, what belongs to some part, may be ascribed to the whole.

Thus we also understand that the tokens of love, which were mentioned above, may be given to Jesus' heart. Strictly speaking, they are intended for His spiritual Heart; but they may be addressed to His total Heart; for what is intended for some part may be addressed to the totality. And through His total Heart they are directed to the Person of Jesus to Jesus Himself.

But is it permissible to designate this whole by the name of 'Heart'? Undoubtedly; it is the figure of speech called 'synecdoche', i.e. the extended acceptation by which the name of a part is transferred to the whole. Thus the name of 'altar', which properly speaking designates the table on which the Holy Sacrifice of the Mass is offered, is given to the whole, composed of the sacrificial table and what adorns and frames it. In like manner, the name of 'heart'—which properly designates the physical heart—designates the whole, formed by the physical and the spiritual Heart.[1]

That the Heart of Jesus is in reality considered in this way clearly appears in particular in two liturgical prayers, namely, the Collect and Preface of the Mass of the Sacred Heart and in the litany of the Sacred Heart.

In the Collect, the Heart of Jesus is shown as 'wounded'—which relates to His physical Heart; and as the means by which 'God deigns mercifully to bestow on us infinite treasures of love'—which refers to His spiritual Heart. Hence the word 'Heart' manifestly designates here not only Christ's physical Heart but also His spiritual Heart, or rather the totality formed by both of them, His total Heart. And it is to this total Heart that we intend 'to render the devout homage of our affection' and also 'to discharge our duty of worthy satisfaction'.

In the Preface of the Mass the Heart of Jesus is presented as opened by the lance ('Everlasting God, who didst will that thine only-begotten Son as He hung upon the cross should be pierced

[1] Cf. Noldin, ibid., p. 83.

by a soldier's spear, that this opened Heart . . .')—which refers to Christ's physical Heart—and as 'the treasury of the divine bounty', as 'pouring forth upon us streams of mercy and grace'—which refers to His spiritual Heart. Here, too, then the word 'Heart' designates Christ's total Heart. It is this total Heart which is venerated by the Church.

And in the Litany the Heart of Jesus is presented at once as 'glowing furnace of charity, full of kindness and love, abyss of all virtues, patient and abounding in mercy, obedient unto death', etc.—which relates to His spiritual Heart; and as 'pierced by the lance, formed by the Holy Ghost in the womb of the Virgin Mary, hypostatically united to the Word of God'—which refers to His physical Heart. It is then really to the total Heart that our invocation is directed; it is through this Heart that it goes to the Person of Jesus.[1]

CONCLUSION

We may conclude then:

1. In devotion to the Sacred Heart the word 'Heart' designates not only Jesus' physical Heart but also, as closely united to It, His spiritual Heart, i.e. the appetitive faculty of His soul, the principle and seat of His affective or emotional life, or rather, this word designates His total Heart, i.e. the compound formed by His physical and spiritual Heart.

2. Hence Jesus' physical Heart does not constitute the entire immediate object of the devotion. What is called His spiritual Heart also forms part of it. Therefore the complete immediate object is His total Heart.

3. The Heart of Jesus, thus understood, is considered and worshipped at once as the symbol, principle and seat of His love and of His whole inner life; as the symbol, in so far as It comprises His physical Heart; as the principle and seat, in so far as It comprises His spiritual Heart.

4. Christ's physical Heart forms what is termed the material object of the devotion, i.e. it is that which is honoured; both His

[1] Cf. Noldin, op. cit., p.92.

love and His whole inner life make up its formal object, i.e. the special aspect under which His Heart is worshipped. His love is its primary essential constituent; His whole inner life, the secondary element.

5. If we consider only the essential formal constituents of the object of the devotion we may say: devotion to the Sacred Heart of Jesus is essentially and in substance devotion to His Heart, regarded as the symbol, principle and seat of His love; or, it is devotion to His love considered as produced and symbolized by His Heart.

6. And as the Person of Jesus is the general and ultimate object of the devotion we may also say: it is devotion to Jesus, considered in His Heart, the symbol, principle and seat of His love; or, it is devotion to Jesus, viewed in His love, produced and symbolized by His Heart.

Remark

ON THE TITLE OF 'THE SACRED HEART'

When the devotion to the Sacred Heart had spread to some extent, the faithful soon came to speak of 'the Sacred Heart' simply. At first this title was nothing but an abbreviation of the phrase 'the Sacred Heart of Jesus'. Everybody understood it in this way: the Heart of Jesus was the Sacred Heart *par excellence*.

Gradually this meaning became modified, and finally by this shortened phrase was meant the Person of Jesus. In accustoming themselves to consider in the Heart of Jesus His whole interior life, and particularly His love, the principle of all that He did and suffered, the faithful began to look upon the Heart of Jesus as the summary of His entire Person and to see in Jesus, as it were, nothing but His Heart, so that they designated Himself by His Heart and used the phrase 'the Sacred Heart' as a surname of Jesus. And this expression is now in common use. Both titles, however, are not identical: the phrase 'the Sacred Heart of Jesus' signifies directly the Heart and indirectly the Person of Jesus, whereas the phrase 'the Sacred Heart' designates directly the Person and indirectly His Heart.

What we want to express by the last-named title is that we

considei the Person of Jesus in the light in which He is viewed as the object of the devotion, namely, in His interior life and more in particular in His love for men. '*The Sacred Heart*' is Jesus, contemplated and considered, through His Heart, in His inner life, in His love.[1]

The Sacred Heart, then, is Jesus Himself. Both titles, however, are not synonymous and so are not to be indiscriminately used one for another. The Sacred Heart is Jesus, considered under a definite aspect, in relation to His love, to His inner life. This title, therefore, is only appropriate for Him when there is question of His love, of His affections, His interior sufferings, His wishes, and His virtues. Hence we cannot say, for instance, that the Sacred Heart was born of the Blessed Virgin Mary, that It toiled at the carpenter's bench at Nazareth, that It went teaching and preaching through Galilee and Judea, that It died on the cross and rose again the third day, etc.; but we may say that we are indebted to the Sacred Heart for our salvation, that the Sacred Heart offered Itself on the cross to His Heavenly Father, that It renews in Holy Mass, in an unbloody manner, the Sacrifice of the Cross, etc.

That in certain cases the choice may not be easy is undeniable. Yet in practice there is scarcely any danger of erring on this point. On the other hand, 'it is entirely profitable to the faithful to speak so of "the Sacred Heart", for thus it represents directly what God has been pleased to place in the forefront of the Christian religion, *the redeeming love*. Should not this be the great benefit of the devotion to the Sacred Heart? In order to win souls Christ has found nothing better than to reveal to them His love.'[2]

---

[1] The expression 'Heart of Jesus' is frequently used in this sense by St. Margaret Mary; for instance, when she points to the Heart of Jesus as 'making known, asking, urging, refusing, promising', etc. She writes: 'The Sacred Heart of our Lord has made me know that It demands everything of Its friends.' 'The lovable Heart of Jesus requires purity of intention.' 'The Sacred Heart of our Lord urges me on to inform you that you should spend all your time for Him and all the means at your disposal.' 'The Heart of our good Master will never refuse you the grace necessary to fulfil what It has commanded you.' 'The Sacred Heart told me again that It has such great pleasure in being loved, known and honoured, that It promised me to grant to men of the world, by means of this devotion, all the succour they need in their state of life.' (*Vie et Oeuvres*, passim.) In Jesus, the Saint sees, as it were, only His Heart and His love; in this Heart, she views the whole Jesus. To her Jesus is only His Heart, to her the Heart of Jesus is the whole Jesus.

[2] Galtier, op. cit., p. 133.

COMPLEMENTARY QUESTIONS

1. Does the love which Jesus bears us in His Divine nature form part of the object of the devotion?

Jesus is both God and Man. He is a Divine Person, the Second Person of the Blessed Trinity. From all eternity He possesses the Divine nature. But by His Incarnation He also assumed a human nature: He has, then, a twofold nature, a Divine and a human nature; and consequently a twofold will, a Divine and a human will; and hence also a twofold love, a Divine and a human love.

Thus He loves us in a twofold manner, as God and as Man. As God He loves us with a Divine love, which He has in common with the Father and the Holy Ghost; and as Man He loves us with a human love, which is in reality proper to Him.[1]

It is self-evident that Christ's *human* love forms part of the proper and direct object of the devotion.

It is no less certain that His Divine love, in fact, is *attained* by devotion to the Sacred Heart, and that it is of necessity honoured by the homage which is paid to His human love. For the honour which is paid to the Heart of Jesus and to his human love is directed to His Person. Now His Divine love, as well as His Divine nature, is identified with His Person. To honour, then, the Person is, by that very fact, to honour His Divine love. Thus the latter belongs at the very least to the ultimate object of the devotion.[2]

But, is Christ's Divine love aimed at directly in our devotion? And hence, does it belong to the proper and direct object of the devotion?

This question may be answered in general terms: Our Lord wishes us, in the first place, to honour the love with which He loves us with His human Heart. Yet, in addition, He desires that from His human love we should ascend to the love with which He loves us as God, to His Divine love, and that we should combine both loves in our worship.

This general statement may suffice for the ordinary faithful. To

---

[1] Just as all that belongs to Jesus, by the union of His human nature with the Person of the Word, possesses a Divine dignity, so does His human love, and may in this sense be called a Divine love. Yet, in this treatise, we take the word 'Divine' in the sense of 'appertaining to the Divine nature'. Hence, by the phrase 'Christ's Divine love', is meant here the love which Christ bears us as God, in His Divine nature. It is usually termed by theologians 'His uncreated love'; His human love is called 'His created love'.

[2] Cf. Galtier, op. cit., p. 125; and Vermeersch, op. cit., p. 96.

those who want to go more deeply into the doctrine and are somewhat familiar with theological arguments and distinctions, we suggest the following explanation and elucidation.

Opinions on the question before us are divided. Since the Church has made no pronouncement, it is still therefore a matter of opinion.

I think the following answer may be given: Only the human love of Jesus is, in the strict sense, the direct and proper object of the devotion; but His Divine love forms part of the object in a broad sense, at once as indirect object and as direct and proper object in a broad sense.

That Christ's human love only is the proper and direct object of the devotion, I think we may deduce, firstly, from the way in which Our Lord, in His apparitions to St. Margaret Mary, speaks of the love of His Heart, for which He demands a special worship; and secondly from the statements made by the first apostles of the devotion.[1]

How does Jesus Himself present His love? He points to it as the love of His human Heart, as a love produced, or at least experienced, by this Heart: 'Behold this Heart which has so loved men . . .'[2] As a love that is thirsting for our return of love: 'I burn, I thirst with a consuming desire for men's love in the Blessed Sacrament.'[3] As a love that suffers from being despised: 'In return I receive from the greater part of men nothing but ingratitude. . . . Yet, what is more painful to Me is that even souls that are consecrated to Me are acting in this way.'[4] As a love which asks for reparation for this neglect: 'Afford Me at least the happiness of making up for their ingratitude, as much as you can.'[5]

Now to which love does all this appertain? Is it not to His human love, and this only? And are we not permitted to conclude from it that the love for which Jesus asks a special cult is His Human love and that consequently this, and this only, is the proper object of the devotion?

And what proofs of love does He ask for in return for His love? As we shall see further on: consolation and reparation, consecra-

---

[1] No doubt, the question did not arise at that time. Yet, their statements allow us to infer with satisfactory certainty what their answer would have been had they been questioned on that point.

[2] See p. xxvii.

[3] *Vie et Oeuvres*, II, p. 580.

[4] See p. xxvii.

[5] See p. xxvi.

tion and apostolate, imitation of His virtues, devotion to His Sacred Passion and to the Eucharist.[1] Now these proofs of love, as we shall see, are addressed directly to His Humanity, and consequently to His human love. Are we not allowed to conclude from the way in which Jesus speaks of His love and from the sort of proofs of love which He demands in return, that the love which He presents directly to our worship is His human love?

How does St. Margaret Mary present the love of Jesus? No doubt she is fully aware that the Heart and the love of Jesus are the Heart and the love of a Divine Person, and so possess a Divine dignity; she calls both of them adorable; she adores them with the profoundest reverence. Yet the features by which she describes the love of Jesus all point to a love that makes the Heart of Jesus beat, that makes It glow; to a sensitive, suffering, compassionate, grateful love; to a love that produces in His Heart other really human sentiments, such as joy, content, affliction, etc.[2] Is not this all evidence that she considers the love, which she herself honours and wishes to be honoured by others, a really human love?

Bl. Claude de La Colombière, for his part, in speaking of the cult of the Sacred Heart, makes sole mention of the virtues and affections which animated Christ's human nature, and so also of His human love.[3]

Fr. Croiset, as was said above, begins his book on devotion to the Sacred Heart as follows: 'The particular object of this devotion is the boundless love of the Son of God, which prompted Him to deliver Himself to death for us and to give Himself entirely to us in the Blessed Sacrament of the Altar, without refraining from working this marvel in spite of all the ingratitude and outrages which He was to endure in this state of immolated Victim to the end of time.'[4] Now for these two great benefits we are indebted directly to the love which Jesus bears us as Man. Moreover, Fr. Croiset explicitly attributes them further on to Christ's humanity, and so to His human love. 'God has, as it were, made Himself tangible in becoming Man; and this Man did, beyond all that can be imagined, whatever is capable of inducing men to love Him.'[5]

---

[1] See chap. iii.
[2] *Vie et Oeuvres*, passim.
[3] See p. 22, the beginning of his form of Consecration to the Sacred Heart.
[4] Op. cit., pt. i, chap. i, p. 11.
[5] Ibid., chap. iii, § iii, p. 38.

F

Fr. de Galliffet, for his part, writes: 'Devotion to the Sacred Heart is an exercise of religion which has for its object the adorable Heart of Jesus Christ glowing with love for men . . .'[1] And he adds: 'These words mean that the Heart of Jesus Christ is to be regarded as burning with that boundless love which induced Him to do and to suffer all that He did and suffered for us, but particularly to institute the Sacrament of the Altar, which has been the last effort of His love.'[2] And that by this love Fr. de Galliffet means Christ's human love is amply proved by the connection which he sees between this love and Christ's physical Heart. 'Through Faith we know for certain,' he writes further on, 'that Jesus Christ, true God and true Man, has been like all other men in all things, except sin and imperfection. He has loved, then, after the manner of other men and in keeping with man's nature; hence His Heart has shared in His love; It has co-operated with His love; It has been its principle and seat; It has experienced its impressions, like the hearts of other men.'[3] Now, it was only of His human love that the Heart of Jesus was capable of experiencing the impressions, only with His human love that It was capable of co-operating.

So, then, neither the holy confidante of Jesus, nor the first apostles of the devotion to the Sacred Heart, who are surely most qualified to give us a correct idea of the Devotion, make mention of Christ's Divine love. Evidently one must not conclude from this that they want to exclude it altogether from the object of the devotion. But is not it a proof that they consider only His human love as the proper and direct object? If they considered His Divine love as also forming part of this object, can we imagine that they would not speak of it?

Besides, Christ's Divine love cannot form part of the proper and direct object of the Devotion.

In order to form part of it, the love of Jesus must fulfil three conditions: it must be proper to Jesus, otherwise it could not be the object of a special devotion to Jesus: moreover, it must be naturally symbolized by His physical Heart, for the special reason why honour is paid to the physical Heart of Jesus is that this

---

[1] Op. cit., p. 48.
[2] Ibid., p. 50.
[3] Ibid., p. 55.

Heart is the natural symbol of His love; finally, it must have the spiritual love of Jesus for its principle and seat, for the reason why His spiritual Heart is honoured is that It is the principle and seat of His love.[1]

Now, then, does Christ's Divine love fulfil these three conditions?

Firstly, is it proper to Jesus? In a strict sense, no. It is common to the three Divine Persons, for it is identified with the Divine Nature, which the three Persons possess indivisibly, or rather with which they are identified.

'It is evident,' writes Fr. Galtier, 'that the love presented for our adoration, and to which we are called upon to make amends, is the love with which Christ in His own Person loved and still loves us. Now, though He is God and also loves us as God, Christ has no really personal love to show us but His human love; for whatever is not human is not distinctively proper to Him. His Divine love, then, is not exclusively His own, as it is common to Him with the Father and the Holy Ghost. He himself on earth, when He spoke of this love, distinguishing it from His own, was, as it were, bent on attributing it to the Father. 'The Father Himself loveth you,' He said with reference to it. In the same way, He attributed to the Father His Divine will, opposing to it as His own, His human will. 'Not My will, but Thine be done.' This human will is indeed exclusively proper to Him. Likewise His human love. He only, in the Divine Trinity, loves us with this love; and when He speaks of His own love or others speak of it, it is only of His human love that we have to think.'[2]

Is Christ's Divine love naturally symbolized by His physical Heart? To this question, too, we think we must answer: in a strict sense, no. For the reason why the heart is used as the symbol of love lies in the fact that it receives its reaction, that it is its revealing organ, and that consequently there is between the heart and love a real connection.[3] Therefore the physical Heart of Jesus only symbolizes that love which causes It to react. Now Christ's Divine love has no such reaction; only His human love makes itself felt in His Heart.[4]

Finally, does Christ's Divine love have His spiritual Heart as

[1] Cf. pp. 15 and 25. See Bainvel, op. cit. pp. 148–49.
[2] Galtier, op. cit., p. 123.
[3] See p. 19.
[4] Vermeersch, op. cit., vol. II, pp. 85–88.

its principle and seat? Evidently not. It has its principle and seat in the Divine essence with which it is identified.

Therefore it seems to us that the conclusion is forced upon us: Christ's Divine love does not appertain to the proper and direct object of the devotion; only His human love forms part of it.

Yet His Divine love belongs to the object taken in a broad sense, at once as indirect object and as direct and proper object in the wider acceptation.

First, as indirect object, for between the human love of Jesus and His Divine love there is a close connection.

To what do we owe Jesus' human love? To His Divine love. It was His Divine love that prompted Him to take upon Himself a human nature with a human will and a human heart. It is then to His Divine love that we are indebted for the fact that Jesus has been able to love us with a human heart and a human love. His human love is the most moving and most striking manifestation of His Divine love.

Further there is between His Divine and human love a perfect harmony. All that He loves as God He also loves as Man. His human love is the echo of His Divine love. It is its image, and the most perfect that exists or could exist.

It is, moreover, entirely under the influence of His Divine love. All the favours which we owe to His human love are also, and in the first place, willed by His Divine love; and they are only willed by His human love because they are willed by His Divine love. If then Jesus loves us with a human love, it is essentially because He loves us with a Divine love.

On the other hand, Jesus' Divine love also belongs to the object as direct and proper object in a wider acceptation.

In fact it fulfils the requisite conditions.

In a broad sense it may be considered peculiar and proper to Jesus. In some respect it may be attributed to Him, namely with reference to the Incarnation, the Redemption and all the other gifts and graces which we owe directly to His human love.[1]

Indeed, to His Divine love we are indebted not only for the Incarnation but also, at least indirectly, for all His other benefits. Surely this love is common to the three Divine Persons, but only

---

[1] But it is only in this respect that it may be regarded as belonging to the object of the devotion to the Sacred Heart, for it is only in this respect that it may be attributed to Jesus. With reference to the other benefits of God, for instance, the Creation, it does not appertain to the devotion. (Cf. Vermeersch, op. cit., pp. 149 and 153.)

the Son of God, impelled by His love, took upon Himself a human nature; He only redeemed us through His Passion and Death; He only has imparted to us His merits, His doctrine, His example, His Sacraments and His Church. Therefore His Divine love may, in this respect, be specially attributed to Him and, consequently, be considered peculiar and proper to Him in a broad sense.

In a wider acceptation it may also be symbolized by His physical Heart and so be considered the direct object in a broad sense. There is between the Divine and the human love a certain analogy; we conceive of Divine love as being similar to ours. Is not this sufficient to allow us to symbolize Christ's Divine love by His Heart? Moreover the heart may be said to be, at least in a broad sense, an universally understood symbol of all love, and hence also of a Divine love. Suppose we wished to represent the love of God, would we not be permitted, to this end, to give Him a human appearance, with a visible heart on His breast? Would not this heart be looked upon and understood by all as a symbol of His Divine love? And is this not evidence that the heart may serve as a symbol of Divine love, at least in a wider sense?

Moreover, as we have seen above, the human love of Jesus is the most striking and most brilliant manifestation, and the most perfect image of His Divine love. Hence what symbolizes His human love also quite naturally symbolizes His Divine love.

We may then combine in our devotion to the Heart of Jesus His Divine and His human love. We ought even to do so. We are not allowed to separate them. Is it not in order to convince us of the love of God for us, and to make us think of it, that Jesus has revealed His Heart and His human love?

Indeed it is not in order to separate them that we make the preceding distinctions, but only to assign to each its exact place in the devotion.

But is not our thesis inconsistent with certain texts of official documents in which Christ's Divine love seems to be presented, at the very least, as the proper and direct object in the strict sense?

We might content ourselves with answering that this seems to us to be impossible; for we have seen that Christ's Divine love could not possibly be the direct and proper object of the devotion. Yet it will be useful to examine closely these texts. We shall see that nothing forces us to conclude from them that the Church considers and presents this love in such a way.

There are, first, some texts in which Christ's love is presented as 'divine', 'infinite', 'immense'.

For instance, the postulators of the feast of the Sacred Heart, in 1765, state that this Heart is to be considered 'the symbol or the natural seat of all virtues and sentiments of Christ our Lord, and above all of that immense love which He has borne to His Father and to men'.[1]

Pope Pius IX speaks of the Heart of Jesus as 'the seat of the Divine charity'.[2] And Leo XIII presents it as 'the symbol and sensible image of the infinite love of Jesus Christ'.[3]

Nothing, however, permits us to conclude that these epithets have in view the love which Jesus bears us in His Divine nature.

For, as we have seen above, Christ's human love as well as His Heart, may and even must be called Divine, in the sense of belonging to a Divine Person and consequently possessing a Divine dignity. Moreover, it is clear that the text in the place quoted has in view Christ's human love. It is only of His human love that His Heart may be said to be the seat. His Divine love has its seat in His Divine nature, with which it is identified.

As for the epithets 'infinite', 'immense', they are often taken in a broad acceptation, that is, in the sense of 'extremely great'. The context in each case fixes the meaning. Now nothing, in the texts mentioned above, obliges us to take these words in their strict sense. Even the contrary is true regarding the statement of the postulators of the feast; it is there clearly stated that there is question of 'the virtues and sentiments' of Jesus. Now these unquestionably appertain to His human nature. Hence the words 'the immense love which He has borne to His Father and to men' in reality have in view His human love.

There are, however, some other texts in which there is plainly question of Christ's Divine love.

The hymn at Matins of the Office of the Sacred Heart celebrates 'the love which impelled the Son of God to take to Himself a mortal body'.[4] This love is at once described as 'the artisan who made the earth, the sea and the stars'.[5]

---

[1] Cf. Nilles, op. cit., Liber I, cap. iii, § iii, n. 18.
[2] Brief of Beatification of Bl. Margaret Mary.
[3] Encyclical Annum sacrum, n. 10.
[4] 'Auctor beate saeculi, Christe, Redemptor omnium Amor coegit Te tuus mortale corpus sumere.'
[5] 'Ille amor, almus artifex terrae, marisque et siderum.'

The love which is celebrated in these verses is the love which induced the Son of God to take to Himself a human nature; it is to this same love that we owe the Creation; it is consequently the love which Jesus bears us in His Divine nature, His Divine love.[1] Hence the Church really considers this love as forming part of the object of the devotion. Yet this is no proof that she views this love as the direct and proper object: even if this love were only the indirect object or the proper and direct object in a broad sense, it may none the less be considered as appertaining to the object, at least to the object taken in a broad sense.

The decree of the Sacred Congregation of Rites, 1765, which grants the celebration of the feast of the Sacred Heart, states that 'in allowing this Mass and Office nothing else is aimed at than to renew symbolically the memory of that Divine love by which the Only-begotten Son of God took to Himself a human nature and, obedient unto death, wished to prove to men by His example that He was meek and humble of heart'.[2]

First of all, it seems to us to be evident that the Sacred Congregation did not intend to give a definition properly so called of the devotion. Had this been its purpose, it could not have confined the effects of Christ's love to His Incarnation, His redemptive death and His example; it must also have mentioned for instance the Eucharist, which is undoubtedly a still more precious gift than His example.

The love which induced the Son of God to take to Himself a human nature is unquestionably Christ's Divine love. The love which prompted Him to be willing to die for us and to serve as an example is His human love. 'The Divine love' therefore denotes not only His Divine love, but also His human love which both may and must be termed Divine.

Now the fact that the Sacred Congregation joined both loves under the same name is no proof that it intended to place them on the same plane, nor that it considered both of them as forming part of the direct and proper object of the devotion. Even if one is the direct and proper object and the other only indirect object, or direct and proper object in a broad sense, they may none the less be joined and presented as forming together the complete object, taken in a broad sense.

---

[1] The hymns at Lauds and Vespers celebrate Christ's human love.
[2] Cf. p. xxxix.

The last two remarks also apply to the decree of 1821 of the same Sacred Congregation, almost literally reproduced in the decree of April 4th, 1900, on the scapular: 'This feast', the passage reads, 'has not for its object some particular mystery of which the Church did not make mention at the proper time and place; it is as it were a summary (compendium) of the other feasts in which some special mysteries are worshipped; here is commemorated the Divine love which induced the Word to become incarnate for our ransom and for our salvation, to institute the Sacrament of the Altar, to take upon Himself our sins, and to offer Himself on the cross as a Host and Sacrifice.'[1]

In the Encyclical *Miserentissimus* several passages are to be found in which there is question of Christ's Divine love.

'Among all other proofs of the infinite mercy of our Redeemer there is one particularly resplendent: when the charity of the faithful was growing cold, the very love of God has been presented for the homage of a special cult, and the riches of His bounty have been opened wide by means of that form of religion, which is the cult of the Most Sacred Heart of Jesus, "in whom are hid all the treasures of wisdom and knowledge" ' (Col. ii, 3).

The devotion to the Sacred Heart, then, is presented to us as a special cult of the love of God. Yet it does not follow that this love is considered and worshipped as the direct and proper object. Even if it were only its indirect object, if it were not worshipped except in and through Christ's human love, one may none the less say that devotion to the Sacred Heart forms a special cult of the love of God.

This remark also applies to the following text: 'When the most insidious and pernicious of all heresies, Jansenism, was creeping in and, contrary to love and devotion for God, representing Him not as a Father to be loved but as a merciless Judge to be feared, the most merciful Jesus showed His Sacred Heart to all nations as a token of peace and a pledge of victory' (n. 5).

And further on we read: 'Among all these practices of the cult of the Sacred Heart stands out the pious Consecration by which we give back to God's eternal love all that we are and have received, and devote ourselves to the Divine Heart of Jesus' (n. 8).[2]

---

[1] Quoted in Nilles, II, pt. I, chap. iii, § v, A.
[2] The Latin text reads: 'nos nostraque omnia aeternae Numinis caritati accepta referentes . . .' The verb 'referre' employed with the dative case means, among other things, 'to give back'.

Neither is this text in conflict with our thesis. The ultimate object which we have in view in our Consecration is undoubtedly the eternal and uncreated love of God. Yet we consecrate ourselves directly to the Heart of Jesus in gratitude for His human love, and thereby, *ipso facto*, also consecrate ourselves indirectly to God for His Divine love, to which we owe directly all that we are and have, and consequently also all that we owe to Jesus' human love.

The part of the Encyclical which treats of the reparation begins as follows: 'If in the Consecration the first and chief thing is that the love of the Creator should be repaid by the love of the creature, there follows of itself another duty—namely, to compensate this same uncreated love for the indifference, neglect, offences and outrages of all sorts which may be committed against It. This debt is what is commonly called the duty of reparation' (n. 11).

The reparation which the Encyclical here deals with is evidently that which we owe to the Divine or uncreated love of God. Yet it should be noted that the Encyclical does not treat solely of the reparation which is proper and peculiar to the devotion to the Sacred Heart, but considers the reparation to its full extent. It distinguishes a twofold object and a twofold motive: 'The duty of atonement and reparation is incumbent on us by reason of justice and love; of justice, in order that the outrage offered to God by our crimes may be atoned for, and that the violated order may be re-established by our penance; of love, in order to compassionate Christ suffering and "overwhelmed with reproaches", and to afford Him, according to our littleness, some consolation' (n. 12).

The object of the reparation by reason of justice, then, is 'the outrage offered to God by our crimes'. This reparation is addressed directly to God, considered as our Master and Lord. Jesus Himself practised it in giving His Father an infinite satisfaction for the whole sinful human race. We are all bound to practise it in union with Christ by our works of penance' (n. 13–20).

The reparation for a motive of love considers Christ as Man 'suffering and overwhelmed with reproaches'. Its object, then, is these sufferings and outrages, this unworthy behaviour of men towards Him. It is addressed directly to the Sacred Heart. It is the Sacred Heart which is the immediate victim of these outrages; it is then for the Sacred Heart that the homage is intended, which tries to make up to Him (n. 21–27). Consequently it is this reparation which is proper and peculiar to the devotion to the Sacred Heart.[1]

The Encyclical treats separately of these two forms of reparation.

Now, in the part which treats of the reparation which we are bound by love to offer to the Sacred Heart, nowhere is mention made of Christ's Divine love (n. 21-25).

But as Christ is a Divine Person, we also owe Him the reparation in justice. That is the reason why the Act of Reparation, prescribed by Pope Pius XI on the feast of the Sacred Heart, bids us say to Jesus: 'We offer the satisfaction Thou didst once make to Thy eternal Father on the cross and which Thou dost continue to renew daily on our altars.' Yet this reparation, as we have seen, does not appertain properly to the devotion to the Sacred Heart.

So, then, not one of the texts quoted—and we do not think there are others which ought to be taken into consideration—forces us to admit that the Church presents Christ's Divine love as the proper and direct object of the devotion to the Sacred Heart.

We have, moreover, good reasons to think that it is only Christ's human love which the Church considers in such a way.

This appears in the first place from the manner in which it approved the devotion to the Sacred Heart. It gave its approbation by the decree of the Sacred Congregation of Rites (February 6th, 1765), which granted the celebration of the feast of the Sacred Heart.[2]

The Bishops of Poland had presented to the Sacred Congregation a request aiming at obtaining the institution of the feast, and had added to it a *Memoriale* or explanatory memorandum, in which they gave a detailed account of all that could be adduced in favour of the feast and the devotion which was connected with it. At the same time they replied to the objections which could be, and really were, urged against the new feast.

The decree stated: 'Knowing well that the cult of the Heart of Jesus is already spread in almost all parts of the Catholic world, favoured by Bishops and enriched by the Apostolic See with a thousand Briefs of indulgences, granted to countless Confraternities canonically erected in honour of the Heart of Jesus; moreover, understanding that by allowing this Mass and Office nothing else

---

[1] Galtier, op. cit., p. 62, note.
[2] See p. xxxviii.

is aimed at than to renew symbolically the memory of the Divine love, by which the Only-begotten Son of God took to Himself a human nature and, obedient unto death, wished to prove to men by His example that He was meek and humble of heart: for these reasons the Sacred Congregation of Rites has deemed it right to accede to the request of the Bishops of the kingdom of Poland.'[1]

The decree, then, states simply, without making any remark or reserve, that it complies with the request of the Bishops.[2] We may conclude, then, that it was the purpose of the Sacred Congregation to approve the feast requested, and consequently also the devotion to the Sacred Heart, in the sense in which the Bishops had presented them in their *Memoriale*.

Now how did these describe Christ's love? 'The love,' they stated, 'which Jesus, our Lord, bore to His Father and to men, was in keeping with the laws of man's nature; hence His spiritual love, which was certainly most intense and most vehement, must have been accompanied by an equally intense sensible love. . . . Therefore, the Heart of Christ our Lord may be said to have largely contributed, in its own way, to the love with which He has loved us, and to have experienced impressions and emotions similar to those which other men naturally feel when they love.'[3]

Hence the love of Christ, which the Bishops point out as the direct and proper object of the feast, is the love the impressions of which His Heart has felt. It is, then, His human love, and this love only: indeed His Divine love had no echo in His Heart. Now the Sacred Congregation approved the feast, and consequently the devotion to the Sacred Heart in the sense in which the Bishops had presented them. We may conclude then that the Sacred Congregation also views Christ's human love as the proper and direct object of the devotion.

Besides, the Sacred Congregation stated that by granting the feast of the Sacred Heart 'nothing else is aimed at than to develop a cult already established', a devotion 'which is already spread in nearly all parts of the Catholic world, favoured by Bishops and enriched by the Holy See with a thousand Briefs of indulgences'.

Now this devotion, already established and encouraged by

---

[1] Nilles, op. cit. (1873), pars I, cap. iii and iv.

[2] It makes mention, it is true, of Christ's Divine love, but as we have seen above, this by no means proves that the Sacred Congregation views the devotion otherwise than do the Bishops of Poland.

[3] Nilles, op. cit., Liber I, pars I, cap. iii, § iii.

Bishops and the Holy See itself, considers Christ's human love, and this love only, its direct and proper object. The Bishops of Poland bear witness to it in their *Memoriale*: indeed, the devotion which they describe is no other than that which is observed everywhere and is encouraged by Bishops and the Holy See. It is then the devotion viewed in this way which the Sacred Congregation wishes to see spread ever more widely and which consequently it approves. And by this approbation it shows that it understands the devotion in the same way, that it too considers Christ's human love the direct and proper object of the devotion.

The Office and the Collect of the Mass for the feast of the Sacred Heart, approved by it a few days after the publication of its decree, clearly show that it really understands the devotion in this way.

In the Office we read: 'Pope Clement XIII has granted to several churches the celebration of the feast of the Most Sacred Heart of Jesus, in order that the faithful, under the symbol of this sacred Heart, might recall with more piety and fervour the love of Christ suffering and dying for the Redemption of the human race and, in memory of His death, instituting the Sacrament of His Body and Blood' (2nd Nocturn, 6th lesson). The love which is presented here as the special object of the feast and consequently of the devotion to the Sacred Heart is that which induced Jesus to suffer and to die for us and to institute the Blessed Sacrament of the Altar. Now for these benefits we are indebted directly to His human love. On the other hand, not a word is said of any benefit which we owe directly to His increate love; for instance, the Incarnation. The love therefore which the lesson presents as the peculiar object of the feast is really the human love of Jesus.

The Collect runs as follows: 'Grant, we beseech Thee, O almighty God, that we who glory in the Most Sacred Heart of Thy beloved Son, and celebrate the singular benefits of His love towards us, may rejoice both in their accomplishment and in the fruit they produce.' So, then, the benefits which we celebrate in devotion to the Sacred Heart are not those which we owe directly to God and which are common to the three Divine Persons, but those which are proper and peculiar to the Son of God. Now, only those benefits are proper to the Son of God, which He granted to us as Man and which consequently we owe directly to His human love. It is then to this human love that we want to pay honour directly in devotion to the Sacred Heart.

Another exercise of the Liturgy confirms our opinion. In the Litany of the Sacred Heart, which the Church has made its own, we find three invocations which bear upon Jesus' love: 'Heart of Jesus, glowing furnace of charity', 'abode of justice and love', 'full of kindness and love'. Now, in all three it is, directly at least, His human love that is pointed out. For it is with this love only that the Heart of Jesus may be said to be glowing, that It is its abode, that It is full of it; His uncreated love has no echo in His Heart, and its seat is the Divine nature with which it is identified. Once more the human love of Jesus is presented as the proper object of the devotion.

Neither, in a Brief of Pope Pius VII which grants the feast of the Sacred Heart to some churches, is mention made of Christ's uncreated love: 'We have,' he writes, 'complied with the wishes of the faithful who wanted to see the cult of the Heart of Jesus increased, that they might worship more ardently the excessive love of our Lord Jesus Christ, suffering and dying for the Redemption of the human race.'[1] The love which prompted our Lord to be willing to suffer and to die for our Redemption is directly His human love. It is then directly this love which the faithful wished to celebrate with more ardour by means of the feast of the Sacred Heart; it is then this love, and this only, which is the proper object of the devotion.

Finally, we find in documents issued from the Holy See two principles which corroborate our thesis.

Pope Benedict XIV in his book on Beatification and Canonization writes: 'There is no feast in honour of Christ which refers to the Son as to the Second Person of the Blessed Trinity; these feasts are all feasts of Christ, i.e. of God made Man, and present to us the singular graces and profound mysteries which the Word Incarnate has wrought for the salvation of the human race.'[2] In other words, the proper and peculiar object of all feasts of Christ is always something performed by Him as Man, some benefit which we owe directly to His humanity. Hence this also applies to the feast of the Sacred Heart. Now which particular love of Christ is one of the benefits of His humanity? Obviously His

Nilles, I, p. 345.
[2] Op cit., Liber IV, pars II, cap. 30, n. 2.

human love, and this only. It is then this love, and this only, which is the proper and peculiar object of the feast of the Sacred Heart and consequently also of the devotion to the Sacred Heart.[1]

In his Encyclical *Divinum illud*, Leo XIII writes that the only reason to worship one of the three Divine Persons with a special cult is His 'external mission'. Now, the love which appertains to the external mission of the Word is His human love. It is then in this human love that lies the reason of the special homage which devotion to the Sacred Heart pays to the Son of God; in other words, it is this human love which is the proper and peculiar object of this devotion.[2]

So, then, not only is our thesis not inconsistent with the teaching of the Church but is fully in keeping with it.

I think we may conclude therefore: Only the human love of Jesus is in the strict sense the direct and proper object of the devotion to the Sacred Heart; but His Divine and uncreated love forms part of the devotion taken in a broad sense, at once as indirect object and as direct and proper object in a broad sense.

Fr. Ramière, s.j., the greatest apostle of the devotion to the Sacred Heart, the founder of the *Messager du Cœur de Jésus*, and organizer of the world-wide League of the Sacred Heart, the Apostleship of Prayer,[3] had already written in 1868: 'The proper object of the devotion to the Sacred Heart is the human and created love of Christ. To convince oneself it suffices to read attentively the very words of our Saviour, the writings of Blessed Margaret Mary, the decrees of the Sovereign Pontiffs and the forms of the Missal and Breviary:[4] in a word, all the documents in which we have to search for the idea of God and His Church on the subject of this devotion. Everywhere one will find that the love presented to men by the good Master, under the symbol of His Heart, is a suffering love, a love that exhausts itself, a love that shares in our trials, sympathizes with our distress, mourns over our infidelities: the love, in fine, which transformed the life of our Saviour into a long martyrdom and caused Him to endure at Gethsemane a Passion still more cruel than that of which His executioners were the instruments. And is it not this which is proclaimed in a sensible way by the blessed image under which

---

[1] Vermeersch, op. cit. (1930), II, p. 55.
[2] Ibid., p. 57.
[3] See appendix II, n. III, p. 261.
[4] The Mass *Miserebitur* and ancient Office.

our gentle Saviour has been pleased to represent to us His love, this image of a wounded Heart, surmounted with a cross, and crowned with thorns?'[1]

Fr. Galtier, s.j., on his part, has no hesitation in concluding: 'When we take into account the dogmatic data which forbid us to attribute to Christ any other personal love than His love as Man, and when we observe the accordance of the encyclicals and the revelations of Paray-le-Monial in bringing into prominence His suffering love, one cannot hesitate, it would seem, to see in the love of His human nature the proper and direct object of the worship to be paid to His Sacred Heart.'[2]

At the end of his great work, *Histoire de la dévotion au Sacré-Cœur*, Fr. Hamon, s.j., arrives at the same conclusion: 'In the devotion to the Sacred Heart, as it is practised officially in the Church, the love which, together with the physical Heart, forms the object of the cult, is in the first place and more directly the created love, the human love of Jesus towards His Father[3] and for men; in a wider sense, it is also the uncreated love, appropriated to the Word, uncreated love by which "the Word is made flesh".'[4]

2. To what extent does the love of Jesus towards His Heavenly Father belong to the object of the devotion?

It is evident that Christ's love towards His Father forms part, at least of the secondary object. To this object belongs, as we have seen, the whole interior life of Jesus, i.e. not only His affective life, His sentiments, but also His moral life, His virtues, and consequently also His love towards His Father, His love of God.

[1] *Messager du Cœur de Jésus*, 1868, p. 275.
[2] Galtier, op. cit., p. 124.
[3] See the next section.
[4] Hamon, op. cit., t.V., p. 120. It is also the conclusion of the remarkable study of Fr. Vermeersch, s.j., on this subject (op. cit. (1930), II, pp. 101–2). (In the edition of 1930 the author has slightly altered his previous view on the matter in hand. If then we wish to know his definitive opinion on this subject, it is this edition which should be consulted.) Among the theologians who confine the proper object of the devotion to Christ's human love, we should mention, besides Vermeersch, Galtier and Hamon, the following authors: Marques, s.j., *Defensio cultus SS. Cordis Jesu*; Zaccaria, s.j., *Antidoto contra i libri prodotti o da prodursi dal sign. Blasi*; Nilles, *Cor Jesu, divini Redemptoris nostri caritatis symbolum*, p. 56; Card. Franzelin, s.j., *De Verbo incarnato*; De San, s.j., *De Verbo incarnato*; Dalgairns, *The devotion to the Sacred Heart*; Vignat, s.j., in *Etudes*, 1906, p. 665; De Franciosi, s.j., *Le sacré-Cœur de Jésus et la Tradition*, etc. 'The soul of the cult (of the Sacred Heart) is the love symbolized by the Heart of Jesus. Which love? It is the redeeming love, a human love; not the love "which created Lazarus, but the love which wept over him" ' (Mgr. Mathieu, bishop of Aire and Dax, France, in *Le Sacré-Cœur de Jésus et la doctrine du Corps mystique*, p. 70).

It even takes the first place in it, for charity was indeed the first, the principal virtue of Jesus; and He practised it in the highest degree. Charity was for Him the mother, the queen of His other virtues; it was the soul of them, which imparted to them all its own perfection, its own dignity, and its own merit.

'Devotion to the Sacred Heart,' writes Fr. Bainvel, 'is, in its direct and immediate object, devotion to the loving Heart of Jesus, to the Heart the emblem of love; but it is also, by a legitimate and natural extension, devotion to the Divine Heart of Jesus in His whole interior life, and hence in His virtues, and particularly in His love for God. As the symbol of love, it is His love for us that Jesus discovers to us in discovering to us His Heart; but in discovering this adorable Heart He shows It to us in all its reality, as the ideal of our life no less than as the object of our love.'[1]

The love of Jesus for His Father was considered as forming part of the object of the devotion from the very outset.

Bl. Claude de la Colombière, as we have seen, begins his form of consecration in these terms: 'This offering is made with the intention of honouring the Divine Heart, which is the seat of all virtues, the fountain of all blessings, and the refuge of all holy souls. The *chief* virtues which we seek to honour in this Heart are: firstly, *a most ardent love of God His Father*, joined to perfect reverence and humility.'

And in their answer to the objections advanced against the devotion to the Sacred Heart, the Bishops of Poland stated: 'The Heart of Jesus is to be regarded . . . secondly, as the symbol or the natural seat of all the virtues and interior affections of Christ, *in particular of the immense love He has borne to His Father*.'[2]

Does this love also form part of the essential constituent of the object?

We think the answer to this question must be: Directly and immediately, no. If we take into account the revelations made to St. Margaret Mary, the Papal Letters and liturgical texts, then there is no doubt possible: our devotion has in view directly Christ's love for men, and this only. It is of this only that Jesus speaks in His apparitions to the Saint. It is only of this love that the Popes make mention in their Letters. The Church, too, in her liturgy of the Feast of the Sacred Heart—The Mass, Office and

---

[1] Bainvel, op. cit., pt. II, chap. i, p. 141.
[2] Nilles, op. cit., Liber I, pars I, cap. iii, *Disputatio*, etc., *Exceptiones*, n. 18, p. 127.

Litany—shows us Our Lord in His relation to us; to persuade us to love Jesus, she only reminds us how much He has loved us: *Quis non amantem redamet?* she sings in the hymn at Lauds, 'Who would not love in return One who loves us so much?'[1]

Moreover, as we shall see in the next chapter, the special aim and end of the devotion is to make a return of love to Jesus, and to make reparation for the neglect and disdain of His love. Now, for which love are we to return love? Evidently for His love towards us. And for which disdained love is reparation asked? Obviously also for His love towards man, as His love for His Father is not scorned. Therefore, the direct and immediate object is really His love for men, and this only; His love for His Father forms no part of it.

Yet it may be said to form part of it indirectly, since it is in close connection with the love which Jesus bears us. It is the source and incentive of it. Jesus loves us for the sake of His Father, because He loves His Father, because we are the images of His Father, because His Father loves us and wishes Him to love us too. His love for us is, properly speaking, only a form of His love for His Father. Hence He desires that from His love for us we should ascend to His love for His Father; that we should not separate the two loves in our worship; and consequently that we should address our homage through His love for us to His love for His Father. In other words, Jesus must wish us to view and honour His love for His Father as the indirect object of devotion to His Heart.

'Neither the Church nor Christ prompts us to return love for love in this way but for the purpose of winning us to love for God Himself. No one, moreover, should contrive to twist the essential order of true charity. If Christ has loved us, it is not, properly speaking, for our own sakes and because of the good He wishes to procure us; it is because of God Himself and of the supreme love He has charity for Him. What He demands of us on behalf of our neighbour He did Himself first and to perfection on our behalf: He has loved us as Himself, more than Himself in a manner, out of love for God.'[2]

---

[1] Cf. Galtier, op. cit., p. 126.
[2] Galtier, op. cit., p. 128.

G

CHAPTER II

Ends of the Devotion

DIRECT AND INDIRECT ENDS

Now that we know the precise object of the Devotion, the question arises: In what does the Devotion consist?

It is evidently our Lord Himself whom we ought to ask in the first place.

As we can see in the writings of St. Margaret Mary, Jesus wished by His apparitions and manifestations of His Heart to attain as many as seven different ends. He wished us to return love for His love, to make reparation to His Heart for the neglect of His love, to pay honour to His Heart, to place our trust in His Heart, to love His Heavenly Father more and more, to work to establish and extend the reign of His Heart, and to afford Him the occasion of pouring forth upon men the treasures of His Heart.

Yet all these aims of Jesus are not to be put on the same level; they are not all ends properly so called of the devotion which He wanted to establish. The first four relate to the affections which we should endeavour to arouse in our hearts by the contemplation of the Heart of Jesus and which we should manifest to His Heart if we want to practise this devotion as it is asked for by our Lord. It is then properly speaking in this that the devotion consists. The other three are the results, the attainment of which Jesus had in view by means of these affections, by means of this devotion understood and practised in this way, and which we shall almost necessarily attain if we practise the devotion as Jesus asked for it. These then are the real ends of the devotion.

Usage, however, has become general to designate by this word all the aims which Jesus had in view in His apparitions and the manifestations of His Heart. To preclude confusion, we shall then conform to this usage. In that case we must distinguish between direct and indirect ends of the devotion. The direct ends are the four affections which we are to arouse within us and to manifest to the Heart of Jesus—namely, love, reparation, veneration and confidence; the indirect ends are the three results which Jesus wishes to obtain by means of this devotion—namely, the increase of our love for God, the establishment and extension of the reign of the Sacred Heart, and the outpouring of the treasures of the Sacred Heart.

Among the direct ends the two principal are love and reparation: the other two are the secondary ends. In like manner, among the indirect ends there is one that holds the first place, namely, the increase of our love for the Heavenly Father.

§ I. DIRECT ENDS

A. PRINCIPAL ENDS

1. To Return to the Heart of Jesus Love for Love

I. JESUS DESIRES IT

In revealing His Heart, Jesus intended first of all that we should recognize the love of His Heart, that we should show Him our gratitude for it, and that we should requite it by our love. And as the last-named includes the other two, we may simply say: Jesus wished first and foremost to obtain that we should return to His Heart love for love.

St. Margaret Mary states it explicitly: "He gave me plainly to understand that His earnest desire of being loved by men had made Him form the design of revealing to them His Heart . . ."[1] To her spiritual director she writes: 'Jesus made known to me in a manner that admits of no doubt that it was His wish to establish everywhere this solid devotion and, through its means to win countless faithful servants, *perfect friends* and supremely grateful children.'[2] And to her former Superior, Mother de Saumaise: 'To win souls to His love, this is the chief end of this devotion.'[3]

Our Lord manifested this wish on more than one occasion and in various ways.

He expressed this desire to the Saint, promised priceless gifts and graces to those who love Him, complained of being so little loved, and showed that He is sensible to the disdain of His love. He asked of His friends to console Him and to make up for the

---

[1] *Vie et Oeuvres*, vol. II, p. 572, *4e Lettre au P. Croiset.*
[2] Ibid., p. 626–27.
[3] Ibid., p. 355.

little love He receives, invited them to work to make Him loved more and more, and promised in return treasures of blessings and graces.[1]

Here are some passages of the writings of the Saint in which this appears clearly: 'He made me see that His earnest desire of being loved by men . . . had made Him form the design of manifesting to them His Heart, in order that those who would render and procure for It all the honour, love and glory they were capable of, might themselves be enriched with the abundance and profusion of those Divine treasures of which this Heart is the source.'[2]

Again: 'Then He revealed to me the unspeakable marvels of His pure love, and the excess of love He had conceived for men, *from whom He received nothing but ingratitude and contempt.* "This is more grievous to Me," He said to me, "than all that I endured in My Passion. If they would only give Me some return of love, I should make no account of all that I have done for them, and I would do still more, if possible. But *they have only coldness and contempt* for all My endeavours to do them good. Do you, at least, give Me the happiness of *making up for their ingratitude,* as much as you can." '[3]

Again: 'Behold this Heart which has so loved men. . . . And in return I receive from the greater part of men nothing but *ingratitude,* by their irreverence and sacrileges, by the *indifference and contempt* with which they treat Me in this Sacrament of Love. Yet what is more painful to Me is that even souls consecrated to Me are acting in this way. Therefore I *ask* of you that the first Friday after the octave of Corpus Christi be dedicated to a special feast in honour of My Heart . . . by making amends in an Act of Reparation.'[4]

Again: 'He assured me that the pleasure He takes in being loved, known and honoured by His creatures is so great that He *promised* me that no one who has dedicated and consecrated himself to Him will ever perish.'[5]

Again: 'It is His eager *desire of imparting graces* of sanctification and salvation to well-disposed hearts that causes Him to wish to be known, adored and glorified by His creatures.'[6]

---

[1] In this desire of our Lord there is however no shadow of egoism. As we shall see, if He wishes to be loved, it is to induce us to love God His Father and to be able to pour forth on us the riches of His Heart.

[2] *Vie et Oeuvres,* vol. II, pp. 571–72.   [3] Ibid., p. 72.

[4] Ibid., p. 103.   [5] Ibid., p. 300.   [6] Ibid., p. 397.

'One of my greatest tortures was to hear this Divine Heart declare: "I thirst, I burn with a consuming desire for men's love, and I find none to quench this thirst, according to My wish, by making any return of love." '[1]

'There were there many whose names are graved in golden letters in the Sacred Heart, . . . the hearts of those who had done their utmost to make It known and loved.'[2]

In revealing His Heart, Jesus intended in the first place that we should repay His love with love. This, then, is the first and principal end of the devotion to the Sacred Heart.

This was perfectly understood by the first promoters: 'The end aimed at in this devotion,' writes Fr. Croiset, 'is, firstly, *to recognize and to honour*, to the best of our power, by our frequent acts of adoration, by a return of love, by our thanksgiving and every kind of homage, all the sentiments of *love and tenderness* which Jesus Christ bears us in the holy Eucharist.' And further: 'It is, properly speaking, only an exercise of love; love is its object, love is its principal motive; *love* must also be its end.'[3]

In the first request (1697) for the institution of the feast of the Sacred Heart we read: 'The aim and purpose of this devotion is to respond to the boundless love of our Lord Jesus Christ.'[4]

And Fr. de Galliffet, in his turn, wrote in 1745: 'Devotion to the Heart of our Lord Jesus Christ is an exercise which has for its end to honour this Divine Heart by all kinds of homage which *love and gratitude* can inspire.'[5]

It is, moreover, in this way that the Church understands the end of the devotion. '*Quis non amantem redamet?*' she sings in the hymn at Lauds of the Feast of the Sacred Heart: 'Who would not love in return One Who loves us so much?' And in the Secret of the Mass *Egredimini* she bids her priests pray: 'May the Holy Ghost, we beseech Thee, O Lord, *inflame us with the love* which our Lord Jesus Christ enkindled on earth and so ardently desired to be inflamed.'

When Pope Pius IX, in 1856, extended the feast of the Sacred Heart to the universal Church, his purpose was 'to urge on the

---

[1] *Vie et Oeuvres*, Vol. II, p. 580.
[2] Ibid., p. 408.
[3] Croiset, op. cit., pt. I, chap. i.
[4] Nilles, op. cit., Liber I, pars II, cap. i, § I.
[5] De Galliffet, op. cit., Book I, pt. I, chap. iv, p. 48.

faithful *to make a return of love* to the wounded Heart of Him who has loved us and cleansed us from our sins in His blood'.[1] And when he raised the Feast to a higher rite, it was again 'that the devotion of love to the Heart of our Redeemer might spread more and more, and penetrate more deeply into the hearts of the faithful, and that thus charity, which has grown cold among many, might be rekindled by the fire of Divine love'.[2]

In the Brief of beatification of Margaret Mary he states: 'Jesus had nothing more in view than to enkindle in the hearts of men the fire of love with which His own Heart was inflamed. . . . Therefore He wished that the veneration and cult of His Most Sacred Heart should be established and propagated in the Church.'[3] And for the commemorative medal which was struck on the occasion of this beatification, the Sovereign Pontiff ordered an image of Jesus showing His Heart, with the inscription '*Cor ut redametur exhibet*', i.e. 'He shows His Heart in order to be loved in return.'[4]

Pope Leo XIII speaks in the same way in his Apostolic Letter of June 28th, 1889: 'Jesus has no more ardent desire,' he writes, 'than to see inflamed in the hearts of men the fire of love with which His own Heart is burning. Let us then go to Him, Who asks of us recompense for His love nothing but reciprocal love.' The Letter is full of this idea.

To this, moreover, do the official documents which treat of the Sacred Heart refer again and again. Frequently the words of our Lord: 'I am come to cast fire on the earth, and what will I but that it be kindled?' are quoted in this sense (Luke xii, 49).[5]

II. THE HEART OF JESUS IS WORTHY OF IT

Is this aim justified? Does Jesus deserve that we should love Him?

One might as well ask whether Jesus really loves us? Now, as we have seen, we know this for certain; it is a point of Catholic faith.

---

[1] Nilles, op. cit., Liber I, pars I, cap. iv, § i, p. 147.
[2] Ibid., p. 150.
[3] *Vie et Oeuvres*, vol. III, p. 146.
[4] Bainvel, op. cit., pt. II, chap. iii, § i, p. 180.
[5] Bainvel, ibid., p. 181.

(a) Reality of Jesus' Love

Jesus loves us as God. 'We have known, and have believed the charity, which God hath to us . . . God is charity. . . . Let us therefore love God, because God first hath loved us' (1 John iv, 16, 19). As God He loves us with an eternal love, for whatever is in God is eternal, as everything in Him is identified with His Divine Nature.

He loves us as Man, too.

He loved us during His mortal life. He Himself assures us: 'As the Father hath loved Me, I also have loved you . . . This is My commandment, that you love one another, as I have loved you. . . . You are My friends, if you do the things that I command you' (John xv, 9, 12, 14). True, these words were addressed directly to His Apostles, but from the context and the circumstances in which they were pronounced it clearly appears that our Lord had also in view all His future disciples.

Jesus has loved us. It is certified by His Apostles. 'Walk in love,' writes St. Paul (Eph. v, 2), 'as Christ also hath loved us.' And St. John: 'In this we have known the charity of God: He hath laid down His life for us' (1 John iii, 16). Again: 'Jesus Christ, who hath loved us, and washed us from our sins in His own blood . . . to Him be glory and power for ever and ever' (Apoc. i, 5–6). Jesus has loved us. The Church sings it in her hymns. 'Love hath willed Thee to be struck with a visible wound, that we may venerate the wounds of Thy invisible love . . . Who would not love in return One Who loves us so much?'[1] 'At last the wondrous power of Thy love hath washed the world in Thy Blood.'[2] "Hail, Wounds of Christ, pledges of His boundless love!"[3]

It is no less certain that His love embraced not only mankind in general but was also extended to every man in particular,

---

[1] 'Te vulneratum caritas
  Ictu patenti voluit,
  Amoris invisibilis
  Ut veneremur vulnera . . .
  Quis non amantem redamet?'
(Off. in festo SS. Cordis Jesu; Hymnus ad Laudes.)

[2] 'Mira tandem vis amoris
  Lavit orbem sanguine.'

[3] 'Salvete, Christi vulnera,
  Immensi amoris pignora!'
(Ibid., Hymnus ad Laudes.)

chiefly to each one of those whom He foresaw would one day be counted among His disciples, and hence to each one of us.

It was possible for Him thus to love us, thanks to His infused knowledge which, according to the teaching of theologians, He received from the very outset, and which extended to whatever was connected with the work of the Redemption, and hence also to each one of those who would profit by the Redemption.

Hence He saw us, each and every one of us, in the far-off distance of time, and loved us beforehand. Hence each one of us may say truthfully: 'Jesus, during His mortal lifetime, saw and loved me.' And with the Apostle St. Paul: 'He loved me, and delivered Himself for me' (Gal. ii, 20). Consequently, all Scripture texts in which mention is made of Christ's love for men, may and must be applied to each one of us in particular. Likewise all the tokens of love which He gave to men may and must be understood and considered as intended for each one of us. When He gave them, He had before His eyes each one of us, and intended them for us personally. At each of these tokens of love we may and must acknowledge: 'For me He said this; for me He did this; for me He suffered this; His love for me inspired this in Him.'

This love Jesus still bears us. It is still the same as it was during His mortal life. It is true that His Humanity is now glorified, and so is no longer capable of suffering, but for the rest it is still as it was on earth. And why should He not love us now? He loved us when we were not yet in existence; how then should He not love us now that we exist?

Moreover, we know for certain that He goes on loving us. The Apostle St. Paul bears witness to it: 'In all things we overcome, because of Him that hath loved us' (Rom. viii, 37). The Church proclaims it in the Preface of the Mass for the Feast of the Sacred Heart: '*That this opened Heart . . . as It hath never ceased to burn with love for us*, so It might be a resting-place for the devout and afford a refuge of salvation for the penitent.'[1] And in the hymn at Vespers: 'But let us emulate in our hearts with the flames, the tokens of His love'[2]—of His love, simply; and consequently not only of the love which He bore us during His mortal life, but also

---

[1] 'Ut apertum Cor . . . quod amore nostri flagrare numquam destitit, piis esset requies et poenitentibus pateret salutis refugium.'

[2] 'Sed aemulemur cordibus
Flammas amoris indices.'

of that which He still bears us. And in her Litany she bids us call upon the Sacred Heart as 'full of kindness and love', as a 'glowing furnace of charity', and she approved this other invocation: 'Heart of Jesus, burning with love for us, inflame our hearts with love for Thee.'

Besides, Jesus has given us the most undeniable, the most striking and most touching proofs of His love.

Love is proved by deeds, by affording the beloved one some pleasure, rendering him a service and loading him with benefits. The worth of these proofs of love is still further enhanced by the trouble they cost us, by the sacrifices they require of us and the sufferings they bring on us. The more numerous and precious these benefits, the greater the trouble, the more onerous the sacrifices, the more painful the sufferings, so much the more ardent and profound is proved to be the love which inspired them.

Now, to the love of Jesus we are indebted for the most precious benefits, and these benefits cost Him the most burdensome sacrifices and the most atrocious sufferings.

(b) Benefits for which we are Indebted to Jesus' Love

Jesus has given us His doctrine, which acquaints us with our everlasting destiny, the possession of God, and which shows us the way leading to it.

He has given us His example, which illustrates His commandments and counsels, prompts us to the practice of all virtues, and moreover merited for us the graces necessary to reproduce them in ourselves.

He has given us His Sacraments, as so many channels through which the grace indispensable for the attainment of our supernatural end flows into our souls.

He has given us His Church, who by her doctrinal power is our infallible teacher and absolutely trustworthy guide on our way to our everlasting destiny, and who by her priestly power places at our disposal the inexhaustible sources of grace which are bequeathed to her by her Divine Founder.

He has given us His Blessed Mother, to whom He has entrusted us as to our Heavenly Mother, and whom He appointed the universal Mediatrix with Him and the Distributress of all graces.

But He showed His love first and foremost by His Incarnation, by our Redemption and by the institution of the Blessed Eucharist.[1]

The Church has summarized in a lapidary style these three great benefits in one of the strophes of the hymn *Verbum supernum*:

'Se nascens dedit socium,
Convescens in edulium,
Se moriens in pretium,
Se regnans dat in praemium.'[2]

1. *His Incarnation*

The Incarnation is the great favour which we owe directly to Christ's uncreated love. It underlies all the other benefits for which we are indebted to His human love.

By it the Redemption was made possible. Without it, no one would have been able to offer to God the adequate satisfaction which He claimed for sin. God, as God, could neither suffer nor humble Himself, and hence atone for sin; a man, it is true, was capable of humbling himself and suffering, but not thereby offering to God an adequate condign satisfaction; for this, according to the Divine decrees, ought to be infinite, as is the offence done to God by sin. Only God made Man was capable of it; for as Man it was possible for Him to humble Himself and to suffer, and thus to atone for sin, while as God, He could impart to this satisfaction an infinite value.

The Incarnation, moreover, facilitated to a large extent our love for God and made possible, even during this life, the ineffable intimacy of real ties of friendship between man and God. On account of His human qualities which make Him supremely love worthy, Jesus helps us to love God for His infinite perfections. If the Eternal Word had not become incarnate, it would have been extremely difficult for us, if not impossible, to love God really for Himself; for we know Him so little and so deficiently; it even requires on our part the greatest effort to conceive Him as a personal, concrete Being. But now that God, through His Incarnation, became visible, we may form some idea of His infinite perfections,

---

[1] As we have observed, the Incarnation is only connected with the Devotion to the Sacred Heart if we consider the object of the Devotion in a broad sense. (Cf. pp. 10 and 33.)

[2] 'By His Birth He became our Companion, at the Last Supper our food, by His death our ransom, in His Heavenly Kingdom our reward.'

since we have before our eyes a living and ideal reproduction of them.

We can hardly realize in particular the intrinsic nature of the love which God bears us. It is so different from our own; for as it is identified with His Divine Nature and with the Divine perfections, it consists in one eternal and immutable act; nor does it bring about any emotion in God. Hence it is so difficult for us to be moved by the thought of that love, and to answer it by a return of love. But, in becoming man, the Son of God received a human heart, a heart like ours, which loves us with a true human love, with a love which really moves His Heart. This love we understand, to this love we are sensitive, by this love we can be moved, and this love we can easily repay with a return of love.

Not only does His Heart love in the same way as we love, but It is, like ours, sensitive to affection, to love. In God, our love does not produce anything; it cannot move Him, nor increase His happiness. But the Heart of God incarnate is sensitive to the love which we show Him, and constantly finds in it new joys. Is not this thought appropriate to facilitate and arouse our love for God?

To this is to be added the honour which Jesus has done us, all of us, by His Incarnation. In uniting a human nature to a Divine Person, He has ennobled it and as it were deified it. We may then say with a legitimate pride: a God, a Divine Person is a member of the great human family, a God is one of ours, we are God's kinsmen!

2. *Our Redemption*

The greatest benefit of Jesus' love is our Redemption.

By the sin of Adam the human race had incurred the disgrace of God and had forfeited His friendship, His fatherly love. We all come into the world as 'children of wrath' (Eph. ii, 3). We had lost all the gifts which God had bestowed, gratuitously, for pure goodness, upon our first parents, and which were intended to be handed down to their posterity if they had remained faithful— supernatural gifts such as sanctifying grace, divine sonship, indwelling of the Blessed Trinity in us, and the claim to everlasting bliss; preternatural gifts, such as infused knowledge, command over the passions, and immunity from suffering and death.

The Son of God made Man took upon Himself the debt of our first father, and atoned for the offence done by sin; He thus reconciled us to God, and restored to us His friendship.

He also merited that the supernatural gifts, lost by the sin of Adam, should be restored to us, and that the actual graces necessary to attain to everlasting bliss should be placed at our disposal. As for the preternatural gifts, God deemed it preferable not to restore them to us during this life, in order to afford us matter for merit and reward; on the other hand, by means of the actual graces which Jesus merited for us, we are able to check the lusts of the flesh, resignedly to bear the trials and troubles of life, and thus to gather treasures of merit for Heaven.

Yet Jesus made atonement not only for the sin of Adam but also for all the sins of all men, not only for sins committed before His coming into the world but also for those which will be committed until the end of time. Thanks, then, to this atonement we can obtain pardon of all our faults, provided we make use of the means which He has placed at our disposal to this end.

To Jesus, then, to the satisfaction which He presented to His Father and to the merit which He acquired by it, we owe priceless benefits: thanks to Him we are God's adopted children, God bears us real fatherly love; our souls are as it were deified by sanctifying grace, the three Divine Persons dwell within us; we are able to restrain our evil passions and to resist temptations; to gain merits for everlasting life, and one day to share in the happiness of God Himself.

In short, we owe to Jesus and His love all that we are, all that we have, all that is in our power, and all that we hope for with reference to supernatural life.

3. The Blessed Eucharist

And what a benefit is the Eucharist!

In the Tabernacle Jesus is our great solace and comfort. Here we enjoy the priceless advantage of possessing in our midst our Saviour, who went about through the lands of Galilee and Judea, doing good to all, whom the apostles and the inhabitants of those countries were allowed to see and hear, whose ineffable kindness they experienced, whose sublime lessons they heard, and whose magnificent miracles they witnessed. We have not, as they had, the good fortune of seeing and hearing Him; but Faith gives us the certainty that He really dwells in the Tabernacle, that there He lives, that He sees and hears us.

Thanks to the Eucharist we have the great honour of possessing in our midst the Son of God, God Himself, the King of kings, the Master and Lord of the world, whom the Angels adore with the deepest reverence and whose contemplation transports the Saints into ecstasy. True, Jesus remains concealed under the veil of the Host, but Faith assures us of the truth that He is really present there, under this veil, close by.

Thanks to the Eucharist we have the immeasurable good fortune of possessing in our midst our great Friend, who really, ardently and tenderly loves us, who wishes us to be happy, who is interested in whatever concerns us, whom we may consult about everything, and to whom we may entrust all our cares, all our desires. To be sure, we do not see His eyes which look upon us, His arms which stretch out to receive us, His smile which encourages us. But we know for certain that He is there, and that He loves us.

At any hour of the day we may approach Him, come very near Him, and talk to Him as often and for as long as we wish. Always ready to receive us, He is never weary of listening to us; nor are we to observe any etiquette, any ceremonial, any formalities. We may talk to Him, very simply, familiarly, about everything we want, and He listens to us as though we were the only one to converse with Him.

How easy then becomes our intercourse with Jesus! We know precisely the spot where He is; thither we can direct our gaze, our thoughts and our hearts; thither we can stretch forth our entreating hands. Hence how easy it becomes to pray, to pray respectfully, fervently and trustfully.

On the Altar Jesus is our infinitely precious Offering.

Holy Mass is indeed the Sacrifice in which Jesus, the Son of God, offers Himself to His Heavenly Father through the ministry of His priests; hence the Sacrifice in which the Son of God is at once the Offerer and the Offering, the Priest who offers and the Victim which is offered.

Holy Mass, therefore, is the renewal and perpetuation of the Sacrifice instituted at the Last Supper, in which Jesus, for the first time, offered Himself to His Father, under the species of bread and wine. Hence, when we attend Mass we are in reality present at the great mystery which took place at the Last Supper.

Holy Mass is the renewal, the memorial and real representation of the Sacrifice of the Cross. On the Cross and on the Altar there is one and the same Sacrifice, here as well as there the same Sacrificer and the same Victim—Jesus who offers Himself to God His Father; with this difference that, whereas He immolated Himself in a bloody manner on the Cross, He does it in an unbloody, mystical manner on the Altar.[1] Hence, when we assist at Holy Mass, we are in fact present at the great mystery which was accomplished on Calvary.

In Holy Mass we possess an Offering which enables us to discharge in the most perfect and most efficacious way two great duties towards God, duty of adoration and duty of gratitude, and at the same time to supply a twofold need, the need of pardon and the need of help. When we devoutly celebrate or attend Mass, we offer to God, as co-offerers with Jesus, and with the priest, a sacrifice of adoration of infinite perfection, a sacrifice of thanksgiving which surpasses in an infinite degree all benefits received, a sacrifice of propitiation which offers to God for our sins the infinite satisfactory merits of the Sacrifice of the Cross, and finally a sacrifice of impetration, which unites our prayer with the all-powerful prayer of Jesus and thus can obtain for us all graces.

At the Holy Table Jesus is our divine food.

By Holy Communion Jesus unites Himself with us most closely. Not only is He near us, but He dwells within us. By the Incarnation He united Himself to human nature in general; by Holy Communion He unites Himself with each one of us in particular. When we communicate we are really living ciboriums. Then we bear within us the Son of God, the King of kings, the Lord of Heaven and earth, God Himself. We possess then within us the Giver, the living and inexhaustible source of all graces. We bear then within us, in our hearts, Him who loves us as no one else loves us.

He unites Himself with us, in order to purify our flesh, stifling in it the flame of sinful lusts and carnal desires, and thus helping us to preserve our body untainted and chaste; in order to sanctify our body coming into touch with the sacred species and hence indirectly with His Divine Flesh and Blood; in order to prepare it for the glorious resurrection and everlasting glory, of which

---

[1] Conc. Trid., Sess. XXII, cap. ii.

Holy Communion is a pledge, as the Church sings in the anthem *O sacrum convivium*[1] and as Christ Himself said: 'He that eateth My Flesh and drinketh My Blood hath everlasting life, and I will raise Him up on the last day' (John vi, 55).

He unites Himself with us especially in order to feed the supernatural life of our souls. What food does for the body, the Eucharist does for the soul. Nor is this pious fancy, neither a mere metaphor, nor exaggeration, but the real truth. When He instituted the Eucharist, Jesus said: 'Take ye and eat: this is My body' (Matt. xxvi, 26), thus fulfilling His promise when He assured us: 'My Flesh is meat indeed and My Blood is drink indeed' (John vi, 56).

But, whereas material food is absorbed and converted into the body, the opposite process is brought about by the Eucharist; for in Holy Communion it is not Christ who is made like unto us, but we are made like unto Himself. He imparts to us His virtues; He enlightens our understanding and causes it to think and judge as He does; He cleanses and rekindles our hearts, makes them love what He loves and wish what He wishes; He moves and strengthens our will, and induces it to act in accordance with His will. If we do not hinder Him from working within us, He becomes ever more the principle and mover of our interior life; it is He who thereafter thinks within us, loves within us, is willing in us and impels us to action, so that we may say in truth with St. Paul: 'I live, now not I, but Christ liveth in me' (Gal. ii, 20).

(c) What these Benefits Cost Him

These, then, are the benefits for which we are indebted to the love of Jesus; surely more than enough to oblige us to recognize that Jesus has really, ineffably loved us, and that on account of this love He supremely deserves our gratitude and return of love.

This appears still more clearly when we consider Who it is who shows us this love, namely, the Son of God, the Second Person of the Blessed Trinity, God Himself, Who became man precisely in order to be able to love us with a true human love and to load us with those benefits.

But, as we have observed, what peculiarly enhances the value of those gifts and graces, and so manifests still more outstandingly

[1] 'O sacrum convivium, in quo . . . futurae gloriae nobis pignus datur.'

the love which inspired them, are the sacrifices and sufferings which they cost our Redeemer.

To appreciate those sacrifices and sufferings at their true value we must bear in mind that Christ's Humanity, because of its hypostatic union with the Eternal Word, had a right to a life full of glory and happiness. If Jesus had willed it, this would have been His lot. But His Heavenly Father willed it otherwise; and Jesus, for love of His Father, but also for love of us, submitted to the will of His Father and accepted it with all the plenitude of His human will.

1. *Sacrifices*

He consented to appear among men under a form which concealed His Divinity from their eyes and gave Him the outward semblance of an ordinary human creature. He, the Eternal, the Infinite, the pure Spirit, united Himself to a created, limited, material nature!

He had a right to a glorified humanity, free from the physical laws, exempt from the needs of nature, immune from fatigue, suffering and death; He agreed to take to Himself a nature like unto ours in all things except sin and concupiscence; a nature, therefore, subject like ours to the necessity of sustaining life with food, open to weariness and suffering, and liable to death.

He might have come into the world as a full-grown man, in the vigour of life—He appeared as a tiny, helpless babe, unable to walk, to talk, to feed Himself, and in all things dependent on His Mother. He was even willing to be conceived in the womb of a woman, and to remain there for nine months without individual existence, forming only one being, as it were, with His Mother, and feeding on her blood.

His Mother was a woman of the people, His legal father an artisan earning his bread by the labour of his hands. He was born in utter poverty, in a cave, a lonely stable; His Mother had nothing but some shabby swaddling clothes to wrap Him in; His cradle was a manger.

He spent thirty years in a small town which was held in contempt in the neighbourhood: 'Can any thing of good come from Nazareth?' said Nathanael when he heard that the expected Messiah had appeared in the person of Jesus of Nazareth. He lived there hidden and unknown to the world, ignored by His fellow townsmen. He passed His childhood and youth in the midst of a poor family, standing at the carpenter's bench and acquainted with all the cares and hardships peculiar to that social position. After His foster-father's death He had to provide for Himself and for His Blessed Mother by manual labour, nor was He known otherwise than as the carpenter's son.

For three years He went about through Galilee and Judea, instructing and training His Apostles, preaching to the people, now in a synagogue, now on the public road, then on some mountain slope, or by the seashore, and even out in the desert. On foot He crossed the country, knowing from His own experience what weariness, hunger and thirst mean. So, one day, He sat down on the brink of Jacob's well, whilst His disciples were gone to the city to buy provisions; and He asked the Samaritan woman, who came there to draw water, to give Him to drink (John iv, 6). And in the boat which carried Him and His Apostles over the lake of Genesareth He fell asleep with fatigue (Matt. viii, 23). He was supported by the charity of some ministering followers. He had no home, no patch of ground of His own: 'The foxes have holes, and the birds of the air nests; but the Son of Man hath not where to lay His head' (Matt. viii, 20). He passed the night more often than not under the open sky.

2. *Sufferings*

In addition to these sacrifices there were the sufferings and sorrows caused Him by men.

What did He not suffer from the ignorance, coarseness, worldly-mindedness and failings of His Apostles; from the narrow-mindedness, fickleness and ill-will of many of His hearers; from the envy, malice and hatred of the Pharisees, high-priests and scribes; from their endeavours to thwart His working, to destroy the influence of His teaching, to stir up the people against Him and to withdraw from Him those who believed in Him?

Never indeed was He without sufferings. The author of the *Imitation of Christ* does not exaggerate when he says: 'Not even our Lord Jesus Christ was ever one hour without suffering so long as He lived . . . His whole life was a cross and a martyrdom' (II, 12). The Passion of His body lasted only a few hours; the Passion of His Heart lasted a lifetime. True, these mental sufferings were not always equally intense, but they were never interrupted.

H

Throughout His whole life He suffered from the ever-present thought of the offences offered to God His Father by the sins of men, from the ever-present knowledge of all that He was to endure for the expiation of these sins, from the ever-present prevision of the ingratitude of men and the futility of His Passion and Death for so many souls.

This Passion of His Heart reached its climax in the Garden of Olives. There He let His sensitive nature take its course: weariness and sadness (Mark xiv, 33) overwhelmed Him and reduced Him to such a state that He prayed His Father to remove this chalice from Him. And whilst bloody sweat covered His body and the bitter pangs of agony befell Him, He would have sunk under the burden, it seems, had not an Angel come from Heaven to sustain and strengthen Him (Luke xxii, 43).

And what did He not suffer during the further process of His Passion?

First, in His body. His back was torn with scourges, His Head surrounded by a crown of thorns. He was forced to drag the heavy cross to the place of execution, and repeatedly fell to the ground under the crushing burden of the instrument of torture. Stretched upon the cross, His bruised limbs were pierced with rough nails by His fierce executioners, whilst His blood was gushing forth and running down in streams. For three deadly hours He hung upon His transfixed hands, till in His last throes and with a final convulsion His soul was torn from His tortured body.

What did He not suffer in the consciousness of His dignity? A brutal band of mercenaries, armed with swords and clubs, came to apprehend Him as though he were a robber (Matt. xxvii, 6). Fettered as a dangerous criminal, He was dragged from Gethsemani to Jerusalem, through the streets of the city, and hauled from court to court. Before Caiphas, the high-priest, His judges were His mortal enemies, who had sworn His ruin and suborned false witnesses (Matt. xxvi, 60). Before Pilate, the Roman governor, His accusers treated Him as a malefactor (John xviii, 30), an imposter (Matt. xxvi, 63), a rebel (Luke xxiii,2). Herod at first took Him for a sorcerer, a magician, and then treated Him as a fool (Luke xxiii, 8-11). The satellites of the chief priests reviled Him, spat in His face, buffeted Him and, after blindfolding Him, defied Him to guess who it was that had struck Him. The soldiers of the governor, making a mockery of His kingship, hung a scarlet cloak upon His shoulders, put a crown of thorns upon His head and in His hands a reed for sceptre, and bowing the knee before Him, shouted: 'Hail, king of the Jews!' (Matt. xxvii, 29). Pilate acknowledged His innocence, and nevertheless let the incited people choose between Him and Barabbas, ordered Him to be scourged, and condemned Him to the cruel and ignominious death of the cross. And Jesus was crucified, in the full light of day, on the mountain slope of Calvary, hard by a bustling road, that many might be eye-witnesses of His execution and infamy. He was crucified in the midst of two thieves, as the most guilty of the three. Close by stood His enemies, the chief priests and the scribes, watching Him in an arrogant and defiant attitude, taking delight in the spectacle of their defeated enemy and of His miserable end. Scorning and blaspheming they sneered at Him: 'If He be the king of Israel, let Him now come down from the cross, and we will believe Him! He trusted in God; let Him now deliver Him, if He will have Him; for He said: I am the Son of God' (Matt. xxvii, 41). And Jesus died, as one whose mission which He pretended to have received from God, was an ignominious failure, dishonoured in the eyes of the whole people, found guilty and condemned by the highest and holiest authority of the country, execrated by those who had believed in Him and now saw that they were deceived by Him.

And what did He not suffer in His Heart?

That people, whom He loved so much, to whom He had done nothing but good, on whose behalf He had wrought so many miracles: that people, led astray by their leaders, no longer believed in Him and, forgetting His admirable lessons, His incomparable kindness and His innumerable miracles, spurned and repudiated Him, assailed Him with shouts of hatred when, after the scourging and the crowning with thorns, He appeared again, blood-stained, exhausted, unrecognizable. They cried aloud for His death: 'His blood be upon us and upon our children!' (Matt. xxvii, 25).

And His Apostles! Already during His agony in the Garden they had disappointed His hopes, and left Him alone, without solace. When He suffered Himself to be seized, they all fled. Not one of them claimed or begged for the honour of sharing His fetters; not one during the trial before Caiphas or Pilate came forward to plead on behalf of his Master, to bear witness to His blameless conduct, to His submission to the Law, to His love for God and for men. Not one accompanied Him on His painful way to Calvary, nor presented himself to help Him to carry His heavy cross. And at the foot of the cross only one was found, the youthful, beloved disciple John, to give His agonizing Master a last token of compassion and love, and to receive His last sigh (John xix, 26). One of them, alas, the one on whom He intended to build His Church, denied Him publicly and swore thrice that he did not even know Him. And another sold Him for thirty pieces of silver, betrayed Him with a kiss, and delivered Him into the hands of His enemies.

Even His Mother contributed to the Passion of His Heart! Surely, she remained faithful and stood by the Cross, suffering and agonizing together with Him. It was a comfort for His Heart not to be alone and, in the midst of the surrounding hostile crowd, to meet at least some loving and compassionate glance. But, on the other hand, the sight of the sorrow of His Mother was to Him a source of new torture. Certainly, Mary proved to be courageous beyond words; she succeeded in not fainting and in standing upright; she joined in the sacrifice of her Son and offered Him to the Eternal Father for the salvation of mankind. Yet, what torture in her mother's heart! To see her beloved Son hanging on the cross as a malefactor, His hands and feet pierced with nails, His whole body covered with wounds, His breast heaving violently, and His face becoming overspread with the paleness of death; to see her Jesus suffering horribly and not even to be able to soothe His pain a little: what a torment for her mother's heart! . . . Jesus was fully aware of it, and the thought of the sorrow of His Mother intensified His own sufferings.

Did He at least receive any solace from Heaven, from His Heavenly Father? His Heart, alas, so far from finding in Him any comfort, experienced an increase of suffering in consequence of His attitude towards Him. So dreadful was this suffering that He could not refrain from complaining of it, and He let escape from His dying lips the painful sigh: 'My God, My God, why hast Thou forsaken Me?' (Matt. xxvii, 46).

What does this complaint mean? Did Jesus really think that His Father no longer loved Him, that He spurned Him, that He had really abandoned Him? Oh, certainly not. He was fully aware that His Father could not for a moment cease loving Him, especially at that hour when He offered Himself as a willing victim for His glorification and the salvation of mankind. But certain it is that God at this moment willed that His Son should endure all these tortures, and that He did not wish to do anything to alleviate them.

Jesus had accepted the mission of atoning for all the sins of mankind, of paying the ransom to the full. The hour of expiation had come. And to make us see and, as it were, touch the immeasurable malice of sin, God willed this expiation to be as rigorous as possible, and let His Son suffer without any consolation, Jesus had substituted Himself for sinful man, who had so grievously offended his Creator and provoked His righteous anger; hence it was fitting that this anger should turn against Him and should fall upon Him. All-holy God abhors sin infinitely, holds it in abomination. Now, Jesus had taken on Himself all the sins of the world, and, at this moment, He saw Himself covered with them as with a hideous leprosy. God, then, must have an aversion to Him and turn away His eyes from Him in horror.

What a situation! What torment for the Heart of Jesus! He, who loved His Father with His whole soul; who came into this world to make Him known and loved; who throughout His life had sought nothing but His will and good pleasure, and now gave His life for His glorification—to see and feel that this Father was angry with Him and was taking an aversion to Him—what unutterable torture! This was really the culminating point of the Passion of His Heart.

These, then, are the benefits for which we are indebted to the love of the Heart of Jesus. These are the sacrifices and sufferings they have cost Him. Is it not evident that He has loved us ineffably, and consequently that it is supremely just and right that we should repay His love with a return of love?

Well then, this is the very essence of Devotion to the Sacred Heart. This is essentially a devotion of love: it aims at paying homage to the love of Jesus, it wishes to honour it by a return of love. The love of the Heart of Jesus is its object, our love for Jesus its principal and primary end. Devotion to the Sacred Heart is the answer of our hearts to the Heart of Jesus. Its watchword is: heart for Heart, love for love.

2. To Make Reparation to the Heart of Jesus

Devotion to the Sacred Heart, however, has yet another principal end.

We have seen that, in accordance with our Lord's desire, the love of His Heart is to be considered as neglected by men, as receiving in return ingratitude and insults. To this peculiar consideration corresponds a second special end of the devotion, namely, to compensate the Heart of Jesus for the disdain of His love, to make reparation for it to His Heart.

In the devotion, as it is practised, this compensation, this reparation holds, in point of fact, an important place.

This is manifest with St. Margaret Mary, whose whole life was an uninterrupted series of trials and afflictions, cheerfully accepted and lovingly offered in a spirit of atonement and reparation.[1]

The Liturgy of the Sacred Heart, too, clearly bears this character of reparation. The Feast, instituted by the Church in honour of the Sacred Heart, is a feast of reparation; the Collect of the Mass is a prayer of reparation; the priests, in all the churches of the world, are to recite on that day, together with the faithful, the Act of Reparation composed by Pope Pius XI.[2]

This character is also conspicuous in the devotion as it is practised by the faithful. The Feast of the Sacred Heart is celebrated everywhere with peculiar solemnity and piety; the first Friday of each month is considered a day of reparation; daily Communion is readily offered by fervent souls in a spirit of reparation; and the Holy Hour, an exercise of reparation, is more and more propagated.

In fact, then, devotion to the Sacred Heart is a devotion of atonement and reparation. And it ought to be so. Reparation, as well as love, is one of the principal ends of the devotion.

I. JESUS DESIRES IT

Our Lord clearly manifested His desire and purpose on this point.

This appears at first from His complaints about the manner in which men repay His love. 'One of my great tortures,' writes St.

---

[1] Cf. *Vie et Oeuvres*, vol. III, *Table analytique*, at the words 'Amour de la croix et des souffrances; Marguerite-Marie; elle s'offre en victime; Patience; Souffrances.'
[2] See § ii, The Feast of the Sacred Heart.

Margaret Mary, 'was to hear this Divine Heart say to me: "I thirst, I burn with a consuming desire for men's love in the Blessed Sacrament; and I find none who strives, in accordance with My wish, to quench this thirst, by making any return of love." '[1]

And in her account of the third apparition: 'Then He revealed to me all the unspeakable marvels of His pure love, and the excess of love He had conceived for men, from whom He received nothing but ingratitude and contempt. "This is more painful to Me," He said to me, "than all that I endured in My Passion. If they would only give Me some return of love, I should not reckon all that I have done for them. . . . But they have only coldness and contempt for all My endeavours to do them good." '[2]

Again, in the fourth apparition: 'Showing me His Divine Heart, He said to me: "Behold this Heart, which has so loved men that It has spared nothing, going even so far as to exhaust and consume Itself, in order to testify Its love for them. And in return I receive from the greater part of men nothing but ingratitude, by their irreverence and sacrileges, and the coldness and contempt they have for Me in this Sacrament of Love. . . . Yet what is more painful to Me is that even souls consecrated to Me are acting in this way." '[3]

What did Jesus aim at by those complaints but to arouse in St. Margaret Mary, and in all those in whom they would find an echo, the desire and resolve to console and compensate Him for the neglect of His love, not only by a more ardent love and by their zeal for making Him loved by others, but also by their exercises of reparation?

Moreover, Jesus explicitly expressed this purpose when, in the third apparition, after giving expression to His complaint, He added: 'Do you, at least, give Me the happiness of making up for their ingratitude, as much as you can.'[4] And in the fourth: 'Therefore I ask of you that the first Friday after the octave of Corpus Christi be dedicated to a special feast in honour of My Heart . . . by making amends in an act of reparation . . .'[5]

He recurred to this demand of reparation again and again. Now He asked for it on behalf of sinners[6] or of the Christian people

---

[1] *Vie et Oeuvres*, vol. II, *4e Lettre au P. Croiset*, November 3rd, 1689, p. 580.
[2] Ibid., p. 72.   [3] Ibid., p. 103.   [4] Ibid., p. 72.
[5] Ibid., p. 103.   [6] Ibid., vol. I, p. 84.

in general;[1] now on behalf of definite classes of persons and in particular of souls that are consecrated to Him;[2] or for sins committed on definite occasions, as during carnival time.[3]

This demand, it is true, is usually addressed directly to the Saint; but beyond her it has in view all those who love Jesus and wish to practise devotion to His Heart.

This may be deduced from many passages of her biography and her writings. The Saint applied herself to promoting, together with the love of the Sacred Heart, the spirit of reparation. Now, considering her character, her natural timidity, her humility, her fear of self-delusion, and her almost scrupulous care to do in all things the will of her Divine Master, we may affirm that she would not have done so if she had not been sure that she was complying on this point with the wish of our Lord.

Thus she invited Mother Greyfié, one of her former Superiors, to designate a sister who should be charged with the office of a mediatrix, a go-between, in order to beg of God the Father to make known the Sacred Heart, and of the Holy Ghost to make It loved; and she advised her to appoint a different one every month for this office. Then she added: 'Moreover, He asks for a *reparatrix*, that is, one who will most humbly beg of God pardon for all the outrages offered Him in the Blessed Sacrament of the Altar; and every month you should appoint a different one.'[4]

Sister Joly, one of the most zealous auxiliaries of the Saint in propagating the devotion, writes: 'Those who strive to honour the Sacred Heart are to make *reparation*, to the best of their power, by their homage of praise and adoration, for the outrages to which His love exposed the Son of God, throughout all His life and in His Passion, and to which it still exposes Him every day in the Blessed Sacrament of the Altar. . . . All the ingratitude of men being known to Him, He experienced beforehand all the affliction and sorrow in His Heart, without being disheartened, nor prevented by it from manifesting to us His love and tenderness. . . . It is, then, fit and proper that this God of love should find friends of His Sacred Heart, who *sympathize* with His sorrows, so that we should no longer have the confusion of hearing Him complain by His prophet: "I looked for one that would grieve together with Me, and I found none" (Ps. lxviii, 21). . . . This has roused the

---

[1] *Vie et Oeuvres*, vol. ii, p. 107. [2] Ibid., vol. i, p. 196.
[3] Ibid., vol. ii, p. 323. [4] Ibid., vol. ii, p. 323.

zeal and devotion of several persons who, taking to heart the interests of their Divine Master, cannot suffer to see His love despised or at least neglected, without manifesting to Him their *sorrow* and their desire to make *reparation* to Him by some return of love and all kinds of homage.'[1]

Is not this what we pointed out as the second principal end of the Devotion, namely, to compensate the Heart of Jesus and to make reparation to Him for the neglect of His love?

Fr. Croiset states it, moreover, explicitly: 'The end aimed at in this devotion is, firstly, to recognize and honour as much as we can, by our frequent acts of adoration, by a return of love, by our thanksgivings and all kinds of homage, the sentiments of love and tenderness which Jesus Christ bears us in the adorable Eucharist, where He is nevertheless so little known by men, or at least so little loved even by those who know Him. *Secondly, to make reparation*, by all possible means, for the outrages to which His love exposed Him during His mortal life, and to which it exposes Him still every day in the Blessed Sacrament of the Altar. So that the whole devotion only consists, properly speaking, in ardently loving Jesus Christ, whom we incessantly possess in the adorable Eucharist, and in showing this ardent love by the *regret* which we have to see Him so little loved and so little honoured by men, and by the means that are employed *to make up* for this contempt and this lack of love.'[2]

'Devotion to the Sacred Heart of Jesus Christ,' writes Fr. de Galliffet in his turn, 'may be defined as follows: it is an exercise of religion, which has for its object the adorable Heart of Jesus Christ burning with love for men and outraged by the ingratitude of those same men; which has for its aim to honour this Divine Heart by all kinds of homage inspired by love and gratitude; and in particular *to make reparation* to Him for the outrages which He receives in the Sacrament of His love.'[3]

This is confirmed by Pope Leo XIII in his Apostolic Letter of June 28th, 1889: 'One of the principal ends of devotion to the Sacred Heart is *to expiate* by our homage of adoration and love, the crime of *ingratitude*, so common among men, and to appease God's anger through the Most Sacred Heart of Jesus.'[4]

---

[1] *Livret de la Sœur Joly*; excerpt quoted by Yenveux, op. cit., vol. I, p. 309.
[2] Croiset, op. cit., Book I, chap. i.
[3] De Galliffet, op. cit., Book I, chap. iv, p. 48.
[4] Litterae apostolicae, *Benigno divinae Providentiae*.

Moreover, this view of the devotion to the Sacred Heart was solemnly sanctioned by Pope Pius XI in his Encyclical *Miserentissimus*, in which he sets forth that it exactly corresponds with the purpose of Our Lord.

It may be useful, we think, to quote here to the full extent this passage of the Encyclical:

'As the consecration proclaims and confirms the union with Christ, so expiation begins this union by cleansing sin; it perfects it by sharing in Christ's sufferings, and consummates it by offering victims for our brethren. This then was undoubtedly the design of the merciful Jesus when He showed us His Heart, presenting the tokens of the Passion and the flames of love: He wished us, after considering the infinite malice of sin and admiring the boundless love of the Redeemer, to detest sin more vehemently and to make a return of more ardent love.

'It is specially the *spirit of expiation or reparation* which has always occupied *the first and principal place* in the cult to be rendered to the Sacred Heart of Jesus, and nothing is more in keeping with the origin, nature, efficacy and practices which are proper to this devotion. This is attested to by history, usage, sacred liturgy and the acts of the Sovereign Pontiffs.

'When Christ showed Himself to Margaret Mary, He pointed out to her His boundless love, and at the same time, in an afflicted tone, He complained of the numerous outrages inflicted on Him by the ingratitude of men, expressing Himself in these words— would to God that they may be engraved in the hearts of all pious souls, and never be effaced there!—"Behold this Heart," He said, "which has so loved men and has heaped upon them so many benefits, and which, for this boundless love, not only receives no gratitude, but, on the contrary, meets with forgetfulness, neglect, outrages, and this sometimes on the part of those who are obliged towards Him by a duty of particular love."

'To expiate those faults, He recommended, among several other things, as being particularly agreeable to Him, the following practices: to partake, in this spirit of expiation, of the Sacrament of the Altar, by what is called the "Communion of Reparation" and to offer expiatory supplications and prayers during one hour, rightly called "the Holy Hour", which pious exercises the Church not only approved, but also enriched with considerable indulgences.'

Finally, in the Collect of the Feast of the Sacred Heart, full stress is also laid upon the atoning characteristic of the Devotion: 'O God, Who in the Heart of Thy Son, wounded by our sins, dost deign mercifully to bestow on us infinite treasures of love: grant, we beseech Thee, that whilst we render It the devout homage of our affection, we may also discharge our duty of worthy satisfaction.'[1]

But for what precisely are we to make up? For what shortcomings does the Sacred Heart demand compensation and reparation? In other words, what is precisely the object of this reparation which forms the second principal end of the Devotion to the Sacred Heart?

At first sight, it seems to be only men's conduct towards the Blessed Sacrament of the Altar.

Indeed, Fr. Croiset, as we could observe in his explanation of the second aim of the Devotion, makes only mention of the outrages inflicted on Jesus in the Blessed Sacrament, and when he treats of the practice of the devotion he states: 'The practice of devotion to the Sacred Heart of Jesus, however holy, would be

---

[1] The Collect contains two parts: the first specifies the object of the Feast, the second indicates its aim.

The Collect reminds us at first that all the tokens of love (*infinitos dilectionis thesauros*), all the benefits which we owe to God, are given us directly by Jesus, and more particularly by His Heart (*Deus, qui in Corde Filii tui . . . largiri dignaris*); for it is the Heart of Jesus, it is His love, which merited them for us and imparts them to us.

Hence, the object of the Feast is the Heart of Jesus, to whose love we are indebted directly for all the benefits which come to us from God.

This Heart is really the physical Heart of Jesus, for It is presented as wounded, as wounded formerly because of our sins (*nostris vulnerato peccatis*). But It is also His spiritual Heart (cf. p. 25); for it is His Heart, wounded now by the ingratitude and the sins of men; it is His Heart, guided by Its love in the distribution of the benefits which God bestows on us (*nobis in Corde Filii tui . . . largiri dignaris*). It is, then, in reality, His total Heart: i.e. the compound formed by these two Hearts, at once the symbol, principle and seat of His love. (Cf. p. 28.)

The second part points out the aim and purpose of the Feast. This aim is twofold: to pay to the Heart of Jesus the homage of our piety, and hence of our love (in classical Latin the word 'pietas' also means 'love') for the love which He bears us (*illi devotum pietatis nostrae praestantes obsequium*), and, moreover, to make reparation to Him for the neglect of His love (*dignae quoque satisfactionis exhibeamus officium*), reparation, which is not only a matter of piety and devotion but also a real duty (*officium*), a reparation which we must try to make worthy of His Heart, worthy of His Person and worthy of the love He has shown us (*dignae satisfactionis*). (Cf. Galtier, op. cit., p. 200, note.)

This homage of our devotion and love, and this reparation, are addressed to the Heart of Jesus. But, through It, they ascend to God the Father, Who loves us in and through the Heart of His Divine Son.

The Collect, therefore, contains a magnificent summary of the devotion to the Sacred Heart itself (its object and end). Perhaps it may be added that the Collect also reminds us of the chief practice of love towards the Sacred Heart, namely, the consecration. The word 'devotus' in classical Latin means 'devoted', 'consecrated'.

of little avail, unless it were animated by the spirit and motive to which it owes its whole value. This motive, as has been said, is to make up as much as we can, by our love, by our acts of adoration and by all kinds of homage, for all the insults which Jesus Christ endured and still endures in the Blessed Sacrament.'[1]

Likewise, Fr. de Galliffet, in his definition of the devotion quoted above, mentions only 'the outrages which He receives in the Sacrament of His love'. And it is only these outrages which he describes at length in the second chapter of the second book.

Besides, Our Lord Himself seems to confine to those outrages the object of the reparation demanded by Him, when He says in the fourth apparition: 'In return I receive from the greater part of men nothing but ingratitude, by their irreverence and sacrileges, by the coldness and contempt with which they treat Me in this Sacrament of Love.' And He adds: 'Therefore I ask of you that the first Friday after the octave of Corpus Christi be dedicated to a special feast in honour of My Heart . . . to make up for the outrages It has received during the time It has been exposed on the Altars.'[2]

There is no doubt, however, that the object of the reparation asked for by Our Lord is more extensive and includes all forms of neglect of His love, all sorts of ingratitude, all the shortcomings, all the outrages of which men are guilty towards Him.

In the fourth apparition Our Lord speaks, it is true, solely of the conduct of men towards the Blessed Sacrament, but then He has in view only one particular exercise of reparation, namely, the institution of a Feast in honour of His Sacred Heart, and not devotion to His Heart in general. We may take for granted that He asked for this Feast solely in reparation for the outrages which He receives in the Blessed Sacrament. But in other apparitions He also mentions other shortcomings, and asks of the Saint that she should atone and make reparation; for instance, for secret sinners, for the faults or the tepidity of souls that are consecrated to Him, for sins committed during carnival time, etc.[3] And in the third apparition no doubt is left about the purpose of Our Lord. For, after complaining that He receives from men nothing but ingratitude and disdain, He adds: 'This is more painful to Me than all

---

[1] Op. cit., pt. III, chap. i, p. 209.
[2] *Vie et Oeuvres*, vol. II, *Autobiographie*, p. 103.
[3] Cf. Yenveux, op. cit., vol. I, pp. 313–45.

that I endured in My Passion. If they would only give Me some return of love, I should not reckon all that I have done for them, and I would do still more, if possible. But they have only *coldness and contempt for all My endeavours to do them good.* Do you, at least, give Me the happiness of *making up for their ingratitude,* as much as you can.' Here, then, there is really question of an unlimited reparation, extending to all forms of ingratitude and contempt, great and small, without reserve or exception.

Two statements of the Holy See corroborate our assertion.

Pope Leo XIII, in his Apostolic Letter of June 28th, 1889, stated, as we have seen: 'One of the principal ends of the devotion to the Sacred Heart is to expiate . . . *the crime of ingratitude,* so common among men. . . .'[1]

Nor does Pope Pius XI either, in his Encyclical *Miserentissimus,* assign any limit to the object of the reparation asked for by Our Lord. After recalling 'the numerous outrages inflicted on Him by the ingratitude of men', he reminds us of the complaint of Our Lord that 'for His boundless love He not only receives no gratitude, but, on the contrary, meets with forgetfulness, neglect and outrages', and he concludes with the words: 'To expiate these faults, He (Jesus) recommended . . . the following practices . . .' In all these expressions, we see, there is not the least restriction.

This also applies to the Act of Reparation, prescribed by the same Sovereign Pontiff on the Feast of the Sacred Heart. It begins as follows: 'O sweet Jesus, whose overflowing charity for men is requited by so much *forgetfulness, negligence and contempt,* behold us prostrate before Thy altar eager to repair by a special act of homage the *cruel indifference and injuries,* to which Thy loving Heart is everywhere subject.' And the Act enumerates some of the shortcomings for which we make reparation to the Sacred Heart: 'We are now resolved to expiate each and every deplorable outrage committed against Thee; we are determined to make amends for the manifold offences against Christian modesty in unbecoming dress and behaviour, for all the foul seductions laid to ensnare the feet of the innocent, for the frequent violation of Sundays and holidays, and the shocking blasphemies against Thee and Thy Saints. We wish also to make amends for the insults to which Thy Vicar on earth and Thy priests are subjected, for the profanation, by conscious neglect or terrible acts of sacrilege, of the very

[1] Litterae apostolicae, *Benigno divinae Providentiae.*

Sacrament of Thy Divine love; and lastly for the public crimes of the nations who resist the rights and the teaching authority of the Church which Thou hast founded.'

Finally, in the Liturgy, too, reparation is extended to all forms of disdain of Jesus' love. In the Collect of the Mass for the Feast of the Sacred Heart, the Church bids us pray that God may grant us '*to discharge our duty of worthy satisfaction*'.[1] Here, too, no restriction whatever.

It would be wrong, then, to confine the object of reparation, in the Devotion to the Sacred Heart, to the conduct of men towards the Blessed Sacrament.

On the other hand, it is absolutely certain that these short-comings must hold the first place in this object; for, as they are contrary to the great benefit of Jesus' love, His Sacrament of Love, they most deeply injure His Sacred Heart. It is then in this sense that we have to understand the texts which seem to confine the object of the reparation to these particular shortcomings.

II. THE HEART OF JESUS DESERVES IT

The second principal end in view of the Devotion, then, is to make reparation to the Heart of Jesus for the neglect of His love, for the ingratitude of men towards Him, and for the outrages inflicted on Him.

This end logically follows from the first. For, if the first end is to respond by our love to the love of the Heart of Jesus, the second ought to be to make up to Him for the disdain of this love.

Indeed, love aims at the good of the beloved one. When any harm befalls him, love prompts us not only to be afflicted by it, but also to make up for it to the best of our ability and to com-pensate the beloved. This is the case when anyone whom we love tenderly has been deprived of what belongs to him, or has been denied his due; when no full justice is done to his merit; when his honour or reputation is injured; when he suffers from a lack of respect or gratitude; when he has been grieved or wronged in some way. Then we are not content with being afflicted by it, but we express to the loved person our regret and sympathy, we assure him of our esteem and affection, and thus we try to console and compensate him for the harm done to him. By proceeding other-wise we should prove that we did not love him sincerely.

[1] 'dignae satisfactionis exhibeamus officium'.

It is the same in the case of Our Lord. If we really love Him, we must be eager to make up to the best of our power for men's ill-conduct towards Him.

(a) For the Outrages offered Him Directly

How indeed do men behave towards Our Lord?

There are so many, alas, who refuse to recognize Him as the Son of God, Whom they are to adore; as the Master, to Whom they are to listen; as the Legislator, Whose laws they are to observe; as the Redeemer, of Whom they are to expect salvation. They refuse to accept His doctrine, to keep His commandments, to obey His Church, and to avail themselves of His Sacraments.

There are so many who blaspheme and scorn Him, deride His religion, revile His Church and His priests, insult His Cross, defile His Sacrament of Love through sacrilegious robberies and nefarious practices which can only be inspired by the Evil-one. There are even those who make war against Him, prevent His Church from fulfilling her mission, by depriving her of her liberty; who leave nothing undone to alienate her from the confidence and affection of her children by suspicion, slander and calumny; who by all possible means try to kill the faith within souls, and to tear them away from Christ; who do not even shrink from violence and bloody persecution, in order to destroy the work of Christ!

No doubt there are many who believe in Him; but, alas, even among these, Our Lord finds so little genuine Christian spirit, so little gratitude, so little love, so little generosity. There are so few who follow Him faithfully, put into practice His doctrine, are animated with His spirit, love Him with their whole heart, entirely devote themselves to Him, promote His interests, endeavour to make Him known, to extend His reign and to cause Him to be increasingly loved.

On the other hand, there are so many who scarcely know Him, seldom think of Him and of all that He did and suffered for them, repay His benefits and love with coldness and indifference, are imbued with the spirit of the world, make light of the recommendations and warnings of the Church, and dishonour Him by their ill-conduct; in short, who are Christians only in name.

In particular, towards that masterpiece of His love, the Blessed Sacrament, what indifference and slights, what lack of reverence, and even what unworthy conduct! How many there are who never visit Him in His Tabernacle, He their Redeemer, their Benefactor, their King and their God; who indifferently pass by His churches and leave Him alone in His solitude. How many who do not appreciate the favour of being allowed to assist at the most sublime act which can be accomplished on earth, the renewal of the Sacrifice of the Cross, Holy Mass; who have to be compelled to attend it at least once a week, and who consider this assistance as a vain ceremony, an unpleasant business. How many who remain deaf to His pressing invitation to come frequently, even every day, to His holy Table, and who deem it too much to feed and fortify their souls, once a year, with His Divine Flesh and Blood . . .

And would to God that they repaid His love only by their indifference! Alas, they even add outrages to this indifference. Outrages, by their irreverence at church, in His presence, during the religious ceremonies; by their unbecoming behaviour, their immodest dress, their impertinent remarks, voluntary distractions, wanton thoughts and looks, and guilty desires. Outrages, by their Communions made without proper preparation and thanksgiving; by their Communions made by mere routine or from mere natural motives; by their Communions received in hearts full of earthly cares and inordinate affections; by their Communions, alas, received in hearts stained with mortal sins and in which Christ's arch-enemy is the master. Outrages, finally—alas, even this—on the part of those on whom He conferred the inestimable honour of choosing them as ministers of His Divine Sacrament, and who sometimes treat this Divine Sacrament with an offensive and unpardonable frivolity, and who, what is even worse, forgetful of their superhuman dignity and profaning their sacred garments, dare to touch with polluted hands Christ's Divine Body and Blood, and offer sacrilegious Masses . . .

Can a soul that really loves Jesus Christ remain insensible to this conduct of men? Will it not be grieved by it? Will it not wish to express its regret and indignation? And will it not be eager to make up for it and compensate our Lord to the best of its abilities?

(b) For All Sins of Men

Yet it is not only by their conduct towards Jesus that men do wrong to Him, but also by all the sins they commit.

They injure Him, firstly, as God. This is true of all sins, not only of mortal sins but also of deliberate venial sins; not only of sins which offend God directly, such as unbelief, blasphemy and hatred of God, but also of those which we commit directly against ourselves or against our fellow-men, such as impurity, injustice, detraction, slander, etc.; for they are all more or less grievous transgressions of a Divine law. Hence, by each sin we offend God more or less, our Sovereign Lord, whose authority we slight; by each sin we scorn Him more or less as the supreme Good, by the preference which we give to some creature; by each sin we defy in some way His infinite justice, which must punish us when we commit sin; by each sin we are more or less guilty of ingratitude towards Him, our great Benefactor, from whom we received all that we have and are, whose favours we abuse by offending Him. By each sin, therefore, we do wrong to God, and hence to Jesus as God.

And so many sins are committed, alas—so enormous and so abominable! Sins of impurity and licentiousness, of infidelity and guilty sterility in marriage, of luxury and drunkenness, of injustice and exploitation of the weak, covetousness and avarice, slander and calumny, hard-heartedness and cruelty, ambition and pride, scandal and corruption; sins of unbelief, impiety, blasphemy, sacrilege and hatred of God . . .

Our sins also injure Jesus as Man. They offend Him by the displeasure they cause Him. He loves His Father as can no one else, for He loves Him above all things; He loves Him more than Himself, He really loves Him with His whole heart, His whole soul, and with His whole mind. Hence sin, each sin, must necessarily displease Him in a supreme degree; the more so, because He realizes better than anyone else God's infinite dignity, holiness and goodness; because He knows and understands better than anyone else what reverence, submission, gratitude and love are due to God, and hence He apprehends better than anyone else the infinite malice of sin.

Furthermore, the sins of men caused Him terrible suffering during His mortal life. He was to atone for them by His Passion and Death; not only for the sin of our first parents, but also for all the sins which were committed before His coming into the world and for all those which would be committed to the end of time. The sins of men, then, were the cause of His Passion and Death. Each sin has had its share in it; each sin obliged God to demand of His beloved Son a painful expiation. The sins of men were the real executioners of Jesus.

They caused Him to suffer in yet another way. In the Garden of Olives they reduced Him to a real agony. The thought of the offence which they did to His Heavenly Father overwhelmed His soul with sorrow. He was to take upon Himself all the sins, all the crimes and infamies of fallen and sinful man; and at the sight of the avenging arm of God coming down upon Him alone in chastisement of them all, He trembled with fear. He, innocence itself, saw Himself covered with all these sins as with a hideous leprosy, and He became to Himself an object of disgust. In this state He appeared before His Father, the All-Holy, and He almost died of shame. Moreover, He foresaw that men, taking no account of what their sins had cost Him, would not desist from transgressing the law of God; that thus they risked making His Passion and Death futile as far as they were concerned; that they would oblige Him, so to speak, constantly to suffer in order to atone over and over again for their sins, and would in some way crucify Him again and again, by renewing without cease the cause of His Passion and Death.[1] This prevision made Him 'sorrowful even unto death' (Matt. xxvi, 38).

Add to this that through the sins of men Jesus still suffers in His mystical Body, the Church. The Church is disregarded, scorned, slandered and derided just as He was. In many countries she is even deprived of her liberty, oppressed and persecuted. Her bishops, priests and faithful are put into prison or confined in concentration camps, deported, condemned to miner's work, or even put to death. For we know that Jesus takes as done to Himself whatever is done to His Church, as He Himself stated when He said to Saul on his way to Damascus: 'Saul, why persecutest thou Me?' (Acts ix, 4). Moreover, whatever affects the body and its members also affects the head.

Is it then possible for anyone who loves Jesus even a little to remain insensible to the evil that sin did and does to Him still, not to be deeply grieved by it, and not try to make reparation to Him—in the first place, needless to say, for his own sins, but also for those of others?

---

[1] 'Crucifying again to themselves the Son of God, and making Him a mockery' (Heb. vi, 6).

To atone for our personal sins is, properly speaking, as we are taught by the Encyclical *Miserentissimus*, a duty of justice. Justice, indeed, demands reparation; requires that the offender should give to the offended the satisfaction which he reasonably claims. Thus for the offence we have done to God by our sins we are bound to make reparation to Him. No doubt, Our Lord, by His voluntary self-abasement and self-immolation, by His Passion and Death, offered to God a satisfaction of infinite value for all sins, and hence for ours also. But this does not relieve us from the obligation of giving satisfaction for our own sins and atoning for them. God has willed that we should join our satisfaction to that of Jesus in order that the fruits of His atonement may be applied to us.

Besides, even when our sins are already forgiven, it is entirely profitable to us to expiate them; in this way we not only obtain remission of temporal punishment still due after the guilt of sin has been forgiven, but we acquire new merits for everlasting life. And sins for which we have not atoned here on earth are to be expiated in Purgatory, without any merit.

In devotion to the Sacred Heart, however, we consider not so much our duty and our profit, as our love. We wish to make amends and reparation to Jesus first and foremost out of love, because we love Him, because we are grieved at having offended and despised Him who loves us so much· and has heaped His benefits upon us; because by committing sin we proved to be ungrateful towards Him, we slighted His love and were the cause of His sufferings.[1]

---

[1] The Encyclical *Miserentissimus* clearly distinguishes the reasons of justice and love. 'We are bound to make reparation for a reason of justice and love. For a reason of justice, that the outrage offered to God by our crimes may be expiated and the violated order may be restored by penance. For a reason of love, in order to compassionate Christ "suffering and overwhelmed with reproaches", and to give Him, according to our littleness, some consolation.'

'In distinguishing these two motives for making reparation the Pope also distinguishes two objects; he marks out, as it were, the two planes on which this reparation should be made.

'The first is the supreme plane of the Divinity, on which the object of reparation is the offence offered to God by all the sins of men. This reparation then is addressed directly to God as the Creator and Supreme Lord. Christ performed it Himself by giving satisfaction to His Father for the whole sinful human race, and we are bound to discharge this duty by our acts of penance.

'The second plane is that of Christ's humanity, that on which He Himself appears to us as "suffering and overwhelmed with reproaches". These sufferings, reproaches, acts of ingratitude or sorrows are the object of the reparation to be made. It is then to the Sacred Heart itself that it is addressed directly. As **He** is the immediate victim of these insults, He is also the immediate recipient of the homage proper to compensate them.' (Galtier, op. cit., p. 62, note.)

As for the sins of others, charity should urge us on to atone for them as much as we can. In spite of our personal sins and unworthiness, God, in His infinite goodness, allows us to pay the debts of others. He accepts the expiation we offer to Him to this end. By this expiation we are able to propitiate His justice, to appease His righteous anger, predispose Him to mercy, obtain for sinners graces of conversion and for those whose sins are already forgiven remission of temporal punishment. Hence expiation and atonement is a form of apostleship, even one of the most efficacious.

To make reparation for the sins of others is, moreover, for all Christians a real obligation resulting from their membership of Christ's mystical Body. For God has willed that the Redemption of mankind by atonement for sin should be accomplished not only by the Head of that mystical Body, namely by the personal Christ, but by the total Christ, that is, the personal Christ with Whom all the members of His mystical Body are united. All Christians then are bound to co-operate with Christ in the work of the Redemption of mankind; they are all obliged to atone and make reparation for others, in union with the Great Penitent; they are all to be saviours of souls, in union with the one Saviour, Christ our Lord.[1]

But, in devotion to the Sacred Heart, we consider this atonement for the sins of others especially with respect to our love for Jesus. We want to expiate them because they offend Jesus, because they displease Him, because they made Him suffer; we wish to give Him satisfaction and make amends because we love Him, because we are grieved to see that men repay His favours with ingratitude and slight His love.

Remark

EFFICACY OF OUR REPARATION

Yet the objection may be raised: Why should we wish to make reparation for all this, since Jesus at the present moment does not suffer from it? As He is no longer liable to suffering and sorrow, how can He be sensitive to the conduct of men towards Him? Our purpose of consoling and compensating Him, therefore, seems to be of no avail.

It is absolutely certain that Jesus since His resurrection enjoys

[1] Cf. Encyclical *Miserentissimus*, n. 15–19.

a perfect happiness, which can neither be disturbed nor lessened. He is no longer capable of suffering either in His body or in His soul. Affliction no longer has any hold on Him.

Yet to several privileged souls, among others to St. Margaret Mary, He showed Himself more than once in a pitiful state, and made known that He was reduced to this condition by the sins of men.

'One day,' relates the Saint, 'our Lord presented Himself to me, bloodstained and covered with wounds, His Heart rent with grief, and almost exhausted. "To this state," He said to me, "My chosen people has reduced Me." '[1] Again: 'One carnival, after Holy Communion, my Divine Spouse appeared to me under the figure of an Ecce Homo, laden with His cross, bruised and wounded, His blood trickling down. And He addressed to me the pathetic complaint: "Will there be none who has pity on Me and sympathizes with Me in the pitiable state to which sinners reduce Me, especially at the present time?" '[2]

It is clear, however, that these apparitions do not represent the reality, nor do they mean that Jesus even now suffers and is afflicted by the conduct of men. In appearing in this state, He probably wished to show most vividly the unworthy behaviour and cruelty of men towards Him, and how grievously they would cause Him to suffer by their conduct if He were still liable to suffering. Perhaps, too, He wished to remind us of all that He really suffered during His mortal life because of the sins of men, sins which are being committed at the present moment, but for which He was to atone in anticipation, and also by the prospect of the ingratitude with which men would repay His love.

Doubtless, too, Jesus gave us to understand that He was sensitive to the contempt of His love. In the fourth apparition, for instance, after complaining of the ingratitude of men, He added: 'Yet what is more painful to Me is that even souls consecrated to Me are acting like this.' And in the third apparition, after 'revealing the ineffable marvels of His pure love, and the excess of love with which He loved men', He continued: 'This is more grievous to Me than all that I endured in My Passion.'

Have we to explain these words of our Lord in the same way

---

[1] *Vie et Oeuvres*, vol. I, *Mémoire des Contemporaines*, n. 105, p. 111.
[2] Ibid., vol. I, n. 216, p. 196. Cf. also vol. I, pp. 64, 71, 83; vol. II, pp. 34, 41, 45, 116, 127, 142, 153.

as the apparitions just mentioned, or is it permissible to say that He is really sensitive to the ingratitude of men, without, however, His happiness being in any way diminished or disturbed?

Be that as it may, although the conduct of men no longer causes Him to suffer, we are by no means released from our duty of reparation. If we really love Him, must not the very fact that He is scorned and outraged prompt us to make up for it? Suppose anyone were to slander one's deceased father, would one abstain from avenging his memory because calumny can no longer reach him? Surely not. Hence the fact that the conduct of men no longer causes our Lord to suffer, cannot be a reason why we should abstain from making up for it.

Moreover, the fruit of this reparation is not lost for Jesus. Our making amends consoled and rejoiced His Heart during His mortal life. That we were able to do so, before we existed, is owing to His prescience, His knowledge of the future. Theologians hold for certain that by the infused prescience with which God invested His soul, Jesus knew all that was in any way connected with the work of Redemption. He foresaw, then, all the good and evil which would occur in the course of time, and hence also whatever would be done for or against Him. He knew, then, in particular, how men would repay His love. One may even say that this prevision was one of the causes of His deadly sorrow at Gethsemane. But at the same time He foresaw the tokens of love which He would receive from His faithful followers, and particularly the reparation they would make to Him for the inagratitude of others. It cannot but be that this prospect consoled, encouraged and fortified Him, and helped Him to give Himself up to suffering and death, in spite of His prevision of the ingratitude of so many. Whenever, then, we pay to Jesus some homage of reparation we may cherish the gratifying conviction that, especially during His agony in the Garden, He saw us in the far-off distance of time, that He gratefully looked upon us, and that our reparation really soothed His sorrow to some extent, and comforted and strengthened Him in His agony.

Pope Pius XI assures us of it, moreover, in his Encyclical *Miserentissimus* (n. 25): 'If, for our sins, which were future but foreseen, the soul of Christ was sorrowful even unto death, there is no doubt that He already then received some consolation from our reparation, also foreseen, when an Angel from Heaven appeared to Him to console His Heart overwhelmed with sorrow and anguish. So, then, we may and must even now, in a wonderful but real manner, console this Sacred Heart, which is continually wounded by the sins of ungrateful men. For, as the sacred Liturgy recalls, Christ Himself, by the mouth of the Psalmist, complains of His being abandoned by His friends: "My Heart hath expected reproach and misery; and I looked for one that would grieve together with Me, but there was none; and for one that would comfort Me, and I found none" (Ps. lxviii, 21).'

But our reparation did not only console the Heart of Jesus during His mortal life; now, at the present moment, it still comforts Him, still affords Him pleasure. True, His happiness is complete, nothing is wanting. His essential happiness, caused by the intuitive vision of the Divinity and by His hypostatic union with it, cannot increase. But in addition to that, He enjoys an accidental happiness and this is capable of being augmented. It is augmented whenever He is afforded a new joy. For, if He is no longer liable to suffering and sorrow, He can still feel joy.

Now, it is certain that each act of reparation is for Him the source of a new joy. If He suffers no longer on account of the harm done to Him, He is certainly not insensible to the good done to Him, nor to the tokens of love given Him. Thus we have the consoling certainty that by our acts of reparation we really rejoice His Heart and increase His happiness.

Can we say that our reparation not only rejoices but also really consoles Him?

If we take the word 'console' in its proper sense, no. Consolation properly so called presupposes sorrow, a moral suffering which we want to soothe. Now, as we have seen, Jesus is no longer accessible to mental suffering. Hence there can be no question of consoling Him in the strict sense of the word.

But if we take the word in a broader meaning, in the sense of affording Jesus a pleasure that would be for Him a real consolation if He were still in need of it, then we may say that our reparation really consoles His Heart.[1] 'In consolation,' rightly notes Fr. Zeij, s.j., 'we may distinguish two elements: first, the relief or alleviation of pain and distress, received by the afflicted; secondly, the joy he experiences at it, and which is the very reason of that relief.

[1] See the words of Pope Pius XI quoted above, p. 88.

Alleviation and relief we cannot afford Jesus any longer, for He can no longer be afflicted; but He enjoys the pleasure afforded by the consolation.'[1]

CONCLUSION

From what precedes it is evident that reparation is not a mere accessory to the devotion to the Sacred Heart. It belongs to its very essence. It is even more than a special practice of devotion, however important it may be held to be; it is one of the primary ends of the devotion, in fact it is that end which gives to it its special characteristic. Hence our devotion to the Sacred Heart must be animated by this spirit of atonement, and bear this characteristic of reparation. Without this characteristic, without this spirit, it would not be the devotion as it is meant by Our Lord and approved and practised by the Church.

It is, however, true that the first aim of the devotion is to return love for love. Reparation presupposes this love. It is a reparation springing out of love. We ought to offer to Jesus our acts of reparation because we love Him; we ought to show Him our love especially by making reparation. Reparation, then, is only a form which our love takes to itself, yet a very special and, even, the principal form which it must assume. One may say: to return to Jesus love for love, this is the general principal end of the devotion; to compensate Him for the neglect of His love by our reparation, this is its special principal aim, its specific end.

B. SECONDARY ENDS

1. To Honour the Heart of Jesus

I. JESUS DESIRES IT

To return love to the Heart of Jesus, and to make reparation for the contempt shown to His love, are therefore the two principal ends of the devotion. Yet, in addition to these, there are two other aims, secondary it is true, but none the less real.

The first is to pay honour to the Heart of Jesus.

Indeed, Our Lord manifested His desire that His Heart should be honoured by men. 'Therefore I ask of you,' He said to St.

---

[1] Zeij, s.j., *Gemeenschappelijk Eerherstel*, p. 96.

Margaret Mary, 'that the first Friday after the octave of Corpus Christi be dedicated to a special feast in honour of My Heart . . . I also promise you that My Heart will open wide to pour forth lavishly the influence of Its divine love on all those who will render and procure for It this honour.' Again: 'In being faithful to these devotional practices,' the Saint said to her novices, 'you afford Him more pleasure than you could do by all the rest, for He *wishes* this adorable Heart to be known, loved and *honoured.*'[1] 'If you only knew,' she writes to Mother de Saumaise, 'how much merit and glory there is in *honouring* this lovable Heart of the adorable Jesus, and what reward He will give to those who, after consecrating themselves to It, endeavour to honour It!'[2] Again: 'It is His eager desire to impart to well-disposed souls these sanctifying graces that makes Him *wish* to be known, loved and honoured by His creatures.'[3]

II. THE HEART OF JESUS IS WORTHY OF IT

We know then for certain that our Lord wishes His Heart to be honoured. It is no less certain that His Heart is worthy of honour in the highest degree.

(a) Because of Its Divine Dignity

It is worthy of it first and foremost because of Its Divine dignity. True, It is a human Heart, but by reason of Its union with Christ's Divine Person It possesses a Divine excellence. In His Incarnation the Son of God, the Eternal Word, took to Himself a human nature and united it to His Divine Nature. There are then two natures in Him: the Divine and the human, completely distinct and undivided, but intimately, substantially—hypostatically, as it is termed by theologians—united in one and the same Person. Together with His Divine Person they form a whole, the God-Man.

To the Divine Person of Jesus, then, belongs not only His human nature viewed as a whole, but also all that forms part of that nature—His soul with all its faculties, His body with all its parts, and hence also His Heart.

---

[1] *Vie et Oeuvres*, vol. II, p. 279.
[2] Ibid., vol. II, p. 279.
[3] Ibid., vol. II, p. 397.

The Heart of Jesus is thus really the Heart of a Divine Person and hence is possessed of a really Divine dignity.

On account of that Divine dignity the Heart of Jesus, as well as the other parts of His human nature, has a right to the homage of supreme worship, or adoration.

The Church solemnly pronounced in the fifth oecumenical Council of Constantinople (553) that the cult of adoration is to be paid to the Sacred Humanity of Christ, and also condemned the doctrine of those who contended that 'the Incarnate Word of God was not to be adored together with His humanity in one and the same adoration'.[1]

True, from this condemnation it is only permissible to conclude directly that Christ's humanity taken as a whole is to be adored. But it follows of necessity that whatever forms part of that human nature has equally a right to the cult of adoration, for human nature is nothing else than the compound formed by all that is a portion of it.

Moreover the Church has clearly shown that it is to the Heart of Jesus that this homage of adoration is most suitably paid, for, in approving the devotion to the Sacred Heart as it was already practised everywhere[2] by the faithful, who included in their homage to the Sacred Heart the cult of adoration, the Church approved by that very fact also this homage of adoration.

And in her Liturgy she herself pays this supreme homage to the Heart of Jesus when, in the Invitatory of the Office of the Feast of the Sacred Heart, she bids her priests pray: *'Cor Jesu, amore nostri vulneratum, venite, adoremus*—Let us *adore* the Heart of Jesus, wounded for love of us.'

It may be objected that Christ's Heart is created and that to pay Divine honour to a creature is idolatry.

To this it may be answered that the Heart of Jesus is certainly a created thing as It was formed in the womb of His Virgin Mother Mary. This Heart, however, is not regarded as existing by itself, but in and by the Person of the Word, and inseparably united to this Person. Nor is It adored on account of an excellence of which It is possessed by Itself, but by reason of the Divine dignity of the Person to Whom It belongs and Who imparts to It

---

[1] Denziger, n. 221. 'Si quis . . . non *una adoratione* Deum Verbum incarnatum cum propria ipsius carne adorat, sicut ab initio Dei Ecclesiae traditum est, talis A.S.'
[2] Cf. *Decree of 1765*. See Introduction, p. xxxix.

His own dignity. There can therefore be no question of idolatry.[1]

The Jansenist contention, especially in the synod of Pistoia (1786), that the faithful in giving Divine honour to the Sacred Heart committed idolatry, was condemned by Pope Pius VI in his Bull *Auctorem fidei*, in which he states that 'the faithful adore the Heart of Jesus, not looked upon as apart and separate from the Godhead, but as the Heart of the Person of the Word to Whom It is inseparably united'.[2]

(b) As the Symbol, Principle and Seat of His Love and of His Whole Inner Life

The Heart of Jesus, then, deserves in the highest degree to be honoured on account of Its Divine dignity.

Yet, as we have seen in the first chapter, the object of our devotion is not the Heart of Jesus viewed in itself, but in connection with His love and with His whole inner life, and more precisely as the principle and the symbol of both.

Considered in this way, the Heart of Jesus is also in the highest degree worthy of our veneration.

Indeed the principle and the symbol of that which deserves to be honoured are themselves worthy of our homage. So we respect the national flag out of consideration for the native land of which it is the symbol; we honour the mother of a king out of consideration for her son.

Now the love and the inner life of Jesus deserve to receive Divine homage, to be adored, as being the love and the inner life of a Divine Person, and as such being possessed of a really Divine dignity.

Moreover, Jesus' love in particular is worthy of our homage because of its liberality, its abnegation and its generosity.

We pay honour to those who distinguish themselves by their charity and benevolence, who render great services to their fellow men by their institutions, their inventions, their wise rule.

Yet, for what are men not indebted to Our Lord? By sin they had incurred the enmity of God and had forfeited all the supernatural gifts which He had bestowed on them. Jesus reconciled them to God, and enabled them to become God's children, to be

---

[1] Cf. Nilles, op. cit., p. 245; Terrien, op. cit., p. 16; Bainvel, op. cit., p. 161; Galtier, op. cit., p. 111; Leroy, *De SS. Corde Jesu eiusque cultu*, n. 201–3; and *Les Litanies du Sacré-Cœur de Jésus*, p. 36; Noldin, op. cit., p. 113.

[2] Cf. Denziger, n. 1563. See Hamon, op. cit., vol. IV, p. 276.

partakers of the Divine nature by sanctifying grace and, in the life to come, to share in the happiness of God Himself. To this end, He lavishly provided them with the most precious and most efficacious means—His sublime doctrine, His splendid example, His inexhaustible merits, His Sacraments, His Church, to say nothing of all that they owe to Him in the natural order—true liberty, true equality, true fraternity, the abolition of slavery, the moral elevation of woman, respect for children, the nobility of labour, in short, whatever constitutes true civilization. For all these benefits we are indebted to the love of the Heart of Jesus. Does not then this love deserve our veneration and homage?

We honour those who sacrifice themselves for the welfare of their fellow men and give everything for it: their time, their fortune, their strength, their health, and even their life. Yet what did Jesus not sacrifice for man? Everything to which He had a right: riches and pleasure, honour and glory: everything He possessed, His time, His rest, His strength, His blood, and even His life.[1] He gave it all to save them. Does not such devotion and such love deserve to be honoured by us?

Yet, not only His love but also His whole inner life is worthy of our homage on account of its ideal beauty. Everything in the Heart of Jesus is pure and unblemished; there is nothing in It in any way sinful, inordinate or imperfect. All Its affections and sentiments are inspired by the most perfect love for God and by the purest love for man. All virtues adorn It in the highest degree and make of It the living ideal of moral greatness and perfection. It is sufficient to run over the pages of the Gospel narrative to find plenty of instances of it. In particular, what kindness towards all, especially towards children, to the afflicted and to sinners. What meekness and self-control, what profound humility and thorough self-denial! What perfect conformity and submission to His Father's will, what ardent zeal for His Father's glory and for the salvation of souls! What patience and strength of soul in suffering! What magnanimity towards His enemies! And that faultless perfection never showed the slightest slackening, neither in His hidden life at Nazareth nor on His journeys through Galilee and Judea; neither in the midst of the fickle multitude nor in the familiar circle of His chosen disciples; neither in His struggle against the malignant and hypocritical Pharisees nor in the splendour of His

[1] See pp. 65-70.

triumphal entry into Jerusalem; neither in the bitter pangs of His agony in the Garden of Olives nor before His unjust judges, nor when suffering the pains and humiliations of His Passion.[1] So manifest is the moral perfection of the Heart of Jesus that even unbelievers neither dare nor can deny or contest it, nor even refrain from admiring it; and although they refuse to bend the knee before His Divinity, they agree in calling Him 'the Wise Man above all'.

Now it is of that love, so liberal, so generous, so heroic, and of that inner life, so beautiful, so perfect, so divine, that the Heart of Jesus is at once the principle and the symbol. It is, therefore, in the highest degree worthy of our veneration.

Consequently the Church honours and praises It as a Heart 'infinite in majesty', 'wherein abides the fullness of the Godhead', 'in which the Father was well pleased'; as the 'Holy Temple of God', the 'Tabernacle of the Most High'; as an 'abyss of all virtues', 'full of kindness and love', 'wherein are all the treasures of wisdom and knowledge', 'of whose fullness we have all received', as 'most worthy of all praise'.[2]

To pay honour to the Heart of Jesus, then, is the third direct end of the devotion. It is in close connection with the two primary ends: this veneration is an excellent means of rousing ourselves to love and reparation, and at the same time an excellent way of showing our love to this Heart and making reparation to It.

2. To Place our Trust in the Heart of Jesus

I. JESUS DESIRES IT

Finally, in revealing His Heart, Jesus intended that we should place our trust in It.

This is attested by St. Margaret Mary: 'The Sacred Heart of Jesus,' she writes to Fr. Croiset, '*wishes us to have recourse to Him in all our needs*, entirely committing ourselves to His loving care, like children to their Father, who having brought us to life on the cross with so many pains, cannot fail to provide for all our wants.'[3] And to Mother de Saumaise: 'This divine Heart desires, as the source of all good, to establish Its reign in Its creatures, in order

---

[1] See further on: the imitation of the Heart of Jesus, p. 156.
[2] Litany of the Sacred Heart.
[3] *Vie et Oeuvres*, vol. II, *3e Lettre au P. Croiset*, p. 557.

to supply their needs. Therefore It wishes us to turn to It with great confidence.'[1]

So did the Saint herself: 'I expect of the sacred Heart of Jesus all the succour of graces and mercy which I shall need; for I place *all my trust* in It.'[2] Again: 'I find in the sacred Heart of my Jesus all that is wanting to my poverty, for It is full of mercy . . . In It I sleep without worry and take my rest without anxiety . . . This divine and loving Heart is *all my hope*; It is my refuge.'[3] Again: 'I *hope* everything from the goodness of this loving Heart.'[4]

She was zealous in communicating this confidence to others. In her letters she repeatedly points out the riches and treasures which the Heart of Jesus contains and offers to men. 'That is why He reveals to us the devotion to His sacred Heart, which contains incomprehensible treasures which He desires to pour forth on all well-disposed hearts.'[5] Again: 'Would that I could manifest the infinite riches which are concealed in this treasure-house and which He places at the disposal of His faithful friends for their enjoyment.'[6]

And she multiplies the metaphors to explain to us how much the Heart of Jesus deserves our trust. 'This divine Heart,' she writes, 'is the *treasure-house of Heaven*, the precious gold of which is already given us to pay our debts and to purchase Heaven.'[7] 'It is an *inexhaustible fountain* from which there flow incessantly three streams: the first is the stream of mercy towards sinners . . .; the second is the stream of charity, which brings succour to those in need . . .'[8] 'It is an *abyss of* riches, in which the poor must cast their wants, . . . an abyss of love, in which we must plunge our troubles.'[9] 'It is a *fortress and safe refuge* to those who take shelter in it, in order to escape Divine Justice.' 'It is a *throne of mercy*, where the distressed are welcomed, provided that charity brings them there from the depths of their sufferings.' 'Enter into It, as a traveller goes aboard a *trustworthy vessel*, of which Love is the captain; It will lead you safe and sound through the rough

---

[1] *Vie et Oeuvres*, vol. II, p. 397.
[2] Ibid., vol. I, *Mémoire des Contemporaines*, n. 303, p. 286.
[3] Ibid., vol. II, *Petit Livret*, p. 790.
[4] Ibid., vol. II, *Lettre à la Mère de Saumaise*, 1689, p. 425.
[5] Ibid., vol. II, *Lettre à son frère*, p. 445.
[6] Ibid., vol. II, *2e Lettre au P. Croiset*, September 15th, 1689, p. 533.
[7] Ibid., vol. II, *3e Lettre au P. Croiset*, p. 556.
[8] Ibid., vol. II, p. 558.
[9] Ibid., p. 558.

seas of the world and guard you from rocks and storms.' 'It is a *priceless coin*, marked with the stamp of goodness, with which men can pay their debts and arrange the important business of their eternal salvation.'[1]

The Church, too, recommends trust in the Sacred Heart and sets the example herself.

She approved and enriched with indulgences the invocation *'Heart of Jesus, I trust in Thee.'*[2] In the Litany of the Sacred Heart she bids us invoke the Heart of Jesus as 'full of kindness and love; of whose fullness we have all received; rich unto all that call upon It; source of all consolation; our peace and reconciliation; hope of those who died in It.'

She also exhorts us to it by the mouth of the Popes.

When Pius IX, in 1875, invited all the faithful to consecrate themselves to the Sacred Heart he stated: 'In this divine Heart they will find an unassailable *refuge* against the spiritual dangers which surround them, *strength of soul* in the present troubles of the Church, *solace* and unshakable *hope* in the midst of all their afflictions.'[3]

In his Encyclical *Annum sacrum*, after describing 'the manifold troubles which afflict the world and incite us to implore the help of Him who alone has it in His power to avert them' (n. 14), Pope Leo XIII shows to the world the Heart of Jesus as its last hope, and exclaims: 'When the Church in the early ages of her existence sighed under the yoke of the Caesars, a young emperor saw in the heavens a cross as a token of a magnificent and speedily approaching victory. So today another emblem, sacred and divine, appears before our eyes: it is the Most Sacred Heart of Jesus, with the Cross above It, all glowing with splendour, in the midst of surrounding flames. In It we must place all our hopes; to It we must look for the salvation of the human race' (n. 15).

In his Encyclical *Caritate Christi compulsi* (May 3rd, 1932), 'on offering prayer and expiation to the Sacred Heart of Jesus in the present distress of the human race', Pope Pius XI writes: 'Let the faithful pour out to that merciful Heart that has known all the griefs of the human heart, the fullness of their sorrow, the steadfast-

---

[1] *Vie et Oeuvres*, vol. II, passim.
[2] Three hundred days. To those who recite it every day, a plenary indulgence once a month, on the ordinary conditions. (*Preces et pia opera*, n. 195.)
[3] *Decree of the Sacred Congregation of Rites*, dated April 22nd, 1875. Cf. Vermeersch, op. cit., vol. II, p. 198.

ness of their faith, their confident hopefulness and their ardent charity. Let them pray to Him, begging also the powerful intercession of the Blessed Virgin Mary, Mediatrix of all graces, on behalf of themselves and their families, their country and the Church; let them pray to Him for the Vicar of Christ on earth and for all the other Pastors, who share with him the dread burden of the spiritual government of souls; let them pray for their brethren in the faith, for their brethren who still hold erroneous doctrine, for unbelievers, for infidels, even for the enemies of God and the Church, that they may be converted ... The Divine Heart of Jesus cannot but be moved by the prayers and sacrifices of His Church, and He will finally say to His Spouse, weeping at His feet under the weight of so many griefs and woes: "Great is thy faith; be it done unto thee according to thy desire." '[1]

And the following year, 1933, he asked the members of the Apostleship of Prayer to pray during the month of June of that year and to offer their actions and sufferings, in particular 'that the world might place *its trust* in the Heart of Jesus'.

II. THE HEART OF JESUS IS WORTHY OF IT

On what is our trust in the Heart of Jesus founded? Why may and must we foster that trust? We find the answer to this question in the invocations of the Litany of the Sacred Heart quoted above. It may be summarized as follows: The Sacred Heart is willing to help us, because It is kind and loves us; It is able to help us, because It is rich and powerful; and It will really help us, because It promised it and is true to Its promises.

(a) *It is Willing to Help Us*

The Sacred Heart is willing to help us, because It is kind and loves us.

As God, Jesus is infinite goodness; but as Man, too, He is goodness itself. This goodness shines forth from almost every page of the Gospel narrative. It is extended to all, but preferably to the afflicted, to those who suffer, to those in distress.

And Jesus, who is so kind and gentle, loves us. We have seen that He loved us during His mortal life, even before we came into existence, and the proofs He gave of that love. He still loves us,

[1] *Acta Apost. Sedis,* 1932, pp. 177–94.

each one of us, with a sincere, really human love, with a tender, effective, generous, faithful love, in spite of our weakness, our infidelity, and our wickedness. Should we not then trust in His Heart?

(b) *It is Able to Help Us*

Not only is His sacred Heart willing to help us, but It is also able to do so because It is rich and powerful.

The Heart of Jesus is rich. He Himself declared to St. Margaret Mary that His Heart contains 'incomprehensible',[1] 'inexhaustible'[2] 'infinite treasures'. 'It is a hidden and infinite treasure, that only wants to reveal itself to us and to enrich our poverty.'[3] 'Would that I could manifest the infinite riches concealed in this priceless treasure with which He enriches His faithful friends!'[4] 'The treasures of blessings and graces which this sacred Heart contains are infinite.'[5] They are really infinite, for the merits by which Our Lord acquired for us all graces are infinite.

That we are able to obtain all these treasures of grace, we owe to His Heart; for it was His Heart, His love, which moved Him to sacrifice Himself, in order to atone for our sins and to merit for us all graces. And when we actually receive these graces, for this too we are indebted to His Heart. They are His property, and so He may dispose of them in the manner and in the measure which He chooses. In distributing them He is only guided by His love, by His Heart. He imparts them to those whom He loves in the measure in which He loves them. For these two reasons, then, we may ascribe these treasures of grace to the Heart of Jesus, and say that they come from His Heart, that they are contained in His Heart, that His Heart is rich and consequently is able to help us.

It is powerful, too. 'Do you believe that I can do this?' Our Lord one day asked His chosen servant. 'If you believe, you will see the power of My Heart in the magnificent effects of My love.'[6] As God, Jesus is all-powerful. As Man, His power is limited; it extends, however, to all that is connected with the aim and purpose of the Incarnation, namely, the glorification of God through

---

[1] *Vie et Oeuvres*, vol. II, p. 445.
[2] Ibid., p. 405.
[3] Ibid., vol. II, *Lettre à la Mère de Saumaise*, juillet 1688, p. 405.
[4] Ibid., *2e Lettre au P. Croiset*, 10 août 1689, p. 533.
[5] Ibid., vol. II, *Lettre à son directeur*, p. 627.
[6] Ibid., vol. II, *Lettre à la Mère de Saumaise*, 1689, p. 429.

K

the salvation of souls. Within these limits it has no bounds. Jesus Himself said: '*All* power is given to Me in heaven and in earth' (Matt. xxviii, 18).

If we read the Gospel narrative we see that the whole of visible creation is subject to Him. He changes water into wine at the marriage at Cana of Galilee (John ii, 1–10). He feeds the multitudes in the desert with a few loaves and a few small fishes (Matt. xiv, 15). He walks upon the Lake of Genesareth (Matt. xiv, 25); commands the raging winds and waves, and stills the storm with a single word (Matt. viii, 26). With a single word, with a single touch of His hand, He heals those who are ill with various diseases; restores sight to the blind, hearing to the deaf, speech to the dumb, the power of movement to the paralysed (Luke, viii and xviii; John, v and ix; Mark, ii, iii and vii). He even raises the dead to life (Luke vii, 12; Matt. ix, 18; John xi, 1). The devils, too, are subject to Him. They tremble with fear when the possessed persons are brought to Jesus; they rage and rave, and try to resist, but they always obey His orders and go out from their victim (Mark i, 23–27).

Jesus is the Master of hearts. With a look, with a word, He brings about complete and permanent changes in souls. 'Come ye after Me,' He said to Peter and Andrew who were casting their nets into the sea, 'and I will make you to be fishers of men. And they immediately, leaving their nets, followed Him' (Matt. iv, 19). He sees James and John, in a ship with their father, mending their nets. He calls them, and immediately they leave the ship and their father, and follow Him. He sees a man, named Matthew, sitting in the custom house: 'Follow Me,' He says to him; and Matthew rises and follows Him (Matt. ix, 9). Saul is on his journey to Damascus, 'as yet breathing out threatenings and slaughter against the disciples of the Lord', in order to seize the Christians there and bring them bound to Jerusalem. Jesus appears to Him: 'Saul, Saul, why persecutest thou Me? . . . I am Jesus whom thou persecutest.' And the persecutor Saul is transformed into the Apostle Paul (Acts ix, 1-6).

The grace of Jesus works wonders: wonders of conversion, penance, self-denial, purity, charity, zeal for souls, love of God and sanctity. And it makes heroes of delicate children, weak women and decrepit old men, who face the most horrible tortures and most cruel deaths in order to remain faithful to Him.

The power of Jesus, finally, manifests itself in the history of the Church. Through the assistance which He promised her, she has escaped all the dangers which, in the course of ages, threatened her very existence, her faith, her unity, her action, her fecundity and holiness. By this powerful assistance she has surmounted obstacles of all kinds: bloody persecution, oppression, heresy, schism, corruption of morals, intrigues, slander and calumny. And now today, after nineteen centuries, she is established further afield, is stronger, more youthful, more active and fertile, more sound and pure than ever.

This is the power which Jesus has at the disposal of His loving Heart; the power He uses to execute the loving designs of that Heart. We may then attribute it to His Heart and say that His Heart is endowed with this power, that His Heart is powerful, and hence is able to help us.

(c) It Will Really Help Us

Moreover, the Heart of Jesus will really help us, because It promised to do so, and It is faithful to Its promises.

Our Lord has made the most magnificent promises to those who honour His Heart. True, these promises aim at inviting men to practise devotion to His Heart, and hence constitute one of the motives which should induce us to cultivate it. Yet they are naturally most suitable to foster and increase our trust. It will not be without advantage to mention them here. When we treat of the motives for practising the devotion, we shall consider these promises more closely and examine their authenticity, their bearing and purport.

They have been summarized in the following formulae:[1]

1. I will give them all the graces necessary for their state of life.

2. I will give peace in their families.

3. I will console them in all their afflictions.

4. I will be their secure refuge during life and especially at the hour of death.

5. I will pour abundant blessings on all their undertakings.

6. Sinners shall find in My Heart the source and infinite ocean of mercy.

[1] These formulae do not give the words of Our Lord literally, but they render faithfully the sense of them.

7. Tepid souls shall become fervent.

8. Fervent souls shall rise to great perfection.

9. I will bless the homes in which the image of My Sacred Heart shall be exposed and honoured.

10. I will give to priests the power to touch the most hardened hearts.

11. Those who propagate this devotion shall have their names written in My Heart, and they shall never be effaced.

12. I promise thee, in the excess of the mercy of My Heart, that Its all-powerful love will grant to all those who receive Holy Communion on the first Friday of every month for nine consecutive months the grace of final repentance, and that they shall not die under My displeasure, nor without receiving the Sacraments, and that My Heart shall be their secure refuge at that last hour.

The Sacred Heart, then, promised that It would help us. And It is faithful to Its promises. To the Sacred Heart we may apply the word of Holy Writ: 'Let us hold fast the confession of our hope without wavering, for He is faithful that hath promised' (Heb. x, 23). Moreover, It could not be unfaithful, for this would be contrary to Its infinite holiness. And countless facts prove the fidelity of the Sacred Heart and that devotion to It is an abundant source of blessings and graces.

The Heart of Jesus is really worthy of our trust in It. Let us therefore place our hope in It. Let us follow the advice of St. Margaret Mary: 'If you are in the depths of loneliness and desolation, enter the Divine Heart: It is our solace . . . If you are in an abyss of aridity and impotence, plunge into the lovable Heart of Jesus, which is an abyss of power within you . . . Are you in an abyss of poverty, throw yourself into the abyss of abundance of the Sacred Heart: It will enrich you . . . Are you in an abyss of weakness, throw yourself into the abyss of strength of the Heart of Jesus . . . Are you plunged in an abyss of sadness, throw yourself into the abyss of Divine joy of the Sacred Heart . . . Are you in trouble and anxiety, throw yourself into the abyss of peace of that adorable Heart . . . Are you in an abyss of fear, throw yourself into the abyss of confidence of the Sacred Heart . . .'[1]

---

[1] *Vie et Oeuvres*, vol. II, pp. 752–55.

To place our trust in the Sacred Heart, this then is the second subsidiary end of the devotion. This aim is closely connected with the previous one, of which it is one particular aspect and form. By placing our trust in someone we show our conviction that he is able and willing to help us; we give evidence that we appreciate his abilities, his influence, his power, and the kind services he renders us. In this way we pay him the homage of our respect and honour. In exactly the same way, in placing our trust in the Sacred Heart, we show that we believe in Its power and Its kindness. And thus we pay homage to It and honour It.

§ II. INDIRECT ENDS

To persuade us to make a return of love to the Heart of Jesus, to make reparation to It for the neglect of His love, to honour His Heart and to place our trust in It, this then was the aim and purpose of Jesus in revealing His Heart; this is what He intended first of all to obtain from men, what He wished to see realized by devotion to His Divine Heart.

Yet this was but His immediate and direct aim. He still has something else in view, an end for the attainment of which the devotion serves as a means, and which therefore is to be considered as the mediate and indirect end of the Devotion. This end itself is threefold: the first refers to His Heavenly Father, i.e. to enkindle our love for God the Father; the second relates to His Divine Heart, i.e. to extend Its reign; the third is connected with men, i.e. to pour forth on them the treasures of His Heart.

1. To Enkindle our Love for the Heavenly Father

Jesus desires, by means of devotion to His Heart, to induce us to love His Heavenly Father. This is the chief indirect end of the Devotion.

Jesus, as we know, loves His Father with an all-inspiring, all-embracing, dominating love. He has observed in all its plenitude and perfection the commandment as to the love of God. He has really loved God His Father 'with His whole heart, with His whole soul, and with His whole mind'. Hence He necessarily longs most ardently for His Father to be loved by men also and for this love to grow ever more intense and effective.

Now the purpose of Jesus, when He asked for the devotion to His Heart, was precisely, in the first place, to rouse and enkindle the love of His Heavenly Father within the hearts of men by means of this devotion.

Pope Pius IX explicitly states it in the Brief of beatification of Margaret Mary: 'When the Author and Finisher of Faith, Jesus, moved by an excess of love, after He had taken to Himself the weakness of our human nature, offered Himself as a spotless Victim to God on the altar of the cross, in order to deliver us from the heinous slavery of sin, He had nothing more in view than to inflame by all means within the souls of men the fire with which His Heart was burning, as He Himself said to His disciples: "I am come to cast fire on earth, and what will I but that it be kindled?" Now, *as a means of enkindling more and more this fire of love*, He willed that the veneration and cult of His Sacred Heart should be established in the Church and propagated.'[1]

And when he raised the Feast of the Sacred Heart to a higher rite, the Sovereign Pontiff intended thereby 'that the devotion of love to the Heart of our Redeemer might spread ever more widely and penetrate more profoundly into the hearts of the faithful, and that thus the love for God, which had grown cold among many, might be enkindled by the fire of the love of God'.[2]

Pope Benedict XV alludes to it in his Letter to Cardinal Amette, Archbishop of Paris, on the occasion of the consecration of the basilica of the Sacred Heart at Montmartre: 'We firmly believe,' he writes, 'that the Sacred Heart of Jesus has been divinely presented to the world at the proper time, to be the object of a special worship, i.e. when it seemed that the *love of God* which had grown cold in many hearts could only be *revived* by this fire of Divine love.'[3] What does this mean but that God has willed the devotion to the Sacred Heart in order to combat this fading away of charity, and so to enkindle the love for God?

Nor does Pope Pius XI speak differently in his Encyclical *Miserentissimus*: 'In the stormy times of a more recent age, when the most insidious and pernicious of all heresies, Jansenism, was creeping in, which, *contrary to love and devotion for God*, represented Him not as a Father to be loved, but as an implacable Judge to

---

[1] Brief *Auctor nostrae fidei* (August 19th, 1864). Cf. *Vie et Oeuvres*, vol. III, p. 145.

[2] Nilles, op. cit., Liber I, pars I, cap. iv, § iv, p. 150.

[3] Letter dated October 7th, 1919. *Acta Apost. Sedis*, vol. XI, p. 412. See Galtier, op. cit., p. 155.

be feared, the loving Jesus showed His Most Sacred Heart to all nations as a token of peace and a pledge of victory' (n. 5). The Pope, then, presents the devotion to the Sacred Heart as directed to God Himself against Jansenism, contrary to the love for God, and hence as a devotion appropriate to enkindle the love for God, to make God loved ever more by men

To revive and increase the love for God by means of the devotion to the Sacred Heart, this then was the chief indirect aim of Jesus in revealing His Heart; this then is the principal mediate or indirect end of the devotion to the Sacred Heart.

Is this means well chosen? This cannot be called into question, for indeed the devotion induces us first of all, automatically as it were, to love Jesus as God. True, the principal immediate and direct end of the devotion is to make us love Jesus on account of His divine and human love.

Loving Jesus because of His Divine love, we shall remember that both His Heavenly Father and the Holy Ghost love us with the same love, for this love is common to the three Divine Persons and identified with their Divine Nature. We shall then naturally be induced also to love the Father and the Holy Ghost.

Moreover, we must not forget that if the Son of God loves us with a human love, it is because His Father willed, for love of us, that He should assume a human nature, and hence a human heart capable of loving us with a human love. Hence we shall refer our love to God the Father and at the same time to the Holy Ghost.

Finally, if we love Jesus we shall endeavour to comply with His wishes and to resemble Him as much as we can. Now what does Jesus desire more ardently than to see His Father loved by men? And what virtue shines forth in Him more vividly than His own love for His Heavenly Father?

2. To Establish and Extend the Reign of the Heart of Jesus

Jesus also intends, by means of devotion to His Sacred Heart, to establish and extend the reign of His Heart.

This is attested by St. Margaret Mary: 'The adorable Heart of Jesus wishes to establish the reign of Its love in all hearts, and to destroy and ruin that of Satan.'[1] Again: 'Our sovereign Master

---

[1] *Vie et Oeuvres*, vol. II, *Lettre à la Sœur Joly*, p. 489.

has an ardent desire to be known and loved by men, in whose heart *He longs to establish, by means of this devotion, the rule of His pure love*, so as to promise great rewards to those who will strive to make Him reign.'[1] Again: 'He wants to establish His reign in all His creatures, as the source of all good, in order to provide for all their needs.'[2]

To accomplish our Lord's desire was the aim of her whole life. The Saint devoted herself entirely to it, sparing neither toil nor trouble, undeterred by opposition, mockery and humiliation, or any kind of suffering. 'My only consolation,' she writes to Mother de Saumaise, 'is to see the Heart of my adorable Saviour reigning. Whenever this devotion spreads, some special cross is laid upon me. But I am ready to suffer anything for it.'[3] And to Fr. Croiset: 'In what depths of confusion and humiliation I shall be plunged! But what does it matter provided the Heart of my lovable Jesus be known and loved, and reigns.'[4]

Besides, our Lord had assured her that His wishes would be realized, and that His Heart would reign in the hearts of men, and this assurance was to her a source of courage, consolation and joy. She writes: 'Amid the difficulties and opposition, which were very great at the outset, He repeatedly said to me: "*I shall reign in spite of My enemies and of all those who oppose this devotion*"; and these words filled me with comfort and hope.'[5] Again: 'Whenever Satan stirred up any opposition, the kindness of Jesus raised my courage by these comforting words: "What do you fear? I shall reign in spite of Satan and whatever else stands in the way." '[6]

Thus the establishment and extension of the reign of the Sacred

---

[1] *Vie et Oeuvres*, vol. II, *2e Lettre au P. Croiset*, 10 août 1689, p. 530.

[2] Ibid., *Lettre à la Mère de Saumaise*, mai 1688, p. 397. In the mouth of the Saint, the phrase 'the reign of the Sacred Heart' means especially the rule of the Heart of Jesus over the hearts of men, and hence the development of the devotion to the Sacred Heart. In the revelation of June 1689 the word 'reign' seems to have a broader meaning: 'The Sacred Heart wishes to enter with splendour and pomp the residence of princes and kings . . . , to reign in the palace of the King, to be pictured on his banners and engraved in his arms' (*Vie et Oeuvres*, vol. II, p. 438). It is only towards the close of the nineteenth century that the kingship of the Sacred Heart begins to penetrate into the minds of the faithful. For the friends of the Sacred Heart it is now positively settled that Jesus, by means of this devotion, really wanted to establish and extend the kingdom of His Heart. (See Hamon, op. cit., vol. v, p. 259 and seqq., the historical development of the idea of the reign of the Sacred Heart).

[3] *Vie et Oeuvres*, vol. II, p. 393.

[4] Ibid., *4e Lettre au P. Croiset*.

[5] Ibid., *àe Lettre au P. Croiset*, p. 537.

[6] Ibid., *Lettre à la Sœur Joly*, 1689. Cf. *Lettre à la Mère de Saumaise*, pp. 355 and 436.

Heart is one of the indirect ends of the Devotion to the Sacred Heart.

But what is meant by this *'reign of the Sacred Heart'*?

To answer this question rightly we ought first to consider: In what does the reign of Christ consist?

The Prophets in the Old Testament had foretold that Christ should reign as a King. The testimony of Isaias (ix, 5), Jeremias (xxiii, 5), Daniel (vii, 13) and Zachary (ix, 9) is well known.

Jesus represented Himself as a King in the description of the last Judgement: 'When the Son of Man shall come in His majesty, and all the Angels with Him, then shall He sit upon the seat of His majesty. And all nations shall be gathered before Him . . . Then shall *the King* say to them that shall be on His right hand: Come, ye blessed of My Father, possess you the kingdom prepared for you from the foundation of the world. For I was hungry, and you gave Me to eat . . . Then shall the just answer Him, saying: Lord, when did we see Thee hungry, and fed Thee? . . . And *the King* answering, shall say to them: Amen I say to you, as long as you did it to one of these My least brethren, you did it to Me' (Matt. xxv, 31–40).

Moreover, He proclaimed His royalty in the most tragic circumstances when, at the question of the Roman governor Pilate, 'Art thou a king then?' He answered firmly and clearly: 'I am a King' (John xviii, 37). And on the day of His Ascension He said to His Apostles: 'All power is given to Me in Heaven and on earth. Going therefore, teach ye all nations . . . to observe all things whatsoever I have commanded you' (Matt. xxviii, 18–20).

Hence the Church celebrates Him as King of the entire world. In the hymn *Te Deum* she praises Him as the King of glory: *Tu Rex gloriae, Christe!* In the Invitatory of the feasts of the Saints: *'Regem Apostolorum . . . , Martyrum . . . , Confessorum . . . , Virginum, venite adoremus:* Come, let us adore the King of the Apostles, the King of Martyrs, the King of Confessors, the King of Virgins.' In the Invitatory of Corpus Christi: *'Christum Regem, dominantem gentibus, venite, adoremus:* Come, let us adore the King ruling over the nations.' Think of the numerous Advent antiphons in which Jesus is hailed and invoked as King. This eulogy was sanctioned and crowned by Pope XI's institution of the Feast of Christ the King,[1]

---

[1] The Feast is celebrated on the last Sunday of October.

the Office and Mass of which magnificently celebrates Jesus' royalty.

The feast was instituted with a view to protesting against the disdain and rejection of the kingship and empire of Christ by modern States, of inculcating upon the minds of the faithful the vitally important truth of this empire, and urging them on to work to the utmost for the establishment and extension of the Reign of Christ.[1]

Jesus is really our Lord and King. He has a right to rule over us. His empire embraces all men. 'It includes,' to use the words of Pope Leo XIII in his Encyclical *Annum sacrum* (n. 4), 'not only Catholic nations, not only baptized persons who, though by right belonging to the Church, have been led astray by error, or have been cut off from her by schism, but also all those who are outside the Christian faith; so that truly the whole of mankind is subject to the power of Jesus Christ.' Pope Pius XI in his turn solemnly proclaimed and set forth the kingship of Christ in his Encyclical *Quas primas* (December 11th, 1925), whereby he instituted the Feast of Christ the King.

What is the foundation of this royalty of Jesus?

As God, He is, like His Father, the Creator, and hence the Lord and King of all creation.

He is also the King as man, as God-man, and this by a twofold right, namely, by right of birth and by acquired right.

By right of birth, for as man He is hypostatically united to the Person of the Word, and hence shares in the royal dignity and authority of the Second Person of the Blessed Trinity. It follows, says Pope Pius XI, 'not only that Christ is to be adored by angels and men, but that to Him as man angels and men are subject, and must recognize His empire; by reason of the hypostatic union Christ has power over all creatures.' (*Quas primas*.)

But also by acquired right Jesus is our Lord and King, namely by His Redemption of us. 'Would that those who forget what they have cost their Saviour might recall the words: "You were not redeemed with corruptible things, but with the precious blood of Christ, as of a lamb unspotted and undefiled" (1 Peter i, 18–19). We are no longer our own, for Christ has purchased us "with a great price" (1 Cor. vi, 20 and 25).' (*Quas primas*.)

What obligations does the kingship of Jesus lay on men?

[1] Cf. *Quas Primas*.

Individuals must acknowledge His dominion by submitting to Him in their moral life. 'Not one of our faculties is exempt from His empire. He must reign in our minds, which should assent with perfect submission and firm belief to revealed truths and to the doctrines of Christ. He must reign in our wills, which should spurn natural desires and love God above all things, and cleave to Him alone. He must reign in our bodies and in our members, which should serve as instruments for the interior sanctification of our souls.' (*Quas primas.*)

Families must recognize His kingship, by submitting to Him in their family life. Husband and wife, parents and children, must be guided in their mutual relations, in their whole conduct, in their deliberations and decisions, by the teaching, the commandments and the counsels of Christ, by the doctrine of His Church, and must practise the virtues which Our Lord wishes to see flourish in the domestic circle.

Nations, finally, must recognize His kingship, by submitting to Him in social life.[1] And as it is the State that governs and represents the nation, this duty is in the first place incumbent on the State. Hence the State ought to conform its legislation and government to the doctrine and the laws of Christ and His Church, particularly in the matter of marriage, education, public morality, Sunday observance, etc.; not only not to permit nor to do anything that hinders the divine mission of the Church, but to co-operate as far as possible with the Church and bring all its citizens to respect the Christian religion and Christian morals.[2]

It is in this submission to the royal authority of Christ, in their individual, domestic and social life, that consists the '*Reign of Christ*'.

---

[1] What is the nature of the kingship of Jesus? 'This kingdom,' writes Pius XI, 'is primarily spiritual and concerned with spiritual things . . . It would be a grave error, on the other hand, to say that Christ has no authority whatever in civil affairs, since by virtue of the absolute empire over all creatures committed to Him by the Father, all things are in His power.' The administration and direction of civil affairs He leaves to the government of the State, and only claims an absolute authority over all that refers to the supernatural end of man. Hence the State has nothing to fear: 'No earthly crown comes He to take, who heavenly kingdoms doth bestow' (Hymn for the Epiphany).*

* 'Non eripit mortalia, qui regna dat caelestia.'

[2] Christ Himself has clearly shown that this kingship has no political character. 'On many occasions, when the Jews, and even the Apostles, wrongly supposed that the Messias would restore the liberties and the kingdom of Israel, He repelled and denied such a suggestion. When the populace thronged around Him in admiration and would have acclaimed Him king, He shrank from the honour and hiding Himself, fled from them. Before the Roman magistrate He declared that His kingdom was not of this world.' (*Quas primas.*)

Now, then, in what does the '*Reign of the Sacred Heart*' consist? Our Lord wishes us to submit to Him, not because we must, but because we are willing to do so; not under constraint, nor for fear, but for love; He wishes His reign to be founded on love. Hence He wishes us to allow Him to rule over our hearts, not only by conforming our sentiments, affections and desires to His will, but by loving Him with our whole heart and above all things; to allow Him to rule over our whole being and our entire life, not only because He has a right to it but because we love Him and recognize Him as our beloved King.

And it is precisely in this that 'the reign of the Sacred Heart' consists. This reign, then, is nothing else than the reign of Christ, as we have described above, but a reign founded on love, on His love for us and our love for Him; it is nothing else than the sovereignty of Christ, but a sovereignty to which we submit because He loves us and because by His love He deserves the complete submission of our hearts; nothing else but the rule of Christ, but a rule which we recognize and accept willingly, cheerfully and lovingly, because He is our loving and beloved King.

By the expression 'the reign of the Sacred Heart', therefore, we mean to signify that we consider Jesus Christ not only as having a right to reign over us, but also as justly claiming it because of His love, and that we submit to His empire out of love; in short, that we regard Him as the King of love.[1]

Now, Jesus wishes to realize the establishment and extension of this reign through devotion to His Sacred Heart. It is one of the indirect ends of the devotion.

In revealing His Heart, Jesus intends first of all to enkindle our love for Him, and by love to reign in our hearts. This is the first immediate and direct end of the devotion to the Sacred Heart. But He wishes to reign in our hearts in order to rule, by this love, over our entire being, our whole lives, our individual life, our family life, and our social life. And this is the second indirect end of the devotion.

In the next chapter, when we treat of the practice of the Devotion, we shall see that this reign of the Sacred Heart is principally established by the consecration to the Sacred Heart—personal consecration, consecration of the family, and consecration of municipalities and nations.

[1] Cf. Ramière, s.j., *Le Règne social du Cœur de Jésus*, p. 43.

3. To Pour Forth on Men the Treasures of the Heart of Jesus

Jesus wishes, by means of the devotion to His Sacred Heart, to attain yet another end, namely, to pour forth on men the riches of His Heart.

In the first apparition He said to the Saint: 'My divine Heart is so passionately inflamed with love for men and for you in particular, that, not being able any longer to contain within Itself the flames of Its ardent charity, It must needs spread them abroad. By means of you It will manifest Itself to men, in order *to enrich them* with the precious treasures which I discover to you and which contain the sanctifying and salutary graces necessary to preserve them from the abyss of ruin.'

In the second apparition He repeats this declaration: 'He gave me to understand that it was the great desire He had to be perfectly loved by men and to withdraw them from the path of ruin along which Satan was drawing so many, that made Him form the design of manifesting to men His Heart with all the treasures of love, mercy, grace, sanctification and salvation which It contains, in order that those who would render Him and procure for Him all the honour and love possible *might themselves be abundantly enriched* with those divine treasures of which this Heart is the source . . . This devotion was the last effort of His love that He would grant men in these latter ages, in order to withdraw them from the empire of Satan . . .'

The Saint dwells on this aim of the devotion in many passages of her letters: 'It is His ardent *desire of imparting* these sanctifying and salutary graces to well-disposed souls that makes Him wish to be known, loved and honoured by His creatures.'[1] 'That is why He reveals to us the devotion to His Sacred Heart, which contains inconceivable treasures which He wishes to pour forth on all hearts of good will; for it is the last effort of His love for sinners, to induce them to do penance and to provide them abundantly with His powerful graces.'[2] 'He made me know His ardent desire of imparting lavishly to you the inexhaustible riches of this adorable Heart, not only for yourself, but that you may communicate them to the souls which He wants to gain by means of you.'[3] 'The ardent desire of Our Lord that His Sacred Heart

---

[1] *Vie et Oeuvres*, vol. II, *Lettre à la Mère de Saumaise*, mai 1688, p. 397.
[2] Ibid., vol. II, *Lettre à son frère*, juin 1689, p. 445.
[3] Ibid., *1e Lettre au P. Croiset*, 14 avril 1689, p. 518.

should be honoured by a special homage aims at renewing in souls the fruits of the Redemption, by making of this Sacred Heart as it were another Mediator[1] between God and men whose sins have increased to such an extent that His whole power is necessary to obtain for them mercy, and the graces of salvation and sanctification *which He longs to impart to them* in such abundance.'[2]

Thus Our Lord by means of the devotion to His Sacred Heart wishes 'to enrich men abundantly with the treasures of His Heart', 'to pour forth on them the precious, divine, inconceivable, inexhaustible treasures of which His Heart is the source', 'treasures of salvation and sanctification'. As for sinners in particular, He wishes 'to preserve them from the path of ruin', 'to induce them to do penance', 'to withdraw them from the empire of Satan', 'to bestow on them abundant graces of salvation', and thus 'to renew in souls the fruits of the Redemption'.

The Devotion to the Sacred Heart, therefore, is really a new and great benefit of the Heart of Jesus, a new and magnificent proof of His love for men. If He asks for this devotion in order to satisfy a desire of His loving Heart, which has a right to a return of love, it is also for us, in our favour, that He may heap upon us new and more abundant gifts and graces, and particularly afford us a powerful aid in working out our salvation and sanctification.

---

[1] This expression must not be taken literally. Between God and man there is only One Mediator, Jesus Christ (1 Tim. ii, 5), with whom moreover the Sacred Heart is identified. The Saint means to say that the manifestation of the Heart of Jesus is, as it were, a new manifestation of His Mediation, a new and more abundant communication of the fruits of this mediation. She herself shows that the expression is to be understood in this sense when she says that the devotion 'aims at renewing in souls the fruits of the Redemption'.

[2] *Vie et Oeuvres* Vol. ii, p. 321. See also *Lettre à la Mère Greyfié*, 1685, p. 300.

CHAPTER III

Practice of the Devotion

Now that we know the object and ends of the Devotion, the question arises: How is it to be practised? How is it to be lived?

It is clear that this practice ought to correspond to the immediate and direct end of the devotion. This end, as we have seen, is fourfold: to return to the Heart of Jesus love for love, to make reparation for the disregard of Its love, to pay honour to It, and to place our trust in It. Logically, then, the practice of the devotion will comprise various exercises which are in connection with each of these ends.

Moreover, it is obvious that Jesus desires not only sentiments but also acts, and consequently that these exercises should not be confined to arousing affections, but that they must also serve to manifest them to His Heart.

With reference to each of the four ends of the devotion, we may then distinguish two groups of practices, namely, practices intended to arouse these affections and practices suitable for their manifestation.

§ I. PRACTICE OF LOVE

A. HOW TO INCITE OURSELVES TO LOVE FOR THE HEART OF JESUS

1. The Consideration of the Love of the Heart of Jesus

How are we to incite ourselves to return to the Heart of Jesus love for love? Evidently by the consideration of His love for us. Love engenders love. Our heart is so made that it is sensitive to affection and love, and that it responds, as it were, automatically to affection with affection, to love with love. If then we wish to arouse in our souls love for the Heart of Jesus, we have only to consider and meditate on the magnificent and touching proofs which He has given of His love for us.[1] It cannot be but that our

[1] See p. 59.

hearts will be inflamed with the love which Jesus rightly demands as the response to His love.

There is no lack of books that may help us for this contemplation. There is, first of all, the Book *par excellence*, the Holy Gospel, the simple and yet moving record of what Jesus said, did and suffered for love of us.

There is, however, yet another book, to which for this study we should give the preference, namely, the Sacred Heart of Jesus itself. It was the favourite book of St. Margaret Mary, the book in which she had learned to know the love of Jesus. Not seldom it even happened to her that she was unable to read any other. 'Though using every endeavour,' she writes to Fr. Croiset, 'I am often incapable of reading the book I hold in my hands. But instead of this, the lovable Heart of my Jesus lies open to me as a great book in which He makes me read the marvellous lessons of His pure love.'[1]

'Indeed,' writes Fr. de Galliffet, 'what is more fit and proper to enkindle the devotion of the Christian people than the Heart of their Redeemer? What other sensible thing is to be found in the world, so holy and lovable, the mere sight of which reminds us so strongly and so sweetly of Jesus' love for us, of His benefits, His virtues and His sufferings? For all this is contained in this sacred Heart, all this is engraved in It and impressed as it were upon It with letters never to be effaced, so that he who at the first glance at this adorable Heart would not be moved, would show that he had no faith or no heart.'[2]

That is true when we consider the Heart of Jesus as It is in reality; still more so, when we contemplate It as It manifested Itself in one of the apparitions to St. Margaret Mary. Let us read her narrative over again: 'This Divine Heart was shown to me as on a throne of flames, more dazzling than the sun and transparent as crystal, with that adorable wound, and surrounded with a crown of thorns which signified the pricks caused to It by our sins; and above there was a cross, which signified that from the first moment of His Incarnation, that is, as soon as this sacred Heart was formed, the cross was planted in It and that It was filled with all the bitterness which humiliation and poverty, pain and scorn would cause to It, and which His sacred Humanity

---

[1] *Vie et Oeuvres*, vol. II, *6e Lettre au P. Croiset*, 17 janvier 1690, p. 599.
[2] De Galliffet, op. cit., Book II, chap. i, art. ii, p. 83.

was to suffer through all His lifetime and in His sacred Passion.'[1]

As the Saint attests, the cross symbolizes all that Jesus suffered in His Heart during His mortal life; the thorns are the emblem of the grief caused Him by our sins. Of the wound and the flames she gives no explanation, but the wound evidently reminds us of His Death, for it is called 'that adorable wound', i.e. the well-known wound inflicted on Him on the cross by the lance of the soldier. As for the flames, from other passages of the writings of the Saint it appears that they are the symbol of Christ's ardent love. 'My Divine Heart,' Our Lord said to her, 'is so passionately inflamed with love for men and for you in particular, that, not being able any longer to contain within Itself the flames of Its ardent charity, It must needs spread them abroad by means of you.'[2] Again: 'The adorable Heart of my Jesus was in the midst of the flames of Its pure love.' Again: 'From His sacred Humanity there burst forth flames on all sides, especially from His adorable breast, which resembled a furnace. He opened His breast and showed me His Divine Heart as the source of these flames.'[3]

These emblems are unquestionably most suitable to remind us still more vividly of the love of the Heart of Jesus and to urge us on to repay to It love for love.

The Bishops of Poland, in 1765, emphasized it in their *Memoriale:* 'If we consider things attentively, we shall find that there is no corporal and sensible thing more proper and fit to be presented to the homage of the faithful than this Heart, so loving and at the same time so afflicted. For there is none that contains and represents more sublime mysteries; none the contemplation of which is more appropriate to produce holier affections in the hearts of the faithful; none that more vividly represents before the eyes of the soul as well as of the body the boundless love of our Lord Jesus Christ; none that is more capable of reminding us of all the benefits we owe to our loving Redeemer; none that expresses more strikingly the interior sufferings which He endured for our sakes. All this and still more is seen not merely contained and represented, but as it were written and engraved in this Sacred Heart, as it is usually pictured and presented for our veneration. All this

---

[1] *Vie et Oeuvres*, vol. II, p. 571.
[2] Ibid., vol. I, p. 122.
[3] Ibid., Vol. I, n. 130.

L

brings about that to the worship of the faithful no object can be presented, holier and more suitable strongly to arouse gratitude and love towards our loving Saviour, to inflame pious desires and efficaciously to stimulate our hearts to holy affections.'[1]

Besides, even to facilitate our contemplation of the Heart of Jesus we have a means at our disposal, very simple it is true, yet efficacious, namely, the picture of this Heart, represented with the emblems described above. Appealing to our eyes, it considerably helps us to represent the Heart of Jesus to our imagination, to contemplate It and to be moved by the thought of the love symbolized by It.[2]

2. Prayer

Yet, if the contemplation of the Heart of Jesus and of His love is to produce its full effect and to arouse in our hearts a real, effective and lasting love, it must be fecundated by grace. We obtain this grace by prayer.

Let us then beg this grace of God the Father, who is well pleased in His beloved Son (Matt. iii, 17); of the Holy Ghost, who is the love which the Father and the Son bear to each other; of the Blessed Virgin Mary, the first and most perfect worshipper of the Heart of Jesus. Let us ask the Saints who have distinguished themselves by their love for the Heart of Jesus to obtain it for us, too, and particularly St. Margaret Mary and Bl. Claude de la Colombière, both of them chosen by Jesus Himself to be apostles of His Heart; both of them only living to love Him and to cause Him to be loved, and desiring nothing so much as to obtain for us this precious grace.

Let us ask for it in our Communions and visits to the Blessed Sacrament. And let us repeat frequently and fervently the invocations by which we implore this grace: 'Sweet Heart of Jesus, make me love Thee ever more.'[3] 'Sweet Heart of Jesus, be Thou my love!'[4] 'Heart of Jesus, burning with love for us, inflame our hearts with love for Thee.'[5]

---

[1] Nilles, op. cit., Liber I, cap. iii, § iii, n. 40.
[2] See chap. iii, § iii, n. 2.
[3] Three hundred days' indulgence. (*Preces et pia opera*, n. 193.)
[4] Three hundred days. Ibid., n. 206.
[5] Five hundred days. Ibid., n. 194.

B. HOW TO TESTIFY OUR LOVE TO THE HEART OF JESUS

Yet Jesus not only desires that by the contemplation of His Heart and His love we should enkindle our own love for Him, but He wishes us moreover to testify it to Him.

We show our love both by affections or emotions, and by acts inspired by love. The affections form what is called affective love, the acts effective love.

1. Practice of Affective Love

Love can assume three forms: good pleasure, benevolence, and desire of union.

I. GOOD PLEASURE

He who loves takes pleasure in considering all the good which the beloved one possesses: his dignity, his beauty, his qualities, his happiness, the esteem he enjoys, etc.; he rejoices at it, as if it were his own, expresses to him his joy and congratulates him on it.

We will then testify our love to the Heart of Jesus by considering, by admiring whatever there is beautiful, noble, great and good in Him, and by rejoicing at it: the personal union of His Heart and whole humanity with the Second Person of the Blessed Trinity; His Divine dignity which exalts Him infinitely above all creatures; His wisdom, His power, His kindness, and His holiness with all the virtues which it contains; His unutterable bliss and happiness resulting from the beatific vision and from His union with the Eternal Word; the glory given Him in Heaven by the adoration of the Saints and the Angels, and the honour procured for Him by the just on earth; the love of which He is the object in Heaven on the part of the Saints, the Angels, the Blessed Virgin and the Holy Trinity; the joy afforded Him by the acts of virtue performed by the just, by the conversion of heathen, infidels and sinners, etc. All this we will make the favourite subject of our meditations, considering it with affection and admiration, and trying to realize it increasingly clearly; we will rejoice at it more and more intimately, and join all those who love Him on earth and in Heaven, to congratulate, praise and glorify Him.

II. BENEVOLENCE

To love means to wish well to the person loved, to be watchful of his interests, to adopt his sentiments, to hope for the realization of his desires, and to be ready to help him towards it.

We shall then manifest our love for Jesus by taking to heart all His concerns, by making His desires our own, wishing that they may be fulfilled, and showing ourselves ready to work for that fulfilment to the best of our ability.

What does Jesus desire? He longs for His Heavenly Father to be known, honoured, served and loved as perfectly as possible; for His Church to extend unendingly, to be flourishing, free in its action, true to its mission, pure and holy; for heathen, heretics, infidels and sinners to be converted; for the faithful to lead a truly Christian life, and for the Religious and priests energetically and perseveringly to aspire to perfection; for all men to attain to eternal bliss in the life to come.

He wishes in particular that His Heart should be better known, honoured and loved; the devotion to His Heart spread ever more and practised ever more perfectly; the reign of His Heart to be established in the hearts of individuals, in the family and in social life; His Heart to be glorified by the fervour, generosity, charity, self-denial and holiness of those who practise this devotion; and to be consoled by the reparation made by loving souls, etc.

We will then ardently desire and earnestly ask in our prayers that all these wishes of the Heart of Jesus may be realized; we will regret that they are so little satisfied and express that regret to Him, and we will promise Him to try to realize them as much as we can, in ourselves as well as in others.

III. DESIRE OF UNION

He who loves aims at being united with the person loved and seeks his presence, wants to see him and talk to him, and tries to make this union as intimate and lasting as possible.

We will then manifest our love to Jesus by aspiring and endeavouring to make sure of an ever closer union with Him. We will often think of Him, be eager to converse with Him in prayer, and be desirous to visit Him in the Tabernacle, to receive Him in Holy Communion, and to go to Him in Heaven in order to be with Him, to see and hear Him, and to live with Him for ever in a beatific union.

2. Practice of Effective Love

Love consists not only in affections but also in deeds. Love impels us to acts, expresses itself by acts and is proved by acts. Love without acts would not be true and genuine love, which should be not only affective but effective also.

This effective love we may manifest to the Heart of Jesus in various ways.

A. General Practices

This love we may and must manifest to Him in general by avoiding whatever may displease Him and by doing whatever is agreeable to Him.

I. AVOIDING WHATEVER DISPLEASES THE HEART OF JESUS

Love requires first and foremost that we should carefully refrain from whatever may injure or displease the person loved. If then we really love the Heart of Jesus we shall most watchfully avoid whatever is displeasing to Him. Now, what displeases Him supremely is sin, even the smallest.

Sin displeases Him because it displeases His Heavenly Father whom He loves above all things; because it is contrary to His own holiness; because it was the cause of His Passion and Death; because it is a base ingratitude towards Him and a grievous contempt shown to His love; finally, because sin, at least mortal sin, threatens to make His Passion and Death futile and vain.

If then we really love the Heart of Jesus, we shall, with all the power of our love, detest sin, each voluntary sin, and avoid it most carefully.

II. DOING WHATEVER IS AGREEABLE TO THE HEART OF JESUS

Love does not content itself with abstaining from what displeases the beloved, but endeavours to do what is pleasing and agreeable to him. If then we really love the Heart of Jesus we shall endeavour to do what is pleasing to Him.

To do what is pleasing to the Heart of Jesus is, in the first place, to accomplish His holy will, to keep His commandments. He Himself said: 'If you love Me, keep My commandments.' Again: 'He that hath My commandments, and keepeth them, he it is that loveth Me' (John xiv, 15 and 21). We shall then faithfully, readily and generously observe His commandments, all of them, even the smallest, and we shall keep them especially out of love, because they are the expression of His will and afford us the opportunity of showing Him our love.

To do what is pleasing to the Heart of Jesus is moreover to perform what He wishes us to do, without His imposing it upon us as a strict obligation. These desires are made known to us through circumstances, through the inspirations of His grace, and through the advice of our spiritual director.

To do what is agreeable to the Heart of Jesus is, finally, to act with the purpose of glorifying Him or giving Him pleasure. Each act of virtue, each mortification, each act of self-conquest, each sacrifice, each suffering performed or accepted for that purpose, is agreeable to Him and constitutes an act of love. Even our usual business, our professional duty, our manual labour, accomplished or offered with that purpose in view, become in this way acts of love. By that intention we are able to transform into acts of love for Jesus, and so into practices of devotion to His Heart, all that we do and all that we suffer, sin alone excepted; to this end it is sufficient to accomplish or accept each thing with the intention of glorifying the Heart of Jesus, of affording Him pleasure. In this way our whole lives can become a continual exercise of love for the Heart of Jesus, and so of devotion to His Heart.

It is in this manner that St. Margaret Mary understood this devotion, that she practised it herself, and taught and recommended it to others. For her this devotion does not merely consist in performing certain pious exercises in honour of the Heart of Jesus, but also and especially in a life wholly animated by love for the Sacred Heart, a life in which all thoughts, all affections, all acts of the will and all actions are inspired by that love and form proofs of that love.

B. Particular Practices

Yet in addition to these general practices of love, devotion to the Sacred Heart includes certain particular exercises asked for by Our Lord Himself. The principal ones are: consecration to His Sacred Heart, devotion to His Passion, devotion to the Blessed Eucharist, and the apostolate of His Heart.

I. THE CONSECRATION TO THE HEART OF JESUS

(a) *The Personal Consecration*

Consecration is the chief exercise, the fundamental act of effective love towards the Heart of Jesus. Pope Pius XI states in his Encyclical *Miserentissimus* (n. 8): 'Among all these practices of the cult of the Sacred Heart there stands out and is to be pointed out the pious consecration, by which, giving back to God's eternal love all that we are and have received, we devote ourselves to the Divine Heart of Jesus.'[1]

Its Nature

The consecration is indeed an act by which we devote and give ourselves up to the Sacred Heart, in order to belong entirely to Him and to live no longer but for Him.

Love gives itself. In proportion as it gives itself, it proves to be great, strong and deep. True love gives itself entirely, unreservedly. In this way we are to give ourselves up to the Heart of Jesus if we wish to love It with our whole heart. It is in this that the consecration consists. Jesus is our Master and Lord. He has then a strict right to all that we have and all that we are. But out of love we wish to give it all to Him, as though it belonged to us as our own property.

That the consecration is to be understood in this sense clearly appears from the terms of the form which St. Margaret Mary used to this end and which she recommended to others. In a letter to Fr. Croiset she says that our Lord Himself inspired it in her: 'I beg of you to enter (in your book) the small consecration which, if I am not mistaken, as it comes from Him, He would not approve of being omitted: "I, N . . . , give and consecrate myself to the Sacred Heart of our Lord Jesus Christ. I offer my person and my life, my actions, pains and sufferings, and it is my desire henceforth to use no part of my being save in honouring, loving and glorifying Him. It is my steadfast purpose to belong only to Him, to do everything for love of Him, and to renounce absolutely all that could displease Him." '

---

[1] Directly, then, we consecrate ourselves to the Heart of Jesus in gratitude for His love, but by so doing we also consecrate ourselves, indirectly, to God to whom we owe, either directly or indirectly, all that we are and have.

[2] *Vie et Oeuvres*, vol. II, *10e Lettre au P. Croiset*, 21 août 1690, p. 621.

Significance and Purport

In many passages of her writings the Saint sets forth the significance and import of the consecration. To Mother de Saumaise she writes: 'You should offer to Him the sacrifice of yourself by consecrating to Him all your being to be used in His service, to procure for Him all the glory, love and praise that lies in your power to give Him. This is what I think the Divine Heart asks, in order to perfect and achieve the work of your sanctification.'[1]

And to one of her novices: 'Our Lord wishes you to offer Him the entire sacrifice of yourself, of all your bodily and mental being, to be used only to render and procure for Him all the honour, love and glory in your power, by making a *complete donation* and unreserved gift of all the good which till now you may have done by His grace, that He may dispose of it according to His will.'[2]

She insists on it in a letter to Mother de Soudeilles: 'If you wish to live entirely for our Lord and to attain to the perfection which He demands of you, you are to make to His sacred Heart the *entire* sacrifice of yourself and of all that depends on you, unreservedly, willing no longer anything than by the will of this lovable Heart, loving only by His love, acting only in accordance with His wish, never undertaking anything without asking His advice and His help . . . If you want to be among His friends, you are to offer Him the sacrifice of yourself, consecrating yourself entirely to Him, in order to procure for Him all the love, honour and glory that lies in your power. After that, you ought to consider yourself only as belonging to and depending on the adorable Heart, having recourse to It in all your needs and establishing yourself in It.'[3]

Again, she writes to Sister de la Barge: 'After losing our hearts in those divine flames of pure love, we are to take a wholly new heart which makes us live henceforth with an entirely new life, with a new heart fostering new thoughts and affections and performing new actions, that is to say, we are no longer to will and act by ourselves, but this Divine Heart must take the place of ours, so that He alone may live and act in us and for us; His will must so annihilate ours as to be able to act without any resistance on our part; and lastly, His affections, His thoughts and wishes must take the place of ours, but especially His love which will love

---

[1] *Vie et Oeuvres*, vol. II, p. 297.
[2] Ibid., *Avis particuliers*, p. 649.
[3] Ibid., vol. II, *Lettre à la Mère de Soudeilles*, 3 novembre 1684, pp. 281–82.

Himself in us and for us. And thus this lovable Heart, being for us all in all, we shall be able to say with St. Paul: "I live, now not I; but Christ liveth in me." '[1]

From these texts the following conclusions may be drawn concerning the significance and purport of the consecration, as asked for by our Lord.

1. The consecration is a fully conscious act of our will, a maturely deliberate resolution from which there results a true engagement and hence which involves real obligations. It is not a vow, however, binding under penalty of sin but rather an explicit promise, an engagement of honour.

2. It is a true donation of ourselves to the Sacred Heart, and hence an act by which we become in truth the property of the Sacred Heart. We no longer belong to ourselves but to the Sacred Heart, which becomes in a strict sense our Proprietor.

3. It is a total donation; total, firstly, in respect of its object; we give ourselves up entirely with all that we are and have, with all that we do and all that we suffer; we give our person, our understanding, our heart, our will, our senses, our health, our strength, our affections, our words and our actions; in short, our whole lives. We except nothing; it becomes all the property of the Sacred Heart. Total, too, relative to the consequences of our donation, i.e. as regards the rights which it confers on the Sacred Heart and which, out of love, we promise to respect to the best of our ability in all our ways of acting.

What are these rights? The rights which any proprietor may assert over his possession and over his property.

1. The proprietor has a right to dispose of his property at his will and pleasure. By the consecration, then, we confer on the Sacred Heart the right to dispose at Its own pleasure of our persons, of all that we are and have. Hence we give ourselves up to the Sacred Heart with reference to all our temporal interests, our health, success in our undertakings, etc.; with respect of all our spiritual concerns, graces, consolations or spiritual trials, degree and form of holiness, spiritual help, etc.; likewise as regards our apostolic activity, sphere of action, form of apostleship, success, etc. For all this we abandon ourselves to the good pleasure and guidance of the Sacred Heart of Jesus, and we pledge ourselves

[1] *Vie et Oeuvres*, vol. II, *Lettre à la Sœur de la Barge*, 22 octobre 1689, pp. 472–73.

to allow Him to do what He pleases with us, to follow Him where and in what way He wants. We engage ourselves the more readily because we know that He will exercise His right only in accordance with His love, that He knows better than we do what is beneficial to us, and that He desires our true happiness still more than we ourselves do; and on the other hand, that He will always be ready to help us to make the sacrifices which He demands of us, to bear the trials which He permits for our good.

2. The proprietor has a right to claim that others should make no use of his property but in compliance with his will. We then bind ourselves never to do anything against the will of Jesus, either command or wish; in other words to avoid most carefully all that may displease Him, especially every deliberate fault, even the smallest; to act always in accordance with His wish, and following the inspirations of His grace; and to this end we engage ourselves to consult Him in all things, and to ask Him for light and strength, His blessing and assistance.

3. The proprietor, finally, has a right to demand that his property should be useful and profitable to him, affording him the advantages and enjoyment which he may expect and wishes to obtain from it. By the consecration, then, we confer on the Heart of Jesus the right to wish us in whatever we do to have only in view His joy, His interests and His glory. Hence we bind ourselves to afford Him all the joy, consolation and honour we are capable of, on the one hand, by doing everything with this intention and in such a way as to effectively procure them for Him, by the love, generosity and perfection with which we act, in other words, by our personal sanctity; on the other hand, by promoting His interests, by making His Sacred Heart known and loved by others so far as we can; in other words, by our apostolate.[1]

By the consecration, therefore, we pledge ourselves towards the Heart of Jesus to lead a life of entire dependence, trustful self-surrender and absolute devotedness. Once consecrated we are no longer allowed in anything to follow our own will, to seek our proper satisfaction, but in all things we are to consult and follow the will of Jesus, to seek His satisfaction and to promote His interests. Our watchword becomes: Nothing for me, all for the Sacred Heart!

[1] See chap. iii, § ii, n. 5, the apostolate of the Sacred Heart.

Such a life implies a complete and continual self-denial. It is then to this life of self-denial that we engage ourselves, in order to belong entirely to the Heart of Jesus and to live henceforth only for Him.[1]

Our Lord's Desire

The Sacred Heart Itself asked this consecration of Its friends. Pope Pius XI states it explicitly in his Encyclical *Miserentissimus* (n. 8): 'Our Saviour made known to the loving disciple of His Heart His eager desire that this homage (the consecration) should be rendered to Him by men, not so much in virtue of His right as by reason of His boundless love for us.'

Many passages of the writings of the Saint give evidence to it. Whenever she recommends this pious practice, she reminds us of our Lord's desire, or points out that it is something very agreeable to the Sacred Heart. 'If you have not yet done so,' she writes, for instance, to Mother de Saumaise, 'you will, by consecrating yourself and offering yourself to the Sacred Heart, do an act very pleasing to God.'[2]

The Saint was the first to comply with the wish of our Lord. 'After Holy Communion,' she writes, 'He asked me to renew to Him the sacrifice I had already made of my liberty and of all my being. Which I did with all my heart.'[3]

Sometimes this consecration was asked of her in some peculiar form. The most original is the donation by testament whereby, at the request of our Lord, she appointed the Sacred Heart 'heir of all that she might be able to do and to suffer, and of all the prayers and spiritual goods which would be performed for her in her life-time and after her death'.[4] This testamentary disposition is dated December 31st, 1678. In return for this donation our Lord appointed her 'heiress of the treasures of His Sacred Heart'.[5]

She asked this consecration of all the friends of the Sacred

---

[1] Cf. Vermeersch, op. cit., vol. I, § i, art. i. Another sort of consecration is to be found in the booklet, *My Personal Consecration to the Sacred Heart of Jesus*, by F. Alcaniz, s.j., in which the author sets forth the contract proposed by the Sacred Heart to the Ven. B. de Hoyos, s.j., the first apostle of this devotion in Spain: 'Take you care of My honour and of what concerns Me, and My Heart will concern Itself about you and whatever concerns you.' (On P. de Hoyos, see J. B. Couderc, s.j., *Le vénérable Bernard-François de Hoyos, S.J.*; and Hamon, op. cit., vol. IV, p. 173 and seq.)

[2] *Vie et Oeuvres*, vol. II, *Lettre à la Mère de Saumaise*, 24 août 1685, p. 297.

[3] Ibid., vol. I, n. 121, p. 119.

[4] Ibid., n. 150, p. 172. Cf. *Autobiography*, n. 84, p. 95.

[5] Ibid., n. 152, p. 173.

Heart. Blessed Claude de la Colombière did it without delay and frequently repeated it.[1] Of the feast of the Sacred Heart, observed for the first time, July 20th, 1685, at Paray-le-Monial, by the novices of the Saint, the consecration was the principal part. 'She read aloud to us,' we are told, 'a form of consecration composed by herself in honour of this Divine Heart and she invited each one of us to write our consecration.'[2]

Motives

What are the motives which must move us to make the consecration?

First and foremost, our Lord's desire. As we have seen, the Sacred Heart wishes Its friends to give themselves entirely to Him, to consecrate themselves to Him.

Then, the beauty and excellence of this act. It is the most generous and most perfect act of love towards the Sacred Heart, for we give Him everything.

Furthermore, the decisive influence which the consecration may have on our spiritual life and will really have if we make it with all our heart. The remembrance of it will be an incentive and efficacious help in the aspiration to perfection. 'Such an engagement is a turning-point in our spiritual life, the starting-point of a life of pure love and of effective aspiration to sanctity. It causes us to become, in Bl. Claude de la Colombière's words, "a new product of God's love".'[3]

It is, moreover, the special claim which the consecration confers on us to the love, liberality, protection, help and blessings of the Sacred Heart. Jesus does not suffer Himself to be surpassed in generosity.

Finally, the magnificent promises made by the Sacred Heart to all those who will give Him this great token of love. 'Sister Margaret Mary,' witnessed Sister de la Faige at the process of beatification, 'had no greater pleasure than to speak of God and the establishment of the devotion to the Heart of Jesus, by recalling the great graces which He bestowed on those who consecrated themselves to Him.'[4] 'I cannot believe,' writes the Saint in one of

---

[1] That he should have first done it on June 21st, 1675, as some writers assert, is not certain. (See Guitton, s.j., *Le Bienheureux Claude la Colombière*, pp. 266–69.)
[2] Hamon, op. cit., vol. I, p. 350.
[3] Vermeersch, op. cit., vol. I, p. 12.
[4] *Vie et Oeuvres*, vol. I, p. 548.

her letters, 'that persons consecrated to this sacred Heart should perish or should fall under the dominion of Satan by mortal sin.'[1] And in another place: 'Our Lord made known to me that He would impart many graces when they should have consecrated themselves to the devotion and love of His Sacred Heart.'[2] Again: 'He reveals to me treasures of love and graces on behalf of those who consecrate and sacrifice themselves in order to procure for Him all the honour, love and glory in their power.'[3] Nor does she hesitate to state that 'there is no shorter way to attain to perfection, nor a more secure means of salvation, than to be entirely consecrated to this Divine Heart, in order to render to Him all possible homage of love, honour and praise'.[4]

Yet the consecration presupposes an ardent love for the Sacred Heart, a great generosity and a firm resolution, for it obliges us, as we have said, to a life of entire abnegation. We should not pass on to it if this threefold condition is not fulfilled. As long as we do not feel generous enough to accept, to the full and decidedly, this life of continual abnegation, our consecration is to be deferred; in the meantime we will endeavour to acquire the requisite dispositions, by meditating on the motives for making the consecration, and especially by asking the Sacred Heart for an efficacious grace that makes an end of our hesitation and moves us to take on us those bonds of love.[5]

In the meantime we may, if we wish, consecrate ourselves to the Sacred Heart in a more or less restricted measure, for instance, by engaging ourselves to accomplish His holy Will in all things, as far as He commands or forbids, in other words, to keep His commandments. But whatever this restriction may be, it is necessary that in some respect we give everything to Jesus, that we want to belong to Him completely. If then our engagement is confined to observing His commandments, it should at least be extended to all that He commands, to all that He forbids, even in the smallest things. And it should be inspired by love. We are to give ourselves out of love; we are to submit to the Sacred Heart not so much because He has a right to our submission as because He is deserving of it by His love; not constrained by force, but freely; because we love Jesus and are happy to have Him for our Master.

[1] *Vie et Oeuvres*, vol. II, *Lettre à la Mère de Soudeilles*, 15 septembre 1686, p. 328.
[2] Ibid., vol. I, *Procédure de 1715*, p. 535.
[3] Ibid., vol. II, *Lettre à la Mère de Saumaise*, mai 1688, p. 396.
[4] Ibid., vol. II, *Lettre à son frère*, p. 344.   [5] Cf. Vermeersch, op. cit., vol. I, p. 22.

Choice of the Day

Yet if we are firmly resolved to accept all the obligations which the consecration involves and faithfully to fulfil them with God's never-failing grace, we shall do well to choose for this act a day which by its own sanctity will enhance the solemnity of this self-consecration. The particularly suitable day for it is the Feast of the Sacred Heart, or of Christ the King. Another day which lends itself excellently to the purpose is the first Friday of the month. The choice of this day was recommended by St. Margaret Mary.[1] 'You will then offer Him this sacrifice of yourself,' she writes to Mother de Soudeilles, 'on a first Friday of the month, after Communion made with that intention, by consecrating yourself to Him . . .'[2] We may perhaps prefer to connect our consecration with the annual retreat, which we shall then direct to this act, perhaps decisive for our spiritual life.

Form of Consecration

Though the consecration is an act of the will, we shall do well to express it orally, and even to write it. St. Margaret Mary wrote hers, and signed it with her blood.

What form is to be used for this purpose? The best would surely be that which each one composed for himself, in accordance with his personal dispositions and the inspirations of grace, for in this way he would understand better the precise significance of the terms used and would find in it a more faithful echo of his sentiments.

On the other hand, by taking a form of consecration which has the approval of the Church and the sanctity of its maker to recommend it, it will remind us of the generous fidelity with which this chosen soul has been able to keep his engagement, and we shall feel stimulated to imitate it.[3]

---

[1] It should be noted that the Feast of the Sacred Heart was not yet instituted at the time.

[2] *Vie et Oeuvres*, vol. II, p. 282.

[3] It should be noted that the 'Morning Offering' suggested by the *Apostleship of Prayer*, earnestly performed and faithfully observed, is a true self-consecration to the Sacred Heart, and even one of the most efficacious, while at the same time very simple. (Cf. appendix n. II, III, p. 264.) This opinion is confirmed by the testimony of Pope Benedict XV who, in his address to the directors of the *Apostleship of Prayer*, June 22nd, 1919, stated: 'The first degree of the Apostleship of Prayer consists in consecrating daily to the Sacred Heart all that we have. In this way, by means of the Apostleship of Prayer, we shall lead a life of consecration, as life in the main consists of a series of days.' (Cf. *Messager du Cœur de Jésus*, 1919, p. 491.)

Renewal and Self-examination

We will endeavour to preserve the memory of our consecration and will do all in our power to remain in the dispositions which inspired it. To this end it will be useful frequently to renew it.

St. Margaret Mary recommended this earnestly: 'The Sacred Heart of Jesus,' she writes, 'takes a particular pleasure in your frequently renewing this consecration.' She even advised its renewal every day: 'In the morning,' she said to her novices, 'you are to enter the Sacred Heart of Jesus, in order to pay to It your homage of adoration and self-sacrifice, and to offer to It all that you will do and suffer, and all the parts of your being, to be used only to love, honour and glorify It.'[1] And as though she deemed it not yet sufficient, she suggested habitually to wear the consecration in order to preserve more easily the memory of it, and to renew it, as it were, at every moment: 'I send you,' she wrote among others to an Ursuline Sister, 'a small consecration, that you may wear it on your breast together with an image.'[2]

Finally, it is to be recommended to examine ourselves from time to time about our fidelity to our consecration, not only during our annual retreat but also every month on the day of recollection. It would even be excellent to do so every night, and to ask ourselves: 'Can I sincerely assert that I have acted at every hour of this day like a truly consecrated soul? If, at this moment, Our Lord opened to me His Heart, should I see written in It all the actions, all the words, all the thoughts and all the affections of this day?' And then let us pass them in review, one by one, and listen in our inmost heart to the divine answer.

(b) The Consecration of Families

Its Origin

There is no text of the writings of St. Margaret Mary which allows us to conclude or even conjecture that the Consecration of Families was asked for by our Lord, neither was it propagated or recommended by the Saint.

Yet it is connected with the promises which Jesus made to her on behalf of those who practised devotion to His Heart. 'The Sacred Heart of our Lord,' she writes to one of her former Superiors, 'promised me that not one of those who dedicated

---

[1] *Vie et Oeuvres*, vol. II, *Défis et instructions*, p. 766.
[2] Ibid., *Lettre à une Ursuline*, p. 508.

themselves to this sacred Heart would ever perish and that, as It is the source of all blessings, It would abundantly pour them forth *wherever* the image of this lovable Heart should be exposed, in order to be loved and honoured; that, by this means, It would reunite *families* divided by discord, and assist and protect those that would be in any need, and that It would shed the sweet unction of Its ardent charity on all *communities* in which this divine image should be honoured . . .'[1]

Although the Consecration of Families properly so called does not go back to the Saint, it is certain that she herself practised and promoted a similar collective consecration, namely, that of religious communities. On the first private feast, celebrated in 1685 at Paray-le-Monial, in honour of the Sacred Heart, she consecrated both herself and all her novices to the Heart of Jesus.[2] In her writings is to be found such an act of collective consecration on behalf of her novices.[3] And in her letters to Superiors of other Visitation convents we see how she urges them on to consecrate their communities to the Sacred Heart.[4]

Its Nature

In what does the Consecration of Families to the Sacred Heart consist?

To consecrate oneself to the Sacred Heart is, as we have seen,[5] to give oneself up to It, in order to belong entirely to It and to live only for It. The consecration of the family, then, is an act whereby a family gives itself to the Sacred Heart of Jesus and devotes itself to His service, in order to live henceforth for Him alone and to accomplish in all things His holy will.

Yet we may look upon the Sacred Heart from a peculiar point of view, and devote ourselves to Him, for instance, as to our Redeemer, our Benefactor, our Friend, our King, etc. In the Consecration of Families, as commonly practised nowadays by the faithful, the Sacred Heart is preferably considered as our King.

The consecration of the family, then, is an act whereby a family devotes itself to the Sacred Heart as to its King, recognizes It as

---

[1] *Vie et Oeuvres*, vol. II, *Lettre à la Mère de Saumaise*, 24 août 1685, p. 296.
[2] Hamon, op. cit., vol. I, pp. 349–50.
[3] *Vie et Oeuvres*, vol. II, *Prières*, iii, p. 780.
[4] Ibid., vol. II, *Lettre à la Mère de Soudeilles*, 4 juillet 1686, p. 324.
[5] See p. 121.

its King, and promises to make It reign and rule over the whole family life.[1]

In the form of consecration already suggested in 1882 by the great organizer of the Apostleship of Prayer, Fr. Ramière, s.j., we read: 'Deign to accept, *O Divine King*, . . . the consecration which we make of our family to thy sacred Heart. May this Heart take absolute possession of our persons, our lives, our interests in time and eternity . . .'[2]

And the form, prescribed by Pope Pius XI for gaining the indulgence, begins as follows: 'Sacred Heart of Jesus, Who didst manifest to St. Margaret Mary the desire of *reigning* in Christian Families, we today wish *to proclaim Thy most complete regal dominion over our own*.'

Hence the consecration includes a twofold element: an act of the intellect whereby the head of the household recognizes the right of the Sacred Heart to rule over his family, and an act of the will whereby he submits both himself and his whole family to the dominion of the Sacred Heart.

Its Foundation

The consecration is founded on the royal power of Jesus, on His right to rule over us.[3] His dominion is extended not only to all individuals but also to all associations formed by them, and in the first place the family. 'The whole of mankind,' wrotes Pope Pius XI in his Encyclical *Quas primas*, 'is subject to the power of Jesus Christ. Nor is there any difference in this matter between the individual and the family or the State; for all men, whether individually or collectively, are under the dominion of Christ.' Besides, it is God Himself who has willed that men form families; these then are God's work, and hence belong to Him. They must therefore, as well as individuals, recognize this sovereignty of God and Christ, and submit to it.

But this sovereignty of Christ we may recognize and submit to, not so much because we must, as because we are willing to do so; not so much from duty, as from love; not so much because Jesus has a strict right to it, as because on account of His love and His benefits He deserves that we should give ourselves up to Him and

---

[1] Cf. Calot, s.j., *Oeuvre de la Consécration des familles*, p. 12.
[2] Cf. *Messager du Cœur de Jésus*, 1922, p. 357.
[3] See p. 107–10.

M

cause Him to rule over us; in short, we may recognize His dominion and submit to it because He is our loving and loved King.[1]

It is in this way that the consecration is understood in the devotion to the Sacred Heart. Families consecrate themselves to the Sacred Heart as to their loving and loved King. And Jesus is worthy of it in the highest degree, because of the priceless gifts and graces for which the family is indebted to His love. Did He not restore to marriage its indissolubility, which ensures the stability of the family? Did He not elevate marriage to the dignity of a Sacrament, and does He not give to husband and wife, by means of this Sacrament, grace and strength for their faithful discharge of the duties of the married state, bearing more courageously its burden, and attaining more perfectly its end? Did He not abolish the bondage of woman and make her queen of the home? Did He not inculcate respect for childhood? Did He not sanctify the family, by his willingness to form part of a family which set the example of all domestic virtues?

Its Consequences

Families, by their consecration, pay honour to the Sacred Heart, and give It a magnificent homage of love. But they contract moreover a real obligation, namely, to allow the Sacred Heart to rule over them.

What does this mean?

To allow the Sacred Heart to reign is, in the first place, to accomplish His explicit will, to keep His commandments and the precepts of His Church, and to discharge the duties of one's state of life. It is, moreover, to avoid whatever displeases the Sacred Heart or threatens to destroy Its dominion in the home, thus not only what is positively contrary to faith and morals, but also what is merely dangerous, in the matter of pictures, books, newspapers, conversations, friends, etc.

This is a minimum without which there can be no question of a true dominion of the Sacred Heart. All this, families, desirous of consecrating themselves to It, are bound to promise if their consecration is not to be a vain ceremony, a senseless formula, but is to have its true significance and to be performed as it is desired by the Church.

[1] See p. 110.

But a full dominion of the Sacred Heart of Jesus requires more. To allow Him to reign to the full is also to comply with His wishes.

It is therefore to cause His Spirit to reign in the home, a spirit of detachment from earthly goods, of mortification and abnegation.

It is also to imitate the virtues of which He set the example and which vividly shone forth in the Family at Nazareth.

It is finally to cultivate devotion in the home and to promote its practice: night prayers in common, grace before and after meals, if possible daily assistance at Holy Mass, frequent Communion, devotion to the Sacred Heart.

In particular, in consecrated families the picture of the Sacred Heart will occupy a place of honour in the drawing-room in order to show to visitors that the Sacred Heart is King of this home. It will remain exposed in the living-room in order to remind the members of the family of their consecration, and to form the centre of the whole family life. This image will be adorned with flowers and candles; before it night prayers will be recited, as far as possible, in common; it will be greeted respectfully whenever one enters or leaves the room; to this image one will lift hopeful and entreating eyes when aid, strength, courage or consolation are needed; and heartfelt thanks will be offered to it whenever the grace asked for is obtained, whenever one feels happy; in short, all will avail themselves of this image to consider in practice the Sacred Heart as their beloved King, who is at the same time their great Friend and their kind and powerful Protector.

Thus the whole family life is to be brought into harmony with the consecration; it must bear its visible mark. According to the word of Pope Benedict XV the consecrated families are 'to live up' to their consecration. 'What we want to insist on,' he said in 1919 to the directors of the Apostleship of Prayer, 'is that the consecrated families are "to live their consecration". Who does not know that this consecration should not consist in a mere passing manifestation of Christian life? It is, on the contrary, to be the principle of a series of acts suitable to show that the home consecrated to the Divine Heart has become the abode of faith, charity, zeal in prayer, order and domestic tranquillity. The old should find strength, the young prudence, the afflicted comfort, the infirm patience in the Sacred Heart of Jesus. Let mothers and fathers of families, distressed with care and anxious for their welfare, cast their sufferings and worries upon the Sacred Heart. If they wish to do all this thoroughly, is it not obvious that such families should assemble frequently on their knees before the image of the Sacred Heart, and pray there that they may be aided by Divine grace to bear their misfortunes and to learn Christian virtue? These practices of piety, this love of virtue, this ever-watchful desire to spend day and night under the eyes of Jesus— —all this constitutes *the life* of Consecration to the Sacred Heart.'[1]

Its Spread

To the Apostleship of Prayer is due the honour of having been the first to propagate and promote the Consecration of Families. Its idea was set forth for the first time, in 1882, in a letter addressed by Fr. Wibaux, s.j., to Fr. Ramière, the director-general of the Apostleship of Prayer, who published it in the *Messager du Cœur de Jésus*. In consequence of this article ten thousand families consecrated themselves, from 1882 to 1886, in Marseilles alone.[2]

A few years later, in 1889, the Apostleship of Prayer addressed a call to the faithful of the whole world, urgently inviting them to pay to the Sacred Heart this homage of veneration, love and reparation. 'To establish the reign of the Sacred Heart in the bosom of the family,' it reads, 'is to prepare and inaugurate Its triumph in civil society; and the day on which all families are officially consecrated to the adorable Heart of Jesus, Its public reign in the State will be close by, or even have already begun.' At the same time the form in which the Consecration was to be made was indicated, and it was asked that the names of the consecrated families should be inscribed in costly albums which were to be sent to the sanctuaries of Montmartre or Paray-le-Monial, to be deposited there at the foot of the statue of the Sacred Heart. The picture of the Sacred Heart circulated on that occasion represented Jesus sitting on a throne and crowned with a diadem, while a poem by Fr. Delaporte, s.j., proclaimed the rights of Christ the King.

This call met with an enthusiastic acceptance everywhere. It was signed and propagated by many prelates. Pope Leo XIII

---

[1] Address of Pope Benedict XV to the directors of the Apostleship of Prayer, June 22nd, 1919.
[2] Calot, op. cit., p. 41, and *Messager du Cœur de Jésus*, 1882.

himself twice invited the faithful of the whole world to subscribe to the formula. It was said in it: 'In order to hasten in our dear country the reign of Thy adorable Heart, O Jesus, we consecrate, under the protection of the Immaculate Heart of Mary and under the patronage of St. Joseph, our whole family.'

The success was phenomenal. More than a million families, from all nations of the world, responded to the petition and solemnly consecrated themselves to the Sacred Heart. Their names fill forty-two volumes, the so-called 'Golden Books of the Sacred Heart'.[1]

This took place in 1889. Since then the Work of the Consecration of Families has become a section of the Apostleship of Prayer, which through its organ *The Messenger of the Sacred Heart*, and by means of its promoters, continues to recommend and inculcate the Consecration.

The Enthronement

The movement rapidly spread abroad during the world war of 1914–18, especially owing to the unflagging zeal of Fr. Mateo who gave the consecration a new form, with a special ceremonial which he propagated under the name of Enthronement.[2]

His purpose was to emphasize the significance of the consecration as a solemn and practical recognition of the royal dominion of the Sacred Heart over the Family, and deeply to inculcate it in the hearts of the members of the family. To this end he preceded the consecration properly so called by a ceremony which symbolically represented its significance: the picture or statue of the Sacred Heart was to be placed as on a throne, and to be exposed

---

[1] Cf. Calot, op. cit., pp. 51–55.

[2] Fr. Mateo Crawley-Boevey, born at Arequipa in Peru, on September 8th, 1875, was a priest of the Congregation of the Sacred Hearts of Jesus and Mary (called Picpus). In 1907, sent by his Superiors to Europe for the benefit of his health, he felt cured of his illness as he was praying in the chapel of the apparitions at Paray-le-Monial. On the evening of the same day, whilst making the Holy Hour, it seemed to him that our Lord charged him with the mission of conquering the whole world, family by family, for the Sacred Heart; at the same time he clearly perceived the whole plan of the Work of the Enthronement. Encouraged by Pope Pius X, he undertook a true crusade to make the Sacred Heart honoured everywhere as King of the home, and thus to prepare Its social reign throughout the world. In a few years' time the Work was flourishing in most countries of South America. In 1914 Fr. Mateo travelled through Europe, preaching with extraordinary success. Pope Benedict XV wrote to him in 1915 a remarkable letter, in which he set forth the bearing and purpose of the consecration, and at the same time gave a warning against the danger of making it a mere transient ceremony. (*Acta Apost. Sedis*, 1915, pp. 203–5.) See also Hamon, op. cit., vol. v, pp. 297–304.

there in order to remind the members of the family, and to make known to visitors, that the family had consecrated itself to the Sacred Heart as to its King. This symbolical ceremony was to be carried out with great solemnity, if possible in the presence of a priest who would previously bless the picture. To the consecration which was made in this way, Fr. Mateo preferred to give the name of 'enthronement' in order to manifest that by the consecration the Sacred Heart had been installed as King of the home.

Thus the Enthronement is a peculiar form of the Consecration. It consists in the installation of the Sacred Heart as King of the family, in the solemn and effective recognition of Its dominion. This takes place in two ways: first, symbolically, by exposing the statue or picture of the Sacred Heart on a throne; then, explicitly, by the consecration properly so called. Pope Benedict XV, in his Letter to Fr. Mateo, defines it as follows: 'His image being exposed in the place of honour of the home as on a throne, Christ our Lord really seems to reign in the homes of Catholics.'[1]

Thus in the Enthronement the Consecration properly so called is the essential thing; the rest is only a means of emphasizing the significance of the Consecration, and of engraving it in all hearts.

To propagate it more efficaciously and to confirm its beneficial results, Fr. Mateo founded the Work of the Enthronement, which has its own secretaries and periodicals in several countries, and which endeavours to prepare, through the Enthronement, the social reign of the Sacred Heart.

Both 'the Work of the Consecration of Families', patronized by the Apostleship of Prayer, and 'the Work of the Enthronement', established by Fr. Mateo, are recognized and approved by the Holy See, and work side by side. For Italy, however, there exists a special arrangement: Pope Benedict XV, by rescript of May 10th, 1918, committed the direction of the Italian movement to the Apostleship of Prayer.[2]

Aim and Purpose

The immediate and direct aim of the consecration is to make the home more Christian, to cause a really Christian spirit to reign there, to cultivate in it all domestic virtues, and to sanctify it.

'*The Apostleship of Prayer*,' says Pope Pius XI, 'intends to make

---

[1] *Acta Apost. Sedis*, 1915, p. 203.
[2] *Acta Apost. Sedis*, 1918, p. 298. Cf. Calot, op. cit., p. 90.

the home a *sanctuary* from which the fragrance of Christian purity ascends; a family, formed after the pattern of the Family of Jesus, Mary and Joseph,'[1]

'By the enthronement,' writes Fr. Mateo, 'we wish to implant in the family not only an exercise of piety, but a strong love and *a truly Christian life*, which is its natural outcome.'[2]

This is the more important, as the enemies of Christ and His Church are bent on drawing away from God the whole human society, and try to attain their end by dissolving families and estranging them from God.

There is also an indirect or remote end, namely, to prepare the social reign of Jesus, to cause Him gradually to rule over human society.

'Several times,' said Pope Benedict XV in 1919 to the directors of the Apostleship of Prayer, 'We have declared that We wish to see the social reign of Jesus Christ recognized by all; yet as society is composed of families, the consecration of these is the most efficacious *means of extending and propagating this social reign*, which We earnestly desire.'[3]

'What is more comforting,' said Pope Pius XI in his turn on a similar occasion, 'than to see that the *Apostleship of Prayer* has made it its task to consecrate the family to the Sacred Heart, in order to make of it a small kingdom, which will extend itself and unite the whole human race?'[4]

'The Enthronement,' says the Catechism of the Enthronement, 'strives to establish the reign of the Divine Heart in the family, in order to prepare in this way *the social reign* of our Saviour; to cause Him to rule over the whole of society.'

In fact, the day on which Jesus reigns in all families, He will immediately become King of society, and will be recognized, revered, honoured and obeyed by the whole people in all the manifestations of social life.

The Popes' Recommendation

The consecration of families was on several occasions approved

---

[1] Address of Pius XI to the directors of the Apostleship of Prayer, December 3rd, 1922.
[2] *Circulaire pour 1922* by Fr. Mateo.
[3] Address of Benedict XV, June 22nd, 1919. See *Messager du Cœur de Jésus*, 1919. p. 491.
[4] Address of December 3rd, 1922, to the directors of the Apostleship of Prayer.

and recommended by successive Sovereign Pontiffs, yet by none so insistently as by Benedict XV.

In his Letter to Fr. Mateo he stated: 'We read with pleasure your letter and the enclosed writings, whereby We learned to know the zeal and ability with which for several years already you have exerted yourself to promote the consecration of families to the Sacred Heart of Jesus . . . The success of your labour has gone beyond expectation: We rejoice at it and *exhort you assiduously to continue* your undertaking.'[1]

In the solemn session, held on January 6th, 1918, for the approbation of the miracles presented for the canonization of Margaret Mary, he said: 'In a particular degree and with sentiments of the most lively gratitude *We praise God for the marvellous extension* of the Work of the Consecration of Families to the Sacred Heart. Oh! if all families would consecrate themselves to the Divine Heart, and if all would discharge the duties attached to such a consecration, the social reign of Jesus Christ would be assured.'[2]

A few days later, January 14th, he wrote: '*We desire* that Christian families should solemnly consecrate themselves to the Divine Heart of Jesus, and beforehand We bless all and each one of them, who in this way contribute to the social recognition of the dominion of love of the Sacred Heart of Jesus in Christian families.'[3]

Again (February 27th): 'To all those who labour in the centra and secretariates of the Work (of the Consecration of Families) We impart the Apostolic Benediction, and *We wish* that success may crown their efforts.'[4]

In his address to the directors and promoters of the Apostleship of Prayer he stated: 'We are resolved to *patronize, encourage* and as it were *make our own* the Work of the Consecration of Families to the Sacred Heart of Jesus . . . It is our most earnest desire that the Work should everywhere become better known and adopted, and that the Christian families should lead lives of Consecration.'[5]

His successor, Pius XI, showed himself no less favourable to the Work of the Consecration, as witness the fact that he invited the members of the Apostleship to pray and offer their actions and sufferings during a whole month for the propagation of the Consecration.[6]

---

[1] *Acta Apost. Sedis*, 1915, p. 203.   [2] See *Messager du Cœur de Jésus*, 1918, p. 112.
[3] Ibid., p. 168.   [4] Ibid., p. 169.
[5] See *Messager du Cœur de Jésus*, 1919, p. 491.
[6] Intention of the Pope for the month of March, 1924.

Fruits of the Consecration

What fruits are to be expected from the Consecration?

Firstly, the Consecration will be for the family an excellent means of sanctification. Supported by the thought of being the object of special love on the part of the Sacred Heart, stimulated by the memory of Its promise, and strengthened by the graces which the Sacred Heart will lavishly pour forth on it, the hope may be cherished that the consecrated family will apply itself faithfully to observe our Lord's precepts concerning family life and to imitate as perfectly as possible the virtues of the ideal Family, the holy Family of Nazareth.

Moreover, the Consecration will be for it a source of blessings. The Sacred Heart promised it. 'Our Lord promised me,' writes the Saint to one of her former Superiors, 'that all who consecrate and dedicate themselves to His Sacred Heart *will never perish*; and as He is the source of all blessings, He will lavishly pour them forth wherever the image of this lovable Heart is exposed and honoured; and that by this means He will *reunite* families whose members are at variance among themselves and that He will *protect and assist* those in need. He will shed the sweet unction of His ardent love on every community in which this Divine image is honoured.'[1] What then will He not do for families consecrated to Him?

Lastly, the reign of the Sacred Heart in the home will preserve and keep alive the mutual affection of husband and wife, by teaching them and facilitating reciprocal forbearance; it will maintain and increase attachment to the home; restore to the authority of father and mother its sacred character; renew among all members of the family that spirit of affectionate devotedness which remains with them even after infancy and childhood, and ensures the lasting union of all. Where the Sacred Heart reigns there also reigns concord and peace. Is not this the greatest of all blessings for a family?

Ceremonial of the Consecration

At first, not for the validity of the Consecration but in order to gain the indulgences attached to this ceremony, this should be carried out by means of a priest. Yet as appears from an answer of the Holy See, the Bishop may decide under what circumstances

[1] *Vie et Oeuvres*, vol. II, *Lettre à la Mère de Saumaise*, 24 août 1685, p. 296.

the presence of a priest is not required, provided the picture of the Sacred Heart should have been previously blessed by him.[1]

Although the Consecration may be performed in the way and in the terms each one prefers, the observation of the ceremonial is to be recommended, and the use of the forms approved by the Church and the efficacy of which has been proved by experience.[2]

It is desirable that the Consecration should be carried out with all possible splendour in order to make it a really royal homage to the Sacred Heart and to intensify its impression on the minds of the persons present. It will be well to choose a day which will enhance the solemnity of this act, for instance, the feast of the Sacred Heart, or that of Christ the King, a first Friday of the month, or a family feast, such as a solemn First Communion, a birthday, etc. Finally, it is to be recommended that a priest should say Mass that day for the spiritual and temporal welfare of the family, and for the extension of the reign of the Sacred Heart, or at least let the family assist at Mass and receive Holy Communion for these intentions.

Renewal of the Consecration

To confirm and maintain the impression and beneficial influence of the Consecration on the family life it will be very helpful to renew it from time to time. Its solemn renewal, at least once a year, preferably on the anniversary of the Consecration, should never be omitted. If there is no opportunity to do it on that day, then the feast of the Sacred Heart, or that of Christ the King, may be suitable for the purpose. The best thing would be, in accordance with the wish of Pope Benedict XV, to renew it each day when reciting the night prayers in the presence of all the members of the family gathered around the statue or picture of the Sacred Heart.[3]

[1] *Acta Apost. Sedis*, 1918, pp. 155–56.   [2] For the ceremonial of the 'Enthronement' apply to the office of the Work of the Enthronement.

[3] *Indulgences*. The following indulgences are granted to those who publicly consecrate their homes to the Sacred Heart: An indulgence of seven years to each member of the family who with contrite heart assists at the above ceremony of the Consecration of the Family on the day on which it is carried out. A plenary indulgence or the same day to each member of the family who, in addition to assisting at the ceremony, having been to Confession and received Holy Communion, visits any church or public oratory and there prays for the Pope's intentions. (*Acta Apost. Sedis*, July, 1915.) A plenary indulgence to the members of the family on whatever day each year they renew, before the image of the Sacred Heart, the Act of Consecration. Moreover, three hundred days' indulgence for each individual renewal of the Act of Consecration before the image of the Sacred Heart in their own homes. (*Acta Apost. Sedis*, July, 1915.) Cf. *Preces et pia opera*, n. 655.

(c) The Consecration of Municipalities

As we have seen, the royal dominion of Jesus is extended to all associations formed by men. Thus the Sacred Heart has a right to be recognized and honoured by them as their King, and hence also deserves that all should consecrate themselves to Him. This applies in particular to religious communities, schools, parishes and dioceses. It also applies to cities and villages.[1]

A special reason pleads on behalf of the Consecration of Municipalities. As, taken all together, they form the nation, their consecration is, still more than that of families, a preparation for the social reign of the Sacred Heart and even a beginning of its realization.

For that twofold reason the faithful began, especially after the world war of 1914–18, to consecrate towns and villages to the Sacred Heart.

But, like the personal consecration and the consecration of families, that of municipalities is neither a mere homage paid to the Sacred Heart nor an act whereby the municipality especially places itself under Its protection. It is a true engagement whereby the municipality solemnly promises to cause the Sacred Heart to rule over it. The consecration, then, involves obligations.

In a consecrated municipality the population assumes the obligation to do what lies in its power to make this reign of the Sacred Heart ever more effective and more general. It is the duty of the municipality to be guided in its decisions by Christian principles, to do whatever it can, within the bounds of the law, to promote the Christian life in the district, to extirpate abuses, to maintain public morality, to assure the Christian education of the children, etc.

(d) The Consecration of Nations

Jesus is the King of all nations, too. This we know through Faith. Holy Scripture says: 'For in that He (God) hath subjected all things to Him (Christ), He left *nothing* not subject to Him' (Heb. ii, 8). Nothing, and therefore not the nations either.

Jesus Himself declared, when He was about to return to His Father: '*All power* is given to Me in Heaven and on earth' (Matt. xxviii, 18). All power, and hence also power over all nations. And

---

[1] See several instances of acts of social consecration in Ramière, s.j., *Le Règne social du Cœur de Jésus*, 1892, pp. 617–34.

He added: 'Going therefore, teach ye all nations; . . . teaching them to observe all things whatsoever I have commanded you.' Hence, not only individuals, but also nations, as such, are subject to Him.

This is easy to understand; for He who is the master of all the parts of a whole is evidently also the master of the whole. Now Christ, as we have seen, is the Lord and King of all men, and of all the associations by which nations are formed. He is therefore the Lord and King of all nations.

Moreover, it is God who put into men the propensity to join on to other men, to group themselves and form nations. Thus nations, too, are the work of God, and belong to God. Therefore God, and hence Christ, is their Master, Lord and King.

All nations, and in the first place those who rule and represent them, are bound to recognize this dominion and to submit to it.

But this they can do, in the same way as individuals, families and other associations, not so much because they must, as because they are willing; not so much from a sense of duty as for love; not so much because Christ has a right to demand it as because He is deserving of it on account of His love, and they think themselves fortunate to be allowed to submit to His love.

It is in this that the Consecration of Nations consists. It is therefore an act whereby nations solemnly recognize Jesus for their loving and loved King, and proclaim that they are willing to submit, for love, to His dominion.

Just as in the case of individuals, families and other associations, this Consecration involves real obligations.

The government pledges itself to revere and honour Christ the King, by respectfully pronouncing, and ensuring, respect for His Name; by honouring His cross and image; by participating in ceremonies which take place in His honour; and by acting with deference towards His representatives and ministers. It engages itself to obey in all things Christ the King, by bringing its laws into accordance with His, particularly in the matter of marriage, divorce, the day of rest, property, etc. It pledges itself to serve Christ the King, by being watchful of His interests and promoting His cause, by assisting the Church to the best of its ability, in the accomplishment of her Divine mission; by contributing to the establishment and extension of the reign of Christ.

The citizens, on their part, engage themselves to follow their government in all this, to observe its prescriptions, and to do what they can to make the supreme dominion of Jesus ever more general and more effective.

It belongs to the government to carry out the Consecration in the name of the population. This is, of course, only possible in countries where the population is, in its entirety or by a great majority, sincerely and deeply believing, and firmly resolved faithfully to observe its Consecration.

Several countries consecrated themselves in this way to the Sacred Heart. The Consecration of Ireland was made on Passion Sunday, 1873. The example set by the Republic of Ecuador (1873), on the proposal of its president Garcia Moreno, was followed by the Republic of San Salvador (1874), by Venezuela (1900), Colombia (1902), Spain (1919), Nicaragua (1920), Poland (1920), Costa Rica (1921), Brazil (1922) and Bolivia (1925).

(e) The Consecration of Mankind

During the Vatican Council (1869–70), Fr. Ramière, s.j., submitted to the Bishops present in Rome a request whereby the Holy Father was asked to raise the Feast of the Sacred Heart to the highest rite of the liturgy and, at the same time, to consecrate the whole Church to the Sacred Heart. The request was already supported by two hundred and seventy-two Bishops when the Franco-German war broke out and the Council was adjourned.

Meanwhile the action in favour of the Consecration was carried on, and in a short time several millions of signatures were collected. In 1874, at the approach of the second centenary of the Great Apparition, Mgr. Deprez, Archbishop of Toulouse, at the request of Fr. Ramière, sent to all the Bishops of the world a letter to which a new petition was joined, which sought to obtain that the Pope might consecrate the human race itself to the Sacred Heart. In April 1875, Fr. Ramière presented to the Holy Father the petition signed by five hundred and twenty-five Bishops. 'I shall do what you want,' answered the Sovereign Pontiff, 'but in my own way . . .' In January of the same year, Fr. Chevalier, Superior-General of the Missionaries of the Sacred Heart, had already handed to the Holy Father thirty volumes, which contained the signatures of sixty Bishops and three millions of Catholics, begging the Pope to consecrate them to the Heart of Jesus.

On April 22nd a decree of the Sacred Congregation of Rites

was issued, inviting and urging all the faithful solemnly to consecrate themselves to the Sacred Heart on June 16th, the probable date of the Great Apparition. The Sacred Congregation presented at the same time a form, which was approved by the Sovereign Pontiff, who granted a Plenary Indulgence to all those who recited it on the appointed day. Fr. Ramière, by a special favour, was charged with communicating to all the Bishops of the world both the decree and the form of Consecration.

Thus the Pope preferred not to prescribe anything, but only clearly to show his desire that the whole Church should pay this homage of honour and love to the Sacred Heart. The faithful enthusiastically complied with the wish; the Consecration took place most solemnly on June 16th in all the churches of the world. The Pope himself made it in his private chapel. It was a really triumphal day for the Sacred Heart.[1]

The Consecration of 1899

The Consecration of 1875, however, was not yet the official Consecration of the human race or of the Church. Complying with the invitation of Pope Pius IX, the faithful, dioceses and nations, desirous thus to manifest their devotion, had spontaneously consecrated themselves to the Sacred Heart, every one for himself; this consecration, then, concerned only themselves, not the human race nor the Church at large.

The official Consecration of mankind did not take place until 1899 by Pope Leo XIII. It was owing to the earnest entreaties of a religious, Mother Mary of the Divine Heart, Countess Droste zu Vischering, Superior of the Good Shepherd convent at Porto, Portugal, that the Sovereign Pontiff resolved to carry out this great act, which he himself called 'the most important act of his Pontificate'.

He proclaimed this Consecration in the Encyclical *Annum sacrum* of May 25th, 1899, and on June 11th he consecrated the human race to the Sacred Heart. Throughout the world the faithful, united with their supreme Pastor, solemnly ratified the Consecration, every one for himself.[2]

Since then, by order of Pope Pius X (decree of August 22nd,

---

[1] Cf. Hamon, op. cit., vol. v, pp. 77–83; Bainvel, op. cit., pp. 533–36; and Friedrich, op. cit., pp. 206–9.

[2] See Hamon, op. cit., vol. v, pp. 180–88; Bainvel, op. cit., pp. 536–43; Friedrich, op. cit., pp. 209–13; Le Chasle, *Sœur Marie du divin Cœur*, chap. xi.

1906), this Consecration has been renewed every year in all churches on the Feast of the Sacred Heart. In 1928 it was a little modified, then transferred by Pope Pius XI to the Feast of Christ the King, and replaced on the Feast of the Sacred Heart by a solemn Act of Reparation.[1]

II. DEVOTION TO THE SACRED PASSION

(a) The Sacred Heart Wishes Us to Practise It

The Death of Jesus is, as we have seen, the greatest proof He gave us of His love. Hence it is obvious that devotion to His Sacred Passion is to be one of the chief practices of devotion to His Sacred Heart.

Moreover our Lord Himself has clearly shown it.

He repeatedly appeared to St. Margaret Mary in a state which recalled His Passion, now covered with wounds, torn by the bloody scourging,[2] now as the *Ecce Homo* with the crown of thorns on His head,[3] or laden with the cross.[4] And in the second apparition the Heart of Jesus was presented to her 'with that adorable wound; surrounded with a crown of thorns; surmounted by a cross'.

He also imparted to her an intimate knowledge of the mystery of His Passion. Among the great graces which she received from Him during a retreat, 'whilst she was watching a she-ass with her foal in the garden', she numbered 'what He made known to her about the mystery of His sacred Passion and Death'.[5] Concerning His agony in the Garden in particular, He said to her: 'Here it is that I suffered more than in all the rest of My Passion, seeing Myself entirely abandoned by Heaven and earth, and laden with all the sins of men. I appeared before the holiness of God who, regardless of My innocence, crushed Me in His wrath, causing Me to drink the chalice which contained all the bitterness of His just indignation; and as though He had forgotten the name of Father, He sacrificed Me to His righteous anger. No creature is able to understand the violence of the tortures which I then suffered.'[6]

---

[1] Cf. Encyclical *Quas primas* of December 11th, 1925.
[2] *Vie et Oeuvres*, vol. I, p. 68; and vol. II, p. 41.
[3] Ibid., vol. I, p. 64; and vol. II, p. 34.
[4] Ibid., vol. I, p. 64; and n. 216, p. 196; and vol. II, pp. 34 and 116.
[5] Ibid., vol. I, pp. 88–89; and vol. II, pp. 66–67.
[6] Ibid., vol. I, p. 283; and vol. II, pp. 66–67.

Moreover, our Lord taught her or asked her for certain practices in honour of His Passion.

'On a Friday,' she writes, 'during Holy Mass I felt an intense desire to honour the sufferings of my crucified Spouse. He lovingly said to me that He wished me to come every Friday and to adore Him thirty-three times on the wood of the cross, which is the throne of His mercy, lowly prostrate at His feet, where I was to try to remain in the same dispositions in which the Blessed Virgin was during His Passion, offering them to the Eternal Father together with the sufferings of her Divine Son, in order to beg of Him the conversion of all hardened and unfaithful hearts, which resist the inspirations of His grace. To those who will be faithful to this practice He will be merciful at the hour of death.'[1]

In the third apparition, after asking the Saint to make up for the ingratitude of men, especially by a Communion of reparation on the first Friday of each month, Jesus continued as follows: 'Every night, between Thursday and Friday, I will make you partaker of that sorrow unto death which it was My will to suffer in the Garden of Olives. This sorrow will reduce you, without your understanding how, to a kind of agony more bitter than death. To join with Me in the humble prayer which I then offered to My Heavenly Father you shall rise between eleven and twelve, and remain with Me prostrate for an hour, with your face to the ground, to appease the anger of My Heavenly Father, and to ask of Him pardon for sinners. You will thus also share with Me, and in a manner soothe, the bitter grief I suffered when My disciples abandoned Me and I was constrained to reproach them that they could not watch with Me one hour. During that hour you shall do what I will teach you.' This is the exercise which is known under the name of the 'Holy Hour'. We shall expound it at length when we treat of the practice of Reparation.

A practice which our Lord had taught her for the time of a Jubilee Year, and to which she remained greatly attached, was 'to offer to the Eternal Father the superabundant propitiation which He made to His justice on the wood of the cross on behalf of sinners, praying Him to apply to all criminal souls the merit of His precious Blood.'[2]

---

[1] *Vie et Oeuvres*, vol. I, p. 116.
[2] Ibid., vol. I, *Mémoire des Contemporaines*, n. 95, p. 106; and vol. II, *Ecrits par ordre de la Mère de Saumaise*, n. 23, p. 145.

The Saint had composed in the form of a litany, for personal use, a series of invocations in honour of the Sacred Passion of Jesus. It is to be found in the booklet written with her own hand, in which she had assembled all sorts of prayers and pious exercises, nearly all referring to the Sacred Heart.[1]

She nowhere mentions the Way of the Cross, but this too must surely have been one of her favourite practices. Her sisters in Religion, moreover, noted that the Saint, laden with a heavy cross, sometimes held a penitential procession together with her novices in the garden of the convent. Besides, we know for certain that she spent the whole of Lent in contemplating our suffering and dying Saviour. In her writings we find many other exercises in which devotion to the Sacred Heart and devotion to the Sacred Passion are closely associated.

(b) How We Are to Practise It

True devotion to the Sacred Heart, then, necessarily implies an earnest devotion to the Passion of our Saviour.

We shall like to meditate on this Passion, and in our meditations we shall preferably dwell on Christ's interior Passion: on what He suffered in His soul and in His Heart.

We shall consider with deep sympathy that the Divine Sufferer is a man like ourselves, sensitive to whatever we ourselves are sensitive; we shall reflect with astonishment that He is innocent, Innocence, Sanctity itself, the Son of the living God; we shall remember with shame and sorrow that He suffered all this through our fault, because of our sins; we shall recollect with boundless gratitude that He endured all this for our sakes, in our place, to save us; finally, we shall lovingly remember that He chose to suffer all this for love of us.

We will therefore say to Him how much we compassionate Him, how much we admire Him, how much we regret it all, how much we are grateful to Him, and how much we love Him in return. We will say to Him that, since He deigned to suffer and to die for us, we wish to live henceforth for Him only, in order to love Him and to cause Him to be loved.

Finally, following the example of St. Margaret Mary, we will readily and often perform some exercise or other in honour of the

---

[1] *Vie et Oeuvres*, vol. II, p. 784. This litany is to be found in Yenveux, *Le règne du Cœur de Jésus*, vol. II, p. 248.

Sacred Passion: the Way of the Cross, the Litany of the Sacred Passion, the Holy Hour, etc.

III. DEVOTION TO THE BLESSED EUCHARIST

To devotion to the Blessed Eucharist, as well as to devotion to the Sacred Passion of Jesus, is due a prominent place in devotion to the Sacred Heart. The former must go together with the latter, and should even be one of its special practices. Without devotion to the Eucharist there is no true devotion to the Sacred Heart. The latter is essentially eucharistic.

(a) It is Most Fitting that We Practise It

Firstly, if the Death of Jesus is the greatest token of love He gave us, the Eucharist is the masterpiece, the miracle of His love.

By the Eucharist He wished, in His love for us, to dwell among us, to renew at every moment the Sacrifice of the Cross, and even to come into us and intimately unite Himself with each one of us. He thus afforded us the most precious advantages.[1] To be able to bestow on us those tokens of love and to provide us with those favours, He did not shrink from working the most stupendous miracles, making the greatest sacrifices, and exposing Himself to the most grievous outrages; and although, in instituting the Eucharist, He foresaw the base ingratitude with which men would repay His love, He did not renounce His loving designs.

Hence it is evident that devotion to the Eucharist must be one of the chief practices of devotion to the Heart of Jesus. For this Heart is the living symbol and the principle of the love which induced Jesus to institute the Eucharist.[2]

Furthermore, the Eucharist contains the Heart of Jesus.

It is supremely fit and proper, and moreover very natural, that we should consider and honour the object of the devotion to the Sacred Heart there, where it is really present. Now, where is this object to be found?

We should not forget: this object is not the image of the Heart of Jesus, but this Heart itself. Surely, the cult of the image is one of the forms, one of the practices of the Devotion.[3] But the image is not its object. We do not honour it by itself, but because of the Heart of Jesus represented by it. It is this Heart that we wish to honour in the image; it is to this Heart that our homage is addressed; it is this Heart which is the object of the Devotion.

[1] See p. 62.   [2] See p. 25.   [3] See chap. iii, § iii, n. 2, p. 195.

Well, then, where do we find the Heart of Jesus? In the Eucharist. The Heart of Jesus is there, veiled, hidden it is true, but really present. It is there, not as a mere relic, but living; not separate from the Body of Jesus, but united with His entire human nature and His Divine Person; not become insensible, but still loving us as It loved us during His mortal life and remaining sensible to our love as of old.

Hence it is there, in the Eucharist, that we are to consider and honour the Heart of Jesus.

No doubt, since the Ascension, the Heart of Jesus is also in Heaven, where It is glorified and enjoys the beatific vision of God. Hence it is expedient that we also contemplate and honour It as It is living in Heaven.

But we should preferably do so in the Eucharist.

First, because it is precisely His love that prompted Jesus to institute the Eucharist.

Next, because the Eucharist eminently facilitates the practice of devotion to the Sacred Heart. Heaven seems to be so far off; the Eucharist, on the contrary, is close by; for it is there, where the consecrated Host is, and there is also the Sacred Heart. Thus when we are in a church we may say, in turning our eyes to the Tabernacle: 'The Heart of Jesus is there!' When at the moment of the Consecration the priest elevates the Sacred Host, we may say: 'The Heart of Jesus is there!' When in Communion we receive the Sacred Host, we may say: 'The Heart of Jesus is within me, and reposes in my heart.' Who does not see that the presence of the Heart of Jesus in the Eucharist particularly facilitates the practice of devotion to the Sacred Heart?

Finally, it is in the Eucharist that the Heart of Jesus is most exposed to the outrages of men. It is to the outrages there inflicted on It, and to the conduct of men towards His Sacrament of Love, that It showed Itself most sensible;[1] it is for these outrages and that conduct, that It asked for reparation and amends, a reparation chiefly consisting in practices of devotion to the Eucharist.[2] This consideration, however, refers to the Reparation. We shall return to it when we treat of this form of devotion to the Sacred Heart.

Thus devotion to the Blessed Eucharist not only must characterize devotion to the Sacred Heart but constitutes one of its principal practices.

[1] See p. xxvi.   [2] Ibid.

(b) *The Sacred Heart Wishes Us to Practice It*

Our Lord manifested, moreover, His desire that both devotions should be associated.

He showed it, firstly, by the connection He made between His apparitions and the Eucharist. It is most striking that almost all the apparitions regarding the devotion to the Sacred Heart took place at the Communion table or close by the Tabernacle. Again and again the account of those apparitions begins in the same way: 'One day, while I was before the Blessed Sacrament . . . Once, particularly, when the Blessed Sacrament was exposed . . . One day, after Holy Communion . . . On a Friday, after I had received Our Lord . . . Once, whilst preparing myself for Holy Communion . . .'[1] May and must we not say that this circumstance, recurring again and again, is not to be considered fortuitous, but that it is intended by our Lord, and intended with a special aim and purpose? And what may have been this purpose if not to draw our attention to His presence in the Eucharist and at the same time to manifest His desire to see His Heart specially honoured in the Sacrament of His love?

Moreover, He explicitly manifested this desire: 'I thirst with an ardent desire to be loved by men in the Blessed Sacrament, so as to be consumed by this thirst,' He said to St. Margaret Mary, 'and I find none who strives, in accordance with My wish, to quench this thirst, by making any return of love.'[2]

In particular, He wishes us frequently to visit Him in the Blessed Sacrament. He longs for it, as a friend longs for the visit of his friend; He longs for it in order to enjoy our presence, to see that we appreciate the honour and pleasure of enjoying His company and that we are sensible to the love He shows us in the Eucharist; in order to be able to converse with us, and to hear us say that we are grateful to Him, that we love Him, that we give ourselves up to Him, and that we are willing to work for Him. But He also desires it on account of the good which these visits do us, in order to be able to load us with His gifts and graces, to enlighten, advise, encourage and strengthen us.[3]

He also wishes us frequently to assist at the holy Sacrifice of the Mass. He desires it in order to enjoy the pleasure of seeing that

---

[1] See, for instance, in the Introduction the narrative of the great apparitions.
[2] *Vie et Oeuvres*, vol. II, *4e Lettre au P. Croiset*, November 3rd, 1689, p. 580.
[3] See p. 63.

we appreciate the honour and opportunity of being present at the most august, holiest and most important action in the world, the mystical renewal of His bloody Sacrifice; and that we are grateful to Him for the priceless benefit of the Redemption, which cost Him such great sacrifices and so many sufferings. But He also desires it because of the precious spiritual goods which assistance at Mass procures for us, by providing us with the means of offering to God an infinite adoration, an infinite thanksgiving for the favours for which we are indebted to Him, an infinite satisfaction for our sins and for the punishment we have deserved by them, and a supplication of infinite value, which can obtain for us all graces.[1]

Finally, He wishes us frequently to receive Him in Communion. He desires it in order to enjoy the pleasure of reposing in our hearts, of closely uniting Himself with us and making us live by His life. He also desires it to enable us to enjoy all the advantages of this union, that we may enjoy the pleasure of possessing Him in our hearts, that our souls may be fed with His Divine Body and derive from this Divine food an increase of supernatural life, of charity, of courage and strength to do good; that our hearts may gradually be transformed into His Heart, and that our bodies may be prepared for a glorious resurrection.[2]

Finally, Our Lord manifested His desire that both devotions should be joined, by inspiring a great devotion to the Holy Eucharist into her to whom He revealed devotion to His Heart and at the same time the way of practising it.

Already before she received these revelations, the saint felt attracted towards the tabernacle with a force which concentrated upon the Eucharistic Christ all her thoughts, all her affections, her whole life. But after Jesus had shown her His Heart, living and loving under the veil of the Host, she only lived as it were in the Blessed Sacrament. She often repeated that 'she wished to part no more from the Heart of her God and from the God of her heart'.

She spent before the Tabernacle all the time at her disposal;[3] on feasts and Sundays almost the whole day.[4] Her interior recollection was as a living testimony to our Lord's real Presence.[5]

Her love for the Blessed Sacrament must necessarily produce and maintain in her an ardent desire of Holy Communion. This

---

[1] See p. 63.
[2] See p. 64.
[3] *Vie et Oeuvres*, t. i, *Procédure de 1715*.
[4] Ibid.
[5] Ibid.

desire became to her a true torture. In order to have the good fortune to communicate no sacrifice seemed to her too great. Though she was often ill she did her utmost not to break her fast.[1] Hence we understand that no greater penitence could be imposed on her than to deprive her of Holy Communion.[2]

As regards the Holy Sacrifice of the Mass she envied with saintly jealousy the priests for the honour they had of offering it.[3] Nor could priests afford her greater pleasure than by promising her to say Mass for her intentions.[4] And to anyone whom she wanted to show her affection, she believed she could not give a present of greater value than one of the masses which were said for her.[5] She was particularly happy when she heard that someone had had a Mass said in honour of the Sacred Heart.[6]

(c) How We Are to Practise It

If we love the Sacred Heart we shall cultivate an earnest devotion to His Sacrament of Love. If we want to practise devotion to the Sacred Heart as asked for by Jesus, we shall pay honour to His Heart especially in the Blessed Eucharist.

We shall be eager to assist at Holy Mass, because of the honour it procures for God, because of the love shown to us in it by the Sacred Heart, and because of the precious gifts and graces it bestows on us.[7] We shall endeavour to attend it with the feelings which would have animated us if we had been present at the death of Jesus, or still better, with the sentiments of His Blessed Mother and His beloved disciple at the foot of the cross. We shall assist at it with the greatest exterior reverence. St. Margaret Mary did so herself; she even remained on her knees on the bare ground, however cold it might be. We shall exert ourselves to arouse in our hearts the most earnest sentiments of reverence, gratitude and love, while we unite ourselves with the Heart of Jesus and offer our sentiments to God.

We shall like in particular to offer the Holy Sacrifice in honour of the Sacred Heart. How is this to be understood? Not as though it were offered to the Sacred Heart; for we cannot offer the Sacred Heart to Itself; the Sacrifice is offered to God. No doubt, Jesus is God, and hence, strictly speaking, the Mass is offered to Jesus as God, just as it is offered to the Father and the Holy Ghost. But

---

[1] Ibid., p. 103, n. 90.
[2] Ibid., t. II, p. 111, n. 103.
[3] *Vie et Oeuvres*, p. 608.
[4] Ibid., pp. 618 and 622.
[5] Ibid., p. 433.
[6] Ibid., p. 452.
[7] See p. 64.

in devotion to the Sacred Heart we consider Jesus especially in His Humanity. Besides, the Sacrifice is usually looked upon as offered to God the Father. Therefore, the Holy Sacrifice is not offered to the Sacred Heart but in Its honour, to pay honour to It.

How are we able to honour the Sacred Heart by the offering of Holy Mass? Particularly in three ways.

First, by offering it to God in thanksgiving for having given us the Sacred Heart, for having made It so kind and merciful, for having filled It with compassion and love for us, and for having inspired in It all the gifts and graces which we owe to Its love; in thanksgiving, moreover, to God for all the perfections with which He has endowed and adorned It, as well as for all the glory, power and blessedness He has conferred on It.

Next, by offering Mass in order to obtain that the Sacred Heart may be better known and more ardently loved and that Its reign may be extended abroad ever more; to gain that we ourselves may honour, rejoice and console It increasingly by our care to avoid whatever may displease It, by our generosity in doing all that is agreeable to It, and by our zeal in making It known and loved by others.

Finally, by offering Mass in a spirit of reparation, to compensate the Sacred Heart for the conduct of men towards the Eucharist, and particularly towards Holy Mass.

Furthermore, let us often join in spirit with all the Masses which are celebrated throughout the world. St. Margaret Mary regretted that she could assist at only one Mass every day. To make up for it in some way, she joined in spirit several times a day with all the Masses which were celebrated at the moment; and she recommended this practice to others, too.[1]

We shall also be eager to receive our Lord in Holy Communion.

We shall desire to communicate in order to give Jesus the pleasure of coming into us, of uniting Himself to us, and to feed us with His Divine life, in accordance with His wish. We shall communicate in order to have the eminent honour of receiving within us the Son of God, God Himself; to have the incomparable good fortune of welcoming within us our great Friend who so loved us as to die for us; to have the priceless advantage of

---

[1] *Vie et Oeuvres*, vol. II, p. 736.

receiving within us the Source of all graces, who desires nothing so much as to pour them forth into our souls. We shall communicate in order to feed ourselves with His Divine life, to maintain and increase our supernatural life, our spiritual strength, the ardour and efficacy of our love: in short, to show to Jesus our love and to make it increase more and more.

Holy Communion, then, ought to be primarily an exercise of love. Hence, in order to communicate well, there is no need to have recourse to all sorts of methods; we need only think of the love which our Lord shows us in the Eucharist, and of the love He expects in return; we need only say that we believe in His love, that we are sensitive to it, that we love Him and are desirous to love Him still more, and that for that very reason we want to receive Him in our hearts.

Yet let us beware of seeking in Communion only the sweetness of our sentiments of love, and of contenting ourselves with them. What we are to derive from it first and foremost is the vigour of love, its efficacy, its abnegation and generosity. On our coming back from the Holy Table we should return home with more love than in going to it, and more united with God; firmly resolved to be more attentive and docile to the inspirations of grace, to watch better over our senses, our imagination, our affections and our words; more strenuous in combating our passions and inordinate inclinations; more forgetful of self, more charitable towards our fellow-men, more patient in supporting their failings, more courageous in bearing our crosses, more generous in making the sacrifices which God asks of us, more zealous for His cause and for promoting His interests. For all this is nothing else than love; love translated into action. It is this effective love which is the true aim and purpose of Holy Communion. We go to the source of love that we may be able to discharge more faithfully and more perfectly the duties of Christian life, which is to be a life of love. We feed ourselves with the God of love, that we may act in all things always more perfectly, out of love and according to love.[1]

Therefore when we have received Jesus in Holy Communion, we shall adore Him with the deepest reverence, and tell Him how grateful we are for His unbounded kindness and incomprehensible love; how happy we are to be allowed to press Him to our hearts, to possess Him within us and to be, so to speak, one with Him;

---

[1] Cf. Grou, s.j., *Méditations sur l'amour de Dieu*, p. 124.

how much we love Him and long to love Him for ever. We shall offer Him the homage of adoration, thanksgiving, and the tokens of love of all souls that love Him on earth, and of all the Saints and Angels in Heaven. We shall tell Him of our desire that He may be known, honoured and loved as He deserves. Let us ask Him that He may inflame our hearts with love for Him and with zeal for His interests; that He may cause us to live by His life, and impart to us His thoughts, sentiments and aims, thus making us resemble Him and transforming us into Him. We shall offer Him all that we are and have, that He may be the uncontested Master of it and that it may really be He who lives in us.

Finally, we shall be eager to visit the Sacred Heart in Its Sacrament of Love.

We shall go to Him as to our King, in order to pay Him our homage; we shall go to Him as to our Advocate, to ask Him to plead on our behalf; we shall go to Him as to our Mediator, to offer through Him to God our adoration, thanksgiving, satisfactions and supplications; as to our Priest, to unite ourselves with His acts of adoration, His thanksgiving, His satisfactions, and His supplications, and to offer them to God; as to our Benefactor, to return our thanks for all the favours we owe Him; as to our Protector, to implore His help and succour in our needs and dangers; as to our Confidant, to entrust to Him our cares, our worries and sorrows; as to our Counsellor, to pray Him for light and advice in our doubts, hesitations and perplexities; as to our Physician, to lay open to Him our diseases and infirmities, and to entreat Him to cure them; and finally as to our Friend, to express to Him our love, to keep Him company and rejoice Him by our presence.

We will go to Him with a lively faith, for He who is present in the Tabernacle is Jesus, living as He is in Heaven; with a profound reverence, for He is the Son of God; with an unbounded confidence, for He is there for our sakes, to receive us, to listen to us, to bestow on us His gifts and graces; finally with an ardent love, for it is out of love for us that He chose to become present in the Sacred Host at the cost of the greatest sacrifices and the greatest miracles. This love we can only repay with a return of love.

We have seen that St. Margaret Mary used to spend all the time at her disposal before the Blessed Sacrament. Yet this was not enough for her love; one may say that in spirit she continually remained near the Tabernacle. Without a special grace it is impossible for us, in the midst of our occupations, thus to keep the actual thought of the Tabernacle. We can, however, multiply our spiritual visits to the Blessed Sacrament, now and then converse with the Divine Prisoner, as though we were close by Him. We should do so as often as we can; the Saint recommended this practice as very agreeable to the Sacred Heart and as very beneficial for our spiritual life.[1]

IV. THE IMITATION OF THE HEART OF JESUS

(a) Motives

Jesus wishes us to imitate Him. 'I have given you an example,' He said to His Apostles, after He had washed their feet, 'that as I have done to you so you do also' (John xiii, 15). At each action of His mortal life He seems to say to us too: 'If I set you this example, it is that you may imitate it. If I have been humble, poor, obedient, and meek; if I have disdained human glory and earthly joys and preferred sufferings and scorn; if I have pardoned My enemies, it is in order to urge you to do the same.' And one of the reasons why He chose to become man and to be like unto us, was to show us the way to Heaven; to teach us, to encourage and strengthen us by His example, and thus to facilitate for us the practice of all virtues.

He wishes us to imitate Him because it is the will of His Father that we should resemble Him. 'For whom He foreknew, He also predestined to be conformable to the image of His Son' (Rom. vii, 29).

He also desires it because He loves us. When we love anyone, it is a pleasure for us to discover in him some points of resemblance; to see that he thinks, desires and feels as we do; and we wish him to endeavour to resemble us more and more. Jesus loves us, and hence He necessarily desires us to apply ourselves to imitating Him as perfectly as possible.

If then we love Jesus, we shall comply with His wish. Besides, for him who loves, it is a necessity to make himself as conformable as possible to the person loved. Attracted by his qualities, he wishes to reproduce them in himself. He feels that true friendship

---

[1] Cf. Froment, *La véritable dévotion au Sacré-Cœur de Jésus*, Book III, chap. iv, n. 8; and Yenveux, op. cit., vol. II, p. 230.

could not exist without uniformity in thoughts, sentiments and aspirations, and he imitates them as it were instinctively. It is the same with our love for Jesus. If this love is real, it will of necessity induce us to be eager to resemble Him as perfectly as possible; we shall exert ourselves to the utmost to imitate Him.

Thus without imitation, there is no true love, and without imitation of the Heart of Jesus there is no true devotion to the Sacred Heart.

It is in this way that this devotion was understood by St. Margaret Mary. 'When I spoke to you of devotion to the Sacred Heart of Jesus,' she wrote to a Sister, 'I meant a devotion of perfect conformity to His holy virtues rather than of prayer only.'[1] And to another: 'Don't waste time on always looking out for new means to your perfection. Remember that yours entirely consists in conforming your life and your actions to the holy maxims of the sacred Heart of Jesus, especially His meekness, His humility and charity.'[2] Again: 'Since love conforms lovers, if we love, let us conform our lives to the pattern of His life.'[3]

(b) Its Practice

If then we wish to practise devotion to the Sacred Heart properly, and in accordance with our Lord's desire, we shall exert ourselves to make our hearts as conformable as possible to His Heart.

1. His Sentiments

We will first of all make ours the sentiments of His Heart.

We will love what He loves, His Heavenly Father, His Blessed Mother, the Angels, the Saints, His Church, the souls in Purgatory, and all men, especially children, the poor and the distressed; we will also love all that is good, noble and pure.

We will detest whatever He abhors, that is every sin; every vice, and especially pride and haughtiness, the world and its spirit, its maxims, its allurements and its scandals.

We will appreciate whatever He esteems, the supernatural treasures, graces, virtues and sanctity; we will despise whatever He despises, earthly goods, worldly glory, honours and sensual pleasures.

We will desire all that He desires, all that may promote the

---

[1] *Vie et Oeuvres*, vol. II, *Lettre à la Sœur de Thélis*, p. 372.
[2] Ibid., vol. II, *Avis particuliers*, n. 18, p. 667.
[3] Ibid., *Lettre à la Sœur Morant*, p. 227.

glory of God, the extension of His reign, and the salvation of souls.[1]

We will rejoice at whatever gladdens Him, whatever contributes to the realization of His wishes: the conversion of heathen, unbelievers and sinners: the prosperity of Catholic enterprises; the devotion of the faithful; the magnificent demonstrations of faith and piety which take place here and there; the homage that is paid to Holy Church, to the Sovereign Pontiff, etc.

Finally, we will be grieved at whatever afflicts Him, or at least would afflict Him if He were still accessible to sorrow, namely, sin, the loss of souls, all that is inconsistent with His wishes, and hence whatever might hinder the glorification of His Heavenly Father, the extension of His reign, and the salvation of souls.

2. His Virtues

We will also cultivate in our hearts the virtues of His Heart.

Jesus possessed all virtues in the highest degree, and practised them to perfection. Some of them, however, shone forth in Him with a peculiar splendour. Such are love for His Heavenly Father, conformity to the will of God, the spirit of prayer, humility, obedience, love for men, kindness, meekness, zeal for the glory of God and the salvation of souls.

Yet as there is no lack of books which treat of these virtues, we think it is useless to enter into all the particulars of the example of them which Jesus set us and of our way of imitating them.[2]

3. The Conditions in Which He was Willing to Live

But if we really love Jesus, we shall not content ourselves with sharing His sentiments and imitating the virtues of His Heart; we shall want to live, in so far as we can, among the conditions in which He Himself was pleased to live.

---

[1] See p. 118.

[2] There are many books which treat of the virtues and the imitation of Jesus. One of the best is unquestionably that by the Flemish Jesuit Fr. J. P. Aernoudt who, under his Latin name Arnoldus, wrote in Latin *De Imitatione Sacri Cordis Jesu*. The author was born in 1811. He arrived in the United States in 1835, and died in 1865 at Cincinnati in the odour of sanctity after a successful apostolate in the States. His manuscript, sent to Rome for censorship, remained for fifteen years in the drawers of the then Superior-General, Fr. Roothaan; it was found by chance by his successor, Fr. Beckx, who ordered the work to be edited in 1863, shortly before the author's death.

The following are also recommended: Boussac, s.j., *Les vertus du Cœur de Jésus*; F. Nepveu, s.j., *Retraite sur Notre Seigneur Jésus-Christ*; J. Grou, s.j., *L'intérieur de Jésus et de Marie*; and *Retraite spirituelle sur la connaissance et l'amour de Notre Seigneur Jésus-Christ*; Godfroy, s.j., *Mois du Sacré-Cœur de Jésus*.

What were these conditions? His life was, as we know, a life of poverty and privation, trouble and suffering, humiliation and scorn. Nor does the author of the Imitation of Christ exaggerate when he writes: 'Not even Our Lord was ever one hour without suffering so long as He lived. His whole life was a cross and a martyrdom' (ii, 12). And those privations, humiliations and sufferings He loved, not for themselves it is true, as they were not lovable in themselves, but because they glorified His father and saved us.

There have been countless generous souls who, prompted by their love for Jesus, wished to resemble Him and passionately loved and even eagerly sought poverty, sufferings and humiliations.

So was St. Francis of Assisi, who took Poverty for his 'spouse', and remained heroically faithful to her even to his death.

So was St. Ignatius of Loyola who, whilst imprisoned in the dungeon of the Inquisition under suspicion of heresy, assured those who commiserated him, that all the affronts and outrages inflicted on him, would not slake his thirst for suffering for the sake of Jesus.

So was St. Francis Xavier who, when a moment's respite was given him in his suffering, used to say: 'O my Jesus, I find it hard not to suffer!'

So was St. John of the Cross who, asked by Jesus what reward he wished on earth for all that he had done for His glory, answered: 'To be allowed to suffer, O Lord, and to be despised for Thee!'

So was St. Angela of Foligno, to whom Jesus offered two crowns, one of roses and the other of thorns, and who eagerly took from His hands the crown of thorns and pressed it on her head.

So was St. Theresa of Avila, who could not resign herself to live without sufferings and incessantly repeated: 'Either to suffer or to die!'

So was St. Magdalen of Pazzi, who wanted to live on in order to be able to suffer, and said over and over again: 'Not to die, but to suffer!'

And so also St. Margaret Mary, was prompted by her love for Jesus and her eager desire of resembling Him, passionately to love poverty, sufferings and humiliations. There are many passages in her writings in which she shows this love. We choose some of them.

'If you only knew,' she writes to her former Superior, 'how my

Divine Master urges me on to love Him with a love of conformity to His life of suffering!'[1] And in another place: 'He gave me such an intense desire of sharing His life of suffering, that all I had to endure seemed to me to be nothing.'[2] 'I should have wished to find myself forsaken by all creatures, in order to be conformable to my crucified Love.'[3] To Fr. Croiset: 'Ask for me the same grace, that it may make us true copies of our crucified Love . . .'[4] And to a Sister: 'Ask Him to grant me the grace, according to the great desire He gives me for it, to live and to die with Him on the cross, poor, unknown, forgotten and scorned by all creatures.[5] Again to Fr. Croiset: 'The more I suffer, the more I long for suffering.'[6] Again: 'Contempt, poverty, afflictions and humiliations are the delicious viands with which Jesus continually feeds my soul, which has no relish for anything else. For my only pleasure in this exile is to have no other than that which is to be found in the cross, and to be deprived of any other consolation than that of the Sacred Heart . . .'[7]

The Superiors, Sisters and directors of the Saint, vouched for it that these were really her sentiments and that her whole life was in keeping with them.

'The said venerable Servant of God much loved poverty; she retrenched all superfluities, sought the hardest works in a spirit of poverty; . . . she refused herself, even in her sicknesses, every alleviation of her pain, as she considered herself a poor person; and as soon as she was a little better, she set to work again in order to earn, she said, her livelihood.'[8]

'She rejoiced in being scorned; she submitted to all, enduring with great meekness the outrages and insults offered to her. She was hungry for humiliations, and said that she never had enough of them.'[9] 'From this ardent love of Jesus Christ proceeded the sentiments which she had for contempt and for all sorts of sufferings, which she used to call her delicious bread.'[10] 'Her love for pain and suffering was insatiable; she chose with St. Theresa

---

[1] *Vie et Oeuvres*, vol. II, *Lettre à la Mère de Saumaise*, p. 244.
[2] Ibid., vol. II, *Autobiographie*, n. 29, p. 50.
[3] Ibid., vol. II, *Ecrits par ordre de la Mère de Saumaise*, n. 31, p. 150.
[4] Ibid., vol. II, *5e Lettre au P. Croiset*, p. 591.
[5] Ibid., vol. II, *Lettre à la Sœur de la Barge*, p. 409, note.
[6] Ibid., vol. II, *6e Lettre au P. Croiset*, p. 594.
[7] Ibid., vol. II, *4e Lettre au P. Croiset*, p. 570. See also pp. 247, 261, 588.
[8] Ibid., vol. I, *Procédure de 1715*, p. 471.
[9] Ibid., vol. I, p. 470.
[10] Ibid., vol. I, *Circulaire du monastère de Paray*, p. 575.

"either to suffer or to die"; she said to me that she would be willing to live till the judgment-day, provided she would always have to suffer something for God; but that to live one day without it, would be to her unbearable.'[1] 'She edified all her Sisters by her patience in accepting the rebukes and sharp taunts she had often to endure on account of her devotion.'[2] 'In her sicknesses she showed an extraordinary joy, assuring all that her pleasure in this life was to suffer, in order to keep company with the Sacred Heart expiring on the cross.'[3]

Without the aid of a more than ordinary grace we are unable to imitate or to equal the heroism of these loving and generous souls. Our Love for Jesus, however, would not be sincere, or would not be ardent, at least, if we did not want to resemble Him, to some extent, as regards the conditions in which He lived; if we too did not love poverty, suffering and humiliation. If then we experience any effect of poverty, if sickness and suffering afflict us, if we undergo any humiliation, we shall accept them not only with resignation, but even cheerfully, in order to have one more point of resemblance to Jesus. The more we love Jesus, the more we shall cherish poverty, suffering and humiliation, as He did.

Is it fitting to go further, and expressly to ask God to send us sufferings? With Fr. De Smedt, s.j., we answer: 'As a rule, no. For these petitions easily give rise to self-delusion and often betray a lack of humility. They are made in moments of sensible fervour, but when these have passed, if God, in order to renew the soul in the spirit of humility, seems to gratify in some sort such unconsidered wishes, the poor soul feels herself too weak to carry out the heroic acts of submission and resignation, upon which she was so firmly resolved in imagination. Hence arise severe temptations to despondency and dismay, and even to murmuring against Divine Providence; a kind of reproach addressed to God, which sometimes, objectively speaking, may be blasphemous; this is the cause of much trouble to the directors of those souls. Spiritual directors, therefore, should not permit such requests for suffering until they have ascertained the reality of a special vocation; as a rule, only long practice in conformity to the will of God in unsolicited trials will warrant this experiment.'[4]

---

[1] *Vie et Oeuvres*, vol. I, *Mémoire de la Mère Greyfié*, p. 357; and *Mémoire des Contemporaines*, n. 212, p. 193.
[2] Ibid., vol. I, *Procédure de 1715*, p. 512.   [3] Ibid., vol. I, p. 525.
[4] De Smedt ,s.j., *Notre vie surnaturelle*, vol. II, § iii, pp. 251–52.

V. THE APOSTOLATE OF THE HEART OF JESUS

(a) *In what It Consists*

If we love the Heart of Jesus, we shall take His interests to heart, and we shall do all in our power to promote them and to comply with His wishes. If we failed to do so, our love would not be genuine and true. What are these wishes?

As we have seen, Jesus wishes, in general, whatever promotes the glory of His Heavenly Father and the salvation of souls.[1] In a broad sense we may say that in working for the realization of those wishes we are apostles of the Sacred Heart. In the strict sense of the word, however, this expression means devoting ourselves to what the Sacred Heart of Jesus wishes directly for Himself, namely, that the devotion to His Divine Heart may spread ever more widely and be practised more perfectly, and that the reign of His Heart may be established more fully in the hearts of individuals, in families, and in public life. It is in working for the realization of these desires of Jesus, that, properly speaking, the apostolate of His Sacred Heart consists.

(b) *Why We Are to Practise It*

That Jesus desires and expects this apostolate of His friends is evident. It is, moreover, in keeping with the general system of salvation which demands men's co-operation for the propagation of the Faith and the salvation of souls. In like manner God desires our co-operation for the spread of the devotion to the Heart of Jesus and for the extension of the reign of the Sacred Heart.

Furthermore, this clearly appears from the magnificent promises which Jesus made to St. Margaret Mary on behalf of the apostles of His Heart. The most important are:

Their name shall be for ever written in His Heart: 'He showed me how many persons have their names written in His sacred Heart, by reason of their desire to bring others to honour Him, and how for that reason He will never allow their names to be effaced from His Divine Heart.'[2] Again: 'There were some whose names were written in golden letters in the Sacred Heart . . .;

---

[1] See p. 118.
[2] *Vie et Oeuvres*, vol. II, *Lettre à la Mère de Soudeilles*, 1687, p. 381.

the names of those who worked most for making It known and loved.'[1]

The Sacred Heart will give them great rewards: 'The Divine Heart has such an ardent desire to be known, loved and honoured by men, in whose hearts It wishes to establish by this means the reign of Its pure love, that It promises great rewards to all those who employ themselves in making It reign.'[2] 'As for those who employ themselves in making It known and loved, oh! that I could find words to tell of the rewards that they will receive from this lovable Heart. You would say with me: Happy, indeed, are those whom It will employ in the carrying out of Its designs.'[3] Again: 'The Sacred Heart of our good Master will not let your efforts to make It known, loved and honoured go unrewarded . . . True, He will often make you find the treasure of the cross; but it is only in order to unite you more and more with Himself, which is all that we are to claim for time and eternity . . . Continue then to extend His reign.[4]

The Saint calls these rewards goods of infinite value,[5] incomprehensible treasures,[6] divine treasures.[7] They are treasures of love and grace: 'This Divine Heart lays open to me treasures of love and grace for those who dedicate and devote themselves to render and to procure for Him all the honour, love and glory that lie in their power.'[8]

In particular, speedily rising to great perfection: 'You cannot imagine what salutary effects this devotion produces in souls who have had the happiness to get to know of it by means of this holy man (Bl. Claude de la Colombière) who was wholly devoted to the Sacred Heart and only lived to make It known, honoured and glorified. This is why, I think, he rose in so short a time to so great perfection.'[9]

Its blessings upon the members of their family: 'I shall only say to you that this Divine Heart will reward you, not only you personally, but also your relatives, upon whom He looks merci-

---

[1] *Vie et Oeuvres, Lettre à la Mère de Saumaise*, juillet 1689, p. 408.
[2] Ibid., *âe Lettre au P. Croiset*, 10 août 1689, p. 530. Cf. also *Lettre à la Sœur Joly*, 10 avril 1690, ibid., p. 489.
[3] Ibid., *3e Lettre au P. Croiset*, 15 septembre 1689, p. 550.
[4] Ibid., *Lettre à la Mère Greyfié*, janvier 1686, p. 303.
[5] Ibid., *âe Lettre au P. Croiset*, p. 531.
[6] Ibid., *Lettre à la Sœur Joly*, 1689, p. 462.
[7] Ibid., *4e Lettre au P. Croiset*, p. 572.
[8] Ibid., *Lettre à la Mère de Saumaise*, mai 1688, p. 396.
[9] Ibid., *Lettre à la Mère de Soudeilles*, 15 septembre 1686, p. 328.

o

fully to support them in all their needs, provided they trustfully have recourse to Him.'[1]

Its blessing on their apostolate: 'My Divine Master gave me to understand that those who work for the salvation of souls will labour with success and have the art of touching the most hardened hearts if they are themselves penetrated with a tender devotion to His Sacred Heart and if they endeavour to spread it abroad.'[2] Again: 'There is nothing more efficacious than the sweet unction of the ardent charity of this Divine Heart to convert the most hardened souls and to move the most insensible hearts, through the word of His preachers and faithful friends; that word will be as a fiery sword, melting the most stony hearts in love for Him.'[3]

Finally, a happy death: 'He promises to all who consecrate and dedicate themselves to Him, in order to render and procure for Him all the honour, love and glory in their power, that He will never allow them to perish. His Heart will be their assured refuge against all the snares of their enemies, but especially at the hour of death It will receive them lovingly, making their salvation sure, and sanctifying them in proportion to their work for the extension of the reign of Its love in the hearts of men.'[4]

(c) How to Practise It

We may be apostles of the Sacred Heart by prayer; not only by expressly praying that the Sacred Heart may be better known, more honoured, more ardently loved; that the devotion to the Sacred Heart may spread ever more and may be practised more earnestly, and that the reign of the Sacred Heart may extend more widely, but also by offering for that purpose our works and our sufferings, in so far as they have impetratory merit.

We may be apostles of the Sacred Heart by setting the example of a true and solid devotion to the Heart of Jesus, by faithfully performing its exercises, and showing by our conduct that we effectually recognize the Sacred Heart as our beloved King, etc.

We can practise this apostolate through our purse; by financially supporting, according to our means, the works which have

---

[1] *Vie et Oeuvres, Lettre à la Mère de Saumaise,* juillet 1688, p. 408.
[2] Ibid., *Lettre à son directeur,* p. 627.
[3] Ibid., *3e Lettre au P. Croiset,* 15 septembre 1689, p. 557.
[4] Ibid., *2e Lettre au P. Croiset,* 10 août 1689, p. 532.

specially for their object the spread of the devotion to the Sacred Heart and the extension of Its reign.

We can practise it by our personal action, by making the devotion known to others, by urging them to have recourse to the Sacred Heart in their troubles and needs, to observe the Feast of the Sacred Heart and the first Friday of the month, to make the Holy Hour, to consecrate their family, to subscribe to the Messenger of the Sacred Heart, to join the League of the Sacred Heart, the Apostleship of Prayer, the Guard of Honour, and to participate in public demonstrations in honour of the Sacred Heart, etc.

We may, finally, and no less efficaciously, be apostles of the Sacred Heart through suffering and sacrifice. This is the apostolate *par excellence*. In addition to their power of atonement, suffering and sacrifice possess a higher impetratory merit. In accepting suffering and imposing on ourselves any sacrifice for the interests of the Sacred Heart, we show that we really take them to heart and give unequivocal proofs of the sincerity and ardour of our love. This cannot but be very agreeable to the Sacred Heart and predispose It to comply with our wishes.

§ II. PRACTICE OF REPARATION

The second chief aim of the devotion to the Sacred Heart is to make reparation to the Heart of Jesus for the conduct of men towards Him, for the grief they cause Him by their ingratitude, and for the wrong they do Him by their sins.[1]

But, it may be asked, is this really, at least in respect of the conduct of others, a task which the ordinary faithful may assume? That guiltless, holy souls should endeavour to do so, may be all very well. But we, with all our failings, weaknesses and faults? We are not even able sufficiently to atone for ourselves!

It is obvious that we are to make reparation first and foremost for ourselves, and that we shall never do so enough. Nevertheless, Jesus allows and even desires, in His infinite mercy, that in spite of our unworthiness we should atone for others too. The only conclusion we have to draw from it, is that we are to carefully

[1] See chap. ii, n. 2.

avoid each deliberate, even venial sin, all offensive or indelicate behaviour towards Jesus, in order to have less to make up for ourselves and to make our reparation for others more agreeable to His Heart. The idea of reparation, moreover, will effectually help us to banish from our lives whatever might displease our Lord, and hinder us from consoling His Heart for the shortcomings of others

A. HOW TO INCITE OURSELVES TO MAKE REPARATION

We shall arouse and encourage ourselves to make reparation simply by considering and pondering, on the one hand what the Heart of Jesus deserves on the part of men and, on the other hand, what It receives from them.

What does the Heart of Jesus deserve? To answer this question we have only to recall who Jesus is and what He has done for men.

Who is He? The most worthy, the noblest, the most perfect, the holiest, the greatest of all men, the King of kings, the Lord and Master of Heaven and earth, the Son of God, God Himself.

What has He done for men? He loves them with an incomprehensible love; and this love He showed and still shows incessantly through the innumerable gifts and graces which He bestowed and still bestows on them, and by the sufferings and sacrifices which those benefits have cost Him. He even went so far in His love as to be willing to die for them, in their place and for their salvation, the most cruel and most ignominious death, and to institute the Eucharist, in order to abide with them till the end of time, continually renewing His Sacrifice, and most closely uniting Himself with each one of us.

In consequence, what does He deserve on the part of men? Unquestionably the profoundest reverence, supreme honour, the most perfect submission, the most vivid gratitude, the most ardent love, the most absolute devotedness.

Now, we have seen how little satisfaction He receives from the greater part of men, how few are grateful to Him and love Him; how few there are who listen to Him, follow Him and allow Him to rule over them; with what coldness, what indifference, what irreverence and even what unworthiness they treat the Sacrament of His Love; how He is slandered, scoffed at and persecuted among His disciples and in His Church.[1] We have seen how men offend Him as God, how by their sins they risk making His Passion and Death futile for themselves, and crucify Him as it were over and over again.[2]

If, then, we wish to incite ourselves to make reparation to Him, we shall like to meditate on all this, we shall vividly represent it to the eyes of our soul and impress it on our minds, and allow ourselves to be deeply moved by this grievous and loathsome sight.

B. HOW TO PRACTISE REPARATION

Just for love, we can practise reparation in two ways: by sentiments and by actions. The sentiments by which we want to make reparation form what is called affective reparation the actions, effective reparation.

1. Practice of Affective Reparation

I. GENERAL EXERCISES

Affective reparation is practised, in general, in three ways.

First, by expressing to the Heart of Jesus our compassion, our sorrow, our astonishment and our indignation, on the one hand for the unworthy conduct of men towards Him, for their indifference, their ingratitude and their outrages, and on the other hand for their sins, which supremely displease Him because they offend His beloved Father, and which caused Him to suffer so dreadfully during His mortal life.

Secondly, by offering to Him, in a spirit of reparation, our reverence, our homage, our adoration and thanksgiving; by assuring Him of our faith, our submission, our fidelity, our admiration, our love, our aversion from sin, our devotedness, our earnest desire to see Him better known, more ardently loved and faithfully followed, our will to do all in our power to prevent sin wherever we can, and to make Him better known and loved by others, etc.

---

[1] See pp. 81–82.   [2] See pp. 83–84.

Thirdly, by offering to Him, in a spirit of reparation, the homage, acts of adoration, thanksgiving, sentiments of submission, of admiration and love, as well as the acts of reparation and satisfaction of all the souls who love Him on earth, of all the Saints and Angels in Heaven, and above and beyond all of His Blessed Mother.

By all these acts, performed in a spirit of reparation, we make up to a certain extent for the deficiencies of others.

II. PARTICULAR EXERCISE
THE ACT OF REPARATION OR AMENDS

The Act of Amends is a prayer whereby we express to the Sacred Heart our regret for our conduct and that of others towards Him, particularly with respect to the Blessed Sacrament, in order to try to make it up to Him by our homage and tokens of love.

Fr. Froment, s.j., who was in close relationship with St. Margaret Mary, assures us that no devotional practice could be more agreeable to Jesus Christ than often making amends to Him for the scanty return of love made to Him by men, and for the outrages which they unceasingly inflict on His love.[1] And he certifies that the Sacred Heart particularly recommended us to make it.

Jesus asked that this act of reparation should be made especially on the Feast of His Sacred Heart. In the fourth apparition He said to St. Margaret Mary: 'Therefore I ask of you that the first Friday after the octave of Corpus Christi be dedicated to a special Feast in honour of My Heart, by making amends in an Act of Reparation.'

It is optional for everyone to make this act of reparation in the terms he prefers. In Fr. Croiset's book[2] is to be found the form to which St. Margaret Mary gave her approbation. 'There is no doubt,' she writes to Fr. Croiset, 'that the Sacred Heart has worked for you; for the whole, if I am not mistaken, is so pleasing

---

[1] F. Froment, s.j., *La véritable dévotion au sacré Cœur de Jésus-Christ*, Book III, chap. ii, p. 80. Fr. Froment was born in 1649 and died in 1702. His book was issued in 1699, but was already finished when that by Fr. Croiset was published. In the preface of the new edition issued in 1891 (Vromant, Brussels) a detailed account is given of the simultaneous composition of the two books. That by Fr. Froment gives a large development of the practice of the new devotion (267 pages out of 336). It had neither the success nor the influence of the book by Fr. Croiset. (Cf. Hamon, op. cit., vol. I, pp. 441 and 454; and vol. III, p. 388.)

[2] Op. cit., pt. III, chap. iv, n. I.

to Him, that there is nothing to be changed, neither the consecration nor the act of reparation.'[1]

2. Practice of Effective Reparation

We will not content ourselves, however, with arousing affections, but we want to add acts; we will practise not only affective but also effective reparation.

I. GENERAL EXERCISES

We can compensate the Heart of Jesus for the shortcomings of men, firstly in general, by endeavouring with that purpose, to make our gratitude, love, submission, imitation and devotedness the more intense and earnest.

We will then try to realize what is pledged in a well-known prayer:[2]

'The more Thy Divinity is denied and blasphemed, the more respectfully we will adore it, O Heart of God made man! The more Thy doctrine is rejected and contested, the more firmly we will believe and proclaim it, O Heart of our Divine Teacher! The more Thy commandments are neglected and transgressed, the more faithfully we will observe them, O Heart of our Divine Master! The more the authority of Thy Church is spurned, the more submissively we will obey it, O Heart of our Divine Guide! The more the worldly spirit is indulged in, the more we will imbue our minds with the spirit of Thy Gospel, O Heart of our crucified God! The more Thy Blessed Sacrament is disdained and profaned, the more we will honour and love it, O Heart of our Divine Friend! The more hell works to tear away souls from Thee, the more we will try to extend Thy reign, O Heart of our Divine King! The more Thou art hated, the more we will love Thee, O Heart of our lovable and loving God!'

Furthermore we can practise effective reparation, first, by accepting and bearing, in a spirit of reparation, all the ups and downs of life, indispositions, sicknesses, vexations, contradictions, persecutions, etc. Secondly, by offering in a spirit of reparation the trouble we have to take, the struggle we have to sustain and the sacrifices we have to make in order to resist temptations and evil inclinations, to discharge our duties and to practise the

---

[1] *Vie et Oeuvres*, vol. II, *Lettre au P. Croiset*, 21 août 1690, p. 621.
[2] We reproduce only the ideas, not the terms.

virtues of our state of life. Thirdly, by spontaneously imposing on ourselves, in a spirit of reparation, certain mortifications and penances.

Thus we may translate into acts of reparation whatever we do, and make our lives lives of reparation. To this end it is sufficient to animate it all with an atoning intention and to offer it in a spirit of reparation.[1]

How are we able to make reparation to the Heart of Jesus by our sufferings, our sacrifices, mortifications and penances?

We make reparation to Him as Man for the grief that men inflict on Him by their bad conduct towards Him, in willing to suffer as He did and thus to resemble Him in some way. By this likeness we give Him an eloquent proof of our love, we console His Heart and make up to Him, to some extent, for the grief caused Him by men.

We make reparation to Him as God for the offence which men commit against Him by their sins, by our readiness to atone for the sins of others. By His Passion and Death He superabundantly atoned for the outrages perpetrated against God by the sins of the world. Since by Baptism we are incorporated in Christ and, as it were, identified with Him, He considers our sufferings as His own, unites them to His, and makes them share in the infinite atoning value of His own sufferings. When then we offer, in reparation for sins, our sufferings joined to those of Christ, God looks upon them with pleasure and accepts them in reality as a reparation for the offences of men.

Hence reparation through suffering differs from the apostolate of suffering for the conversion of sinners. Both are practised, it is true, by the offering of sufferings, sacrifices and mortifications. But if we fix our attention on the offence done to God by sin, if we are willing by our sufferings to make up for that offence so far as we can, then we practise reparation; whereas, if we consider the disastrous consequences of sin for sinners themselves, if we intend by our sufferings to preserve them from those calamities, by giving satisfaction for them to Divine justice, to appease God's wrath and to implore for them graces of conversion, then we practise the apostolate of suffering and sacrifice.

---

[1] It is to this life of reparation that the Apostleship of Prayer invites its members as it asks them to offer every day to the Sacred Heart all their prayers, works and sufferings, not only as an apostolic prayer for the intentions of the Sacred Heart, but also in reparation for the offences done to It. (Cf. appendix II, III, p. 264.)

It is clear that we may unite both and offer our sufferings, mortifications and sacrifices at once in order to make up for the offence done to God and to give satisfaction for sinners and to obtain their conversion. In practice, moreover, these two intentions are usually associated. That is why often by 'reparation' is meant not only reparation properly so called, but also the apostolate of suffering and sacrifice for the conversion of sinners.[1]

Furthermore, it should be noted that the apostolate of suffering implies reparation. For, how did Jesus give satisfaction to Divine justice, reconcile men to God and merit for them graces of salvation? Certainly by offering to God, through His sufferings and His sacrifice, a superabundant reparation for the offence done to Him by sin. In like manner, we, too, are unable otherwise to give satisfaction for sinners to Divine justice and to obtain for them graces of conversion.

Hence by our sufferings, sacrifices and mortifications, we can show our love to the Heart of Jesus and thus practise devotion to the Sacred Heart in four ways.

We may, out of love for the Sacred Heart, accept or impose on ourselves any suffering, in order to resemble more our suffering Saviour. Thus we practise imitation of the Heart of Jesus.[2]

We may, for love of the Sacred Heart, offer the impetratory merit of our sufferings for the realization of His wishes. Thus we practise the apostolate of prayer.[3]

We can, for love of the Sacred Heart, accept or impose on ourselves suffering itself with the purpose of promoting in this way Its interests. Thus we practise the apostolate of suffering.[4]

We can, finally, for love of the Sacred Heart, accept or impose on ourselves suffering in order to atone and to give satisfaction for the sins of men and for their conduct towards Jesus. Thus we practise reparation.[5]

---

[1] Cf. Plus, s.j., *L'idée réparatrice*; and *L'intelligence et la pratique de la réparation.*

[2] See p. 157.

[3] See p. 164.

[4] See p. 165.

[5] See p. 161. On reparation may be consulted: Pius XI, Encyclical *Miserentissimus*; Croiset, op. cit., pt. i, chap. ii, § iv; de Galliffet, op. cit., Book i, chap. ii, p. 93; Terrien, op. cit., Book iii, chap. iii; Galtier, op. cit., p. 47; Noldin, op. cit., p. 155; Richstätter, op. cit., p. 74; Plus, *L'idée réparatrice*; and *L'Intelligence et la pratique de la réparation*; Franco, op. cit., p. 128; de Franciosi, op. cit., p. 191; Hamon, op. cit., vol. v, pp. 93–98.

II. PARTICULAR EXERCISES

We can, moreover, make reparation to the Heart of Jesus by certain exercises which He Himself pointed out. The most important are: the Communion of Reparation, the observance of the Feast of the Sacred Heart, the First Friday of the Month, and the Holy Hour.

(a) The Communion of Reparation

Its Nature

The Communion of Reparation, considered as a practice of devotion to the Sacred Heart, has for its object to console and to compensate the Sacred Heart for the ungrateful and often unworthy conduct of a great number of men towards the Blessed Eucharist in its three forms: Christ's presence under the sacramental species, the Holy Sacrifice of the Mass, and Communion; in particular for their unbelief, their indifference, their coldness and irreverence; for the lack of purity, care and devotion with which they receive Communion; for the derision, the outrages, the blasphemies and profanations perpetrated against the Blessed Sacrament.

We can attain this purpose by saying to Jesus whilst He is within us at Communion, how much this conduct of men grieves and revolts us, and by asking Him to pardon it; by expressing thanks to Him for the priceless gift of the Eucharist; by desiring that men may respond better to His boundless love, and promising to the best of our power to help Him realize this desire; and above all by receiving Him ourselves with all the care, purity, reverence, devotion and love which is in us.

If, then, we wish our Communion to be really one of reparation, it is not sufficient to make it with an intention of reparation; we ought to perform it in such a way, that it be truly agreeable to Jesus and make true recompense for the bad conduct of men.

Our Lord's Desire

Jesus has expressly asked for this Communion of reparation.

He asked that it should be made on the Feast of His Sacred Heart. 'In return,' He said in the fourth apparition, 'I receive from the greater part of men nothing but ingratitude, by their irreverence and their sacrileges, and by the indifference and contempt with which they treat Me in this Sacrament of Love.

Therefore I ask of you that the first Friday after the octave of Corpus Christi be dedicated as a special Feast in honour of My Heart, by the reception of Holy Communion on that day and by making amends to It in an act of reparation, in order to make up for the outrages which It received during the time It has been exposed on the altars.'[1]

He also asked that this should be done on the first Friday of each month. 'He bade me to receive Communion on the first Friday of each month, in order to make reparation for the outrages which He received during the month in the Blessed Sacrament.'[2]

He demanded, moreover, of the Saint that she should receive Communion as frequently as possible in a spirit of reparation. 'Do you at least give Me this happiness, supplying for their ingratitude, as much as you can . . . Be attentive to My voice and to what I ask of you for the accomplishment of My designs. First, you are to receive Me in the Blessed Sacrament as often as obedience will allow . . .'[3]

Jesus then wishes us to make this Communion of reparation not only on the Feast of His Sacred Heart and on the first Friday of each month, but as frequently as possible, and even to make each of our Communions a Communion of reparation. Thus it is that the Saint understood it; thus she did herself and recommended others also to do. Thus it is understood by the Church: in order to urge the faithful to multiply their Communions of reparation, she grants to the members of the Apostleship of Prayer a plenary indulgence each time they receive Communion in a spirit of reparation.[4]

Other Views of the Communion of Reparation

The Communion of Reparation, however, may be viewed and practised in yet another way.

It may be made, for instance, with the intention of appeasing the Sacred Heart, angry about the conduct of men towards Him and at their sins. It is this that the Apostleship of Prayer asks of its members. With this object in view, every month or every week they practise the Communion of Reparation, whereby they seek to

[1] *Vie et Oeuvres*, vol. I, p. 136; and vol. II, p. 103.
[2] Ibid., vol. II, *Lettre au P. Croiset*, 3 novembre 1689, p. 580.
[3] Ibid., vol. I, *Mémoire des Contemporaines*, n. 131-32, p. 126.
[4] Rescript of July 1st, 1921.

appease the Most Sacred Heart of Jesus provoked to wrath by the sins of men, and secure a favourable hearing for our prayers.

It may be offered not to the Sacred Heart but to God the Father, with a view to making reparation for the offences of the sins of men against Him. This purpose is attained by offering to God, in reparation for the sins of the world, the Sacred Body of His Divine Son, which we receive in our hearts, with all His merits and all the affections of His heart, Its adoration, Its thanksgiving, and Its love. This Communion of reparation, too, is asked for by Jesus. 'Tell your Superior,' Jesus once said to St. Margaret Mary, 'she has caused Me great displeasure by forbidding you the Communion which I had demanded of you on the first Friday of each month, in order to offer Me to My Eternal Father and thus, through the merits of My Sacred Heart, to give satisfaction to His Divine justice, if any fault should have been committed against charity.'[1]

He often and more insistently repeated His demand, and at the same time pointed out to her how she was to make this Communion of Reparation: 'When I reveal to you that the Divine justice is angry with sinners, you are to come and receive Me in Holy Communion, and having placed Me on the throne of your heart, you are to adore Me, prostrate at My Feet. You are to offer Me to My Eternal Father, as I shall teach you, in order to appease His righteous anger and to move His mercy to pardon them.'[2]

It was to this Communion of Reparation that Pope Pius IX referred, writing in his Apostolic Letter of August 9th, 1861: 'The chief aim of the Communion of Reparation is to obtain that God, appeased by frequent Communion, may avert from us the scourge of His wrath; that thus the outrages inflicted on His Divine Majesty, on the religion of Christ and His Vicar on earth, may be to some extent compensated . . .'

It is evident that we may associate those different intentions, so as to offer Holy Communion at once to console and compensate the Sacred Heart for the conduct of men towards the Blessed Sacrament, to appease God's anger, and to make up for the offences committed against God by the sins of the world.

To this purpose of reparation we may also join an apostolic intention and offer Communion not only to console the Sacred

---

[1] *Vie et Oeuvres*, vol. II, *Lettre à la Sœur des Escures*, p. 293.
[2] Ibid., *Sentiments de ses retraites*, p. 193.

Heart and to make reparation for the outrages inflicted on God, but also favourably to dispose God or the Sacred Heart and to obtain certain graces.

Thus Pope Pius IX in his Apostolic Letter of August 9th, 1861, asks that Communions of Reparation should be made, not only 'to make up for the outrages inflicted on His Divine Majesty', but also 'that the Catholic religion may remain free and unsullied throughout the world, and that thus the flock of Christ may escape the snares of its cunning and relentless enemies.'

Thus the Apostleship of Prayer, too, invites its members to offer Communions of Reparation, not only 'to appease the Sacred Heart provoked to wrath by the sins of men,' but also 'to secure a favourable hearing for our prayers.'

It is in this way that the Association of the Communion of Reparation asks its members to offer Communion, not only 'to console the Divine Heart of Jesus, outraged and offended by men in the Eucharist,' but also 'to make intercession on behalf of the Church and the Sovereign Pontiff, and to obtain the conversion of sinners, the preservation and progress of the Catholic Faith throughout the world and especially in their own country.'[1]

The Mass of Reparation

With the Communion of Reparation is connected the Mass of Reparation.

Holy Mass is of its very essence a sacrifice of reparation. It is nothing else but the mystical renewal and perpetuation of the atonement and reparation of the Sacrifice of the Cross, and hence the practice of reparation *par excellence*.

But this reparation, properly speaking, is offered not to Jesus as man, not to His Sacred Heart, but to God, and more specifically to God the Father. For Jesus as man is the Victim which we offer to God the Father and, in Him, to the two other Divine Persons, in reparation for the offences committed by the sins of men.

Yet it may also be taken as a practice of reparation and atonement, to console and compensate the Heart of Jesus for the conduct of men towards the Blessed Eucharist and in particular with respect to Holy Mass; for the little gratitude they show Him

[1] See appendix II, IV, p. 268.

for this great gift, the little value they set upon it, the carelessness they show while assisting at it, the little reverence, attention and devotion they display in attending it.

We will give to Holy Mass this quality of atonement and reparation by celebrating or assisting at it with a view to showing Jesus that we at least appreciate the priceless gift of the Mass, that we at least are sensible of the boundless love He manifests to us in it. To this end we will assure Him, especially after the Consecration, how much we are grieved by the conduct of men with respect to the Holy Sacrifice, we will ask Him to pardon it, we will offer to Him in reparation our reverence, our gratitude, our love, and we will beseech Him to grant to men abundant graces, that they may realize and appreciate at its proper value the wonderful favour of the Mass, that they may avail themselves of it more fully and respond better to the unbounded love to which they are indebted for it.

Fr. Croiset, whose book on Devotion to the Sacred Heart was inspired, read and approved by St. Margaret Mary, recommends us: 'As soon as the priest has completed the Consecration, you are to adore Jesus Christ with lively faith and with the affections of one who wants to make reparation for all the insults and outrages to which His love has exposed Him in this most august Sacrament. You are to adore Him and give thanks for the love with which His Heart is burning and for all the admirable dispositions of His Heart towards us. Try to realize what are the sentiments of Jesus Christ on this Altar, at the sight of so much contempt and so many outrages; and, penetrated with gratitude and love, say to Him whatever sorrow and love may inspire in a generous and grateful heart. By these interior acts preparation is made for Spiritual Communion, to try and make reparation by the devotion and love which animate you, for the indifference, coldness and deficient preparation with which Communion is received.'[1]

(b) The Feast of the Sacred Heart

Our Lord's Desire

Jesus asked for this Feast in His apparition to St. Margaret Mary, which took place in 1675, during the octave of Corpus

[1] Croiset, op. cit., pt. III, chap. vi, § iii, pp. 419–20.

Christi, probably on June 16th, the apparition which is commonly called 'the great apparition'.

Let us re-read the account of it taken down by the Saint almost immediately after, by order of her confessor, Bl. Claude de la Colombière: 'Being before the Blessed Sacrament, one day during the octave of Corpus Christi, I received from my God extraordinary tokens of His love. As I felt prompted to make some return and to give back love for love, He said to me: "You could show Me no greater love than by doing what I have already so many times demanded of you." And showing me His Divine Heart, He said: "Behold this Heart which has so loved men that It has spared nothing, even so far as to exhaust and consume Itself, in order to testify Its love for them. And in return I receive from the greater part of men nothing but ingratitude, by the contempt, irreverence, sacrileges and coldness with which they treat Me in this Sacrament of Love. Yet what is still more painful to Me is that even hearts consecrated to Me are acting like this. Therefore I ask of you that the first Friday after the octave of Corpus Christi be dedicated to a special feast in honour of My Heart, by amendment offered to It in an Act of Reparation, and by the reception of Holy Communion that day, to make up for the outrages which It has received during the time that It has been exposed on the altars." '

Thus Jesus Himself asked that the Church should institute a feast in honour of His Heart and He Himself appointed the day, namely, the Friday immediately following the octave of Corpus Christi.

Its Institution

The Church, however, not being fond of novelties, was but slowly gained to the idea of this feast. God even permitted its institution to meet with violent opposition, even on the part of influential ecclesiastical dignitaries. Not until 1765 was the celebration of the Feast granted to the dioceses which asked for it, and only in 1856 was it extended by Pope Pius IX, with the rite of Greater-Double, to the universal Church. It was raised, in 1889, by Pope Leo XIII to the rite of Double of the First Class and, in 1929, by Pius XI to that of Double of the First Class with privileged octave of the third order. At the same time it was proclaimed to be a *festum primarium*, placed on a level with the *festa feriata,* so that henceforth it has not to give way to any great feast that might coincide with it.[1]

The Spirit in which it should be Celebrated

The Feast of the Sacred Heart ought to be observed in a spirit of reparation and atoning love.

This is clearly apparent from the words of Jesus in the great apparition. After complaining of the ingratitude of men and particularly of their behaviour towards the Sacrament of His love, He added: 'Therefore I ask of you that the first Friday after the octave of Corpus Christi be dedicated to a special feast in honour of My Heart, by the receiving of Holy Communion that day and by amendment offered to It in an Act of Reparation, to compensate for the outrages which It has received during the time It has been exposed on the Altars.'

This is the view of the Church. Pope Pius XI states in his Encyclical *Caritate Christi compulsi* of May 3rd, 1932:[2] 'The proper spirit of this solemnity, as We amply showed four years ago in Our Encyclical *Miserentissimus,* is the spirit of loving reparation, and therefore it was Our will, that on that day every year in perpetuity there should be made, in all the churches of the world, a public Act of Reparation for all the offences that wound that Divine Heart.'

This quality of reparation and atonement in the Feast of the Sacred Heart stands out most clearly in the Collect of the Mass which makes us ask for the grace of making due reparation to the Sacred Heart: 'O God, who in the Heart of Thy Son, wounded by our sins, dost deign mercifully to bestow on us infinite treasures of love: grant, we beseech Thee, that whilst we render It the devout homage of our affection, we may also discharge our duty of worthy satisfaction.'[3]

---

[1] Decree of the Sacred Congregation of Rites, January 29th, 1929. A feast is called 'primarium' or primary on account of the dignity of its object. The Feast of the Sacred Heart is now, in this respect, numbered among the most solemn feasts of Our Lord, as, for instance, the Epiphany and Corpus Christi. 'Festa feriata' are those which involve the obligation of assistance at Mass and the prohibition of servile works. On the Feast of the Sacred Heart, however—as for some other 'festa feriata' in some countries—that obligation and prohibition do not exist; but as 'festum feriatum' the Feast of the Sacred Heart possesses all its liturgical privileges. This stipulation was introduced to prevent the transfer of the Feast of the Sacred Heart if it were to coincide with that of St. John the Baptist.

[2] *Acta Apost. Sedis,* vol. XXIV (1932), pp. 177–94.

[3] See p. 77, the analysis of the Collect.

For What Shortcomings?

What are precisely the shortcomings against the Sacred Heart, for which the Feast is intended to make reparation?

If we take rigorously the words of our Lord, it seems that it is only those of which the object is the Blessed Sacrament. For He said: 'In return I receive from the greater part of men nothing but ingratitude, by the contempt, irreverence, sacrilege and coldness with which they treat Me in this Sacrament of Love.' And further: 'Therefore I ask of you that the first Friday after the octave of Corpus Christi be dedicated to a special feast . . . by amendment offered to It in an Act of Reparation, to compensate for the outrages It has received during the time It has been exposed on the Altars.'

Christian piety, however, has gradually enlarged the object of the Feast, in accordance with the spirit of the Devotion itself. As we have seen, it by no means confines the object of the reparation—which is the second principal end of the Devotion— to the behaviour of men towards the Blessed Eucharist, but extends it to all forms of neglect of Christ's love, to all forms of ingratitude, all shortcomings, all outrages, of which men are guilty towards the Sacred Heart. In like manner the faithful observe the Feast of the Sacred Heart as a feast of reparation, not only for the behaviour of men towards the Blessed Sacrament, but also for their ingratitude towards the Sacred Heart, in its whole extent and in all its forms.

This extension has been approved and ratified by the Church. The Act of Reparation prescribed by Pope Pius XI on the Feast of the Sacred Heart makes no restriction as regards the object of the reparation. In the same way the Church in the liturgy of the Feast of the Sacred Heart extends the reparation to all sorts of neglect of Jesus' love. In the Collect she bids us pray that we may 'discharge our duty of worthy satisfaction'. Now this duty of satisfaction and reparation is not confined to the behaviour of men towards the Eucharist, but is extended to all their short-comings towards our Saviour.

Yet it is undeniable that Jesus asked for the institution of the feast chiefly in reparation for the bad conduct of men towards the Blessed Sacrament. It is therefore especially with a view to atoning and making up for that conduct, that we are to celebrate it.

P

Hence the Feast of the Sacred Heart ought to have mainly an Eucharistic character.

Its Programme.

Our Lord not only made known the spirit in which the Feast should be observed, but also pointed out the principal parts of the programme. For He said: 'Therefore I ask that a special feast be dedicated in honour of My Heart . . . by the reception of Holy Communion on that day and by amendment offered to It in an Act of Reparation . . .'

He asked, then, chiefly for two practices: first, an Act of Reparation, that is a prayer by which we express to the Sacred Heart our regret for the conduct of men towards Him and try and make up for it by our homage and our tokens of love. Secondly, a Communion of Reparation, that is, a Communion with a view to consoling and compensating the Sacred Heart for the ingratitude of men and their unworthy conduct towards Him, and hence made in such a way that it really compensates It by the earnestness, devotion and love with which we perform it.

This programme, specially as regards the Act of amendment, has been solemnly sanctioned by Pope Pius XI in his Encyclical *Miserentissimus* whereby he ordained a solemn Act of Reparation to be recited every year, on the Feast of the Sacred Heart, in all the churches of the world, and whereby he prescribed the form to be used on that occasion.

How to Observe the Feast

Thus the Feast of the Sacred Heart is the feast of the Devotion to the Sacred Heart, the feast of Its neglected love.

We will then celebrate it with our whole heart. Jesus desires it; this must be sufficient for us. And He deserves it to the full, for His love surpasses all things, and this love is scorned.

In preparation for the feast a novena may be suitable, beginning on the eve of Corpus Christi and continuing throughout the octave of this feast. Every day we can, for instance, make a meditation or read a few passages of this book, assist at Holy Mass, and receive Holy Communion.[1]

On the eve of the feast we will make the Holy Hour with even more devotion than usually.

[1] Cf. Vermeersch, s.j., *Practical Devotion to the Sacred Heart*, 1909, *Meditations for the novena*, pp. 144–200.

On the feast itself we will attend Mass and receive Holy Communion with all the purity of heart, with all the reverence, interior recollection, devotion and love which is in us.

If possible, we should also assist at Benediction of the Blessed Sacrament, and earnestly join in the Act of Reparation which will be recited by the priest.[1]

Moreover, we should try to spend the whole day in a disposition of grateful love and atoning sympathy towards the Sacred Heart. We will most carefully avoid whatever might displease Him, we will as perfectly as possible discharge our daily duties and will not miss an opportunity of making any sacrifice. In short, we should do our best to make the whole day a real day of consolation and compensation for the Sacred Heart.

Touched by those tokens of tender affection, Jesus will thankfully bestow upon us in return His priceless gifts and graces, according to what He said to St. Margaret Mary: 'I promise you that My Heart will expand Itself abundantly to pour forth the influence of Its Divine love on all those who render and procure for It this homage.'[2]

The Month of the Sacred Heart

In the Letter which Cardinal Mazella, Prefect of the Sacred Congregation of Rites, in the name of Pope Leo XIII, addressed to the Bishops on July 21st, 1899, and which may be considered the conclusion of the Encyclical *Annum sacrum* on the Consecration of mankind to the Sacred Heart, we read: 'Our Holy Father particularly recommends the practice, already observed in several churches, of various public exercises in honour of the Sacred Heart, during the whole month of June. To promote it, dispensing the treasures of the Church, he grants to the faithful an indulgence of three hundred days, to be gained each time they assist at these pious exercises, and a plenary indulgence to those who do so at least ten times during the month.'[3] In addition to these indulgences others were granted by Pope Leo XIII, in 1902, and by Pius X, in 1906.[4]

Thus the observance of the month of June as the month of the

---

[1] For the indulgences attached to this solemnity, see *Preces et pia opera*, n. 224.
[2] *Vie et Oeuvres*, vol. I, p. 137. Cf. Croiset, op. cit., pt. III, chap. ii; and de Galliffet, op. cit., Book III, chap. ii.
[3] *Acta Sanctae Sedis*, vol. XXXII (1899–1900), pp. 51–54.
[4] Cf. *Preces et pia opera*, n. 221.

Sacred Heart has been approved and recommended by the Church.

It owes its origin to the initiative of a devout pupil of the school of the 'Monastère des Oiseaux' in Paris, Angèle de Sainte-Croix (1833).[1] She conceived the project of dedicating the month of June to the Sacred Heart, just as the month of May is dedicated to the Blessed Virgin. Mgr. de Quélen, Archbishop of Paris, not only approved the project, but also set out its aim and purpose, and the practical method of its observance: 'During the month of June we will pray for the conversion of sinners and for the spiritual welfare of our country; these devout exercises will go on for thirty-three days, in honour of the thirty-three years of our Lord's lifetime. A number, drawn by lot, will assign to each one his special day, which is to be sanctified by all sorts of good works.'[2] To explain and illustrate more fully this devout exercise, the Superior of the convent, Mother Saint-Jérôme, wrote a booklet, *Mois du Sacré-Coeur*, which met with considerable success.

Since then the devotion of the Month of the Sacred Heart has spread abroad and is observed not only by the faithful privately but also in churches and chapels by public exercises in honour of the Sacred Heart. Since Fr. Tickell, s.j., wrote his *Month of the Sacred Heart*, in 1858, many manuals for the month of June have been published in England and America.[3]

(c) The First Friday of the Month

Our Lord's Desire

In the third great apparition, after complaining of the ingratitude of men and the disdain of His love, Jesus said to the Saint: 'Do you at least give Me pleasure by making up for their ingratitude, as much as you can.' And He pointed out to her some

---

[1] Louis Veuillot related her edifying life and happy death.

[2] Ramière, s.j., *Le mois du Sacré-Cœur*, p. 25; Yenveux, *Le règne du Cœur de Jésus*, vol. ii, pt. iv, n. 5, p. 518.

[3] The most remarkable in French are: Gautrelet, s.j., et Borgo, s.j., *Cœur de Jésus, mon refuge*; Gautrelet, s.j., *Manuel de la dévotion au Sacré-Cœur de Jésus*, pt. ii, *Nouveau mois du Sacré-Cœur de Jésus*; Ramière, s.j., *Le mois du Sacré-Cœur de Jésus*; Godfroy, s.j., *Mois du Sacré-Cœur de Jésus, extrait des écrits de sainte Marguerite-Marie*; Vermeersch, s.j., *Pratique et doctrine de la dévotion au Sacré-Cœur*, pt. i, § ii, *Points de méditation pour le mois du Sacré-Cœur*; A. Lefebvre, s.j., *Mois du Sacré-Cœur de Jésus*; Dehon, pr. du S. Cœur de Jésus, *De la vie d'amour envers le Sacré-Cœur de Jésus*; Rouvier, s.j., *Le Cœur du Maître, d'après Bossuet, Nouveau mois du Sacré-Cœur*.

practices which she had to perform in this spirit of atoning love. The first was the Communion of Reparation, preferably on the first Friday of each month: 'You are to receive Me in the Blessed Sacrament as often as obedience will allow . . . Moreover, you are to receive Communion on the first Friday of each month. And every night between Thursday and Friday I will make you partaker of that sorrow unto death which it was My will to suffer in the Garden of Olives . . .' Jesus thus demanded of the Saint that she should make a Communion of reparation on every first Friday of the month. And by two extraordinary facts He wanted to show how much He insisted on her complying with His wish.

Conquering her natural timidity, she informed her Superior (Mother de Saumaise) of our Lord's desire. In order to try her humility and obedience, the Superior disdainfully received the information and simply refused the Communion requested. Thereupon the Saint fell dangerously ill. The Superior, perhaps following an inspiration from Heaven, ordered her to beg of our Lord that He might restore her to health; her recovery would be a sign that she was really guided by the spirit of God; then the Superior would no longer hesitate to allow her what she had hitherto refused, particularly the Communion on the first Friday of the month. The Saint obeyed, and was restored to health at once.[1]

A few years later, in 1685, perceiving that the new Devotion caused dissension among the Sisters, her Superior (Mother Melin) deemed it expedient to forbid her any exterior practice in honour of the Sacred Heart, and hence also the Communion of Reparation on the first Friday of the month. The Saint humbly submitted to this prohibition; yet she was afflicted at it and, as she had nobody to whom she could lay open her sorrow, she exposed it to her Divine Master Himself. 'Fear not,' He said to her, 'I shall reign in spite of My enemies and of all those who may oppose Me.' Now it happened that a young Sister[2] fell dangerously ill and was within a few days at death's door. The Saint entreated our Lord with tears to heal the Sister, who was wholly devoted to His adorable Heart. Then it was clearly made known to her that the illness would last till the Communion on the first Friday of the month should be given back to her. The Saint was perplexed. She wanted

---

[1] Hamon, op. cit., vol. 1, pp. 152–56.
[2] Sister Verchère.

to obey her Superior; but Jesus insisted upon her informing the Superior how much her prohibition was displeasing Him. Finally she resolved to take the advice of a Sister[1] who enjoyed the esteem and trust of all. At her instance she told her Superior what our Lord had enjoined upon her. Being now fully informed, the Superior allowed the Communion, and at once the sick Sister was found to be out of danger.[2]

But, it may be asked, is this desire of Jesus addressed to all those who wish to show Him their love?

Although in the writings of the Saint we find no explicit declaration of Jesus, there is no doubt about the question.

This may be deduced from the fact that the Saint insistently recommended the Communion of Reparation on the first Friday of the month, and endeavoured to spread this practice abroad— which she would not have done, we may take for granted on account of her character, unless she were sure of thus complying with a desire of Jesus. She writes, for instance, to Mother de Saumaise: 'You should receive Communion on the first Friday of the month and, after Holy Communion, you should offer yourself as victim, dedicating your whole being to the Sacred Heart.'[3] She expressed her joy when she heard that the Fathers of the Society of Jesus had allowed their lay-brothers, and those who were not yet priests, to receive Communion every first Friday of the month.[4]

Nor does Pope Pius XI hesitate to declare in his Encyclical *Miserentissimus* (n. 7) that the observance of the first Friday of the month really corresponds to a desire of Jesus.

Of this desire we find yet another convincing proof in the magnificent promise made by the Sacred Heart on behalf of those who should make the Communion of Reparation on nine consecutive first Fridays. It is not possible to fix with certainty the date on which the Promise was made. The promise itself we may read in a letter of the Saint to her former Superior, Mother de Saumaise: 'One Friday, at Holy Communion, He said, if I am not mistaken, to me, His unworthy slave: "I promise you in the

---

[1] Sister des Escures.
[2] *Vie et Oeuvres*, vol. I, *Mémoire des Contemporaines*, n. 40, p. 218; and n. 257–60. Cf. Hamon, op. cit., vol. I, pp. 370–71.
[3] *Vie et Oeuvres*, vol. II, p. 297.
[4] An instance of uncommon devotion to the Sacred Heart, as frequent Communion was at that time rather unusual.

excess of the mercy of My Heart, that Its all-powerful love will grant to all those who receive Communion on the first Friday of nine consecutive months the grace of final repentance; they shall not die under My displeasure, nor without receiving the last Sacraments; My Divine Heart shall be their assured refuge at that last hour." '[1]

In the fourth chapter, dealing with the motives which should move us to practise devotion to the Sacred Heart, we shall examine the authenticity and credibility of this promise, rightly called 'the Great Promise'. According to our Lord's design, it has a double aim: on the one hand, to convince us of the value He sets on this Communion of the first Friday of the month, and of His earnest desire that we should practise it; on the other hand, to urge us on to practise devotion to His Sacred Heart by the prospect of the precious grace attached to it.[2]

How to Celebrate the First Friday of the Month

The devout clients of the Sacred Heart usually are not content with offering a Communion of reparation on that day, but they add to it yet other exercises made in the same spirit: Holy Mass, a meditation or reading on the Sacred Heart, an Act of Reparation, the renewal of their Consecration to the Sacred Heart, assistance at Benediction or a visit to the Blessed Sacrament, the Litany of the Sacred Heart, the Way of the Cross, and on the eve the Holy Hour.[3]

In short, of every First Friday of the month they make a feast of the Sacred Heart on a smaller scale. And the Church, far from disapproving of their doing so, rather encourages them, particularly by allowing her priests, under certain conditions, to say the Mass of the Feast of the Sacred Heart on that day.[4]

---

[1] *Vie et Oeuvres*, vol. II, *Lettre à la Mère de Saumaise*, mai 1688, p. 397.

[2] The faithful who receive Holy Communion on the first Friday of each month and join in a public exercise in honour of the Sacred Heart may gain a plenary indulgence, if they have been to Confession and pray for the Pope's intentions. (*Preces et pia opera*, n. 220.)

[3] Cf. Croiset, op. cit., pt. III, chap. iii, § i, and chap. iv.

[4] By a special privilege, owing to the devotion of Pope Leo XIII, this Mass may, every first Friday of the month, be joined to the exercises of devotion which, with the approbation of the Bishop, are performed in churches and chapels in honour of the Sacred Heart. It follows the rite of the solemn votive Mass, i.e. with Gloria, Credo and generally one Collect. Several religious Orders and Congregations of priests obtained for their members the personal privilege of this votive Mass, without the obligation of adding to it any other exercise in honour of the Sacred Heart. (Beringer, op. cit., vol. I, n. 677, p. 357.)

(d) The Holy Hour

The Holy Hour is an exercise of mental or vocal prayer, in memory of the agony of Our Lord in the Garden of Olives, with a view to appeasing God's anger, to asking pardon for sinners, and to consoling the Heart of Jesus for one hour.[1]

On the cross Jesus suffered especially in His body; in the Garden of Olives He suffered specially in His Heart and in His soul. Here He suffered at the dreadful vision of the loathsome burden of sins which He had taken upon Himself and for which He was to atone; at the sight of God's wrath and the arm of His vengeance about to come down upon Him; at the clear prospect of the cruel tortures and horrible death that awaited Him, of the base ingratitude of men and the futility of His Passion and Death for innumerable souls. And His Apostles, in spite of His repeated requests, left Him alone and uncomforted in His agony.

These mental sufferings were more grievous than anything else He had to endure in His body. He Himself revealed it to His faithful servant, St. Margaret Mary: 'Attentively considering in one of my meditations the only Object of my love in the Garden of Olives, plunged in sorrow and agony, as I felt strongly urged to share in His anguish, He lovingly said to me: "Here I suffered more than in the rest of My Passion. I saw Myself wholly abandoned by Heaven and earth, and loaded with the burden of the sins of all men. I appeared before the holiness of God who, without considering My innocence, crushed Me in His wrath, causing Me to drink the chalice which was filled with all the bitterness of His righteous anger. The name of Father He seemed to have forgotten, in order to sacrifice Me to His just wrath. No creature is able to understand the violence of the torments which I then endured." '[2]

Our Lord's Desire

For those mental sufferings Jesus asked of St. Margaret Mary compassion, consolation and compensation. The revelation probably took place in the year 1673. 'On this occasion,' she writes, 'my Divine Master bade me rise every Thursday night at the hour He would appoint, in order to recite five "Our Fathers" and five "Hail Marys", prostrate on the earth, together with five

[1] Cf. appendix II, IV, p. 269: The Archconfraternity of the Holy Hour, Statute 1.
[2] *Vie et Oeuvres*, vol. I, *Mémoire des Contemporaines*, n. 297, pp. 283–84.

acts of adoration which He had taught me, thus to render homage to Him in the extreme anguish He suffered on the night of His Passion.'[1]

Shortly after, in the third great apparition, Our Lord appointed to her the hour, and defined the purposes, of that nightly prayer. After He had asked of the saint to make up for the ingratitude of men, particularly by a Communion of reparation cn the first Friday of each month, He continued: 'Every night between Thursday and Friday, I will make you partaker of that sorrow unto death which it was My will to suffer in the Garden of Olives. This sorrow will reduce you, without your understanding how, to a kind of agony more bitter than death. To join with Me in the humble prayer which I then offered to My Heavenly Father in agony, you are to rise between eleven and midnight and to remain with Me prostrate for an hour, with your face to the ground, to appease the anger of My Heavenly Father and to ask Him for the pardon of sinners. You will thus also share with Me, and to some extent soothe, the bitter grief I suffered when My disciples abandoned Me and I was constrained to reproach them that they could not watch with Me one hour. During that hour you are to do what I will teach you.'

Dealing with the practice of the First Friday of the month, we have seen that the Superior of the Saint did not allow her to comply with the double wish of the Sacred Heart, that the Saint fell dangerously ill, and obtained the permission asked for, after she had been wonderfully restored to health.[2]

A few years later, a new Superior, Mother Greyfié, in her turn wanted to put the virtue of the Saint to the test. At first she forbade her to rise any more at night. The Sister humbly obeyed. Our Lord was much displeased with this prohibition and made it so clearly known to Margaret Mary, that she felt obliged to inform her Superior of it. She was afraid, she said, the Superior would be punished. A few days later, indeed, a young Sister, a valuable subject, to whom the Superior was much attached, died in the convent. The Superior saw in it the punishment with which Margaret Mary had respectfully threatened her. She was now no longer in doubt of the supernatural character of what was going on in the soul of the Saint, and allowed her freely to comply with

---

[1] *Vie et Oeuvres*, vol. I, n. 280, p. 264. Cf. vol. I, *Procédure de 1715*, pp. 461, 505, 510.
[2] Cf. Hamon, op. cit., vol. I, pp. 153–56.

the desires of the Sacred Heart.[1] From this time forward Margaret Mary made the practice of the Holy Hour on the night between Thursday and Friday every week. She remained faithful to it till four months before her death; then her weakness became so great that her Superior felt obliged to forbid it.

Diffusion

It is, then, Jesus Himself who taught and asked of St. Margaret Mary the practice of the Holy Hour.

Did He also express the wish that others too should give Him this proof of love, and did He charge her to spread this practice? Neither in her writings nor in her Autobiography do we find any positive evidence in support of it. Yet, the devout clients of the Sacred Heart gradually came to the conviction that our Lord's desire concerned them also, and they began to imitate the Saint. Especially after the establishment of the Archconfraternity of the Holy Hour, in 1829, this practice rapidly spread abroad.[2]

On May 22nd, 1930, at the explicit request of Pope Pius XI, the centenary of the Archconfraternity was solemnly celebrated throughout the world. The Sovereign Pontiff himself participated in the Holy Hour that was made in the basilica of St. Peter.[3]

In a letter, date March 2nd, 1933, addressed to Cardinal Marchetti-Selvaggiani, he expressed the wish that on April 6th of that year, the Holy Hour should be made not only in Rome but everywhere else, to inaugurate the Holy Year, in commemoration of the nineteenth centenary of the Redemption of mankind. The Pope himself joined in it at St. Peter's on the appointed day.

At the present day, throughout the world, innumerable friends of the Sacred Heart practise this exercise, either privately or in common, in churches and chapels.

Now also we may safely say that Jesus desired this diffusion. Pope Pius XI states it in his Encyclical *Miserentissimus* (n.23). After recalling our Lord's complaints about 'the outrages inflicted on Him by the ingratitude of men,' he adds: 'To expiate these faults, He recommended, among several other things, as being particularly agreeable to Him, the following practices: to partake,

---

[1] Cf. Hamon, op. cit., vol. 1, p. 235; *Vie et Oeuvres*, vol. 1, p. 359.
[2] Cf. appendix III, VI, p. 269.
[3] Hamon, op. cit., vol. v, pp. 207-10.

in this spirit of expiation, of the Sacrament of the Altar, by what is called "the Communion of Reparation", and to perform expiatory supplications and prayers during one hour, rightly called "the Holy Hour", which practices of piety the Church has not only approved but also enriched with abundant indulgences.'

Its Nature

The Holy Hour consists in spending one hour in (mental or vocal) prayer, in memory and in honour of Christ's interior sufferings in the Garden of Olives. Hence it is not merely a 'vigil of prayer', nor an hour of union with the Heart of Jesus, during which we strive to do everything for love of the Sacred Heart and in Its honour, as is asked of members of the Guard of Honour of the Sacred Heart, but an hour of prayer in honour of Christ's bitter Passion at Gethsemane.

This Passion we should honour by endeavouring to realize and to have compassion for our Lord's mental sufferings as far as lies in our power, by expressing to Him our sympathy, and our gratitude for His having endured them for love of us, by asking Him pardon for our own sins and for those of others, and by making reparation to Him.

We may consider this Passion not only in itself, but also in its causes. For the subject of our meditations and prayers, then, we may take whatever gave occasion for these sufferings of the Heart of Jesus, for instance, the prospect of the other sufferings that awaited Him, the ingratitude of men, their conduct towards His Sacrament of Love, the futility of His Passion and Death for so many souls, etc. But all this should be connected with Christ's mental sufferings in the Garden, and hence be considered as foreseen by Jesus and as the cause of these sufferings.

Aim and Purpose

The aims of the Holy Hour are clearly pointed out by our Lord. 'You are to rise before midnight,' He said to St. Margaret Mary 'and to remain with Me prostrate for one hour, with your face to the ground, to appease the anger of My Eternal Father, to ask Him for the pardon of sinners, and to some extent to soothe the bitter grief I suffered when My disciples abandoned Me . . .'

Thus the Holy Hour has a threefold aim: one regarding God,

namely, to make reparation to Him, by offering the sufferings of the Heart of Jesus for the sins of men, and to strive to appease His righteous anger; another with regard to sinners, namely, to ask pardon for them and to try to obtain for them abundant graces of conversion; the third regards the Heart of Jesus, namely, to console and compensate Him by our sympathy, our gratitude, and love.

The Holy Hour, therefore, is an exercise of compassionate and atoning love. This characteristic is lucidly set forth by Pope Pius XI in his Encyclical *Miserentissimus*, when he states that Jesus recommended this practice as well as the Communion of Reparation 'to expiate these faults' (ingratitude, neglectfulness, outrages); and this exercise should consist in 'expiatory supplications and prayers' (n. 23); and when he puts the question 'how these practices of atonement are able to console Christ, Who now blissfully reigns in Heaven' and answers it (n. 24). It is, therefore, in a spirit of reparation that the Holy Hour is to be made.

If then we really love the Heart of Jesus, we will want to make the Holy Hour, frequently and earnestly. We know that the prevision of our tokens of love and of our acts of reparation consoled Him in the Garden of Olives, and to some extent soothed His sufferings. We know moreover that He is even now sensible to consolation,[1] to our tokens of love, to our acts of reparation. We may then cherish the sweet conviction that by making the Holy Hour we soothed His sorrow at Gethsemane and that we even now rejoice His Heart.

How to Make the Holy Hour?

In general, all prayers and all exercises of devotion are suitable, provided they are performed for the purposes mentioned above.

There may be recommended in particular: a meditation or meditative reading on Christ's agony at Gethsemane, on some scene from His Sacred Passion, on His love in the Blessed Eucharist and men's conduct towards Him, etc.; acts of reparation and consecration to the Sacred Heart; prayers in honour of the Sacred Wounds of Jesus; the Litany of the Sacred Heart; the Way of the Cross; the sorrowful Mysteries of the Rosary, for instance, for the conversion of sinners, etc.

[1] See p. 89.

The public making of the Holy Hour should take place preferably, when possible, before the Blessed Sacrament.[1]

The priest conducts the exercise from the pulpit. He should remember that the Holy Hour is not a sermon, but meditative prayer. He should be careful to ensure that the faithful actively take part in it; this will keep their interest from flagging. It may be well to divide the hour into three or four parts, to leave pauses for private reflection and prayer after each part, and to have a hymn sung in honour of the Sacred Heart, the Blessed Sacrament, the Sacred Passion, etc., in which all take part, in connection with the previous meditation.

Some special intention, added to the three general purposes, would contribute to make the exercise attractive for the faithful. This may be, for instance, an approaching mission, the Easter-duties, the sick of the parish, the intentions of the month of the Apostleship, etc.

The exercise concludes with Benediction of the Blessed Sacrament.

Conditions

Is the Holy Hour to be made under definite conditions of time, place and attitude? No, except for the gaining of the indulgences attached to this exercise. Therefore, apart from the indulgences, it may be made on any day and hour, in any place and in any attitude.

It is true that Jesus demanded of St. Margaret Mary that she should make it on Thursday night, between eleven and midnight, prostrate with her face to the ground; and she herself always made it in the presence of the Blessed Sacrament. But these circumstances do not belong to the essence of the Holy Hour. This is witnessed by the fact that, as we shall see at once, they are not required for the gaining of the indulgences. The Holy Hour, then, may be made on any day of the week; not only in a church or chapel, but also at home or outside; not only kneeling, but also standing, walking, sitting, and even recumbent if, for instance, one is ill.

Let us, however, where possible, make it preferably under the conditions appointed by Jesus Himself; if possible, on Thursday,

[1] For methods of making the Holy Hour we refer to the excellent booklets: *The Holy Hour* by the late Fr. J. McDonnell, s.j., and *The Devotion of the Holy Hour* by Rev. W. Stephenson, s.j. (1946). Suitable prayers will be found in *An Hour with Jesus* by Rev. P. O'Mara, s.j.

for it is the day on which the tragedy of Gethsemane was enacted, which we commemorate in the Holy Hour; and if it is convenient, between eleven and twelve, for about that time the Passion of the Sacred Heart at Gethsemane reached its climax. If this is not possible, we should at least try to make the Holy Hour late in the evening, in order to make it coincide as much as possible with the time during which Jesus endured His agony.

If we are unable to make the exercise prostrate with our face to the ground, we should at least take up a respectful attitude of supplication, and remain kneeling if possible during the whole hour.

We should make the Holy Hour preferably in a church or chapel, before the Blessed Sacrament, close to our Saviour whom we wish to console and compensate. The prospect of the ingratitude of men towards the Holy Eucharist was indeed one of the causes of the Passion of His Heart at Gethsemane.

But, if we want to gain the indulgences that are attached to the Holy Hour, then we must fulfil certain conditions, which differ according to the indulgences granted.

The Popes have granted, among others, two plenary indulgences, of which one is reserved to members of the Archconfraternity of the Holy Hour, and the other may be gained by all the faithful.

For the first, the conditions are:

1. To be enrolled in the Archconfraternity or in an affiliated association.[1]

2. To make the Holy Hour on Thursday afternoon, between two o'clock and midnight.[2]

3. Confession, Communion, and prayer for the Pope's intentions.

Hence, to gain this plenary indulgence, there is no condition as to place. It may be gained anywhere. Only the time is appointed: Thursday, between two o'clock and midnight.

The second plenary indulgence was granted by Pope Pius XI (S. Penit., March 21st, 1933) to all who, after Confession and

---

[1] Members of the Apostleship of Prayer are not subject to this condition.

[2] For members of the Apostleship of Prayer this time is protracted to sunrise on Friday (about six o'clock). Moreover, they may gain this indulgence every time they make the Holy Hour in common, in a church or chapel, on any day of the week and at any hour appointed by the local Director.

Communion, with prayers for the Pope's intentions, make the Holy Hour in common, in any church, public or semi-public chapel.[1]

Hence, for this second plenary indulgence no membership is required of the Archconfraternity of the Holy Hour or of the Apostleship of Prayer. All the faithful may gain it. No definite time is assigned, but only the place, namely, a church, a public or semi-public chapel. Moreover, the exercise must be performed publicly, in common.[2]

For neither of the two plenary indulgences is any special attitude prescribed. Hence the exercise may be made either kneeling, standing, or sitting.

In short, therefore, to gain a plenary indulgence by making the Holy Hour: if it be made privately, one must be enrolled in the Archconfraternity of the Holy Hour or in the Apostleship of Prayer, and make it on Thursday afternoon between two o'clock and midnight; but it may be performed in any place. If it be made in common, in a church, public or semi-public chapel, it is not necessary to be inscribed in one of these two associations, and the plenary indulgence may be gained on any day of the week and at any hour.

In both cases one must go to Confession and Communion, and pray for the Pope's intentions, either on the day on which the Holy Hour is made, or the next day.[3]

§ III. PRACTICE OF VENERATION

A. HOW TO INCITE OURSELVES TO VENERATION

To incite ourselves to pay honour to the Heart of Jesus—which is the first secondary end of the Devotion—we should consider the titles and claims which He has to that worship.

Those titles and claims we indicated when we showed in the

---

[1] An indulgence of ten years, to those who, with at least a contrite heart (i.e. without Confession or Communion), make this exercise in public or privately. Cf. *Preces et pia opera*, n. 139.

[2] Cf. Vermeersch, s.j., *Periodica de re morali, canonica et liturgica*, 1933, p. 113. Cf. also *Preces et pia opera*, n. 139.

[3] Cf. Lammertijn, C.ss.R., *Gethsémani*; P. Mateo-Crawley, *Heure Sainte*; Parra, s.j., *Gethsémani*; Dargaud, *Au Cœur de Jésus agonisant notre cœur compatissant*; Bouchat, *Vigilate*; Conon, *Au Jardin des Oliviers, Heure Sainte type*; Tesnière, *L'Heure Sainte offerte au Sacré-Cœur de Jésus*; Monastère de la Visitation de Paray-le-Monial, *Allons à Gethsémani*.

second chapter the reasons why the Heart of Jesus deserves to be honoured.

The first and general reason is Its Divine dignity, whereby It is worthy of the supreme cult of adoration. For this Heart is personally, hypostatically united with the Second Person of the Most Blessed Trinity. It belongs to a Divine Person, It is the Heart of a Divine Person.

Then Its quality of symbol and principle of Jesus' love.[1] The symbol and principle of a thing that is worthy to be honoured is itself worthy of that honour. Now, the love of Jesus deserves it in the highest degree, because of its generosity, its abnegation, and its heroism.

Finally, Its quality of symbol and principle of His whole inner life.[2] This inner life deserves in the highest degree our veneration, because of its ideal beauty.

We will then arouse ourselves to worship the Heart of Jesus by contemplating the Divine dignity of that Heart, and also the transcendent beauty of the love and of the whole inner life of Jesus, of which His Heart is at once the principle and the symbol.

B. HOW TO TESTIFY OUR VENERATION

1. General Practices

We may and must worship the Heart of Jesus by paying to It the homage of our adoration. And as this Heart is really present in the Eucharist, it is preferably there that we should adore It. We ought particularly to do so when, on entering a church, we make the genuflection before the Tabernacle; when Jesus at the Consecration of the Mass becomes present on the altar under the species of bread and wine; when in Holy Communion His Heart rests in ours.

We may and must worship It by the reverence with which we address It whilst performing our exercises of devotion. These exercises, it is true, ought to be inspired and animated by love, yet this love should always be fraught with respect. This reverence will also manifest itself in the way in which we speak of the Heart of Jesus. We should take an example from St. Margaret Mary. She never pronounced Its name without adding an adjective: Divine,

[1] See p. 18.   [2] See p. 25.

sacred, adorable, or lovable. 'The adorable Heart of Our Lord Jesus Christ', 'this Divine Heart', 'His Sacred Heart', these expressions recur frequently in her writings.

We may and must worship It, by recognizing, admiring, praising, proclaiming and exalting. Its dignity, Its greatness, Its virtues, Its perfections and Its merits. This we do excellently by devoutly reciting the Litany of the Sacred Heart. Surely this Litany is to implore the mercy of Jesus, to obtain special graces; but the invocations of which it is composed are almost all in connection with some special property of His Heart, by which It deserves our worship. Thus the Litany forms a magnificent eulogy of the Sacred Heart.

We may and must worship It by observing Its liturgical Feast, and by joining in the solemnities and ceremonies in Its honour.

Finally, we should worship It by honouring Its image or picture. Of this practice we treat in particular in the next section.

2. Special Practice: The Cult of the Image of the Heart of Jesus

In honouring the image (picture or statue) of the Heart of Jesus we honour in reality the Heart of Jesus Itself. For the homage which we pay to the picture or statue of a person is directed to the person himself. The image is honoured only because of the person whom it represents. The cult of the image of Jesus is therefore, as it is termed by theologians, a relative cult.

I. OUR LORD'S DESIRE

In the second great apparition Jesus made known to St. Margaret Mary His wish to see the image of His Sacred Heart honoured by men. 'He assured me,' she writes, "that He took a singular pleasure in being honoured under the figure of this Heart of flesh . . ." Wherever this image should be exposed and honoured, He would lavishly pour forth His graces and blessings.' Nor did our Lord confine Himself to this manifestation of His desire, He recurred to it again and again, now repeating and confirming His promises on behalf of those who should honour this image,[1] now

---

[1] *Vie et Oeuvres*, Vol. II., *Lettre à la Mère de Saumaise*, p. 296, and *Lettre à la Mère Greyfié*, p. 300.

Q

expressing His displeasure because of the delay in executing the model of the picture that was to be engraved.[1]

The first image of the Sacred Heart of Jesus was a pen-drawing made by the Saint herself.[2] It was to this picture that the collective homage of her novices was paid on 20th July, 1685, the name-day of the Saint.[3]

At the instance of Jesus, and convinced of the importance of the picture for the spread of her beloved devotion, the Saint spared herself no pains to obtain the printing of it. How many steps she took to hasten the finish of the print![4] What affliction when the realization of her design met with delay![5] What rapture of joy when at last she received a proof satisfying her expectations,[6] and when she received the first copies of the print.[7]

The pictures rapidly spread abroad. They unquestionably helped to popularize the Devotion.

II. UTILITY OF THE PICTURE

The pictures indeed are of outstanding value to the Devotion, as they bring it within the range of all, and particularly help to make it easy, by appealing to the eye; thus they facilitate its practice. They help our memory to think of the Heart of Jesus; our imagination, to represent it to us; our minds, to consider what is symbolized by this Heart, namely, His boundless love; these pictures appeal to our hearts, in order that we may be moved by these thoughts; especially when the Heart of Jesus is represented with the characteristic emblems: the wound, the cross, the thorns and the flames, with which It showed Itself to St. Margaret Mary in the second apparition.

'Is it not true,' writes Fr. Froment, 'that the image of the Heart of Jesus, when we look at it, arouses more vividly in us the memory of Him who was "wounded for our iniquities" (Isa. liii, 5) and who always opens to us His bosom to receive us? Is it not true that, as long as this image, exposed to our eyes, keeps alive such a

---

[1] *Vie et Oeuvres*, Vol. II, *Lettre à la Mère de Saumaise*, p. 315.

[2] It is kept in the Visitation convent at Turin.

[3] In Hamon, op. cit., vol. I, pp. 349–69, and in Yenveux, op. cit., vol. II, pp. 348–62, is found the interesting account of this simple but moving ceremony, of the stir caused by this novelty among the elder Sisters, and also of the sudden change brought about in their dispositions.

[4] *Vie et Oeuvres*, vol. II, pp. 305 and 311.

[5] Ibid., pp. 315, 325, 345.

[6] Ibid., p. 355. Cf. Hamon, op. cit., vol. I, p. 385.

[7] Ibid., p. 382. Cf. Hamon, p. 384; and Yenveux, p. 397.

precious memory in our souls, we are prompted to love this God-Man who suffered His Heart to be pierced for love of us, and to have recourse in our needs to that secure refuge which He presents to us? Can any one see the light and flames which burst forth from this Divine Heart, without being reminded that It is the source of the most pure love? Does the sight of the cross, which is planted in this Sacred Heart, not remind us that Jesus from the first moment of His Incarnation till His death, endured in His Heart all the bitterness of His Passion, and that it is His Divine Heart, that it is His infinite love for men, which induced Him to redeem them through the most ignominious torments?'[1]

Moreover, the images of the Heart of Jesus facilitate the practice of the Devotion, by offering to our homage a present and visible object. Whereas this Heart Itself is absent and invisible, the image is close to us; we see it with our eyes. It represents the Heart of Jesus, so that in honouring the image we honour in reality the Heart of Jesus itself. Hence, because of this picture, it is easy for us to pay our homage to His Heart, to behold It lovingly, to press It to our own hearts, to kneel before It, to stretch forth to It our entreating hands, to surround It with candlelight and flowers, etc.

III. WAY OF REPRESENTING THE HEART OF JESUS

As for the way of representing the Heart of Jesus, it should be noted that in the apparitions made to St. Margaret Mary sometimes it is the Heart only that is shown her, sometimes Jesus himself who appears and shows His Heart.

In the fourth great apparition Jesus appears in person and shows His Heart in His opened breast, saying: 'Behold this Heart, which has so loved men . . .' Likewise in the third: 'Jesus Christ, my sweet Master, presented Himself to me, all resplendent with glory, with His five wounds, shining like so many suns. From all parts of His sacred Humanity there issued forth flames, but especially from His adorable breast, which was like a furnace. And opening it, He showed me His loving and lovable Heart, which was the fountain-head of those flames.'

On the other hand, in the second apparition, it is the Heart only that appears: 'This Divine Heart was shown to me as on a throne of flames, more dazzling than the sun, and transparent as

[1] Froment, op. cit., Book III, chap. x.

crystal, with that adorable wound, and surrounded with a crown of thorns . . .'

So it comes about that the Heart of Jesus is represented now separately, now on or in the breast of the person of Jesus. In the first pictures that were made the person of Jesus never appears; the Heart only is represented.[1] There is no objection to using pictures of this sort. The contention that they are prohibited by the Church is unfounded.[2] There are even indulgences granted to those who wear such images. It is not allowed, however, to place them on the altars and expose them to the public worship of the faithful.[3] Moreover, it is required that the Heart should be visible upon or in the breast. Hence it is not enough that the wound of the pierced side should be visible, nor even that our Lord points with His hand to this wound or to the place of the Heart; the Heart Itself must be seen.[4]

Yet, as the Heart of Christ is not considered under its anatomical aspect but as the symbol of His love, it is not of importance to represent it with scientific accuracy as regards its position, shape and outward appearance; it is sufficient that everyone at first sight may recognize a human heart.[5] On the other hand, to emphasize the symbolical significance of the Heart, it is desirable that It should be represented with the traditional emblems: the wound, the cross, the thorns, the rays and flames.[6]

IV. A THREEFOLD CULT

Jesus asks a threefold cult for this picture of His Heart: a private or personal, a collective or domestic, and a public worship.

A private or personal cult. 'He wishes you to have a copper-plate made of the image of this Sacred Heart,' writes the Saint to Mother de Saumaise, 'in order that all those who want to pay to It any particular homage, may have images in their homes, and small ones to wear.'[7]

Jesus then desires that the faithful should possess pictures of

---

[1] Cf. Yenveux, op. cit., vol. II, p. 371.
[2] Cf. Terrien, op. cit., p. 240; Bainvel, op. cit., p. 548; Noldin, op. cit., p. 184; Richstätter, s.j., *Das Herz des Welterlösers*, p. 95.
[3] Bainvel, op. cit., p. 548; Beringer, op. cit., vol. I, n. 669, note.
[4] Answer of the Sacred Congregation of Indulgences, January 12th, 1878. Cf. Beringer, op. cit., vol. I, n. 669, note.
[5] Cf. Terrien, op. cit., p. 237.
[6] Cf. Richstätter, op. cit., pp. 96-100.
[7] *Vie et Oeuvres*, vol. II, p. 306, note.

His Heart for their personal devotion, and that they should place them in their room, study, office, convent-cell, etc., and even that they should wear them.

Further, He wishes them not to be content with this only, but to honour the picture, for instance, by greeting it, by respectfully kissing it, by adorning it with flowers and candles, etc.[1]

Here are some pious practices recommended by Fr. Froment:

1. Cast frequent glances on this image, in order to remind you of the boundless love with which this Divine Heart is burning for you, and thus to urge you on to renew to Him the consecration and donation which you have made to It of your own heart.

2. At times kneel down before this image, and pray to Jesus that He may give you His Divine Heart, His holy love.

3. Sometimes remember, at the sight of this Sacred Heart, the gifts and graces you have received from Him.

4. At other times, remember, kneeling before this image, the ingratitude of your heart towards the infinitely bountiful Heart of Jesus.

5. At times consider that this Divine Heart, which is represented to you in this image, however lovable, is nevertheless so little loved.

6. At the sight of this image, reflect on the dispositions of your heart, and see that there is nothing in you that may displease the Heart of Jesus. See in particular what you are lacking in order to resemble this most Sacred Heart.

7. At the sight of the sacred wound of this Divine Heart, reflect that Jesus invites you to enter through this opening into His Heart and offers to establish you there.

8. When passing by this image, make some acts of adoration, thanksgiving, supplication, reparation or love.

9. Finally, sometimes respectfully kiss this Heart which you see pictured, to show with what reverence and tenderness you would apply your lips to the sacred Side of our Lord, if you had the good fortune to approach it.[2]

---

[1] An indulgence of 500 days is granted to the faithful who, before an image of the Sacred Heart of Jesus, devoutly recite one *Our Father*, one *Hail Mary*, and *Glory be to the Father*, with the aspiration: *Sweet Heart of Jesus, make me love Thee ever more*. Moreover a plenary indulgence, under the usual conditions, if they observe this practice daily for a month. (*Preces et pia opera*, n. 216.)

[2] Froment, op. cit., Book III, chap. x.

St. Margaret Mary had placed an image of the Sacred Heart on her work-table; before this emblem of the love of Jesus, and almost always kneeling, she used to work, read and pray. 'My dear Sister,' we read at the end of one of her letters, 'that is what presented itself to my mind before the image of the Sacred Heart, in answer to what your heart tells me; for I do my writing kneeling, to answer to those who apply to me concerning the devotion to this Sacred Heart.'

Jesus also asks for the image of His Heart a domestic, collective cult. 'He promised me,' writes the Saint, 'that He would lavishly pour forth the blessings of His Sacred Heart wherever the image of this lovable Heart should be exposed and honoured; that through this means He would reunite families, whose members are at variance among themselves, and that He would assist and protect those who were in any need.'[1]

As the promises are made on behalf of the families as such, so the cult of the image is asked of the homes as such. Hence it is not sufficient that members of the family honour it, each one for himself; it should be a collective cult.

It is also of religious communities as such that Jesus asks a collective worship paid to His Heart: 'He promised me . . . that He would shed the sweet unction of His ardent love on every Community that shows special honour to this divine image.'[2]

This domestic worship may take various forms.

Some prefer to expose the image of the Sacred Heart in the place of honour, for instance, in the drawing-room, thus to manifest that they recognize the Sacred Heart as King of the home. This view is specially propagated by the Work of the Enthronement.

Others prefer to join the Sacred Heart to their whole daily life, and expose Its image in the living-room, so that members of the family may see and greet it whenever they wish. This conception is particularly propagated by the Work of the Consecration of Families, which is a section of the Apostleship of Prayer.[3]

Others, finally, like to place the image in a kind of oratory, where the family meets every day for night-prayers, and where each one may come and pray individually.

---

[1] *Vie et Oeuvres*, vol. II, *Lettre à la Mère de Saumaise*, p. 296. Cf. also *Lettre à la Mère Greyfié*, ibid., p. 532.
[2] Ibid.
[3] Cf. p. 139: The Consecration of Families.

All three ideas are good. The main point is that the family as such should honour the Sacred Heart, by collective homage and prayer.

Finally, Jesus desires for the image of His Heart a public worship. 'He assured me,' writes the Saint, 'that He took a singular pleasure in being honoured under the figure of His Heart of flesh, the image of which He wished to be exposed in public, in order, He added, to touch by it the insensible hearts of men.'[1]

Jesus then wishes the image of His Heart to be exposed in places where it may be seen by all, in public roads and squares, especially in churches and chapels, that it may strike the eyes of all and appeal to the hearts of all. But it is evident that He also desires that this image should be honoured and adorned, and that it should receive public homage.

Lately this practice has spread more and more. The erection of a statue of the Sacred Heart, especially on the occasion of the Consecration of parishes and districts to the Sacred Heart,[2] gives rise to magnificent demonstrations, which are renewed every year on the Feasts of the Sacred Heart and of Christ the King.

§ IV. PRACTICE OF CONFIDENCE

A. HOW TO INCITE OURSELVES TO CONFIDENCE

To arouse ourselves to trust in the Sacred Heart—which is the second subsidiary end of the Devotion—it is sufficient to ponder its motives.

We have seen what these motives are: Its riches and power, which make It able to help us; Its kindness and love for us, which make It willing to help us; finally, Its promises and Its fidelity, which guarantee that It will certainly help us.

If, then, we want to enkindle our trust in the Sacred Heart of Jesus, we should often remember how rich and powerful He is; how kind He is and how much He loves us, and what magnificent promises He made. We should consider, as addressed to us personally, the comforting invitation: 'Come to Me, all you that labour and are burdened, and I will refresh you' (Matt. xi, 28).

---

[1] *Vie et Oeuvres*, vol. II, *Lettre au P. Croiset*, p. 572.
[2] See p. 141.

B. HOW TO TESTIFY OUR CONFIDENCE

1. Invocation

We show our trust in the Sacred Heart chiefly by having recourse to It, by invoking It in our difficulties and needs, in our sufferings and sorrows, and by imploring Its aid and succour. Thus St. Margaret Mary did herself and recommended others also to do. In her letters she assures her correspondents that she prays to the Sacred Heart for them, and she begs them to render her the same service. 'I pray the adorable Heart of Jesus to make you experience the powerful influence of His merciful charity.'[1] 'I beseech the adorable Heart of Jesus to sanctify our hearts.'[2] 'I don't omit asking Him for the recovery of your health.'[3] 'I urgently need your prayers to the Sacred Heart, which is my only hope; do not refuse them to me, I beseech you, assuring you that I will not forget you in His presence.'[4] 'I hope much of your calling on the Sacred Heart, which is all my consolation and hope.'[5]

Every one is free to invoke the Sacred Heart in the terms he prefers. There is, however, a prayer which deserves our preference, because it has become the prayer of our Mother the Church and is in use throughout the world among devout clients of the Sacred Heart, among the true faithful, namely, the Litany of the Sacred Heart. It will not be inappropriate, then, to give a somewhat more detailed account of the origin and contents of this Litany.

The Litany of the Sacred Heart

As we said in the Introduction,[6] this Litany, in its present form, was approved by Pope Leo XIII on April 2nd, 1899, and recognized as an official, liturgical prayer for the universal Church.[7]

The first Litany[8] appeared in a booklet which was published in 1686, by Mother de Soudeilles, the Superior of the Visitation convent at Moulins; it is the so-called *Livret de Moulins*.[9] From

---

[1] *Vie et Oeuvres*, vol. II, p. 370.   [2] Ibid., p. 336.   [3] Ibid., p. 381.
[4] Ibid., p. 329.   [5] Ibid., p. 496.   [6] See p. xliii.
[7] There are only four other Litanies which enjoy the same privilege: that of the Saints, of the Most Holy Name of Jesus, of the Blessed Virgin, and of St. Joseph.
[8] We speak only of the Litanies which are in connection with the apparitions at Paray-le-Monial and with our present Litany. A long time before those apparitions, both the Polish Jesuit Gaspar Druzbicki, who died in 1662, had composed eight Litanies of the Sacred Heart, and St. John Eudes had edited one in a prayer-book published in 1668.
[9] Cf. Hamon, op. cit., vol. I, p. 393.

some passages of St. Margaret Mary's letters[1] it might be gathered that she herself composed it. She used to recite it, that much is certain.[2]

Another Litany appeared, in 1689, in a booklet on devotion to the Sacred Heart, written by Sister Joly, of the Visitation of Dijon,[3] the so-called *Livret de Soeur Joly*. St. Margaret. Mary certainly knew this Litany, and probably recited it.

Two years later, in 1691, a third Litany was published in the second edition of Fr. Croiset's book on the devotion.

In her turn, the Venerable Madeleine de Rémusat, of the Visitation at Marseilles,[4] composed a Litany, which she published in 1718, in her Manual for the Confraternity of perpetual adoration of the Sacred Heart. This Litany, however, was no original work; of the twenty-seven invocations contained in it, there are seventeen taken from the Litany composed by Fr. Croiset and five from that of Sister Joly. Yet it became famous under the name of the *Litany of Marseilles*, because it was sung at the penitential processions organized by Mgr. de Belsunce on the occasion of the terrible plague that broke out in the city, in 1720.[5]

It was this Litany of Marseilles which, with the addition of six invocations taken from the Litany of Moulins and that of Fr. Croiset, was approved by Pope Leo XIII and became the official Litany of the Sacred Heart. These invocations are thirty-three in number, in memory of the thirty-three years of our Lord's lifetime on earth. Of these thirty-three invocations fifteen are in accordance, if not literally, at least as regards their sense, with the Litany of the booklet of Moulins. Hence, we may say that the Litany which we recite is nearly the same as that which St. Margaret Mary used to say.

'Equally precious for its antiquity and for the historical associations connected with its composition and original use, the Litany, as now sanctioned, also merits the respect and pious devotion of the faithful on account of the sacred source whence it has sprung.

---

[1] Cf., for instance, *Vie et Oeuvres*, vol. II, pp. 353–54.

[2] Cf. ibid., vol. II, p. 519.

[3] This Sister, being a fervent promoter of the new devotion, composed in French a Mass, Office, and a Litany of the Sacred Heart. This Mass, translated into Latin, was sung at Dijon on the first Friday of February 1689. (Cf. Hamon, op. cit., vol. III, p. 318.) The Sister died in odour of sanctity on October 19th, 1708. (Cf. *Vie et Oeuvres*, vol. III, p. 468.)

[4] Cf. Hamon, op. cit., vol. III, p. 425.

[5] Ibid., vol. III, pp. 431–49.

We may say all the invocations are derived from Holy Scripture; many, indeed, are literal quotations.'[1]

We cannot say that the invocations are in any logical or pre-arranged order. Nor can we expect logical sequence if we bear in mind how the Litany was composed. Yet we may distinguish two principal parts: what the Sacred Heart is in Itself (invoc. 1-16), and what It is with regard to us (invoc. 17-33).

In these invocations we sum up some titles in honour of this Heart, in order to praise It and favourably dispose It towards us, some motives which must urge us to trust in It, and reasons we advance for being heard.

Here we should recall that the immediate object of the devotion to the Sacred Heart is not merely the physical Heart of Jesus, but also His spiritual Heart, or rather the unity formed by both of them joined, what we have called His total Heart.[2] It is to this Heart that we attribute the excellences, the qualities, and the affections of Jesus; it is to this Heart that we address our invocations.

But, as we have seen, the person of Jesus is the ultimate object of the devotion. The invocation, as well as every other homage, is directed, properly speaking, through this Heart, to the Person of Jesus. To call upon the Heart of Jesus is to call upon Jesus to whom this Heart belongs, by finding in the dignity, in the qualities and in the sentiments of this Heart, motives for praise or trust, and reasons for being heard. Thus the sense of the invocations is: '*Jesus, whose Heart we honour, glowing furnace of charity*, etc., *have mercy on us;*' or, '*Jesus, for Thy Heart, glowing furnace of charity*, etc., *have mercy on us.*'

There is then no reason why we should give the word 'Heart' different interpretations, thereby understanding now the physical Heart, now the will, the soul or the whole Person of Jesus. In all the invocations the word keeps the same sense, namely, that of 'total Heart'; but in certain invocations attention is drawn more specially to the physical Heart, in others to the spiritual Heart.[3]

---

[1] Vermeersch, op. cit., vol. II, p. 96.

[2] See p. 28.

[3] Cf. p. 72. An excellent commentary will be found in Joseph McDonnell, s.j.,' *The Litany of the Sacred Heart*; R. V. O'Connell, s.j., *Reflections on the Litany of the Sacred Heart*; in French: Vermeersch, op. cit., vol. II, p. 84; Leroy, *Les Litanies du Sacré-Cœur de Jésus*; Drive, s.j., *Les Litanies du Sacré-Cœur*; Ch. Sauvé, *Le Sacré-Cœur intime*, vol. III, *Les Litanies*.

2. The Scapular of the Sacred Heart

We also show our confidence by wearing the scapular of the Sacred Heart.

There are two sorts of scapular of the Sacred Heart: the small scapular and the scapular properly so called.

I. THE SMALL SCAPULAR

The small scapular is not a scapular in the strict sense; it does not consist, like the scapular properly so called, of two strips of cloth or wool, attached to two strings and hanging down on breast and back. It is a badge of white flannel, worn on the breast.

Its origin goes back to St. Margaret Mary. As we said above, the Saint, in a letter dated March 2nd, 1686, writes to Mother de Saumaise 'He (Jesus) desires that you should have a copperplate made of the image of this Sacred Heart, that all who want to pay some special homage to Him may possess copies of it in their homes, and small ones to wear.'[1] She herself used to wear such an image on her breast and invited her novices to do the same. She made many of these emblems and recommended the wearing of them as very agreeable to the Sacred Heart.

It was especially in the year 1720, during the gloomy days of the plague of Marseilles,[2] that this small scapular, called 'Sauvegarde' (Safeguard), was spread among the faithful. This 'Safeguard' consisted of a strip of white cloth, on which the image of the Sacred Heart was embroidered, with the legend 'O Heart of Jesus, abyss of love and mercy, I trust in Thee.'[3] The Venerable Madeleine de Rémusat, to whom our Lord had made known beforehand the ravages which the scourge would cause and also the wonderful help the inhabitants of the desolated city would find in the devotion to His Sacred Heart, made with the aid of her Sisters in Religion these emblems by thousands and spread them in profusion in the city and environs. History relates that very often the terrible scourge was wonderfully checked through this sacred badge.[4]

Among the presents which Pope Benedict XIV, in 1748, sent to the Polish Princess Mary Leczinska on the occasion of her

---

[1] *Vie et Oeuvres*, vol. II, p. 306, note.

[2] Cf. Hamon, op. cit., vol. III, p. 431.

[3] Some writers erroneously mention the words: 'Cease, the Heart of Jesus is there.' This inscription dates from later time. (Hamon, ibid., note.)

[4] Cf. Hamon, op. cit., vol. III, p. 425; Beringer, op. cit., vol. I, n. 953, p. 520.

marriage with the French King Louis XV, there were, according to the memoirs of that time, 'many Sacred Heart badges made of red taffeta with golden embroidery.'[1]

At the time of the French Revolution these scapulars were held to be 'the livery of fanaticism' and as an evidence of hostility to the revolutionary régime. During the trial of the unfortunate Queen Marie Antoinette there was produced against her, as a piece of evidence, a strip of thin paper which was found in her possession, on which a picture of the Sacred Heart was drawn, with the wound, the cross and the thorny crown, and with the legend: 'Sacred Heart, have mercy on us.'[2]

From that time forward the pious use of this scapular spread greatly, especially since, in 1866, during the ravages caused by the cholera epidemic at Amiens, Roubaix, Cairo and elsewhere, its beneficial influence was experienced; and also since during the Franco-German war the Sauvegardes proved more than once to have shielded French soldiers against the bullets of their enemies.[3]

Pope Pius IX granted, in 1872, an indulgence of 500 days once a day to all the faithful who wear round their neck this pious emblem and recite one Our Father, one Hail Mary, and one Glory be to the Father.[4]

In a brief, dated June 20th, 1873, we find the answer to two questions regarding the 'Sauvegarde': 1. As it is not a scapular in the strict sense of the word, but merely a badge or emblem of the Sacred Heart, the general rules laid down for the scapular properly so called, are not applicable to it. Hence it needs neither special blessing, nor ceremony, nor inscription in a register; it is enough to wear it round the neck so that it hangs down on the breast. 2. The legend 'Cease, the Heart of Jesus is there', is not required.[5]

On June 14th, 1877, the Director-General of the Apostleship of Prayer obtained an indulgence of 100 days for the members who wear this badge, with the inscription 'Thy Kingdom come', each time they repeat, orally or mentally, this aspiration. The badge may be made of any material, e.g. cloth or enamel.[6]

[1] De Franciosi, s.j., *La dévotion au Sacré-Cœur de Jésus*, p. 289.
[2] Ibid., p. 290.
[3] Cf. *Messager du Cœur de Jésus*, vol. xix, p. 180.
[4] *Preces et pia opera*, n. 219.
[5] Beringer, op. cit., n. 953; *Preces et pia opera*, n. 219.
[6] Beringer, op. cit., n. 231, p. 7 and note.

II. THE SCAPULAR PROPERLY SO CALLED

The scapular properly so called owes its origin to the apparitions of the Blessed Virgin to Estelle Faguette at Pellevoisin, in 1876, and hence is often called 'the scapular of Pellevoisin'. The decree of September 3rd, 1904, whereby it was enriched with indulgences, states that the spiritual favours, granted for the wearing of the scapular, by no means imply any approbation of the extraordinary events that happened at Pellevoisin.

This scapular consists of two strips of white flannel attached to the ordinary strings; on one strip is a picture of the Sacred Heart in red with the characteristic emblems, and on the other the image of the Blessed Virgin, with the title of 'Mother of Mercy'.

It was approved by Decree of the Sacred Congregation of Rites, dated April 4th, 1900. At the same time a special form was prescribed for blessing and giving it. The Superior-General of the Oblates of Mary Immaculate, the Superior-General of the Priests of the Sacred Heart, and some others are empowered to give it and to permit priests to do so.[1]

By Brief of June 10th, 1900, Pope Leo XIII granted special indulgences to those who devoutly wear this scapular. This he did, as he stated in the Brief, 'in order that the devotion and love towards the Divine Heart of Jesus might remain fervent among the faithful and increase ever more.'[2]

3. Other Practices

In addition to the invocation and the wearing of the scapular, St. Margaret Mary recommends, doubtless in accordance with our Lord's desire, three other practices, by which we show our trust in the Heart of Jesus.

I. IN ALL THINGS TO UNITE OURSELVES WITH THE HEART OF JESUS

She recommends us, first, to unite all our affections, our acts of virtue, and our ordinary actions, with those of the Heart of Jesus, in order to supply by the perfection of His for the deficiency of ours. Through this union our sentiments, our acts of virtue and our actions become more perfect, more agreeable to God, and of greater merit for ourselves. They are made divine, as it were, and

[1] Beringer, op. cit., vol. I, n. 943.
[2] Ibid.

become so to speak the sentiments, the acts of virtue, and the actions of Jesus Himself.

'You have only in all that you do,' she writes, 'to unite yourself with the Heart of Our Lord Jesus Christ; at the beginning, to serve you as dispositions; and at the end as satisfaction . . . This lovable Heart will supply for what may have been lacking on your part.'[1]

'It would even be well to unite our defects with the opposite virtues of His Heart, our irascibility with Its meekness, our pride with Its humility, our tepidity with Its ardent charity, etc.' that It may make up for our failings by Its virtues. To recommend us this practice the Saint employs the same metaphor as for urging us to trust in the Sacred Heart, namely, the image of the two abysses, and opposes to the abyss of our defects that of the virtues of the Heart of Jesus: 'If you are in an abyss of resistance and opposition to the will of God, you are to throw yourself into the abyss of submission and conformity to the good pleasure of the Divine Heart of Jesus. If you are in an abyss of distractions, throw yourself into the abyss of the tranquility of the Sacred Heart. If you are in an abyss of pride and vain self-esteem, throw yourself into the abyss of humility of the Sacred Heart. If you are in an abyss of infidelity and inconstancy, throw yourself into that of the firmness and steadfastness of the Sacred Heart of Jesus. If you are in an abyss of peevishness and anger, throw yourself into that of the meekness of the lovable Heart of Jesus . . .'[2]

This union with the Heart of Jesus is particularly suggested to members of the Apostleship of Prayer. They are asked to offer all their prayers, actions and sufferings in union with the Sacred Heart. Not only do they pray and offer everything for the intentions of the Sacred Heart, but they unite their very prayer and offering to that of the Heart of Jesus. By this union their prayer and their offering share in the dignity, perfection and efficacy of that of the Heart of our Lord.[3]

II. TO OFFER TO GOD THE HEART OF JESUS

The Saint also recommends us to offer to God the acts of adoration, thanksgiving, satisfaction, acts of charity, etc., of the Heart of Jesus. Indeed, by Its sentiments the Sacred Heart

---

[1] *Vie et Oeuvres*, vol. II, *Lettre à la Sœur de la Barge*, p. 498.
[2] Ibid., vol. I, pp. 753–74.   [3] Cf. Appendix II, iii, p. 264.

glorifies God in the most perfect way possible. Hence in presenting them to God we give Him a glory truly worthy of Him and supply for what is lacking in our own. By this offering we adore, love, thank and propitiate God through the Heart of Jesus. 'He will love God for you,' the Saint writes to a Sister, 'and you will love God in Him and through Him.'[1] And to Father Croiset: 'The Sacred Heart of Our Lord Jesus Christ will do all this for me if I leave that to Him: It will love for me, and will supply for my impotence and defects.'[2]

It is also very helpful to offer to God the Heart of Jesus with Its acts of adoration, Its merits, Its satisfactions, etc., in order to appease His anger and avert the punishments we deserve for our sins. 'How powerful is this Divine Heart to appease God's anger provoked by the multitude of our sins, and which brought on us all those calamities that afflict us. Common prayers have great power with this Sacred Heart, which will avert the rigours of Divine Justice, placing Itself between them and all sinners to obtain mercy.'[3]

And to atone for our faults, it will be well to offer to God the opposite virtues of the Heart of Jesus. 'When we have committed any fault,' writes the Saint, 'we must have recourse to this Divine Heart to reconcile us to God the Father, to whom we are to offer one of the opposite virtues, for instance, Its humility for our pride, and so on. If we do this lovingly, we shall, according to His promises, by this means discharge our debt to Divine Justice.'[4]

III. TO TAKE THE HEART OF JESUS AS A REFUGE

Lastly, the Saint recommends us to enter in spirit into the Heart of Jesus, in order to find there security, rest, peace, interior recollection, and help.

'I beseech you,' we read in her Instructions and Advice, 'establish yourself in the Sacred Heart of Jesus. Lay down there all the good you do; seek there all that you need.'[5] Again: 'Fear not to enter His Sacred Heart;' she writes to Sister de la Barge, 'Jesus Himself invites you to take your rest there,'[6] And to a

[1] *Vie et Oeuvres*, vol. II, *Lettre à la Sœur de la Barge*, p. 498.
[2] Ibid., vol. II, p. 522.
[3] Ibid., vol. II, p. 480.
[4] Ibid., vol. II, *3e Lettre au P. Croiset*, p. 557.
[5] Ibid., vol. II, p. 654.
[6] Ibid., vol. II, p. 410.

novice: 'Take up your abode in this adorable Heart; bring there whatever grieves or afflicts you; there you will find the remedy for your diseases, strength in your weakness, and a refuge in all your needs.'[1] Again: 'In this Divine Heart everything, even the bitterest grief, is changed into love. We should then establish ourselves there, now and for ever, and nothing will disturb our peace, provided we wholly commit ourselves to Him.'[2] Again: 'This Divine Heart is a secure refuge and a fortress for those who have recourse to it to escape Divine Justice.'[3]

In the Preface of the Mass for the Feast of the Sacred Heart the Church teaches us that one of the reasons why Jesus suffered His Heart to be pierced was to provide souls with a resting-place and shelter: 'God, who didst will that thine only-begotten Son as He hung upon the cross should be pierced by a soldier's spear, that this opened Heart . . . might be a resting-place for the devout and afford a refuge of salvation for the penitent.'

In the Collect of the Mass of the Feast of St. Margaret Mary she bids us pray that we may dwell within His Heart for evermore.[4] And already, a long time before Jesus had revealed His Heart to the Saint, there were souls who took up their abode in this Heart, finding there strength, consolation and peace, and enjoying heavenly delights.[5]

From several passages of the writings of the Saint we may gather an excellent method of spending the day with, through and in the Heart of Jesus.

'On your awaking, enter into the Sacred Heart, and dedicate to It your body, your soul, your heart, your whole being, to make no other use of it than for Its love and glory.'[6] 'For your prayer, enter this Sacred Heart as an oratory, where you offer the prayer of Our Lord, to supply for the deficiency of yours, love God by the love of this Divine Heart; adore by His adoration, praise by His praise; act by His actions, and will by His will.'[7] 'In assisting at Holy Mass, unite yourself with the intentions of this lovable Heart and beg Him to apply to you the merit, according to His

---

[1] *Vie et Oeuvres*, vol. II, p. 708.
[2] Ibid., vol. II, p. 490.
[3] Ibid., vol. II, p. 363.
'Jugem in eodem Corde tuo mansionem habere mereamur.'
[5] See Hamon, op. cit., vol. II, chap. iv; Bainvel, op. cit., pt. III, chap. iii.
'Ibid., vol. II, *Défis et Instructions*, p. 718.
[7] Ibid., vol. II, p. 767.

adorable designs regarding you.'[1] 'Do likewise at Confession and Holy Communion, in which you will offer the sentiments of this Divine Heart, to supply for your shortcomings.' 'In all that you do, you have only to unite yourself with the Sacred Heart of Our Lord Jesus Christ; at the beginning, in order to take up Its dispositions; at the end, to make up for what was deficient. If any trouble, affliction or mortification befalls you, accept what the Sacred Heart sends you to unite you with Itself.'[3] 'If you feel assailed by any suggestion contrary to pure love, take it to this Divine Heart to be consumed there, and that He may give you humility in exchange. Act in the same manner for all other passions or failings.'[4] 'At night, enter this Sacred Heart, to pay to It your homage of gratitude, to give It thanks for all Its favours, to ask It for pardon with a keen sorrow for your ingratitude and for the infidelities you may have committed.'[5] 'To go safely to rest, enter this Holy of Holies of the loving Heart of Jesus, where you may shut yourself up with the key of a loving surrender to His care.'[6]

[1] See *Vie et Oeuvres*, vol. II, p. 718.
[2] Ibid.
[3] Ibid., vol. II, p. 498.
[4] Ibid., p. 720.
[5] Ibid., p. 767.
[6] Ibid., p. 766. Cf. Froment, op. cit., Book III, chap. xi.

R

CHAPTER IV

Motives for Practising the Devotion

One last question: What motives must move us to practise devotion to the Sacred Heart?

We do not have to go far to find them: they may be easily deduced from what has preceded.

1. Our Lord's Desire

Devotion to the Sacred Heart comes from Jesus Himself. Already before St. Margaret Mary the Heart of Jesus was honoured; but the devotion which we have described in the preceding chapters was revealed by Jesus.

He revealed its object: His Heart which loves men and is grieved by the disregard for His love and by the outrages inflicted on It. He revealed its aims, the sentiments which must be the soul of it: love, gratitude, compassion, reparation, deep veneration, and boundless confidence. And He revealed its chief practices: the celebration of the feast of His Heart, the cult of the image of His Heart, the consecration to His Heart, the Communion of Reparation, the Act of Reparation, the First Friday of the month, the Holy Hour, etc.

He revealed all this in the famous apparitions with which He favoured St. Margaret Mary. And both these apparitions and the revelations which accompanied them are, as we have seen, absolutely trustworthy.[1]

Moreover, Jesus wishes us to practise this devotion.

This is quite obvious. Why did He show His Heart and manifest the love with which It is burning, the grief with which It is filled, the treasures which It contains, but that we might honour It, that we might make a return of love, that we might sympathize with Its sufferings, compensate It for the contempt shown to Its love, and place our confidence in It? Why did He entrust St. Margaret Mary with the mission of making known this devotion, but because He wishes it to be propagated? Why did He promise

[1] See p. xxviii.

priceless gifts and graces to those who practise it, but to urge us to take it to heart?

This desire He clearly manifested to the Saint: 'Jesus Christ,' she writes to her spiritual director, 'gave me to understand beyond all doubt that He desired that this solid devotion should be established everywhere and by its means gain innumerable faithful servants, perfect friends and really grateful children.'[1] And, as has been said, He wishes us to enkindle and to give proof to His Heart of the various sentiments which constitute the direct end of the devotion, namely, to make a return of love to His Heart,[2] to make reparation to It,[3] to honour It, especially by the cult of Its image,[4] and to place our trust in It.[5]

2. The Church's Recommendation

To our Lord's desire is to be added the Church's recommendation.

First, the Church approved the Devotion. She sanctioned it especially by instituting the Feast of the Sacred Heart. We know how prudently she proceeded in doing so. Not until 1765 was the right to celebrate this Feast granted to those dioceses which should ask for it; and only in 1856 was it extended by Pope Pius IX to the universal Church.

Moreover, it was not on the apparitions and revelations made by Jesus to St. Margaret Mary, that the Church based herself when approving the Devotion. No doubt, as we have seen, she gives credence to them; but it is not on them that she founded her approval. She considered the devotion in itself, in its diffusion, and in its effects. She saw that it was in complete harmony with her doctrinal teaching and public worship; that it was already spread abroad on all sides, was meeting with a most favourable reception from the faithful, and yielding very beneficial fruits. And that is why she consented to institute the Feast asked for, and thus to approve officially the devotion to the Sacred Heart. This appears clearly from the terms of the decree of 1765, whereby the request of the Bishops of Poland was granted: 'The Sacred Congregation of Rites . . . understanding that the cult of the Sacred Heart of Jesus, favoured by the Bishops, is already spread

---

[1] *Vie et Oeuvres*, vol. II, *Lettre à son directeur*, p. 627.
[2] See p. 53.   [3] See p. 72.   [4] See p. 90.
[5] See p. 95.

in most parts of the Catholic world . . .; understanding moreover' that the concession of this Mass and Office has no other purpose than to develop a cult already established, and to renew symbolically the memory of the Divine love by which the Only-begotten Son of God took to Himself a human nature and, obedient unto death, wished to prove to man by His example that He was, as He had said, meek and humble of heart—for these reasons the said Congregation has deemed it right to accede to the request of the Bishops of the Kingdom of Poland and of the said Roman Confraternity . . .'[1]

About the apparitions and revelations made to St. Margaret Mary, there is not a single word. It was only half a century later, in 1825, that the Church, with a view to her beatification, instituted a canonical inquiry into the writings of the Saint, with the revelations which they relate.

Yet the Church not only approved, but also encouraged and recommended the Devotion.

The Popes have encouraged and recommended it by their actions.

They have granted indulgences for all kinds of exercises, prayers, ejaculatory invocations to the Sacred Heart, particularly for the practices asked for by the Sacred Heart Itself, namely the celebration of the Feast of the Sacred Heart and the observance of the First Friday of each month, the Communion of Reparation, the Act of Reparation, the consecration to the Sacred Heart, the Holy Hour, and also for the recitation of the Litany of the Sacred Heart.[2]

They gave the Feast of the Sacred Heart an increasingly high degree of solemnity. Granted at the outset solely to those dioceses which should ask for it; it was made obligatory for the universal Church, in 1856, by Pope Pius IX, but only with the rite of Double-Major. In 1889, it was raised by Leo XIII to the rite of Double of the first class and, in 1929, by Pius XI to that of Double of the first class with privileged octave of the third order. Thus it has become one of the greatest feasts of the liturgical year.[3]

They raised to the honours of the Altar the first two apostles of the Devotion, chosen by Jesus Himself: Margaret Mary and

---

[1] See p. xxxviii.
[2] Cf. Beringer, op. cit., n. 330–78; and *Preces et pia opera*, n. 192–250.
[3] See p. 177.

Claude de la Colombière, s.j. Margaret Mary was beatified in 1864 by Pope Pius IX and canonized in 1920 by Benedict XV; Claude de la Colombière in his turn was beatified in 1929 by Pius XI.

Pius IX in 1875 invited all the faithful to consecrate themselves to the Sacred Heart on the same day, June 16th, 1875, the second centenary of the Great Apparition, by means of a form approved by himself. For this consecration he granted a plenary indulgence.[1]

Leo XIII, in 1899, consecrated the whole human race to the Sacred Heart. He wished this Consecration to be, as it were, 'the crowning perfection of all the honours that people have been accustomed to pay to the Sacred Heart,' and called it 'the most important act of his pontificate.' He proclaimed it on May 25th, 1899, in his Encyclical *Annum sacrum*, he set forth the reasons why he intended to make that Consecration, as well as the precious fruits he expected from it, and ordered that it should be made in all cities and villages throughout the world, being preceded by a triduum of prayers. The encyclical was accompanied by the form of consecration to be recited on the occasion.

In 1930, the centenary of the erection of the Archconfraternity of the Holy Hour, gave rise to the idea of celebrating a universal feast of reparation by making a solemn Holy Hour on the 22nd of May. Mgr. Chassagnon, Bishop of Autun, in whose diocese Paray-le-Monial is situated, not only approved it, but made himself its promoter and apostle, and sent a letter on the subject to all the Bishops in the world and to the Superiors of Religious Orders. Pope Pius XI encouraged the pious project and expressed the wish that the centenary might be celebrated all over the world.

In 1933 he himself took the lead in instituting a general Holy Hour. On the occasion of the Holy Year, celebrated in commemoration of the nineteenth centenary of the Redemption of mankind, he asked that in the churches of Rome, on Thursday, April 6th, on the eve of the first Friday of the month, a solemn Holy Hour should be made, and he expressed the wish that all the bishops should invite the faithful to perform this exercise of devotion on the same day.

The Popes have encouraged and recommended the Devotion by their words.

Pius VI defended it against the Jansenists, who contended that the worship paid by the faithful to the Heart of Jesus was illicit and contrary to faith and truth. In his Brief of June 29th, 1781, addressed to the Jansenist Bishop of Pistoia, he writes: 'The Holy See has put a stop to all discussions and disputes, and has sufficiently shown what the nature of this devotion is, free from all superstition and materialism . . .'

In his Bull *Auctorem fidei* of 1794 he solemnly stated that the faithful were by no means wrong in adoring the Heart of Jesus.[1]

In the Brief of beatification of Margaret Mary, Pius IX declares: 'In order to enkindle the fire of our love for Him, our Lord wished the devotion to His Most Sacred Heart to be established in the Church and propagated. Indeed, who could be so insensible and hard-hearted as not to be moved to make a return of love to this Most Sacred Heart, which was wounded and pierced by a lance, that we might find in It shelter and refuge against the attacks and snares of the enemy? Who could fail to be moved to practise with the greatest zeal all these devotions which bring him nearer to this Sacred Heart, from whose wound together with the blood and water, sprang up the fountain of our life and our salvation?'[2]

The decree whereby the same Pope, in 1856, extended the Feast of the Sacred Heart to the universal Church, stated that he did so 'in order to incite the faithful to make a return of love to the Heart of Him who loved us and cleansed us of our sins in His blood.'[3] And when, for some religious orders, as the Society of Jesus, he raised the Feast to a higher rank, it was 'in order that the devotion of love to the Heart of our Redeemer might spread increasingly, and that thus the charity, which had grown cold among a great number, might be inflamed by the fire of Divine love.'[4]

In the decree of the Sacred Congregation of Rites of 1875, whereby he invited all the faithful to consecrate themselves to the Sacred Heart, he proclaimed: 'In this Divine Heart they will find an unassailable refuge against the spiritual dangers which surround them, strength of soul in the present trials of the Church, consolation and unshakable hope amidst all their troubles.'[5]

---

[1] Cf. p. xl.
[2] Nilles, op. cit., Liber I, pars II, cap. i, § ii, p. 219; *Vie et Oeuvres*, vol. III, *Bref de béatification*, p. 145.
[3] Nilles, op. cit., Liber I, pars I, cap. iv, § i.
[4] Ibid., § iv.
[5] Cf. Vermeersch, op. cit., vol. II, p. 199.

In the Encyclical *Annum sacrum* (1899) on the Consecration of mankind to the Sacred Heart, Pope Leo XIII writes: 'There is in the Sacred Heart a symbol and sensible image of the infinite love of Jesus Christ, which prompts us to make a return of love. Therefore it is fit and proper that we should consecrate ourselves to His most Sacred Heart . . . We urge and exhort all who know and love this divine Heart willingly to undertake this act of piety; and it is Our earnest desire that all should make it on the same day, so that, the aspirations of so many thousands who are performing this act of consecration may be borne to the temple of heaven on the same day.' And further on: 'In this way, this act of devotion, which We recommend, will be a blessing to all. For having performed it, those in whose hearts are the knowledge and love of Jesus Christ will feel that faith and love increased. Those who, knowing Christ, yet neglect His law and its precepts, may still gain from His Sacred Heart the flame of charity.'[1]

On July 21st, 1899, Cardinal Mazella, Prefect of the Sacred Congregation of Rites, addressed a Letter to all the Bishops, in the name of the Pope, to express the joy of His Holiness at the manner in which the consecration was performed throughout the world, and also to suggest some suitable means of promoting and propagating the devotion to the Sacred Heart. In this Letter, we read, among other things: 'To the end that the hope we have conceived may go on increasing and that the good seed may spring up and yield a richer harvest, it is necessary that these devout affections towards the Sacred Heart of our Divine Redeemer, already enkindled in souls, should be solid and lasting. This constant and persevering prayer will again do violence to the meek Heart of Jesus, to compel Him, as it were, to open anew the source of those graces which He longs to pour out, as He gave to understand more than once to His most beloved daughter, Bl. Margaret Mary.' And further on: 'The Holy Father particularly recommends the practice, already observed in several churches, of performing publicly during the whole month of June various devotional exercises in honour of the Divine Heart . . . His Holiness also earnestly desires that the practice, strongly recommended and already observed in many places, which consists in honouring the Sacred Heart by certain devotional exercises on the first Friday of each month should be more widely propagated,

[1] *Annum sacrum*, n. 10, 11, 12.

and, moreover, that during these exercises the Litany recently approved by him should be recited and the form of Consecration repeated . . . In addition, the Holy Father expressed the strongest wish that young men, especially those who study literature and science, should join the societies, called pious associations or confraternities of the Sacred Heart. Groups of a similar nature might be formed for adults in what is called the 'Catholic Associations'.[1]

In his Letter to Fr. Mateo on the Consecration of Families to the Sacred Heart (April 27th, 1915), Pope Benedict XV writes: 'It is with good reason, dear son, that, taking to heart the interests of the human society, you endeavour first and foremost to renew the Christian spirit in the home, by establishing in the bosom of the families the charity of Jesus Christ, reigning there as queen. By doing so, you obey Christ Himself, Who promised to pour forth His blessings on the homes in which the image of His Heart should be exposed and honoured.'[2]

And Pius XI, in his Encyclical *Miserentissimus* (May 8th, 1928); 'Perhaps many of the faithful are still ignorant of the complaints of Our most loving Lord in His apparitions to Margaret Mary Alacoque, and of the desires He expressed and the requests He made of man, for man's own benefit; others turn a deaf ear to them. Wherefore We deem it opportune to deal briefly with the obligation which binds us to make what is called "reparation" to the Sacred Heart of Jesus." "To expiate these faults, He recommended, among other things, as particularly agreeable to Him, the following practices: to partake, in this spirit of expiation, of the Sacrament of the Altar, by what is called the "Communion of Reparation", and to devote oneself to expiatory supplications and prayers for one hour, rightly called "the Holy Hour"; these practices of piety the Church has not only approved, but also enriched with considerable indulgences.' 'Even as the practice of the consecration, lowly in its origin, afterwards spread far and wide, and finally received by Our confirmation all desirable splendour, so We most earnestly desire to sanction by Our apostolic authority the practice, already established and propagated, of this expiation or pious reparation, and to see it accomplished with great solemnity by the whole Catholic world.' 'There is no doubt

---

[1] Cf. Galtier, op. cit., p. 24.
[2] *Acta Apost. Sedis*, vol. VII (1915), pp. 203–5. Cf. Galtier, op. cit., p. 31.

that from this practice, thus beneficially instituted and now extended to the universal Church, there will result many and precious gifts and graces, not only for individuals, but also for ecclesiastical, civil and domestic society.' 'Even as of old, when the human race came out of the ark, God gave "the bow shining in the clouds" as a sign of a covenant of friendship, so in the stormy times of a more recent age, when the most insidious and pernicious of all heresies, Jansenism, was creeping in, and, contrary to love and devotion for God, representing Him not as a Father to be loved but as a judge to be feared, the most merciful Jesus has shown His Heart to the nations, as a token of peace and love and a pledge of victory.'[1]

In his Encyclical *Caritate Christi compulsi* (May 3rd, 1932), the same Pope expresses the wish: 'Let the faithful pour out to that merciful Heart which has known all the griefs of the human heart, the fulness of their sorrow, the steadfastness of their faith, the firmness of their hope, the ardour of their charity. Let them pray to Him, having recourse to the powerful intercession of the Blessed Virgin Mary, Mediatrix of all graces, for themselves and for their families, for their country, for the Church . . .'[2]

And in his letter of March 2nd, 1933, addressed to Cardinal Marchetti-Selvaggiani, Vicar-general of Rome, on the celebration of the Holy Hour on the occasion of the Holy Year, he writes: 'Among the mysteries of the Redemption of mankind, of which the nineteenth centenary, according to Our ordinance, is in a few days to be celebrated, one of the most moving for every Christian who is not insensible to the sorrows of Our Lord, is that of Christ's agony in the Garden of Olives, when the Divine Heart, at the terrifying spectacle of man's iniquities, and still more at the thought of the bloody manner in which It was to expiate them, deigned to endure the dreadful anguish of the bitterest agony, of which the sweat of blood was but the external manifestation: a most eloquent manifestation it is true, but inadequate as compared with the interior sufferings: "My soul is sorrowful even unto death". It seems then to Us fit and proper that, on the threshold of the Holy Year, one of the opening solemn commemorations should be dedicated to the first blood-stained step of our Redeemer on the way of His Passion. And as devout souls, in order to pay homage

[1] Encyclical *Miserentissimus*, n. 3, 23, 34, 35, 5.
[2] *Acta Apost. Sedis*, 1932, p. 177-94.

to this holy agony and to make reparation for the offences that were the cause of it, are accustomed to perform the pious practice of the Holy Hour on the Thursday preceding the first Friday of the month, We believe that the first Thursday of April, happily coinciding with the first Thursday of the Holy Year, is the obvious day for that commemoration.'

'. . . We do not doubt that the clergy and the people of Our venerable City will respond with saintly fervour to Our paternal invitation; and We trust that all Our Venerable Brethren in the Catholic Episcopate will, as far as possible, follow Our example and exhort their flock to unite with Our sons in Rome, with all the centres of the pious Association of the Holy Hour, and with Ourselves in this fitting and loving commemoration of the bitter sorrows which the Divine Heart deigned to endure for the salvation of mankind.'[1]

Pope Pius XII, in his turn, writes in his Encyclical *Summi Pontificatus* of October 20th, 1939: 'From the widening and deepening of devotion to the Divine Heart, which had its splendid culmination in the Consecration of humanity at the end of the last century, and further by the introduction, by Our immediate Predecessor of happy memory, of the feast of Christ the King, there have sprung up benefits beyond description for numberless souls.'[2] And about the end of the encyclical: 'And you, innocent legions of children, whom Christ so loves, join your unsullied prayers to the prayers of His Church; and, when you come to receive in Holy Communion the Bread of Life, open to Him your simple and innocent hearts; the Heart of Jesus, who loves you so much, will not despise the supplication of your innocence . . .'[3]

The Sovereign Pontiffs have moreover encouraged and recommended the Devotion by their example.

Leo XIII, at the end of his Encyclical *Annum sacrum*, declares: 'Finally, We will not pass it over in silence, there is still one reason, quite personal it is true, but good and weighty, which moves Us to carry out Our design—namely, that God, the Giver of all good, recently preserved Our life by curing Us of a dangerous illness. For this benefit We wish that the increase of the homage paid to the Sacred Heart, prescribed by Us, should publicly attest Our gratitude.'

[1] *Acta Apost. Sedis*, vol. xxv (1933), p. 73–74.
[2] *Acta Apost. Sedis*, vol. xxxi (1939), p. 539.   [3] Cf. ibid., p. 564.

And in the above-mentioned Letter Cardinal Mazella writes: 'The Sovereign Pontiff himself set an example to all. In the Pauline chapel of the Vatican, performing the prayers which he himself had appointed, he dedicated and consecrated the whole world to the Divine Heart of Jesus.'[1]

When, on May 22nd, 1930, according to the express wish of Pope Pius XI, the centenary of the Archconfraternity of the Holy Hour, was solemnly commemorated throughout the world, the Holy Father himself participated in the exercise of the Holy Hour that was celebrated in the basilica of St. Peter. And when, in 1933, the same Pope had expressed the wish that, on April 6th of that year, the Holy Hour should be made not only in Rome but everywhere, he himself assisted at the exercise on the appointed day.

The Church, finally, has encouraged and recommended the Devotion by making it her own.

She accepted the feast of the Sacred Heart as part of her official cult, and directed her priests to celebrate it every year by saying on that day the Mass and Office of the Sacred Heart.

She recognized the Litany of the Sacred Heart as a liturgical prayer and ordained that priests should recite it every year, together with the faithful, on the feast of the Sacred Heart and that of Christ the King.

She ordered her priests to make a solemn Act of Reparation, together with the faithful, on the feast of the Sacred Heart, and to renew on the feast of Christ the King the Act of Consecration of mankind to the Sacred Heart.

3. The Devotion Considered in Itself

But even apart from our Lord's desire and the Church's recommendation, we find in the Devotion itself the most persuasive motives for practising it.

I. ITS EMINENT REASONABLENESS

It is, first, supremely right and reasonable to practise it.

Indeed, Jesus deserves in the highest degree that we should enkindle and manifest the affections which constitute this Devotion: our grateful love for the love He bears us and of which He

[1] Cf. Galtier, op. cit., p. 25.

gave us the most touching proofs;[1] our atoning compassion for the ingratitude of men, for the neglect of His love and the outrages offered Him;[2] our adoring worship because of His Divine dignity and our homage for the beauty and perfection of His interior life;[3] our boundless confidence on account of His kindness and love, His riches and power, His promises and His fidelity.[4]

And it is supremely fitting that we should manifest all these sentiments to His Heart, because of the intimate relation that connects It with His love and His inner life. For this Heart is at once the symbol, the principle and the seat of them.[5] Now the symbol and the principle and the seat of what deserves our homage has itself a right to that homage. Moreover, the homage is directed, through Jesus' Heart, to His Person.

II. ITS ATTRACTIVENESS

The devotion to the Sacred Heart is moreover extremely attractive and captivating.

It is wholly a loving devotion: a devotion to a love, and a devotion out of love. For it consists in considering Jesus' love for us, and in returning our love for His love.

To be loved! And especially to be loved by a person of great nobility of heart; to be loved by him with a disinterested, self-sacrificing love, whose unfailing constancy is utterly trustworthy; is not this the purest and most intense pleasure one may enjoy on earth?

And then, to love! To meet with a person worthy of our love on account of his eminent qualities, and to give ourselves to him with all that we have and all that we are, in order to live only for him and to find our happiness in his happiness, is not this one of the heart's greatest desires?

Now, this exquisite delight is afforded us by devotion to the Sacred Heart, and this earnest desire is satisfied by it. For it gives us the sweet conviction that we are loved, and this by the noblest Being that exists, and with the most ardent, the most generous, the most disinterested love. And to our earnest desire for love it

---

[1] See p. 53.   [2] See p. 72.   [3] See p. 90.   [4] See p. 95.
[5] See p. 28. One should not forget that the physical Heart of Jesus is not the complete immediate object of the Devotion. His spiritual Heart also forms part of it. Thus the total immediate object is the whole formed by both of them, by what we have called the total Heart.

presents the noblest, the most perfect, the most lovable object—namely, our God made Man for love of us, and possessed in the highest degree, in an ideal degree, of all the qualities which the heart can wish for.[1]

III. ITS EXCELLENCE

On the other hand, the Devotion is in itself pre-eminently noble and beautiful.

It is noble and beautiful in its object. The object is the Heart of the greatest, the wisest and holiest Man who ever was. It is the Heart of our gentle Saviour, of our eminent Benefactor, of our great Friend, of our beloved King. It is the Heart of the Son of God, of our God!

Then, what we honour in this Heart, is His love for us. Now this love is the fundamental truth of our holy religion. The work of our Redemption is wholly a work of love. God's love conceived its design; the love of Christ as man carried it out; the love of Christ incessantly imparts to us its beneficial fruits, by means of His Church, of His Sacraments, of His grace. Hence, devotion to the Sacred Heart does not fix our attention upon some secondary point of religious truth; it concentrates it upon what is at once its soul, its foundation and its crown.[2]

No less excellent and beautiful is the Devotion in its aims.

Its aim and purpose is not to make us practise certain exercises in honour of the Sacred Heart, but to inflame our hearts with love for Jesus; to make us love Him with a true, ardent, effective, generous, self-sacrificing, predominant love; to make this love the soul of our entire lives, to put our whole interior and exterior life under the powerful influence of that love.[3]

This aim is also to make reparation for the disregard of Jesus'

---

[1] See p. 91.

[2] Galtier, op. cit., Preface. The Sacred Heart, then, may be said to be the Heart of the Mystical Body of Christ. For it was of the Heart of Jesus, of His love, that the Church was born. It is from the Sacred Heart, from His love, that there spring up all graces which vivify its members. It is the Sacred Heart which is the principle and mover of love, which unites them. It is the Sacred Heart which gives the Eucharist, this Sacrament of Love that completes the closest union between the Head and the members of the Mystical Body.

This doctrine was set forth in a masterly way by theologians of note at the National Congress of the Sacred Heart, held in Paris from June 14th to 17th, 1945. Their reports are found in the book *Le Sacré-Cœur de Jésus et la doctrine du Corps mystique* (Toulouse, Apostolat de la Prière).

[3] See p. 53. Cf. Bainvel, op. cit., pt. I, chap. iii, n. 2, *L'acte propre de la dévotion*.

love and for the outrages inflicted on Him by men. We wish to make up for them, by expressing to Him our sympathy and our regret for them, supplying for the deficiencies and shortcomings of men by our gratitude, our fervour, our generosity, our devotedness, by atoning for them by our sufferings and sacrifices.[1]

Moreover, the indirect aim of the Devotion is to arouse and enkindle our love for God. Its immediate and direct end is principally to make us love Jesus as Man, because of the love He bears us in His human Heart. But, indirectly, its purpose is to make us love Jesus as God too, because of the love He bears us in His Divine nature, and thus to make us love God the Father and the Holy Ghost also.[2]

The Devotion to the Sacred Heart, then, intends to arouse and enkindle within our souls the most important of all virtues, the virtue that constitutes the object of the first and greatest commandment; the indispensable condition of our everlasting salvation and of the merit of our good works; the queen of virtues which embraces them all and imparts to all its own perfection and its own value; the virtue which is the very essence of perfection; the virtue which will be the measure of our eternal bliss and happiness.

Noble and beautiful is this devotion in its practices too.

These are almost all acts which in themselves are of great value and most important for a perfect Christian life. Think, for instance, of the consecration, whereby we entirely give ourselves up to Jesus and bind ourselves to live for Him alone, to seek and to accomplish in all things His holy will and His good pleasure, to exert ourselves to the utmost to make Him known and loved by others, and to extend His reign.[3] Think of the imitation of the Heart of Jesus, whereby we strive to make our hearts as much as possible like unto His, to take up all His affections, to cultivate in our hearts all His virtues, to reproduce His life in ours, and to become other Christs.[4] Think of the devotion to the Blessed Eucharist, which makes us find our happiness in visiting Jesus in His Sacrament of Love and in keeping Him company there, in assisting at the mystical renewal of the Sacrifice of the Cross, and in uniting ourselves with Him in Holy Communion.[5] Think of the devotion to the sacred Passion, which makes us recall and sympathize with all that Jesus, out of love for us, deigned to endure

---

[1] See p. 72. [2] See p. 103. [3] See p. 122.
[4] See p. 157. [5] See p. 152.

in His body and soul;[1] of the various exercises of atonement, the Communion of Reparation, the Act of Reparation, the Holy Hour, by which we express to Jesus our compassion, our affliction, our holy indignation at men's unworthy conduct towards Him, and by which we endeavour to make amends and reparation to His Heart, to the best of our power, by our gratitude, our love, our fervour, our generosity and devotedness.[2]

Consequently, no other devotion is so comprehensive as devotion to the Sacred Heart.

By it we pay homage to Jesus, not only in some mystery or other of His life, as His Birth, His Passion, His Death, or in some benefit or other for which we are indebted to Him, as the Blessed Eucharist, but rather in that which was the principle and driving-power of all that He gave us, of all that He did and endured, namely, His love for us.

Devotion to the Sacred Heart is thus, as it were, the summing-up of all other devotions which have Jesus for their object. It is the soul of them all. It helps us to understand them better and to practise them better. It makes us penetrate into the intimate explanation of the mysteries and gifts to which we wish to pay honour—namely, the love of the Heart of Jesus.[3]

No other devotion makes us penetrate more profoundly into the essence of the Christian religion. This is essentially the religion of Jesus; Jesus is not only its Founder, but also its very Centre, its All.

That is true if we consider the matter on the part of God. God loves us only for the sake of Jesus, the one Mediator. The homage of our adoration is only pleasing to Him if it is presented to Him by Jesus. He only hears our prayers if Jesus is praying with us. For God we only exist, so to speak, in, through and for Jesus.

But it is also true if we consider the matter on our part. It is only by and in Jesus that we are redeemed. It is only by Jesus that we know our Heavenly Father, it is only by Jesus that we are able to love Him. We are only animated with supernatural life if and in so far as we are one with Jesus. Jesus is truly everything in our religion, everything in our Christian life.

Now no other devotion gives us Jesus, makes us know and love Him, brings us into personal and intimate relation with Him, and

---

[1] See p. 147.   [2] See pp. 172 and 186.
[3] Cf. Richstätter, op. cit., *Innerstes Wesen des Welterl sers*, pp. 47-55.

causes us to live in Him and by Him, as does devotion to the Sacred Heart. For it gives us Jesus, not merely in His words and His deeds, in His outward person, but also in His most intimate thoughts and sentiments, in His whole inner life, especially in His love which commands and animates His entire exterior and interior life. It gives us Jesus in His Heart, and in His Heart we possess Him in His entirety.[1]

Nor is there any other devotion with which the Christian religion is so completely identified.

'Devotion to the Sacred Heart,' testifies Pope Pius XI, 'is as it were the summary of the whole religion.'[2] Love of Jesus, and, through Jesus, love of God towards men—so may be summarized what religion teaches us; love of men for Jesus, and, through Jesus, love for God—so may be summarized what religion requires of us. Now Jesus' love for men is the essential object of devotion to the Sacred Heart; and love of men for Jesus, its principal end. Devotion to the Sacred Heart may then rightly be regarded as a magnificent summary of the Christian religion.[3]

No other devotion, finally, is more capable of inspiring us with the true spirit of Christianity.

This spirit is a spirit of love. In all that Jesus did, He was moved by love, by love for His Father and by love for men. He asks that in whatever we do, we too should be guided by love, by love for Him and for His Heavenly Father, by love for our fellow-men. But that is precisely what devotion to the Sacred Heart has in view; that is precisely the spirit that animates it. If then we practise it as it is meant to be practised, we are sure to be animated by the genuine spirit of Christianity.

'The cult of the Sacred Heart, therefore, urges itself upon all Christians. One could not turn away from it or neglect it, without neglecting what is most essential, most luminous and most elevated in the religion founded by Christ. To keep aloof from the cult of the Sacred Heart would be to keep aloof from the immense current of love which God has been pleased to establish between Himself and us, or to refuse to celebrate the benefit of it.

'Experience, moreover, teaches and records the marvellous and powerful attraction it is able to exercise, even over the masses.

[1] Cf. Bainvel, op. cit., p. 189.
[2] 'In ea pietatis forma totius religionis summa continetur' (Encyclical *Miserentissimus*, n. 6).
[3] Cf. Bainvel, op. cit., p. 190.

Instead of being hard to understand, and reserved for some élite, as was asserted by some, wherever it has been preached, it has revealed itself most proper to be understood and relished by the most simple of the faithful. It is never in vain that mankind is reminded of the love which God has never ceased to bear to it. When it is Christ Himself who calls on its heart, this voice awakes in it marvellous echoes. Hence the cult of the Sacred Heart has answered the most profound yearnings of the whole Christian people.'[1]

4. The Fruits of the Devotion

Devotion to the Sacred Heart is moreover rich in fruits of salvation.

The fruit which it produces directly is an ardent, effective and generous love for Jesus.

If this love is the principal end of the devotion, it is at the same time its principal fruit.

This devotion makes us behold the Heart of Jesus, with Its gaping wound, the cross planted in It, the crown of thorns surrounding It, and the flames bursting out of It. This devotion causes us to contemplate the love of Jesus, with all the benefits for which we are indebted to Him, all the proofs He has given us of it, especially in His Incarnation, His Passion and death, and the institution of the Blessed Eucharist. It makes us hear Jesus saying that He is thirsty for the love of men, and complaining of the contempt shown to His love.

Could a truly Christian soul contemplate this Heart, meditate on this love, and hear this longing desire and these complaints, without being deeply moved, without feeling moved to gratitude and to a return of love for Jesus? Will not every glance at this Heart, every recollection of this love, of this desire and of these complaints, increase our gratitude and compel us to a return of love?

Yet, not only does devotion to the Sacred Heart arouse and increase our love for Jesus as Man, but also it arouses and enkindles our love for Jesus as God and for the Blessed Trinity. For, if we love Jesus as Man, on account of His human love, we shall naturally reflect that He loves us as God also, with a Divine love,

---

[1] Galtier, op. cit., Preface, pp. x–xi.

S

and that both His Heavenly Father and the Holy Ghost love us with the same love, as the Three Divine Persons have but one and the same love, identified with their Divine Nature. And thus we are naturally induced to love, not only Jesus, but also God the Father and the Holy Ghost.

We shall, moreover, naturally reflect that, if Jesus thus loves us as Man, it is because His Father, for love of us, willed that He should assume a human nature, with a human Heart, which would enable Him to love us with a truly human love. And thus we shall, once more, naturally be induced to love God His Father because of the love He bears us.[1]

Devotion to the Sacred Heart arouses and enkindles our love for Jesus in yet another way.

Jesus deserves our love in the highest degree, not only because He loves us, but also because He is supremely lovable in Himself, on account of the virtues of His Heart, particularly His kindness, His love for men, His meekness and His magnanimity. As we cannot consider His love without being moved to gratitude, so we cannot reflect on His lovable qualities without feeling attracted towards Him, and without conceiving a tender affection for Him. And the more we meditate on the lovableness of Jesus, the more our love for Him will be enkindled and will grow.

Now devotion to the Sacred Heart makes us consider in the Heart of Jesus not only His love for us, but also His sentiments, His virtues, His entire affective and moral life. All this belongs indeed to the object of the devotion.[2] In this way, it makes us love Jesus, not only because of the love He bears us, but also because of Himself, on account of His intrinsic and supreme lovableness.

And in this way, too, it makes us love Jesus, not only as Man, but as God also. The qualities which render Him lovable as Man, He also possesses as God, and this in an infinite degree, the former being but a finite, yet ideal, reproduction of the latter. If then we love Jesus on account of His human qualities, we shall naturally be induced to love Him because of His Divine perfections also, and together with Him, the two other Persons of the Blessed Trinity, who are indivisibly possessed of them, together with Him. And thus devotion to the Sacred Heart causes us to love Jesus as God, and brings us to perfect charity.

[1] See p. 51.   [2] See p. 21.

Love for Jesus, not only as Man, but also as God; not only because of His love for us, but also because of Himself, on account of His human qualities and His Divine perfections, this, then, is the first and principal fruit of devotion to the Sacred Heart.

To this first fruit are naturally added all the effects of this love. Effects, firstly, upon Jesus Himself.

Jesus is sensitive to tender affection. He yearns to be loved. He is thirsty for love.[1] By practising devotion to the Sacred Heart, by returning to Him love for love, we comply with His longing desire. We gladden His Heart, we console Him for the contempt shown to His love, and we increase His happiness. To make Jesus more happy, what a wonderful prospect!

Nor does He leave our love without response. He repays it with a still more intimate, more profound, more affectionate love. Every act of love, every exercise of devotion to His Heart increases His love for us. The more we love Him and the more we practise devotion to His Heart, the more Jesus also loves us. To be loved more and more by Jesus, what an honour and what happiness!

His ever-increasing love inclines Him to greater kindness and greater liberality. We acquire influence over His Heart. When we ask Him for something, He more favourably complies with our request. He can hardly refuse it; nor does He even wait for us to ask, but He forestalls our wishes. To be able to rely upon the kindness and liberality of Jesus, what a priceless privilege!

But the love for Jesus, and hence the practice of devotion to His Heart, has also the most beneficial effects upon ourselves.

First of all, love of Jesus necessarily leads us to love of our neighbour.

Love causes us to accomplish the will of the beloved and to fulfil his wishes. We know how much Jesus appreciates love of our fellow-men.

He has made it the object of a positive commandment: 'These things I command you, that you love one another'; of a new commandment: 'A new commandment I give unto you: that you love one another'; a commandment, which He particularly calls His commandment 'This is My commandment, that you love one another' (John xv, 17, 34, 12).

He put this commandment on a level with the love of God. A doctor of the law, we are told, asked Him: 'Master, which is the

[1] See p. 53.

great commandment in the law? Jesus said to him: Thou shalt love the Lord thy God with thy whole heart, and with thy whole soul, and with thy whole mind. This is the greatest and the first commandment. And the second is like to this: Thou shalt love thy neighbour as thyself. On these two commandments depend the whole law and the Prophets' (Matt. xxii, 36-40).

He pointed out this virtue as the distinguishing mark of His true disciples: 'By this shall all men know that you are My disciples, if you have love one for another' (John xiii, 35).

He laid down as its rule and measure the love which He Himself bears us: 'As I have loved you, that you also love one another' (ibid. xiii, 34).

He will judge men according to the manner in which they have practised the love of their neighbour. In the description of the Last Judgment, the reason He assigns for rewarding the just is the fact that they performed works of charity, whereas the wicked are condemned because they neglected them (Matt. xxv, 34-46).

He substitutes Himself for our fellow-men and considers as done to Himself whatever we do to them, good as well as evil: 'Then shall the King say to them that shall be on His right hand: Come, ye blessed of My Father, possess you the kingdom prepared for you from the foundation of the world. For I was hungry, and you gave Me to eat . . . Then shall the just answer Him, saying: Lord, when did we see Thee hungry, and fed Thee? And the King answering shall say to them: Amen I say to you, as long as you did it to one of these My least brethren, you did it to Me . . . Then He shall say to them also that shall be on His left hand: Depart from Me, you cursed, into everlasting fire . . . For I was hungry, and you gave Me not to eat . . . Then they also shall answer Him, saying: Lord, when did we see Thee hungry, and did not minister to Thee? Then He shall answer them, saying: Amen I say to you, as long as you did it not to one of these least, neither did you do it to Me' (Matt. xxv, 34-45).

And in His sublime prayer that closes His discourse at the Last Supper, the last grace He asked for His disciples was the union of mutual charity: 'And not for them (His Apostles) only do I pray, but for them also who through their word shall believe in Me. That they all may be one, as Thou, Father, in Me, and I in Thee; that they also may be one in Us; that the world may believe that Thou hast sent Me' (John xvii, 20-21).

Therefore, if we really love Jesus we shall also practise the love of our fellow-men, because He desires it, because this virtue lies so near to His Heart.

Love naturally extends to all who are dear to the beloved. All men are dear to Jesus. If then we really love Jesus, how could we fail to love all men? The love of Jesus will bring about and maintain in particular the union of all the devout clients of the Sacred Heart. How could hearts that are united with the Heart of Jesus be disunited among themselves?

Love tends to resemblance, and inclines to imitate the beloved. We shall then want to resemble Jesus and, following His example, we shall love our brethren with a true, supernatural, effective and self-sacrificing love.

Love for Jesus, and hence devotion to His Heart is moreover one of the most efficacious stimulants to the practice of Christian life and to aspiring to perfection.

The *Imitation of Christ* (III, 5), describes it very well: 'Love is a great thing, a good thing in every way; by itself it makes everything that is heavy, light; and it bears equally all that is unequal.

'For it carries a burden without being burdened, and makes everything that is bitter, sweet and savoury.

'The noble love of Jesus impels a man to do great things, and stirs him up to be always longing for what is more perfect.

'Nothing is sweeter than love, nothing more courageous, nothing higher, nothing wider . . .

'He that loves, flies, runs, and rejoices; he is free, and cannot be held in.

'Love oftentimes knows no measure, but is fervent beyond all measure.

'Love feels no burden, thinks nothing of labours, attempts what is above its strength, pleads no excuse of impossibility; for it thinks all things possible.

'It can achieve anything, and performs and effects many things, where he who does not love, would faint and lie down.

'Love is watchful, and sleeping slumbers not. Though weary, it is not tired; though pressed, it is not strained; though alarmed, it is not confounded; but, as a lively flame and burning torch, it forces its way upwards, and securely passes through all.'

Love of Jesus, and hence devotion to His Heart, will in particular, make us hate sin, and will help us to avoid it. If we really love Jesus, how could we fail to detest sin, which is so vehemently abhorred by Him, which was the cause of His Passion and Death, which repays His love with ingratitude, and conduces to make His His Passion and Death useless and vain for sinners?

Love for Jesus, and hence devotion to His Heart, will make duty attractive and lovable, and will help us to accomplish it always with courage and cheerfulness. In duty it sees only the will of God. The duty may be unpleasant and tedious; yet, as it is the will of the Beloved, how could it fail to be dear to us? It may be heavy and hard; love does not feel it. The Beloved will be satisfied and this thought makes everything light and easy.

Love for Jesus, and hence devotion to His Heart, will render affliction less bitter and even sweet, and will help us to bear it patiently and even joyfully. For the one who permits it, is Jesus Himself, who loves us and desires our good. How could we refuse to accept it readily and submissively? Again: Jesus endured so much for love of us. How could we in our turn be unwilling to resemble Him in some way in that respect?

Love of Jesus, and hence devotion to His Heart, will make us fervent and generous in tending to perfection. If we really love Jesus, we shall aspire to sanctity as strenuously as possible. And love for Him will give us courage and strength to realize it, whatever effort and sacrifice it may require on our part.

Love of Jesus, and hence devotion to His Heart, will make us apostles. Jesus longs for His Heavenly Father and for Himself to be known, honoured, served and loved by all men. He desires that all should attain to eternal bliss and blessedness in Heaven, and that they should thus give to His Passion and Death its full fruitfulness. He desires in particular that devotion to His Heart should be spread abroad and should be practised to perfection. If then we love Him, we shall take His wishes to heart, and do all in our power to realize them. We shall be apostles.

In this way there will gradually be established between Jesus and ourselves relations of true friendship, of real intimacy, which will achieve our likeness to Him, and will be at the same time the source of the sweetest joys. And thus devotion to the Sacred Heart will lead us to the highest perfection. St. Margaret Mary assures us: 'I do not know,' she writes, 'whether there is in the spiritual life a devotional practice more able to raise a soul in a short time to the highest perfection, and to make her enjoy the true sweetness that is to be found in the service of Jesus Christ.'[1] And she confirms her statement by a striking example, namely, that of Bl. Claude de la Colombière: 'If I am not mistaken, this devotion has made him powerful in Heaven, and has elevated him more in glory, than all that he had been able to do during his life.'[2] Again: 'This holy man was entirely devoted to the Sacred Heart, and only lived to make It loved, honoured and glorified. This then it is, I think, that raised him so rapidly to so high a perfection.'[3]

5. The Promises of the Sacred Heart.

Devotion to the Sacred Heart affords us yet other precious benefits. To persuade us to comply with His wish, Jesus made magnificent promises in favour of those who practise it.

They are mentioned in the letters of St. Margaret Mary, particularly from 1685 onwards. A brief record of the most important appears for the first time in a letter addressed to Mother de Saumaise (August 24th, 1685),[4] but nowhere else so outstandingly as in a letter to her spiritual director, probably Fr. Croiset or Fr. Rolin.[5]

Taking into account the classes of persons for whom they are intended, and the exercises for which they are made, they may be classed as follows:

On behalf of people in the world: 'As for people in the world, they will, through the means of this lovable devotion, secure for themselves all the helps necessary for their state, that is to say, peace in their family, alleviation of their toils, the blessings of Heaven on all their undertakings, consolation in their sorrows. And it is especially in this sacred Heart that they will find a place of refuge during their entire life and particularly at the hour of their death. Oh, how sweet is death when one has had a tender devotion to the sacred Heart of Jesus Christ!'[6]

On behalf of religious communities: 'He will pour forth the sweet unction of His ardent charity on those communities who

---

[1] *Vie et Oeuvres*, vol. ii, *Lettre à son directeur*, p. 627.
[2] Ibid., vol. ii, *3e Lettre au P. Croiset*, p. 555.
[3] Ibid., vol. ii, *Lettre à la Mère de Soudeilles*, p. 328.
[4] Ibid., vol. ii, p. 296.
[5] Ibid., vol. ii, p. 626. See also Bainvel, op. cit., pt. i, chap. iv.
[6] Ibid., vol. ii, *Lettre à son directeur*, p. 627.

honour Him and place themselves under His special protection. Moreover, He will turn away from them the arrows of Divine justice in order to retore them to the state of grace, whenever they have fallen from it.'[1]

On behalf of sinners: 'This Divine Heart is an inexhaustible fountain from which there flow incessantly three streams: the first is the stream of mercy towards sinners, on whom is poured out the spirit of contrition and repentance.'[2]

On behalf of tepid souls: 'As it seems to me, there is nothing that I should not be willing to do or to endure in order to give Him the pleasure, so much longed for, of enkindling the flame of charity, which has grown so cold and is nearly quenched in the hearts of most Christian people. He wishes to afford them by this devotion a new means of loving God through this sacred Heart, as much as He desires and deserves it, and thus to make up for their ingratitude.'[3]

On behalf of fervent souls: 'The third (stream) is the stream of love and light that flows into all perfect souls, enabling them to dedicate themselves without reserve to the task of promoting the glory of the Sacred Heart.'[4]

On behalf of priests: 'My Divine Master made me know that those who work for the salvation of souls will succeed and have the art of touching the most hardened hearts, if they are themselves penetrated with a tender devotion to His sacred Heart and endeavour to spread it abroad and establish it everywhere.'[5]

On behalf of those who honour the image of the Sacred Heart: 'He assured me that He took a singular pleasure in being honoured under the image of this Heart of flesh. He wished it to be exposed in order to touch the insensible hearts of men, and He promised me that He would pour down in abundance into the hearts of all those who should thus honour it, all the gifts with which It is replete, and that wherever this image should be exposed with a view to showing it special honour, it would draw down every sort of blessing.'[6]

On behalf of those who observe the Feast of the Sacred Heart

---

[1] *Vie et Oeuvres*, vol. II, *2e Lettre au P. Croiset*, 10 août 1689, p. 532.
[2] Ibid., vol. II, *3e Lettre au P. Croiset*, 15 septembre 1689, p. 558.
[3] Ibid., vol. II, p. 556.
[4] Ibid., p. 558.
[5] Ibid., vol. II, *Lettre à son directeur*, p. 628.
[6] Ibid., vol. I, *Mémoire des Contemporaines*, n. 256, p. 244.

by the reception of Holy Communion and the making of an Act of Reparation: 'I promise you that My Heart will excel Itself in order to pour forth abundantly the influence of Its Divine love upon those who pay to It this homage and procure for It this honour by others.'[1]

On behalf of those who go to Communion on nine consecutive First Fridays: 'I promise you, in the excess of the mercy of My Heart, that Its all-powerful love will grant to all those who shall receive Communion on the first Friday of nine consecutive months the grace of final repentance; they shall not die under My displeasure nor without receiving the Sacraments, My Divine Heart becoming their assured refuge at that last hour.'[2]

On behalf of those who consecrate themselves to the Sacred Heart: 'He assured me that He takes such great pleasure in being known, loved and honoured by His creatures, that He promised me that no one who has specially consecrated and dedicated himself to Him will ever perish.'[3] Again: 'He has made known to me that the desire He has to be known, loved and honoured by men is so excessive that He promises to all who consecrate and dedicate themselves to Him, in order to give Him pleasure, that He will never allow them to perish; that He will be their assured refuge against all the snares of their enemies; that He will receive them lovingly into His Heart, making their salvation sure, sanctifying them and make them great before His Heavenly Father, in proportion as they labour to extend the reign of His love in the hearts of men.'[4]

These favours were summarized—when and by whom we do not know—in formulas, known under the name of 'the Twelve Promises of the Sacred Heart'. They run as follows:

1. I will give them all the graces necessary for their state of life.

2. I will give peace in their families.

3. I will console them in all their troubles.

4. They shall find in My Heart an assured refuge during life and especially at the hour of death.

5. I will pour abundant blessings on all their undertakings.

---

[1] *Vie et Oeuvres*, vol. II, *Autobiographie*, n. 92, p. 103.
[2] Ibid., vol. II, *Lettre à la Mère de Saumaise*, mai 1688, p. 397.
[3] Ibid., *Lettre à la Mère Greyfié*, 1685, p. 300.
[4] Ibid., vol. II, 2e *Lettre au P. Croiset*, 10 août 1689, p. 532.

6. Sinners shall find in My Heart the source and infinite ocean of mercy.

7. Tepid souls shall become fervent.

8. Fervent souls shall speedily rise to great perfection.

9. I will bless the homes in which the image of My Sacred Heart shall be exposed and honoured.

10. I will give to priests the power to touch the most hardened hearts.

11. Those who propagate this devotion shall have their name written in My Heart, and it shall never be effaced.

12. The all-powerful love of My Heart will grant to all those who shall receive Communion on the First Friday of nine consecutive months the grace of final repentance; they shall not die under My displeasure, nor without receiving their Sacraments; My Heart shall be their assured refuge at that last hour.

In 1882, a wealthy American, by the name of Kemper, had these formulas translated into over 200 languages and printed on pictures of the Sacred Heart which he circulated by the million in all parts of the world; it may be said that they are known everywhere.

These formulae, though not usually reproducing literally the Saint's own words, render faithfully their sense, as may be perceived when comparing them with the text of the promises quoted above. The first five contain the promises made in general on behalf of people in the world; the three following relate to sinners, to tepid and to fervent souls; the ninth is that which is made on behalf of those who honour the image of the Sacred Heart; the tenth, of those who work for the salvation of souls; the eleventh, of those who apply themselves to propagate devotion to the Sacred Heart; the twelfth, finally, of those who receive Communion on nine consecutive first Fridays of the month, in honour of the Sacred Heart. Yet, the list is not complete: the promises on behalf of religious communities, of those who observe the Feast of the Sacred Heart by a Communion of Reparation and an Act of Reparation, and of those who consecrate themselves to the Sacred Heart are missing.

Are we sure of the authenticity of these promises?

They form part of the revelations with which Jesus favoured St. Margaret Mary. As these revelations, though not being *de fide*, are fully trustworthy,[1] we may safely give credence also to the authenticity of the promises.[2]

Besides, we know that the Church gives credence to them, at least on the whole.

Pope Leo XIII, in his Constitution *Benigno* (June 28th, 1889), states: 'In order that men may comply more readily with that desire (regarding the devotion to the Sacred Heart), Jesus has promised great favours, and invites and draws all men to His Heart.'

Pope Benedict XV, in the Bull of canonization of Margaret Mary (May 13th, 1920), declares: 'The proofs of Christ's goodness and mercy, which appear so clearly in the life of God's servant, should induce all those who are regenerated by the Blood of Christ, to love the Sacred Heart, that they may obtain from Him, in these troubled times, the graces which He promised to pour forth on those who pay to this Heart a just homage.'[3] And Pius XI, in his Encyclical *Miserentissimus* (n. 35): 'Our Redeemer Himself promised to Margaret Mary that all those who procure this honour for His Heart, would be enriched in profusion with heavenly graces.'

In the Bull of canonization of Margaret Mary, Benedict XV quotes literally the promise made on behalf of those who receive Communion on nine consecutive first Fridays of the month.[4]

As regards the realization of these promises, it would be a profound mistake to make devotion to the Sacred Heart consist in some mere exterior exercises, and to flatter oneself with the hope, on this account, of sharing in the promised gifts and graces. Jesus wishes us to repay His love with our love. His promises are intended to urge us on to make this return of love. If then we wish to claim the promised graces, we ought first and foremost to endeavour to love Him sincerely.

But if we fulfil that condition, then we may, with humble confidence, rely on the realization of the promises. To call them in question would be to suppose that our Lord was not in earnest when making them, or that it is not in His power to keep them.

---

[1] See p. xxviii.
[2] Cf. Hamon, op. cit., vol. v, p. 154.
[3] *Acta Apost. Sedis*, vol. xii (1920), p. 487.
[4] See *Vie et Oeuvres*, vol. iii, p. 745; *Acta Apost. Sedis*, vol. xii, p. 487.

In proportion as our love for Him is ardent, effective and generous, Jesus will pour forth on us the treasures of His Heart.

It should be noted, however, that the temporal gifts, which form the object of the second, third and fifth promises are but conditionally promised. For it is evident that our Lord neither will nor can grant them to us, unless they be helpful to us, not only to work out our salvation, but also to increase our love of Him; for this indeed is the chief aim of the devotion. St. Margaret Mary warns us: 'To speak plainly,' she writes, 'I do not believe that the graces promised by Him consist in abundance of temporal things; for, as He said, those things often render us poor in His grace and love; and yet, it is that with which He wishes to enrich our hearts and souls.'[1] Again: 'But He did not tell me that His friends would not have to suffer anything; for He desires that they make their greatest happiness consist in tasting His afflictions.'[2]

The most remarkable among the promises of the Sacred Heart is surely the one which is made to those who receive Communion in honour of the Sacred Heart on nine consecutive first Fridays of the month. It is therefore called 'the Great Promise'.

There is little mention made of it in the first works on the Devotion. Neither Fr. Croiset nor Fr. de Galliffet refers to it, nor does it figure in the earliest lists of the promises of the Sacred Heart. They seem to shrink from speaking of it, lest it should either scandalize some people or stir up the opposition of the enemies of the Devotion.[3]

Yet it is contained in a letter of St. Margaret Mary addressed to Mother de Saumaise (probably in May, 1688),[4] and is reproduced in her biography, written by her sisters in Religion.[5]

The real object of the promise is indicated by the words: 'I promise you in the excess of the mercy of My Heart, that Its all-powerful love will grant to all those who shall receive Com-

---

[1] *Vie et Oeuvres*, vol. I, *Ecrits de la Mère Greyfié*, p. 373.

[2] Ibid., vol. II, *Lettre à la Mère Greyfié*, p. 303. See Bainvel, op. cit., pt. I, chap. iv; Terrien, op. cit., *Conclusion: Les Promesses*; Yenveux, *Le règne du Cœur de Jésus*, vol. V, Book II, pp. 558–681; Haettenschwiller, s.j., *Die Verheissungen des heiligsten Herzen Jesu*; Leroy, *Litanies du sacré Cœur de Jésus*, p. 336; Truptin, *Les promesses du Sacré-Cœur*; Boubée, s.j., idem; Guillaume, s.j., idem.

[3] Cf. Bainvel, op. cit., pt. I, chap. iv, *La grande Promesse*, p. 85.

[4] *Vie et Oeuvres*, vol. II, p. 397. The promise is preceded by the words: 'One Friday, at Holy Communion, He (Jesus) said to His unworthy slave, if she is not mistaken . . .' As we have seen, the phrase 'if I am not mistaken' denotes neither hesitation nor doubt on the part of the Saint, but only her obedience to her Superior who enjoined on her this manner of speech.

[5] Ibid., vol. I, *Mémoire des Contemporaines*, n. 277, p. 261.

munion on the first Friday of nine consecutive months the grace of final repentance.' The rest of the text is, as we shall see, only an explanation of the promise.

Hence, what is promised is the grace of final repentance, or, as it is usually termed by theologians, the grace of final perseverance, i.e. the gift of dying in the state of grace.[1]

To whom is this priceless favour promised? 'To all those who receive Communion on the first Friday of nine consecutive months.'

These Communions evidently ought to be good Communions, that is to say, received in a state of grace and with the required dispositions; but they must, further, be made for love of the Sacred Heart, in a spirit of reparation, and in such a way that they really afford Him reparation and consolation for the outrages offered to It; for such are the Communions asked for by Jesus on the first Fridays of the month.[2]

Some writers have considered the promise so excessive that they have felt obliged to lessen it, or to impose more stringent conditions. In our opinion, however, there cannot be advanced any determinant reason for restricting it, nor for not taking it in its literal sense.[3]

The Sacred Heart, then, promised that all those who receive Communion on nine consecutive first Fridays of the month will die in the state of grace.

Hence, what is promised is not that he who made the nine First Friday Communions will always persevere in the path of virtue, or will never lose sanctifying grace by mortal sin, but solely that he will die in the state of grace, even if he had lost it by mortal sin; even if he had gone astray and had led a sinful life.

This does not mean, however, that a sinner who at the hour of death refused to return to the Lord would nevertheless be saved, but that this supposition will never be realized, and that never will a sinner, who has fulfilled the appointed conditions, refuse to turn to God, at least at the hour of death, nor will he die impenitent.

But the objection may be made: Is this promise not in contra-

---

[1] The two expressions 'grace of final perseverance' and 'grace of final repentance' differ in so far as the former simply means the possession of sanctifying grace at the hour of death, whereas the latter implies that sanctifying grace, having been lost by mortal sin, is restored at the hour of death by repentance and penance.

[2] See p. 184.   [3] Cf. Vermeersch, op. cit., vol. II, p. 158.

diction with the doctrine of the Church? The Council of Trent
teaches indeed that no one is certain of the grace of final perseverance unless it be made known to him by special revelation?
(Sess. VI, can. 16).

But there is no such contradiction. The Council only teaches
that no one, without a particular revelation, is able to know with
absolute and infallible certainty that he will obtain the grace of
final perseverance. Now the promise of the Sacred Heart does not
afford us this absolute certainty, but only a moral certainty. For
we do not know with absolute certainty whether we have made
the nine Communions with the proper dispositions, and hence
whether we have fulfilled the required conditions. Besides, of the
authenticity of the promise we have no absolute, but only a moral
certainty, which precludes any reasonable doubt.[1] Therefore,
although we may trustfully rely upon the promise, it does not
afford us an absolute certainty of our salvation. There is then no
contradiction between the promise of the Sacred Heart and the
teaching of the Church.

But again is it not to be feared that many will make a bad use
of this magnificent promise, and will rely upon it to lead more
freely a sinful life, since they are sure, after making the nine First
Fridays, to die in a state of grace?

That a bad use may be made of it, is undeniable. But is there
anything good, useful and holy, on earth which is not exposed to
this danger, taking into account human malice?

We think, however, as regards this Promise, that there seems to
be no great danger. Two things may occur: either some one makes
the nine First Fridays with the purpose of securing his salvation
and then indulging himself in dissipation and sin; or someone goes
astray after he has made the First Fridays with the proper dispositions, and perseveres in his evil courses, rashly relying on the
promise of the Sacred Heart.

In the first case, the person would evidently be wrong in relying
on the promise, as he has not fulfilled the requisite conditions.
There are required nine good Communions, hence nine Communions made with a good intention. Now, it is clear that anyone
who received Communion with the suggested dispositions, would
not have this good intention and would make an unworthy
Communion.

[1] See p. xxix.

As regards the second case, Jesus, who does not and could not want His promise to be an incentive to a sinful life, will bring about by His grace that this person should not yield to that presumptuous confidence, or at least should not persevere in it. What confirms this opinion is, among other things, the fact that this case, if ever occurring, must be extremely rare; priests, grown grey in administering the Sacrament of Penance, assure us that they have never met with it.[1]

There are then no well-founded reasons why we should not take the Promise in its literal sense. Therefore, we may safely believe that the Sacred Heart has really promised that all those who have received Communion on nine consecutive First Fridays in accordance with His intentions, will die in a state of grace.

What in the text of St. Margaret Mary follows on the promise properly so called, is doubtless but an explanation of the Promise. 'For they shall not die under My displeasure'—this is the effect of the grace of final repentance. 'Nor without receiving the Sacraments'—this is the ordinary means Jesus will make use of to this end. 'My Divine Heart being their assured refuge at that last hour'—this is the reason why they may rely on final repentance.

At first sight, it might seem that the words 'nor without receiving the Sacraments' should guarantee to all the real reception of the Last Sacraments, in particular the Sacrament of Penance. Yet facts do not admit of that interpretation. It is not seldom that even saintly priests, saintly Religious, wholly devoted to the Sacred Heart, and hence having fulfilled better than any one else the required conditions, are carried off by a sudden death. Are we then to suppose that Jesus does not keep His promise? This would be blasphemy. What we are to deduce from it, it seems to us, is that the promise of the Last Sacraments was not intended for them, as they did not stand in need of them in order to die in the state of grace, according to the general Promise. And consequently we must also conclude from it that Jesus did not promise the Last Sacraments unconditionally and absolutely, but that He only engaged Himself to afford the opportunity of receiving them in so far as one might stand in need of them. The Promise, then, must be understood in this way: 'They shall not die under My displeasure, and hence without receiving the necessary Sacraments.'

[1] Cf. Vermeersch, op. cit., vol. II, pp. 193–94.

This conclusion, moreover, seems to follow from the context. The promise of the Last Sacraments occurs in the middle of two other promises which do not add anything to the general promise, but are a mere explanation of it. As has been said, the words 'for they shall not die under My displeasure' simply express the result of the promise of final perseverance, and the words 'My Divine Heart being their assured refuge at that last hour,' the reason why we may rely on this grace of final perseverance. Is it not logical then to conclude that the promise of the Last Sacraments also, inserted between both of them, does not add anything to the general promise, and hence that it serves solely to explain in what manner this general promise will be realized, namely, by the reception of the Last Sacraments, in so far as this will be necessary to this end?

We find a confirmation of this conclusion in the use of the word final 'repentance', and in the promise that they shall not die under His disgrace. By this Jesus seems to have intended to show that He had especially in view sinners, for whom the Last Sacraments are the ordinary means of dying in the state of grace. It is then natural that He explicitly promises this means, in so far as they need it.

That is, then, what the Sacred Heart promised to all those who make the nine First Friday Communions with the proper dispositions: they shall die in the state of grace, and hence they shall receive the Last Sacraments if they are in need of them. A magnificent promise indeed, which is rightly called 'the Great Promise' and which is, as St. Margaret Mary declares, an eloquent proof of the 'excess of the mercy of the Heart of Jesus' and a priceless gift of 'Its all-powerful love'.

It may be asked what was Jesus' purpose, in making this promise?

So far as we can conjecture, it was first of all to show us how much He appreciates devotion to His Sacred Heart, and in particular the Communion of Reparation, and frequent Communion, preferably on Friday, the day on which He died for us.

Yet He may also, it seems, have intended to set at rest pious and virtuous souls, who often ask themselves anxiously, without any serious reason, whether they will be saved. By giving them the moral certainty of their salvation, He gladdens their souls, makes them more cheerful in God's service, and helps them to accomplish their actions with a more pure and more perfect intention, rather from love than from fear.[1]

And to sinners, who might be tempted to despair, He wished to give a manifest proof of His infinite mercy, and the assurance not only that He will not reject them if they return to Him, but also that He will do all that is possible to facilitate for them the return to God and to secure for them a happy death.

What are the feelings this Promise ought to arouse in us?

First, gratitude towards Him, Who has been willing to secure for us the priceless gift of final perseverance, to which He has attached a condition so easy to fulfil.

Then, confidence in the word of Him, Who is all-powerful, and hence is able to keep His promise; Who is pre-eminently good and loves us sincerely, and hence is willing to keep it; Who is faithful, and hence will surely keep it.

Thirdly, solicitous care to fulfil as perfectly as possible the required condition, making our Communions not only with an intention of reparation, but also in such a manner that they give real satisfaction to Jesus and console Him for the conduct of men towards His Sacrament of Love.

Finally, zeal in responding to Jesus' purposes, by taking to heart this Devotion and in particular the practice for which He made the Promise; by serving Him and His Heavenly Father, not for fear but for love; by setting no limits to our generosity towards Him, Who went to the extreme of His bounty towards us.[2]

---

[1] Cf. Vermeersch, op. cit., vol. II, pp. 183–86.

[2] On the Great Promise, see especially Vermeersch, op. cit., vol. II, pp. 149–96. See also Haettenschwiller, s.j., *Die grosse Verheissung des göttlichen Herzen Jesu*, 5. Aufl.

Devotion to the Immaculate Heart of Mary

It is fitting that to a treatise on the devotion to the Sacred Heart of Jesus should be added an outline of the devotion to the Immaculate Heart of Mary, which is closely connected with it.

HISTORICAL SKETCH

Before the thirteenth century there is no trace to be found of a special devotion to the Heart of Mary. The first pious considerations on this subject occur in the writings of St. Mechtilde (1298), St. Gertrude (1302), Tauler (1361), St. Bernardin of Siena (1444), Justus Landsberger (1539), and especially of St. Francis of Sales (1622).

From the sixteenth century onward, theologians and spiritual writers make mention of this devotion. St. John Eudes (1680) quotes, among the writers who speak of it, twelve Jesuits, whom he calls 'the twelve apostles of the divine Heart of Mary', the most famous of whom are: St. Peter Canisius, Suarez, Nierenberg and Cornelius a Lapide.

Yet it is to St. John Eudes that is due the honour of having given the decisive impulse to the devotion. He was its zealous apostle and learned theologian. Through his preaching of popular missions, he propagated it in about twenty dioceses of France, established everywhere confraternities, wrote a great work on *The admirable Heart of the Holy Mother of God*, composed a Mass and an Office, and laboured to obtain at Rome the institution of a Feast, but without success (1669).

After his death, the devotion met with a powerful auxiliary in the movement which originated from Paray-le-Monial. The first apostles of the Devotion to the Sacred Heart of Jesus, St. Margaret Mary, Bl. Claude de la Colombière, Bouzonié, Croiset, were also devout clients of the Heart of Mary. Fr. Pinamonti, s.j., wrote a book on the Devotion (1699), which strongly contributed to its diffusion in Italy. In his remarkable work on 'The Devotion to the adorable Heart of Jesus Christ', Fr. de Galliffet treats at length of the devotion to the Heart of Mary.[1] In his turn he endeavoured to obtain a feast in its honour, at the same time as a feast in honour of the Sacred Heart of Jesus (1726), but he met with as little success as St. John Eudes.

Papal approbation came at last. In 1799, Pope Pius VI authorized the Bishop of Palermo to institute the feast in his diocese. In 1805, Pope Pius VII granted the same favour to those who should ask for it, but with the Office and Mass of Our Lady of the Snow. In 1855, Pius IX approved a special Mass and Office. And in 1944, Pius XII extended the Feast to the universal Church, under the title of Feast of the Immaculate Heart of Mary,[2] with a new Mass and new Office, and transferred the Feast from the Sunday after the Assumption to the 22nd of August.

In the meantime four particular events had given a new impulse and an extraordinary popularity to the devotion—namely, the spread of 'the miraculous medal'; the erection of the Archconfraternity of the Immaculate Heart of Mary, in Paris, in the church of Notre-Dame des Victoires; the apparitions of the Blessed Virgin at Fatima (Portugal), and the Consecration of the Church and of the human race to the Immaculate Heart of Mary, by Pope Pius XII.

1. The 'miraculous medal' owes its origin to an apparition of Our Lady to Bl. Catherine Labouré, a Sister of Charity, on November 27th, 1830. The Blessed Virgin showed her a medal, bearing on one side a representation of herself with the incription: 'O Mary, conceived without sin, pray for us, who have recourse to Thee'; and on the other side, under the letter M, the Hearts of Jesus and of Mary, the former surrounded with a crown of thorns, the latter pierced with a sword. She ordered the Sister to make and propagate medals after that design, and promised her that all who wore them and devoutly recited this invocation could be sure of her special protection. In a short time innumerable graces, wonderful cures and extraordinary conversions strengthened the confidence of the faithful in the power of the medal, which soon acquired the name of 'the miraculous medal'.

2. The Archconfraternity of the Immaculate Heart of Mary was erected, in 1836, in Paris, in the church of Notre-Dame des

---

[1] De Galliffet, op. cit., pt. I, Book III, chap. iv.
[2] Formerly it was called 'Feast of the Most Pure Heart of Mary'.

Victoires, by the parish priest, Rev. Fr. Desgenettes. The Father was completely discouraged by the lamentable condition of his parish, when, on December 3rd, 1836, feast of St. Francis Xavier, during his mass, he thought he heard an inward voice which, twice over, said to him: 'Consecrate your parish to the most holy and Immaculate Heart of Mary.' After hesitating for a long time, he obeyed the call, and established moreover a Confraternity, in order to honour in a special way the Immaculate Heart of Mary and to obtain the conversion of sinners through her intercession with the Divine Mercy. Contrary to all expectations, the new association met with an extraordinary success. Sinners returned to the Lord in great numbers, and in a short time the parish was completely transformed. Struck by this marvellous result, Pope Gregory XI raised the confraternity to the rank of Archconfraternity for the universal Church as early as 1838. Everywhere confraternities were erected and affiliated to it; in 1890, there were already more than 19,000, with more than 30,000,000 members. Everywhere they could record miracles of conversion. Nor did Pope Pius IX hesitate to call the Archconfraternity 'a heavenly inspiration, a work of God, a source of blessings for the Church', and he enriched it with precious indulgences.

3. In 1917 the Blessed Virgin appeared several times, at Fatima (Portugal), to three children, each time on the 13th day of the month. She asked that people should pray more for the conversion of sinners, and that sacrifices should be made to atone for their transgressions. In the last apparition, she declared: 'I am Our Lady of the Rosary. I have come to persuade them to change their ways of living, to no longer offend Our Lord by their sins, to recite the rosary. I desire that a chapel should be built here. If men change their ways, the war will soon come to an end.' There then occurred an impressive solar phenomenon, which the Blessed Virgin had foretold in confirmation of the divine origin of the apparitions. On October 13th, 1930, the Bishop of Leira, in whose diocese Fatima is situated, proclaimed that the visions of the children were fully trustworthy, and that the cult of Our Lady of Fatima was officially approved.

Later on, one of the seers related that the Blessed Virgin had recommended the devotion to her Immaculate Heart as a means of converting sinners; that she foretold that if men did not return to God, there would be another war, even more terrible; and that she desired the Consecration of Russia (according to another version: that of the Universe) to her Immaculate Heart.

Fatima is at the present moment one of the most famous places of pilgrimage in the world. From the outset many wonderful cures were recorded there; and ever since there has been a remarkable increase of gifts and graces obtained at the shrine. Yet what may be considered the greatest miracle of Fatima is the moral and religious revival of Portugal.

4. On October 13th, 1942, on the occasion of the twenty-fifth anniversary of the apparitions of Our Lady at Fatima, Pope Pius XII addressed a broadcast to the Portuguese nation, and, in a moving prayer for peace, for the Church and the whole world, he consecrated the Church and the Universe to the Immaculate Heart of Mary. He ended his address with these words: 'Even as the Church and the whole human race were consecrated to the Heart of Jesus, that they might place in Him all their hopes and that this Heart might be for them a token and assurance of salvation, so may they also for ever be consecrated to Thee, to Thy Immaculate Heart, O Mary, our Mother and Queen of the world, that Thy love and Thy protection may hasten the triumph of the Kingdom of God on earth, and that all nations, reconciled to each other and to God, may proclaim Thee blessed and, from one end of the earth to the other, may sing together with Thee the eternal Magnificat of glory, of love and gratitude towards the Heart of Jesus, in Whom alone they can find Truth, Life and Peace.[1]

OBJECT OF THE DEVOTION

The object of the Devotion, i.e. that which we intend specially to honour in the Blessed Virgin, is commonly regarded as her physical Heart, considered as a symbol of her love for God and for men.

This object is indicated in the decree of the Sacred Congregation of Rites (May 4th, 1944), whereby the Feast of the Immaculate Heart of Mary was extended to the universal Church. 'By this cult,' we read there, 'the Church renders to the Immaculate Heart of the Blessed Virgin Mary the honour which is due to her, since, under the symbol of this Heart, she pays homage to her eminent

[1] *Acta Apost. Sedis*, November 23rd, 1942, p. 346.

holiness, and particularly to her ardent love for God and her Son Jesus, and to her maternal love for men, redeemed by the Blood of God.'[1]

In this way it was already considered by the Consultors of the same Congregation, who approved the devotion in 1857.[2] It should be noted, however, that in the Office and Mass approved of on that occasion, mention is almost solely made of her love for God. The actual Mass and Office now in use emphasize her love for men, and arouse especially our trust in her intercession.

At Lauds, the Church bids us say: 'O Blessed Virgin Mary, Mother of graces, hope of the human race, hear us Thy sons, who cry to Thee.'

The Introit of the Mass applies to the Heart of Mary what St. Paul says of Christ: 'Let us come with confidence to the Throne of grace, that we may obtain mercy, and may find grace for a timely help' (Heb. iv, 16).

The Gospel is the passage of St. John (chap. xix), where Jesus gives John as son to His Mother, and Mary as Mother to John, and where, according to the Fathers of the Church, Mary is appointed to be the Mother of all Christians. And the lessons of the third Nocturn, derived from the book by the Father of the Church, St. Robert Bellarmine, s.j., on the words of Christ on the cross, afford a magnificent commentary on this text, and dwell on the love of Mary towards men and on the special protection upon which the devout clients of Mary may rely.

The formal object then of the devotion—at least its essential object—is the love of the Blessed Virgin for God, for her Divine Son Jesus, and for men.

Yet, just as in the devotion to the Heart of Jesus, the faithful, with the approval of the Church, extend the object of the devotion, and include in it not only the love of the Heart of Mary, but also her whole inner life, her virtues, especially her love of purity and her humility, and all her affections, particularly her sorrows.

And not without reasons. For the Heart is, as we have seen, not only the symbol of love, but also of the whole affective and moral life.[3] Moreover, Mary's inner life was entirely under the influence of the love of God; all her affections and all her virtues were

---

[1] *Acta Apost. Sedis*, vol. xxxvii, p. 50.
[2] Cf. Nilles, op. cit., Liber ii, cap. iv.
[3] See p. 15.

nothing else but different forms of her love. Thus her whole inner life is the secondary object of the devotion. This symbolism appears clearly in the manner in which the Heart of Mary is usually represented, i.e. surrounded with roses, symbol of her virtues, and pierced with a sword, symbol of her sorrows.

But the physical Heart of Mary, considered as a symbol, is not the whole object of the devotion. What we call her spiritual Heart, that is, the unity formed by the faculties of the soul which concur to the production of her love and of her entire inner life, also forms part of it.[1] In fact, we say of this Heart that it bears us a truly maternal love, that it is full of mercy for sinners, that it loves purity, etc. These qualities, however, do not appertain to Mary's physical Heart, but to her spiritual Heart. The latter, then, forms part of the object of the devotion, as symbol, principle and seat of her love and of her whole inner life.

The complete object of the devotion is, therefore, the total Heart of Mary, that is, the whole formed by her physical Heart and her spiritual Heart, considered at once as symbol, principle and seat of her love and of her entire inner life.[2]

It is evident that, just as in the devotion to the Heart of Jesus, the final and ultimate and at the same time principal object of the devotion is the person of Mary herself. Through her Heart, our homage is directed to her person.

Hence, devotion to the Heart of Mary is nothing else but a special form of devotion to the Blessed Virgin. It considers Mary in her Heart, and in her Heart it sees and honours her affections, her virtues, principally her love, with which it is closely connected and of which it is the living symbol.

ENDS AND PRACTICE OF THE DEVOTION

The contemplation of the Heart of Mary must arouse in us a three-fold sentiment: a profound veneration, a filial love, and an unshakable confidence.

First, *a profound veneration.*

In fact, the Heart of Mary is the Heart of the Mother of God. It shares in His sublime dignity, and hence has a just claim to a quite special cult.[3]

---

[1] See p. 25.   [2] See p. 28.
[3] Theologians call it 'cultus hyperduliae', whereas the cult rendered to the other Saints is termed 'cultus duliae'.

It is the Heart of the Queen of Angels and of all the Saints, whom she surpasses in glory, and by whom she is honoured with the deepest reverence.

It is the most pure, the most perfect, the most holy Heart that has ever beaten in the breast of a human creature; a Heart adorned with all virtues and endowed with all graces; the favourite dwelling of the Most Blessed Trinity.

It is the Heart that has always beaten solely for the love of God, for the love of Jesus, and for the love of men.

It really deserves then that we should offer it our deepest veneration.

This we can do, for instance, by celebrating the Feast of the Immaculate Heart of Mary (August 22nd) and by observing the month of August dedicated to her, by honouring the image of her Heart, etc.

A filial love.

Mary loves us, because we are the children of God; because her Divine Son loves us; because she is our Mother. She loves us with a truly maternal love. She loves us as never a mother has loved her children.

For love of us, she accepted to become the Mother of the Saviour, though she foresaw all the consequences which this motherhood would entail. For love of us, she consented to the death of her Son, and, in union with Him, she offered it to God for our Redemption; she may then rightly be called our Co-redeemer.

And she remains our great Benefactress; she watches over us with a very motherly solicitude; she intercedes for us, and succours us in all our trials and troubles. In Heaven we shall see with grateful emotion all we owe her, how many times she has helped us in our difficulties, protected us in danger, strengthened us in temptation, come to our rescue in critical moments.

To this maternal love of the Heart of Mary we ought to respond with a filial love. Hence we shall often express to her our gratitude and love. We shall rejoice in her sublime dignity, in her privileges, her virtues, her glory; we shall express our admiration, congratulate her, and wish her to be better known, honoured, and especially more ardently loved.

If we love Mary, we shall consecrate ourselves to her Heart.

The consecration properly so called is, as we have seen,[1] a total donation of ourselves and after making this offering we no longer belong to ourselves. By the consecration, then, we give ourselves up to the Heart of Mary, in order to live only for her, to fulfil in all things her holy will and wishes, and to promote her interests as if they were our own.

But, are we permitted to give ourselves entirely up to anyone other than God or Jesus? To Mary, certainly. What we give to Mary, we give to Jesus and to God. Of what we give her, she will make no use but in accordance with Christ's desires, in accordance with God's purposes, for their interests and their glory. And there is no doubt that this consecration will be very agreeable to Them; on account of the love which They bear to Mary, all homage, every token of love that is given her cannot fail to be supremely pleasing to Them. So far from dissuading the faithful from it, the Vicar of Christ set the example of this consecration.

Yet, are we permitted to consecrate ourselves to the Heart of Mary if we have already made our consecration to the Heart of Jesus? Undoubtedly. One does not prevent the other. On the contrary, the consecration to the Heart of Mary will help us a great deal to be more faithful in living up to our consecration to the Heart of Jesus.[2]

Love tends to resemble the beloved. If we really love Mary, we shall want to make our hearts as conformable as possible to her Heart.

Mary desires it because a mother wishes, almost inevitably, that her children should be like herself.

The Heart of Mary is the perfect image of the Heart of Jesus. Hence, to imitate the Heart of Mary is to make our hearts conformable to that of Jesus.

The Heart of Mary is the model of all virtues. To try to imitate it, is to tend to perfection.

For these reasons we shall endeavour to cultivate in our hearts the virtues of the Heart of Mary, particularly her love for God and for her Divine Son; her charity, her humility, her love of purity, her submission to the will of God, her patience, and her strength of soul.

---

[1] See p. 123.
[2] On the Consecration to the Heart of Mary, see Bl. Grignon de Montfort, *Traité sur la véritable dévotion à la très Sainte Vierge.*

But a good-hearted child is also sensitive to the sufferings of his mother. What did Mary not suffer in her Heart? She is called with justice the Queen of Martyrs. Her sufferings began with Simeon's prophecy, and ended only on the day of the Resurrection. They reached their climax on Calvary, at the foot of the cross. They exceeded in acuteness every other suffering, as they were in proportion to the sufferings of Jesus and to the love she bore to Him. Never has a man suffered like Jesus, and never was purely human love so strong as that with which Mary loved her Divine Son.

If then we love Mary, we shall be eager to ponder over the sufferings of her Heart; we shall express to her our sympathy and compassion, and also our love and regret; our gratitude, because she accepted those sufferings for our sakes; our love, because she deigned to endure them for love of us; our regret, because we have been the cause of them by our sins.

We shall also be sensitive to the mockeries, slander and outages of which she is the object on the part of so many men. We shall express to her our grief for them, and also for the conduct of men towards her Divine Son, indeed, particularly for that, for it is on this point above all that she is very sensitive; and were she still capable of suffering, it is that which would continually rend her Heart.

These sufferings of the Heart of Mary should not only excite our sorrow, but should also incite us to make reparation. Love tries to soothe the pains of the beloved, to make up for the wrong done to him. We shall, then, compensate the Heart of Mary by making amends for the outrages inflicted upon it, and console it for the unworthy conduct of men towards her dearly beloved Jesus.

In the liturgy of the Feast of the Immaculate Heart of Mary there is no question of reparation. Hence the official cult of her Heart has not the atoning character which is proper to that of the Heart of Jesus. Nor is reparation, as is the case for the devotion to the Heart of Jesus, one of the essential features of the devotion. It is clear, however, that reparation ought to have some place in it. The Church has recognized and sanctioned it, by approving the practice of the First Saturday of the month as reparation for the outrages inflicted on the Heart of Mary, and by granting indulgences for it.[1]

---

[1] Decree of June 13th, 1912. Cf. *Acta Apost. Sedis*, September 30th, 1912. See also *Preces et pia opera*, n. 335.

In her apparitions at Fatima, the Blessed Virgin repeatedly insisted that reparation should be made to her Heart. 'Are you willing to suffer,' she asked the children in her first apparition . . . 'in order to make up for all the outrages that are offered to the Immaculate Heart of Mary?' And in the third apparition she said: 'Repeat frequently, but especially when you make any sacrifice: O Jesus, it is . . . in reparation for the outrages that are offered to the Immaculate Heart of Mary.' Again: 'I shall ask . . . that the Communion of Reparation should be practised on the first Saturday of each month.'

A third sentiment which the contemplation of the Heart of Mary should enkindle within us, is an unbounded and unshakable *confidence*.

This confidence is based on the kindness and love of the Heart of Mary, and on the power of her intercession.

The Heart of Mary is the most perfect reproduction of the Heart of Jesus. It is therefore goodness itself. Mary is our Mother and loves us as her children. She loves each one of us, without exception, however guilty we may be. She is the '*Mother of Mercy*'.

On the other hand, her intercession is all-powerful with her Divine Son. What could a Son like Jesus refuse to a Mother like Mary? She is rightly called '*the suppliant Omnipotence*'.

Moreover, Jesus has appointed her the Dispenser of all graces. In union with her Son, and in accordance with His designs, she disposes of the treasures of graces which He merited for us.

She is particularly the '*Refuge of sinners*'. She loves them, in spite of their unworthiness. She loves them, because she is mercy itself. She loves them, because they, too, are her children. She loves them, because their souls have cost so much to her Divine Son and to herself.

We will then have an unbounded and unshakable trust in the kindness, love and power of the Heart of Mary. We will have recourse to her in all our trials and troubles. We will call on her, in particular to obtain the conversion of sinners, and specially of those who are dear to us.

We will also offer to the Heart of Jesus, as the Apostleship of Prayer invites its members to do,[1] all our prayers, actions, and sufferings, 'through the Immaculate Heart of Mary'. Being offered through the Heart of Mary, they will be the more agree-

[1] See Appendix II, III. p. 265.

able to Jesus, the more perfect, the more meritorious for ourselves, and of more help to souls.

MOTIVES FOR PRACTISING THE DEVOTION

Treating of the ends and practice of the devotion, we have seen how fit and proper it is that we should honour, love, invoke, imitate the Heart of Mary, and console it by our compassion and reparation.

It is obvious that this is also agreeable to God, to Jesus and to Mary. They have, moreover, clearly shown it, and still show it, by the priceless and innumerable graces, particularly by the many often remarkable and unexpected conversions, obtained by invoking the Heart of Mary. The *Manuel of the Archconfraternity of the Immaculate Heart of Mary* and the *Annales of Notre-Dame des Victoires* are an eloquent proof of it.

Besides, the Blessed Virgin repeatedly made the declaration in her apparitions at Fatima. 'Jesus,' she said in the second apparition, 'demands the establishment in the world of the devotion to my Immaculate Heart.' Again: 'No, my daughter, I shall never abandon you. My Heart will be your refuge and the way that leads you to God.' Thereupon the children perceived 'before the right hand of the Apparition a Heart, surrounded with thorns which pierced it through and through.' They understood that they contemplated the Immaculate Heart of Mary, afflicted by the sins of men. In the third apparition, she said: 'Our Lord wishes to establish in the world the devotion to my Immaculate Heart, in order to convert sinners . . . I shall ask the Consecration of Russia (according to another version: of the Universe) to my Immaculate Heart, and the practice of the Communion of Reparation on the First Saturdays. My Immaculate Heart will triumph in the end. The Holy Father will consecrate Russia (according to another version: the Universe) to me.'

The devout clients of the Heart of Jesus have, moreover, a special motive for practising devotion to the Immaculate Heart of Mary in the close relations which unite the two Hearts.

The Heart of Mary is the living replica of the Heart of Jesus. Is it possible to love the Heart of Jesus and not to love the Heart of Mary?

No other heart has ever loved Jesus like that of Mary. Nor has any heart loved Mary like that of Jesus. How could we separate both Hearts in our love?

It is to Mary that we owe the Heart of Jesus. Thanks to her consent, Jesus could, within her, take to Himself a human heart. But it is to Jesus that we owe the Heart of Mary. He it is who formed it, enriched and adorned it with His graces. He it is who imparted to it its love for us, and made it the masterpiece of His love and His power. Is it not natural, therefore, that we should closely join both Hearts in our worship and love?

That is what the first apostles of the Devotion to the Heart of Jesus have understood and put into practice.

We have seen that both St. John Eudes, 'the author of the liturgical cult of the Sacred Heart of Jesus,' and Fr. de Galliffet, the writer of the masterly work '*De l'excellence de la dévotion au Coeur adorable de Jésus-Christ*' were also apostles of the devotion to the Heart of Mary.

It was Jesus in person who instructed St. Margaret Mary to make His Heart and that of His Holy Mother the double object of her homage and devotion. One day, He showed her her heart in the midst of His own Heart and of that of Mary, and said to her: 'Thus it is that My pure love unites these three hearts for ever.'[1]

During the Advent of 1685, she recommends her novices the following practices: 'You will offer five times to the Eternal Father the sacrifices which the Sacred Heart of His Divine Son offers Him by Its ardent charity on the altar of the Heart of His Mother, asking of Him that all hearts may return to Him and devote themselves to His love. You will make this aspiration as often as possible: "I adore and love Thee, O Divine Heart of Jesus living in the Heart of Mary; I conjure Thee to live and reign in all hearts, and to consume them in Thy pure love".'[2] And repeatedly she urges Fr. Croiset to insert in his book on the Devotion to the Sacred Heart the Litany of the most pure Heart of Mary.[3]

Bl. Claude de la Colombière, in his *Retreat-journal*, ends one of his meditations as follows: 'O Hearts, really deserving to possess all hearts, to rule over all hearts of Angels and of men! You will

---

[1] *Vie et Oeuvres*, vol. II, *Ecrits par ordre de la Mère de Saumaise*, n. 55, p. 166.
[2] Ibid., vol. II, *Défis et instructions*, pp. 750–51.
[3] Ibid., vol. II, pp. 538, 554, 617.

henceforth be my rule, and in similiar situations, I shall try to make Your sentiments my own. It is my will that henceforth my heart should only be in the Hearts of Jesus and Mary, or that the Hearts of Jesus and of Mary should be in mine, that They may impart to it Their feelings, and that it be only moved in conformity with the impressions which it receives from these Hearts.'

And Fr. Croiset indicates devotion to the Heart of Mary as the most efficacious means of arriving at the love of Jesus. 'For,' he says, 'the sacred Hearts of Jesus and Mary are too much alike and too much united for one to have access to the one and not to the other, with this difference, however, that the Heart of Jesus admits only extremely pure souls, and that the Heart of Mary purifies, by the graces which she obtains for them, those that are not pure, and enables them to be received in the Heart of Jesus.'[1]

Through the Heart of Mary, then, to the Heart of Jesus!

Who is more able to make us love this Heart, than She who, better than any one else, knows Its infinite lovableness and boundless charity; She who loves this Heart as no one else has loved or will love It, and who longs for nothing so much as to see It loved by all?

Who is more able to obtain for us to be loved in our turn by this Heart, than She who has such a powerful influence over this Heart, and who could not wish or procure anything better for us, her children, than to be loved by her Divine Son?

Who, finally, is more able to open to us the infinite treasures of this Heart and to allow us to draw from this store at will, than She who has been appointed by Jesus Himself, the Mediatrix and Dispenser of all graces?[2]

---

[1] Croiset, op. cit., pt. II, chap. iv, § v.
[2] On the Devotion to the Heart of Mary, see St. John Eudes, *Le Cœur admirable de a très Sainte Mère de Dieu*; Pinamonti, s.j., *Il sacro Cuore di Maria*; de Galliffet, s.j., *De l'excellence de la dévotion au Cœur adorable de Jésus-Christ*, Book III, chap. iv; Nilles, s.j., *De ratione festorum Beatissimi Cordis Jesu et purissimi Cordis Mariae*; de Franciosi, s.j., *La dévotion au sacré Cœur de Jésus et au saint Cœur de Marie*; Terrien, s.j., *La dévotion au sacré Cœur de Jésus*, Book IV, chap. iv; Nix, s.j., *Cultus SS. Cordis Jesu cum additamento de cultu purissimi Cordis B. Mariae Virginis*; Bainvel, s.j., *Le saint Cœur de Marie*; Pujobras, C.M.F., *Cultus purissimi Cordis B. Mariae Virginis* (1943); Sinibaldi, *Il Cuore della Madre di amore. Il Cuore immaculato di Maria. Corso di conferenze* (1946); Dublanchy, *Dévotion au Cœur de Marie* in *Dictionnaire de théologie catholique*; Sauvé, *Le culte du Cœur de Marie*; Lebesconte, *Le Cœur de Marie, d'après Saint Jean Eudes*.

Associations in Honour of the Sacred Heart

We can be sure that Jesus expressed to St. Margaret Mary the wish to see His friends unite in pious associations in order to honour His Sacred Heart in common. 'If there could be established,' she writes to Fr. Croiset, 'an association devoted to the Sacred Heart, whose members share in each other's spiritual goods, I think this would give great pleasure to this Divine Heart.'[1]

She herself instituted such an association in the novitiate, which was at that time under her guidance. All the novices formed part of it. Others, too, joined it, among whom were Bl. Claude de la Colombière, Fr. Croiset, Mother de Saumaise, Mother Greyfié, the chaplain of the Visitation convent at Dijon, Mother de Soudeilles, superior of the Visitation at Moulins, Sister de la Barge of the same convent, and the two brothers of the Saint, one parish priest and the other mayor of Bois-Sainte-Marie.[2]

After her death (1690) the number of these associations rapidly increased. In 1726 they numbered already more than three hundred, not only in Europe but also in America, India and China. In 1764, even before the official approval of the Devotion, the Holy See had already issued 1089 Briefs of Indulgences on behalf of confraternities of the Sacred Heart.[3] At the present day they are numbered in tens of thousands.

All associations of the Sacred Heart have as their common purpose to worship the Heart of Jesus. Yet some particular aspect of the Devotion may be emphasized, some particular practice preferred. This gave rise to various sorts of associations of the Sacred Heart. The most important are: the Confraternities of the Sacred Heart properly so called, the Guard of Honour, the Apostleship of Prayer, the Association of the Communion of Reparation, the Archconfraternity of the Mass of Reparation, the Archconfraternity of the Holy Hour, the Archconfraternity of the

---

[1] *Vie et Oeuvres*, vol. ii, p. 539.
[2] Yenveux, *Le règne du Cœur de Jésus*, p. 543.
[3] *Memoriale of the Bishop of Poland*, n. 45.

Agonizing Heart of Jesus, and the Archconfraternity of the Eucharistic Heart of Jesus.

It may be useful to give some more detailed account about each of these Associations.

I. THE CONFRATERNITIES OF THE SACRED HEART PROPERLY
SO CALLED

The purpose of the Confraternities of the Sacred Heart is to honour in a special manner the Heart of Jesus, to return love to It, to give thanks to It for Its gifts and graces, and mainly for the institution of the Blessed Eucharist, to compensate and console It for the coldness, ingratitude and outrages with which Its love is repaid by so many.

To join one of these confraternities and to endeavour earnestly to realize its aim and purpose is a sure means of sharing in the promises made by our Saviour on behalf of those who devote themselves to the worship of His Sacred Heart. Besides, many indulgences may be gained by the members if the confraternity, as is commonly the case, is affiliated with an Archconfraternity.

The Roman Archconfraternity

The most important archconfraternity of the Sacred Heart is that which is usually called the Roman Archconfraternity. It dates from 1803 and has its headquarters in the church of Santa Maria della Pace. The majority of existing confraternities are affiliated with it.

To share in the numerous indulgences, which are granted to this Archconfraternity,[1] its members must recite every day, in honour of the Sacred Heart, one Our Father, one Hail Mary, the Creed, and the aspiration: O sweetest Heart of Jesus, make me ever love Thee more and more.

In addition, the following practices are recommended: (1) To celebrate the Feast of the Sacred Heart each year with great devotion and, if possible, to receive Communion on that day. (2) To receive Communion at least once every month, preferably on the First Friday or the first Sunday of the month. (3) To pray frequently for each other and for the deceased members.

[1] Cf. Beringer, op. cit., vol. 1, n. 226, b.

The Archconfraternity of Montmartre

Another archconfraternity has its headquarters in the Basilica of the Sacred Heart at Montmartre (Paris). It was erected in 1877 and has as its purpose: (1) to obtain the liberty of the Pope and the welfare of human society; (2) to obtain the protection of the Sacred Heart for the Church and for the Vicar of Christ, for one's own country, the clergy and religious; (3) to obtain the spiritual and temporal gifts promised by Our Lord Himself and which the members of the association need for themselves and their families; (4) to spread the devotion to the Sacred Heart in the family and in society, in reparation for the offences committed against religion, the Church and the Vicar of Christ; (5) to combat the impiety of modern times, by restoring the observance of the commandments of God and the Church in the family and in society.[1]

The members pledge themselves to recite every day one Our Father, one Hail Mary, the Creed, and the invocation: 'Sacred Heart of Jesus, I consecrate myself entirely to Thee; protect Holy Church against its enemies, have mercy on our country, and make me love Thee ever more.'[2]

The Archconfraternity of Paray-le-Monial

In 1693 there was erected in the chapel of the Visitation convent at Paray a confraternity, which was raised in 1865 to the rank of archconfraternity. But whereas the archconfraternities of Rome and Montmartre are empowered to aggregate all confraternities of the whole world, only the confraternities of France and Belgium are permitted to affiliate with that of Paray-le-Monial.[3]

II. THE GUARD OF HONOUR OF THE SACRED HEART OF JESUS

The Guard of Honour has as its aim to gather, every day and at each hour of the day, around the Divine Master faithful and devoted souls who compensate Him by their acts of adoration and their love, for the neglect and the outrages which His adorable Heart receives so frequently in return for His gifts and graces.

This association owes its origin to the religious of the Visitation

---

[1] Beringer, op. cit., vol. I, n. 226, b.
[2] Beringer, ibid.
[3] Cf. *Vie et Oeuvres*, vol. III, p. 250.

U

convent at Bourg-en-Bresse, France. This idea seems to go back to St. Margaret Mary herself. In one of the apparitions with which she was favoured, the Angels agreed to take her place before the Blessed Sacrament whilst she was engaged in her occupations. This agreement was concluded and solemnly ratified, or, as the Saint herself expresses it, written for ever with golden letters by the Angels in the Divine Heart.[1]

This is the idea which the religious of the Visitation at Bourg hoped to realize when, in 1863, they set up an association of this kind. The following year the association was established as a confraternity and, in 1878, as archconfraternity for France and Belgium. Afterwards similar archconfraternities were recognized by the Holy See for other countries, as Italy, Holland, England, Ireland, Spain, Canada, etc.[2]

The associates choose an hour of the day, which they make known to the director of the archconfraternity, and they pledge themselves to spend that hour every day in union with Jesus in the Blessed Sacrament. They need not change anything in their ordinary occupations, but only endeavour to do everything with a view to glorifying and consoling the Sacred Heart. At the beginning of their hour of guard they present themselves in spirit before the Tabernacle, adore Jesus in the Blessed Sacrament, and offer Him all their actions and sufferings with the desire of consoling the Heart of Jesus by their love. And in the course of that hour they offer now and then to God the Father the Blood and Water which flowed from the pierced Heart of Jesus, in reparation for the sins of men and as a supplication for the needs of the Holy Church.[3]

To this end the following prayers, composed by Fr. Lyonnard, s.J., are recommended: 'Holy Father, we beseech Thee to accept as a propitiation for the needs of the Church, and as a reparation for the sins of men, the precious Blood and Water that flowed from the wound in the Divine Heart of Jesus, and be merciful to us. Amen.' 'Jesus, my most loving and gentle Saviour, I offer Thee and the Eternal Father the precious Blood and Water that flowed from the wound in Thy Sacred Heart on the tree of the cross.' 'Deign to apply this Blood and Water to all souls, and especially

[1] *Vie et Oeuvres*, vol. II, *Autobiographie*, n. 101, p. 109.
[2] Cf. Beringer, vol. II, n. 227.
[3] Cf. Beringer, ibid.

to mine and to those of poor sinners. Purify, cleanse, and save all men by Thy merits, and grant that we may enter into Thy loving Heart and dwell there for ever. Amen.[1]

III. THE APOSTLESHIP OF PRAYER

The Apostleship of Prayer is a league of prayer and sacrifice for the glory of God and the salvation of souls, in union with the Sacred Heart.

It was founded, in 1844, at Vals (France) by Fr. Gautrelet, s.j. Yet its great organizer and energetic propagator was Fr. Ramière, s.j., who, in 1861, by his remarkable book *L'Apostolat de la Prière* and by the monthly issue of *Le Messager du Coeur de Jésus*, made the Work known everywhere. In a short time it became a most flourishing organization.[2]

The Apostleship is now spread throughout the world. Today it numbers over 130,000 Centres in more than 1,300 dioceses, with some 35,000,000 members. Its official organ is *The Messenger of the Sacred Heart*, fifty-seven in number, and published in forty different languages, in all parts of the world.

Successive Popes have enriched it with numerous indulgences and privileges and have recommended and encouraged it more than once in a particular way.

Leo XIII issued nine different briefs conferring different privileges on the Apostleship. Pius X stated: 'The Catholics have established many very useful Works; but none is more useful than that of which you are the Director-General.' (Autograph letter addressed to Fr. Boubée, April 9th, 1911. Cf. A.S.S., III, p. 345.) Benedict XV: 'To all the faithful We strongly recommend the Apostleship of Prayer, expressing the wish that no one should omit joining it.'[3] Pius XI said: 'Your apostolate is easy; and since it is available to all, the obligation urges beyond that of other forms of apostolic activity. Therefore all without exception should belong to it; and your duty will not be fulfilled, nor your work accomplished, so long as a single soul remains to be enrolled in this apostolate.'[4]

Pius XII, in his Encyclical *Mystici Corporis* (June 29th, 1943),

---

[1] Beringer, vol. II, n. 227. For the indulgences, see ibid.
[2] Cf. Parra, s.j., *Manuel de l'Apostolat de la Prière*, 29th ed., p. 11.
[3] Encyclical *Maximum illud*, November 1919.
[4] September 1927. Address to the Directors of the Apostleship.

after having urged on the faithful to bear their trials patiently for
the benefit of the Church, continues as follows: 'For the realization
of this design will be most helpful the daily Offering of self to God,
such as the members of the pious association, called the Apostleship of Prayer, practise—which association we highly appreciate
and recommend as very agreeable to God.'

On the occasion of the centenary of this association, in 1944,
the same Pope wrote to the Director General. 'We avail ourselves
of the opportunity of this auspicious event to praise the association
of the Apostleship of Prayer with due honour and to urge all the
faithful to become its zealous members. We see with great satisfaction that besides the Society of Jesus in which this association
arose, grew up and continued to develop, Bishops and very many
secular and regular priests also, with a resolute will and united
efforts, zealously endeavour to increase, support and direct this
pious association.'

The first Statutes date from 1866. They were revised in 1879
and 1896. On October 28th, 1951, with the approbation of the
Holy See, new Statutes were promulgated. Yet they alter neither
the aim nor the nature of the Apostleship; they only aim at
developing and adapting it to the necessities of the present day,
in accordance with the latest papal instructions. On the occasion
of the publication of the new Statutes His Holiness, Pope Pius XII,
addressed to the Director General a letter in which he sets forth
the great importance of the Apostleship, specially for the cure of
souls and strongly recommends it to the Bishops.

We give here the text of the new Statutes in their entirety.

I. Nature and aim of the Apostleship of Prayer

The Apostleship of Prayer is a pious association of the faithful
who live not only for their own salvation but by their apostolic
prayer and offering also work for the edification of the mystical
Body of Christ, for the extension of His kingdom on earth.

Aware that as members of Christ they are responsible for the
salvation of their neighbour, they unite their life with Christ,
who in Heaven without cease pleads for us and offers Himself in
the Sacrifice of the Mass. Hence it is not only by reciting certain
formulas but by offering with Christ their whole lives to God the
Father that they pray for the intentions of His Heart and offer
their sacrifices. By this offering they want to translate into action

a truth which we know through faith, namely, that by grace we are one in Christ, in an unutterable communion of life and that therefore we are, either by our work or prayer or suffering, to conform ourselves to Him as much as possible.

II. *The Apostleship of Prayer and devotion to the Sacred Heart of Jesus*

This intimate union with Christ in prayer and sacrifice is impossible without the tie of reciprocal love. On the part of Christ the symbol and source of His love is His Heart, from which there have sprung all the mysteries of our Redemption and the Church itself. On our part the best way of returning this love is devotion to the Sacred Heart of Jesus, for it makes us know the mystery of Divine love and incites us to true love for God.

Therefore the Apostleship of Prayer promotes in every way devotion to the Sacred Heart. It urges its associates to train themselves in the spirit of this devotion, to observe and spread its practices. Moreover, it considers this devotion as a means which, in the spirit of the Church, is specially suited to the necessities of our time, prepares and hastens the coming of the Kingdom of God in the world.

Hence devotion to the Sacred Heart of Jesus is so intimately connected with the Apostleship of Prayer and so proper to it, that 'the Apostleship of Prayer with good reason may be said to be the perfect form of devotion to the Sacred Heart, and that, conversely, devotion to the divine Heart of Jesus is wholly inseparable from the Apostleship of Prayer.' (Pius XII; Letter to the Most Reverend Father General, s.j., Sept. 19th, 1948.)

III. *Means and Practices*

To attain its end the Apostleship of Prayer utilizes means or practices which it is true are not all obligatory but, taking them all in all, form a true rule of christian life and are a summary of christian perfection.

Pastors of souls should know that the whole of the different practices of the Apostleship of Prayer suggests to them an excellent means for training the faithful committed to their care in a true christian and apostolic spirit, according to the measure of grace which God gives them.

(a) *First practice: the Daily Offering*

The first and chief thing the Associates are to do, is to make the daily Offering, by which everyone each day offers to God his prayers and works, his joys and sufferings, in union with Christ and for the intentions of His Heart; intentions for which He as Head of His mystical Body without cease pleads for us and offers Himself as Victim. By virtue of our union with Christ this Offering confers on our actions an impetratory and propitiatory value, or better, changes our whole lives into an offering of praise and atonement.

As our union with Christ, the Head, also necessarily requires a close union with the Pope, His Vicar on earth, the Apostleship proposes each month to all its Associates two motives for praying, two intentions which 'the Pope himself examines, approves and blesses': a general intention and a missionary intention. (Cf. Letter of Pius XII 'Cum proxime exeat., June 16th, 1944.)[1]

(b) *Second practice: the Holy Sacrifice of the Mass and the Communion of Reparation*

The 'Daily Offering' draws its perfect value from our union with the Eucharistic Sacrifice, in which our offerings in Christ and with Christ, Priest and Victim, are sanctified and partake of the infinite value of His Sacrifice. The Associates then will also join their Daily Offering as intimately as possible to the Sacrifice of the Mass, and above all they should realize that, as the greatest obstacle to the Kingdom of Christ is sin, Holy Mass affords us the great means of giving satisfaction to the Eternal Father offended by our sins and to make up for the outrages offered to the Heart of Jesus itself.

Therefore the Associates are at least once each month to receive Holy Communion in a spirit of reparation, in order to make amends for their own sins and those of others and to implore His mercy. Furthermore, they are invited to assist at Holy Mass as often as possible, even during the week, and to communicate more frequently than once each month.

---

[1] The usual form of the 'Morning Offering' is: 'Divine Heart of Jesus, through the Immaculate Heart of Mary, I offer Thee the prayers and works, joys and sufferings of this day, in reparation of our offences and for all the intentions for which Thou offerest Thyself unceasingly in the Blessed Sacrifice of The Altar. I offer them to Thee especially for the intentions recommended by our Holy Father the Pope for this month.'

(c) Third practice: Devotion to Mary

Fully aware that the Blessed Virgin Mary intercedes with God for us, as our Mother and Advocate, and by her intercession gives our prayers a special efficacy, the Associates have also recourse to the Immaculate Heart of Mary. They address their Daily Offering through her to the Sacred Heart of Jesus and to God the Father.

Moreover, in token of filial confidence in this compassionate Heart of the Mother of Christ and our Mother, they are urged to recite each day, in private or in common, at least one decade of the Rosary and if possible the whole Rosary.

IV. Practices of devotion to the Sacred Heart of Jesus

As devotion to the Sacred Heart of Jesus is the essential feature of the Apostleship of Prayer, the Associates promote by all the means in their power the chief forms of this cult, which are recommended by the ecclesiastical authority, namely, the Consecration to the Sacred Heart of Jesus, first the personal Consecration, and then that of families also, and all communities; the observance of the Feast of Christ the King; then the different practices of 'Reparation', namely, the Holy Hour, the Communion of Reparation, especially on the First Friday of the month, and, first and foremost, the celebration of the Feast of the Sacred Heart of Jesus.

V. The Organization of the Apostleship of Prayer

(*a*) The Apostleship of Prayer has its own organization, which however—while retaining its essential elements—may and must be adapted to various circumstances.

(*b*) The Director General of the Apostleship of Prayer is the General of the Society of Jesus for the time being, who has the power to delegate another at his choice for this function. The latter in his turn is assisted in the different countries by National or Regional Secretaries, who discharge the duties of their office either for a whole nation, or a determinate region, or some sections of the Apostleship of Prayer. The principal seat or 'Centre' of the Apostleship of Prayer is fixed in Rome in the 'Curia' of the Society of Jesus.

(*c*) The organization of the Apostleship takes place by dioceses. In each diocese one or more diocesan Directors may be established, who are appointed by the Bishop and then designated by the Director General or his delegate.

(*d*) Within a diocese, wherever this may seem expedient, Centres may be established, for instance, in parishes, churches, religious Institutes, schools, etc. These Centres are erected by the diocesan Director. The latter also appoints, with the approbation of the Bishop, their directors; they are called local directors and must be priests. If this appointment is connected with a deter-minate office (for instance, that of parish priest, rector or spiritual director, etc.) it will also hold good for the successor in this office, express revocation excepted.

(*e*) Both the diocesan and local directors are subject to the Bishop even in matters concerning the Apostleship of Prayer, except in what regards the Statutes approved by the Apostolic See.

(*f*) The task of the National or Regional Secretaries is to help the diocesan and local Directors, by providing them with what-ever may be useful for the propagation and development of the Apostleship of Prayer. They also publish the 'Messenger of the Sacred Heart', the official organ of the Apostleship of Prayer, and other papers and writings which promote its aim. Finally, they are the intermediaries between the general Direction and the diocesan and local Directors.

VI. *The Admission of Associates*

For the valid admission of Associates it is required and sufficient that with their agreement their names are inscribed in a register or card-index system of a properly established Centre.

For the enrolment as a member of the Apostleship the one essential duty is the 'Daily Offering' described above. But all are earnestly urged in addition to this Offering to make at least one Communion of Reparation each month and to recite daily a decade of the Rosary. All other exercises of piety are recommended to the Associates as means for leading a better christian life and attaining the aim of the Apostleship of Prayer.

The associates should perform faithfully the different practices, especially the Daily Offering, each one to the best of his abilities, and should endeavour to live more and more according to the spirit of the Apostleship of Prayer.

(*a*) To promote the Apostleship of Prayer and its works the

VII. *The Promoters*

Associates must co-operate. Those who are capable of it, and are admitted by the Director, are called the 'Promoters'. Their duty is to assemble Associates and train them in the spirit of the Apostleship of Prayer.

(*b*) To discharge their duty faithfully and successfully the Promoters should meet at times, once a month at least, if possible. They will receive from the local Director, or another experienced priest, special instructions about the way of strengthening and developing their spiritual life and also of exercising their apostolate. They should endeavour first and foremost to confirm themselves in the apostolic spirit by means of recollections and retreats, and by the zealous practice of devotion to the Sacred Heart of Jesus.

(*c*) As Promoters imbued with the spirit of prayer and apostolate are of great importance for the useful effect of the Apostleship of Prayer and its works, the Directors should earnestly endeavour to have always at their disposal a sufficient number of Promoters and employ them according to the different necessities and conditions of the pastoral ministry. The value of the Apostleship of Prayer wholly depends on the value of the Promoters and Directors.

VIII. *Sections of the Apostleship of Prayer*

(*a*) For a better adaptation to the different persons and places, there may be established in different places, with the approbation of the general Direction, special Sections of the Apostleship of Prayer, which will be designated by proper names, for instance *'the Eucharistic Crusade', 'the League of the Sacred Heart of Jesus'*, etc.

(*b*) These Sections keep the aims, practices and essential organization of the Apostleship of Prayer, but add to them special works of piety and apostolic zeal.

IX. *Relation between the Apostleship of Prayer and the Catholic Action and other religious Works*

As the Apostleship of Prayer nourishes and maintains interior life by which we remain united to God and which is the soul and power of all authentic apostolate; as it incites and trains its Associates to apostolic zeal; it contributes to a great extent to promoting Catholic Action and other Movements which further

v

the apostolate of the Church and to making them from day to day more fruitful. Therefore the Apostleship of Prayer invites and strongly urges its Associates to enrol themselves and work in other Apostolic Works, especially in Catholic Action. (Cf. Letter of Pius XII, June 16th, 1944.)

IV. THE ASSOCIATION OF THE COMMUNION OF REPARATION

Founded in 1854 by Fr. Drevon, s.j., the Association of the Communion of Reparation was canonically erected, in 1865, at Paray-le-Monial, in the Visitation convent, where the Sacred Heart appeared to St. Margaret Mary. At his death, the founder entrusted his work to Fr. Ramière, s.j., Director-General of the Apostleship of Prayer. Ratifying the last will of Fr. Drevon, Pope Leo XIII, by Brief of March 30th, 1886, joined both Works under one and the same Director-General, and made the members of the Apostleship of Prayer partakers of all the spiritual favours granted to the Association of the Communion of Reparation.

The aim and purpose of the Association is to promote the Communion of Reparation, and to establish an uninterrupted series of such Communions.

To this end, the directors appoint to each associate the day of the month or week, on which Communion should be made for the following intentions: (1) to console, in union with the Blessed Virgin, the Divine Heart of Jesus, outraged by men in the Holy Eucharist; (2) to make intercession on behalf of the Church and the Sovereign Pontiff; (3) to obtain the conversion of sinners, the preservation and progress of the Catholic Faith throughout the world, and specially in their own country.

The associates have a particular share in the prayers, Communions, and all good works of the Religious of the Visitation convent at Paray-le-Monial. Moreover, they gain a plenary indulgence for the Communion of Reparation made on the appointed day. Their names are enclosed in the altar erected in the room in which St. Margaret Mary died.[1]

V. THE ARCHCONFRATERNITY OF THE MASS OF REPARATION

This Archconfraternity makes it its object to induce the faithful to assist on Sundays and holidays of obligation at a second Mass,

---

[1] Cf. Beringer, op. cit., vol. II, n. 218.

in order to glorify God, to make up for the offences done to God by the sinful negligence of so many Christian people who, on those days, omit to hear Mass, and to make reparation for the outrages inflicted on the Heart of Jesus in the Holy Sacrifice.

Thus the only obligation of the associates is to assist at a second Mass, for the intentions mentioned above, on the days on which assistance at Mass is obligatory. In case of hindrance this second Mass may be replaced either by a Communion or by assisting at Mass, for the same purpose, on another day of the week. Where only one Mass is celebrated, the associates meet their engagement by adoring for some time the Blessed Sacrament, before or after Mass.[1]

There are now several archconfraternities of the Mass of Reparation, approved by the Holy See.[2]

VI. THE ARCHCONFRATERNITY OF THE HOLY HOUR

In order to propagate the exercise of the Holy Hour, a confraternity of the Holy Hour was established, in 1829, by Fr. Debrosse, s.j., in the Jesuit church at Paray-le-Monial. On April 6th, 1886, it was raised by Pope Leo XIII to the rank of archconfraternity for France and Belgium. In 1911, it was authorized by Pius X to affiliate confraternities throughout the world.

These are the Statutes:

1. The Holy Hour is an exercise of mental or vocal prayer, which has as its object the agony of Our Lord in the Garden of Olives, in order to appease God's anger, to implore mercy for sinners, and to console our Saviour for one hour.

2. The exercise of the Holy Hour is made in common or in private, in the church or in any place, on Thursday night from eleven o'clock to midnight, or even from the time at which the Friday Matins may be begun.

3. Those who wish to join this archconfraternity must send their names to the Visitation convent at Paray-le-Monial, to be inscribed there on a register.

4. Each one is free to make the Holy Hour more or less frequently according to his devotion. Yet it is to be wished that the

---

[1] Cf. *Acta Apost. Sedis*, vol. v (1911), p. 476.
[2] Cf. Beringer, op. cit., vol. II, p. 219.

associates should often give the Heart of Jesus this token of tender and generous love. St. Margaret Mary, their pattern, made it every Thursday night.[1]

VII. THE ARCHCONFRATERNITY OF THE AGONIZING HEART OF JESUS AND OF THE COMPASSIONATE HEART OF MARY FOR THE SALVATION OF THE DYING

This confraternity owes its origin to Fr. Lyonnard, s.j. Being moved by the indifference of so many who allow themselves to be overtaken by death in the state of mortal sin, he resolved to do all in his power to secure a happy death to the dying.[2] To this end he erected, in 1848, at Vals (France), a league of prayer in honour of the agonizing Heart of Jesus for the salvation of the dying. The league was canonically established as a confraternity by several Bishops of France and Belgium. In 1864, their example was followed by the Patriarch of Jerusalem, and in 1869 this confraternity of Jerusalem was raised by Pope Pius IX to the rank of archconfraternity.[3]

Thus the Archconfraternity makes it its object: (1) to honour with a special worship both the suffering and agonizing Heart of Jesus at Gethsemane and the afflicted Heart of Mary during the Passion of her Divine Son; (2) to obtain, by the bitter pangs of the Son and the Mother, the grace of a happy death for all who, daily, depart this life.

The members engage themselves to recite every day the following prayer: 'O most merciful Jesus, lover of souls, I beseech Thee, by the agony of Thy most Sacred Heart and by the sorrows of Thy Immaculate Mother, cleanse in Thy Blood all the sinners of the world, who are now in their agony, and are to die this day. Amen.—Agonising Heart of Jesus, have mercy on the dying.[4]

It is also recommended: (1) to devote a day every month to the dying, to offer for them that day their works and exercises of devotion, and to pray for half an hour to the agonising Heart of

---

[1] For affiliation one may apply to the Office of the Apostleship of Prayer.

[2] Every day more than 140,000 depart this life.

[3] The headquarters are at the convent of the Sisters of the Agonizing Heart of Jesus in Paris, 5 rue du Regard.

[4] Indulgences: 300 days each time. Plenary on the usual conditions once a month to those who, during the month, repeat this prayer at least three times daily at intervals (*Preces et pia opera*, n. 625).

Jesus. (The last-named exercise may be replaced by assistance at Holy Mass.) (2) To do all in their power to ensure that the Last Sacraments are received in good time by their relatives, friends and neighbours.

VIII. THE ARCHCONFRATERNITY OF THE EUCHARISTIC HEART OF JESUS

By Brief of February 16th, 1903,[1] Pope Leo XIII established at Rome, in the church of St. Joachim, the Archconfraternity of the Eucharistic Heart of Jesus, the direction of which he entrusted to the Redemptorist Fathers.

The aim of the Archconfraternity is clearly defined in the Brief: 'It is an association of the faithful who, though having towards the Sacred Heart a devotion not essentially different from that which the Church already pays to this Divine Heart, strive to take as special object of veneration, of love and gratitude, that act of supreme love whereby the loving Heart of Jesus instituted the Eucharist, in order to dwell with us until the end of time.'

The following exercises are suggested to the associates:

(1) Every week a visit of adoration to the Blessed Sacrament lasting at least half an hour. (2) Every day a prayer to the Eucharistic Heart of Jesus, and at the stroke of the clock, the aspiration: '*Praised, adored, loved, and thanked be at every moment the Eucharistic Heart of Jesus, in all the Tabernacles of the world, till the end of ages. Amen.*' (3) To receive Communion on Maundy-Thursday and on the Feasts of Corpus-Christi and the Sacred Heart. (4) To observe the month of April in honour of the Eucharistic Heart of Jesus.[2]

IX. DIALOGUE OFFICE OF THE SACRED HEART

I. Grateful Adoration

The Priest. Let us ask Jesus Christ, who is present among us— to bless us in company with all men throughout the world—so that we may all know Him, love Him and serve Him through the accomplishment of His holy Will.

---

[1] Cf. *Nouvelle Revue Théologique*, 1903, pp. 196 and 269.
[2] Cf. Beringer, op. cit., vol. II, n. 229. See there also the indulgences granted to the associates.

The People. That our soul—may magnify the Lord.
               That our spirit may rejoice—in God, our Saviour.

The Priest. For His mercy is shown from generation to generation
               —to them that serve Him—He, whose way it is to
               disperse His enemies with the strength of His arm—
               and to confound the proud in the conceit of their
               hearts.

The People. That our soul—may magnify the Lord.
               That our spirit may rejoice—in God, our Saviour.

The Priest. He, whose way it is to put down the mighty from
               their seats, and to exalt the humble and the lowly.

The People. That our soul—may magnify the Lord.
               That our spirit may rejoice—in God, our Saviour.

The Priest. He, whose way it is to fill with His supernatural gifts
               those who hunger for them—and to send away,
               empty-handed, the rich and the self-important.

The People. That our soul—may magnify the Lord.
               That our spirit may rejoice—in God, our Saviour.

The Priest. He who has always watched over—the People who
               serve Him—wishing to remember His mercy for
               ever—as He promised to Abraham and to the whole
               race of believers.

The People. That our soul—may magnify the Lord.
               That our spirit may rejoice—in God, our Saviour.

The Priest. He, who came to dwell among us—putting aside for
               a while His glory—in order to become like ourselves
               in everything except sin.

The People. That our soul—may magnify the Lord.
               That our spirit may rejoice—in God, our Saviour.

The Priest. He who humiliated Himself and was obedient—
               obedient unto death, even the death of the cross.

The People. That our soul—may magnify the Lord.
               That our spirit may rejoice—in God, our Saviour.

The Priest. He who first instituted the Eucharist—in order to
               perpetuate among us for ever His complete sacrifice
               and His holy presence—and to give Himself to our
               souls as spiritual nourishment.

The People. That our soul—may magnify the Lord.
               That our spirit may rejoice—in God, our Saviour.

The Priest. He who gave to His priests—the power to forgive our sins—in His name.

The People. That our soul—may magnify the Lord.

That our spirit may rejoice—in God, our Saviour.

The Priest. He, who for this mission of suffering redemption, has been so supremely exalted by the Father—so that at the Name of Jesus every knee shall bend, in heaven, on earth, and in hell beneath—and that all men shall acknowledge that Jesus is Lord, Man-God Saviour, to the glory of the Father in the unity of the Holy Spirit: Gloria in excelsis deo. (Mass of the Angels.)

The People. Et in terra pax hominibus bonae voluntatis.— Laudamus Te.—Benedicimus Te.—Adoramus Te.— Glorificamus Te.—Gratias agimus Tibi propter magnam gloriam Tuam.—Domine Deus, Rex cælestis, Deus Pater omnipotens.—Domine Fili Unigenite, Jesu Christe.—Domine Deus, Agnus Dei, Filius Patris.—Qui tollis peccata mundi, miserere nobis.— Qui tollis peccata mundi, suscipe deprecationem nostram.—Qui sedes ad dexteram Patris, miserere nobis. Quoniam Tu solus sanctus.—Tu solus Dominus.—Tu solus altissimus, Jesu Christe.—Cum Sancto Spiritu, in gloria Dei Patris.—Amen.

(A few minutes of silent, personal prayer.)

II. The Love of Contrition and Reparation

The Priest. 'What is man, Lord, that Thou shouldst remember him? What is Adam's breed, that it should claim Thy care?'

The People. Lord, our God—we marvel at your love.

The Priest. 'Who dares climb the mountain of the Lord, and appear in His sanctuary? The guiltless in act, the pure in heart; one who never set his heart on lying tales, or swore treacherously to his neighbour.'

The People. For him you will reserve—Your mercy and your happiness.

The Priest. That is why, Lord, gathered together here in Your presence—we implore You to take pity on us because of our sins—and to pardon us for them.

The People. Merciful Heart of Jesus—pardon.

The Priest. For all those who forget You, scorn, or oppose You— Lord, we pray.

The People. Merciful Heart of Jesus—pardon.

The Priest. For all those who pass by, indifferent to Your love— and for all those, among Your own, who are unfaithful and tepid—Lord, we pray.

The People. Merciful Heart of Jesus—pardon.

The Priest. For all of us, Lord, who do not love You enough.

The People. Merciful Heart of Jesus—pardon.

The Priest. For all husbands and wives who profane their sacred obligations, for so many broken homes and culpable associations.

The People. Merciful Heart of Jesus—pardon.

The Priest. For our prayers so badly made, for Your neglected or profaned Sacraments, for so many graces which remain sterile through our own fault—for our sloth and our cowardice in responding to Your inspirations and in extending Your reign on earth.

The People. Merciful Heart of Jesus—pardon.

The Cantor. Kyrie eleison (Litanies of the Saints).

The People. Kyrie eleison.

The Cantor. Christe eleison.

The People. Christe eleison.

The Cantor. Kyrie eleison.

The People. Kyrie eleison.

The Cantor. Christe audi nos.

The People. Christe exaudi nos.

The Cantor. Pater de coelis, Deus.

The People. Miserere nobis.

The Cantor. Fili, Redemptor mundi, Deus.

The People. Miserere nobis.

The Cantor. Spiritus Sancte, Deus.

The People. Miserere nobis.

The Cantor. Sancta Trinitas, unus Deus.

The People. Miserere nobis.

Parce, Domine—parce populo tuo, ne in aeternum irascaris nobis. (3 times.)

(A few minutes of silent, personal prayer.)

III. Confiding Love

The Priest. Saint Margaret Mary has told us that one day You taught her this lesson: 'Learn that I am a holy Master who teaches sanctity. I am pure and cannot suffer the smallest stain, the smallest deviation, nor endure lukewarm and cowardly souls. And if I am gentle in bearing with weaknesses, I am no less precise and severe in punishing infidelities.'

The People. Lord—we trust You—to make us generous.

The Priest. You said one day:[1] 'Your misery draws Me, because I am mercy: your weakness captivates Me because I am all-powerful: your faults plead with Me because I am holy and the source of all holiness.'

The People. Lord—we trust You—to sanctify us.

The Priest. For You are He—who has custody of and surpasses all holiness—He who wills to be sought, and served, and loved in holiness—He who takes delight in the heart which is offered Him—provided that this heart is humble, generous and pure.

The People. Lord—we trust Your mercy—to purify us.

The Priest. Your love unceasingly bridges the abyss of our misery—to bend over us and have pity on us. As of old You said to Your people, Israel, You repeat to us: 'I will pour cleansing streams over you, to purge you from every stain you bear, purge you from the taint of your idolatry. I will give you a new heart, and breathe a new spirit into you; I will take away from your breasts those hearts that are hard as stone, and give you human hearts instead.'

The People. Lord, give us a new and pure heart.

The Priest. 'I will make my spirit penetrate you, so that you will follow in the path of my law, remember and carry out my decrees'—for 'The man who loves Me is the man who keeps the commandments he has from Me.'

The People. Lord—teach us to be humble and faithful.

The Priest. 'I will allure thee and lead thee into the wilderness; and I will speak to thy heart. I will espouse thee to

---

[1] To Mother Louise Marguerite Claret de la Touche (1868–1915).

Me for ever—I will espouse thee to Me in faith:'—in the Father, for 'What I do is always what pleases Him.'

The People. That which will nourish our souls—will be to do—His will always.

The Priest. 'Now comes the hour when I will talk to you in parables no longer, but tell you openly about the Father,' for—'Just as I am known to My Father, so I know Him.'

The People. Lord—make us to know the Father.

The Priest. 'Learn from Me, for I am gentle and humble of heart.'

The People. Lord—make our hearts like unto Thine.

The Priest. Let us express our filial and generous confidence—by repeating the prayer which You, O Lord, Yourself taught us:

The People. Pater Noster, qui es in caelis—sanctificetur nomen tuum—adveniat regnum tuum—fiat voluntas tua sicut in caelo et in terra—Panem nostrum quotidianum da nobis hodie—et dimitte nobis debita nostra—sicut et nos dimittimus debitoribus nostris—et ne nos inducas in tentationem—sed libera nos a malo.—Amen.

(A few minutes of silent, personal prayer.)

IV. Radiant Love

The Priest. Jesus, You have said to us: 'The man who loves Me is the man who keeps the commandments he has from Me.'

The People. Lord—we will love You.

The Priest. 'I have a new commandment to give you, that you are to love one another; that your love for one another is to be like the love I have borne you. The mark by which all men will know you for My disciples will be the love you bear one another.'

The People. Lord—we will love one another—for love of You.

The Priest. 'He who loves Me will win My Father's love, and I too will love Him.'

The People. Lord—help us to love You—and to make You loved.

The Priest.	'Father, that they may all be one; that they too may be one in us, as Thou, Father, art in Me, and I in Thee; so that the world may come to believe that it is Thou who hast sent Me' as Saviour.
The People.	Lord—we will love one another—that Your works may be made manifest in us.
The Priest.	'I am not praying for the world, but for those whom Thou hast entrusted to Me. . . . It is not only for them that I pray; I pray for those who are to find faith in Me through their word—that they may all be one.'
The People.	Lord—increase our faith—and that of our brethren.
The Priest.	'Going therefore, teach all nations,' for you are the light of the world and the salt of the earth, you are the leaven, mixed with the dough in order to transform it. 'He that loveth his brother abideth in the light; and there is no scandal in him.'
The People.	Lord, we will be your witnesses—just where You have placed us.
The Priest.	'Let us not love in word nor in tongue, but in deed and in truth', for 'In this we have known the charity of God, because He hath laid down His life for us; and we ought to lay down our lives for the brethren.'
The People.	Lord—we will sacrifice ourselves—so that our brethren may also—be truly sanctified.
The Priest.	'And we have known and have believed the charity which God hath to us. God is charity: and he that abideth in charity abideth in God, and God in him.'
The People.	Lord—may the world be better and happier—because we have passed through it.
Chant.	Lord Jesus, teach us to be generous, to serve You as You deserve to be served, to give without counting the cost, to fight without thought of the wounds, to work without seeking repose, to spend ourselves without expecting any other reward than that of knowing that we are doing Your holy Will.
The Priest.	Christ Jesus—bless our prayer and renew our hearts in ardent charity for the Father and for our brethren —so that one day we too may be able to sing the

praises of Your eternal mercy in the words of the Virgin Mary, Your Mother and our refuge:

Magnificat.

Tu es Petrus.

Cor Jesu Sacratissimum.

Tantum Ergo.

After Benediction the Divine Praises.

Sacred Heart of Jesus, may Your Kingdom come.
Sacred Heart of Jesus, I believe in Your love for me.
Sacred Heart of Jesus, I trust in You.

(3 times.)

Works Consulted

Acta Apostolicae Sedis.

ANIZAN, Félix, *Qu'est-ce que le Sacré-Coeur?*, Paris, 1910; idem, *Vers Lui*; idem, *En Lui*, Paris.

BAINVEL, J. V., S.J., *La dévotion au sacré Coeur de Jésus*, Paris, 1930.

BÉGASSIERE, René de la, S.J., *Coeur de Jésus*, in Dictionnaire apologétique de la foi catholique.

BENEDICT XV, *Letter on the Consecration of Families to the Sacred Heart*, April 27th, 1915; idem, *Letter on the occasion of the solemn consecration of the basilica of the Sacred Heart at Montmartre*, October 7th, 1919.

BERINGER, F., S.J., *Les Indulgences*, Paris, 1924.

BOUZONNIÉ, J., *Entretien sur la dévotion au sacré Coeur de Notre-Seigneur*, Brussels, 1905.

BUCCERONI, J., S.J., *Commentarii in cultum SS. Cordis Jesu*, Paris, 1880.

CASTELAIN, D., CssR., *De cultu eucharistici Cordis Jesu*, Paris, 1928.

CLAEYS-BOUUAERT, M., S.J., *La dévotion au Sacré-Coeur.*

COLOMBI´RE, Blessed Claude de la, S.J., *Retraite Spirituelle*, Toulouse, 1945.

CROISET, Jean, S.J., *La dévotion au sacré Coeur de Jésus*, Brussels, 1891; idem, *La vie de la Bienheureuse Marguerite-Marie*, Paris.

DALGAIRNS, *The Devotion to the Sacred Heart of Jesus.*

FRANCIOSI, Xav. de., S.J., *La dévotion au sacré Coeur de Jésus et au saint Coeur de Marie*, Paris, 1878.

FRANCO, S., S.J., *De la dévotion au sacré Coeur de Jésus*, Tournai, 1862.

FRANZELIN, Card., S.J., *De Verbo Incarnato*, Roma, 1874.

FRIEDRICH, Edw., S.V.D., *Die kirchliche Andacht zum göttlichen Herzen Jesu*, Mödling bei Wien, 1920.

FROMENT, Fr., S.J., *La véritable dévotion au sacré Coeur de Jésus-Christ*, Brussels, 1891.

GALLIFFET, Joseph de, S.J., *De cultu Sacrosancti Cordis Dei ac Domini nostri Jesu Christi*, Rome, 1726; idem, *De l'excellence de la dévotion au Coeur adorable de Jésus-Christ*, Paris, 1861.

GALTIER, Paul, S.J., *Le Sacré-Coeur*, Paris, 1936.

GARRIGUET, L., *Le Sacré-Coeur de Jésus-Christ*, Paris, 1920.

GAUTHEY, Mgr., *Vie et Oeuvres de sainte MargueriteMarie-*, 3 vol., Paris, 1920.

GAUTRELET, S.J., *Manuel de la dévotion au sacré Coeur de Jésus*, Brussels, 1852.

GROU, Jean-Nicolas, S.J., *L'intérieur de Jésus et de Marie*, 2 vol., Neuilly, 1843.

GUITTON, G. S.J., *Le bienheureux Claude la Colombière*, Lyon, 1943.

HAMON, Aug., S.J., *Histoire de la dévotion au Sacré-Coeur*, 5 vol., Paris, 1923-40.

LANGUET, Mgr. Jean-Joseph, *La vie de la Vénérable Mère Marguerite-Marie*, Paris, 1860.

LEJEUNE, Mgr., *La dévotion au Sacré-Coeur de Jésus*, Paris, 1922.

LEO XIII, *Litterae Apostolicae Benigno divinae Providentiae*, June 28th, 1889; idem, Encyclical *Annum Sacrum*, May 25th, 1899.

LEROY, Chan. L., *De Sacratissimo Corde Jesu eiusque cultu*, Liège, 1882; idem, *Les Litanies du Sacré-Coeur de Jésus*, Liège, 1904.

LETIERCE, P. E., s.j., *Étude sur le Sacré-Coeur*, Paris, 1891.

LYONNARD, Jean, s.j., *L'apostolat de la souffrance*, Tournai, 1910.

MARGUERITE-MARIE ALACOQUE, *Vie et Oeuvres*, Paris, 1920.

MATEO (CRAWLEY-BOEVEY), C.ss.CC., *Vers le Roi d'amour*, Lyon, 1920.

MAZELLA, Card., Prefect of the Sacred Congregation of Rites, *Letter on the means of promoting the cult of the Sacred Heart*, Rome, July 11th, 1899.

Memoriale of the Bishops of Poland, 1765.

MESCHLER, M., s.j., *Die Andacht zum göttlichen Herzen Jesu*, 2e Aufl., Freiburg, 1899.

Messager du Coeur de Jésus, Toulouse.

NILLES, Nic., s.j., *De rationibus festorum Beatissimi Cordis Jesu et purissimi Cordis Mariae*, Oeniponte, 1873.

NOLDIN, H., s.j., *Die Andacht zum heiligsten Herzen Jesu*, Elfte Aufl., Innsbruck, 1923.

PARANGUE, F., s.j., *La dévotion au Sacré-Coeur de Jésus étudiée en son image*, Paris, 1901.

PARRA, Charles, s.j., *Le Sacré-Coeur*, Toulouse, 1947; idem, *L'apostolat de la Prière*, 1946.

PESCH, Chr., s.j., *Unser bester Freund*.

PIUS VI, The Bull *Auctorem fidei*, August 28th, 1794.

PIUS XI, The Encyclical *Miserentissimus Redemptor*, May 8th, 1928; idem, The Encyclical *Caritate Christi compulsi*, May 3rd, 1932.

PLUS, Raoul, s.j., *L'idée réparatrice*, Paris, 3e édit., 1929.

Preces et pia opera indulgentiis ditata, Rome, 1938.

RAMIÈRE, Henri, s.j., *Le Coeur de Jésus et la divinisation du chrétien*, Toulouse, 1891; idem, *L'Apostolat de la Prière*, Tournai, 1906; idem, *Le Mois du Sacré-Coeur*, Toulouse, 1890.

RICHSTÄTTER, Karl, s.j., *Das Herz des Welterlösers*, Freiburg, 1932.

SAUVÉ, Charles, s.s., *Le Sacré-Coeur intime*, Paris, 1927.

SUAU, Pierre, s.j., *Le Sacré Coeur de Jésus*, Paris.

TERRIEN, J. B., s.j., *La dévotion au Sacré-Coeur de Jésus*, Paris, 1893.

THOMAS, Jules, *La théorie de la dévotion au Sacré-Coeur de Jésus*, Paris, 1912.

VERMEERSCH, Arthur, s.j., *Pratique et doctrine de la dévotion au Sacré-Coeur*, 2 vol., Tournai, 1930.

YENVEUX, A., o.m.i., *Le Règne du Coeur de Jésus*, Paris, 1899.

OTHER TITLES AVAILABLE

Wife, Mother and Mystic. Bessiers.
The Life of Anne Catherine Emmerich. Schmöger.
The Evolution Hoax Exposed. Field.
The Cure D'Ars. Trochu.
The Glories of Mary. St. Alphonsus Liguori.
The Convert's Catechism of Catholic Doctrine. Geiermann.
The Rosary in Action. Johnson.
Dogmatic Canons and Decrees.
The Three Ways of the Spiritual Life. Garrigou-Lagrange.
Latin Grammar. Scanlon.
Second Latin. Scanlon.
Saint Therese — The Little Flower. Beevers.
Bible Quizzes. Rumble & Carty.
Purgatory Quizzes. Rumble & Carty.
Indulgence Quizzes. Rumble & Carty.
Confession Quizzes. Rumble & Carty.
Marriage Quizzes. Rumble & Carty.
Hell Quizzes. Rumble & Carty.
Birth Prevention Quizzes. Rumble & Carty.
Eucharist Quizzes. Rumble & Carty.
True Church Quizzes. Rumble & Carty.
Virgin and Statue Worship Quizzes. Rumble & Carty.
Set of 10 Quizzes Above.
Dogmatic Theology for the Laity. Premm.
Is It a Saint's Name.
What Catholics Believe. Lovasik.
The Incredible Creed of the Jehovah's Witnesses. Rumble.
Uniformity with God's Will. St. Alphonsus Liguori.
Saint Gertrude the Great.
Chats With Converts. Forrest.
Humility of Heart. Bergamo.
St. Francis of Paola. Simi/Segreti.
Incorruptibles. Cruz.
St. Pius V, His Life and Times. Anderson.
Where We Got the Bible. Graham.
Humanum Genus. (On Freemasonry). Pope Leo XIII.

Available wherever Catholic books are sold.

NOTES